Teaching English as an International Language

How do teachers inspire students to learn to appreciate different Englishes? Has anyone tried to teach world Englishes? If so, what do they do and how do they feel about it? Most importantly, do students see the benefits in learning about world Englishes? This book responds to these questions by (1) offering a clear and solid foundation for the development of English as an International Language (EIL)-oriented curricula in an English Language program and a teacher education program, (2) critically reviewing the current pedagogical principles and practices of teaching EIL, and (3) offering an alternative way of conceptualising and teaching EIL. Using a three-year undergraduate program of EIL in an Australian university as a research site, this book provides a detailed account of actual classroom practices that raise students' awareness of world Englishes and engage them in learning how to communicate interculturally. This book is the first of its kind that explores the teaching of EIL in a country where English is a predominant and national language.

Roby Marlina holds a doctorate in Language Teacher Education (Monash University, Melbourne, Australia) and is a Language Specialist (Teacher-Educator) with the Training, Research, Assessment and Consultancy Department at the Southeast Asian Ministers of Education Organization (SEAMEO), Regional Language Centre (RELC), Singapore. Prior to joining SEAMEO-RELC, Roby was a lecturer in the EIL program at Monash University, Melbourne, Australia. His publications have appeared in international journals including *International Journal of Educational Research*, *Multilingual Education*, and *Asian EFL Journal*, and he has contributed chapters in several books edited by key EIL/World Englishes scholars. He is one of the main editors of the book, *The Pedagogy of English as an International Language: Perspectives from Scholars, Teachers, and Students* (Springer International Publishing).

Routledge Studies in World Englishes

Series Editor: Ee-Ling Low, National Institute of Education, Nanyang Technological University, Singapore and President of Singapore Association of Applied Linguistics

This **Singapore Association for Applied Linguistics** book series will provide a starting point for those who wish to know more about the aspects of the spread of English in the current globalized world. Each volume can cover the following aspects of the study of World Englishes: issues and theoretical paradigms, feature-based studies (i.e. phonetics and phonology, syntax, lexis) and language in use (e.g. education, media, the law and other related disciplines).

For a full list of titles in this series, visit www.routledge.com/Routledge-Studies-in-World-Englishes/book-series/RSWE

The Future of English in Asia
Perspectives on language and literature
Edited by Michael O'Sullivan, David Huddart and Carmen Lee

English Pronunciation Models in a Globalized World
Accent, Acceptability and Hong Kong English
Andrew Sewell

Attitudes to World Englishes
Implications for teaching English in South Korea
Hyejeong Ahn

Teaching English as an International Language
Implementing, reviewing and re-envisioning World Englishes in language education
Roby Marlina

Negotiating Englishes and English-speaking Identities
A study of youth learning English in Italy
Jacqueline Aiello

Teaching English as an International Language
Implementing, Reviewing, and Re-Envisioning World Englishes in Language Education

Roby Marlina

First published 2018 by Routledge

2 Park Square, Milton Park, Abingdon, Oxfordshire OX14 4RN
52 Vanderbilt Avenue, New York, NY 10017

Routledge is an imprint of the Taylor & Francis Group, an informa business

First issued in paperback 2019

Copyright © 2018 Roby Marlina

The right of Roby Marlina to be identified as author of this work has been asserted by him in accordance with sections 77 and 78 of the Copyright, Designs and Patents Act 1988.

All rights reserved. No part of this book may be reprinted or reproduced or utilised in any form or by any electronic, mechanical, or other means, now known or hereafter invented, including photocopying and recording, or in any information storage or retrieval system, without permission in writing from the publishers.

Notice:
Product or corporate names may be trademarks or registered trademarks, and are used only for identification and explanation without intent to infringe.

British Library Cataloguing in Publication Data
A catalogue record for this book is available from the British Library

Library of Congress Cataloging in Publication Data
Names: Marlina, Roby, author.
Title: Teaching English as an international language : implementing, reviewing, and re-envisioning world Englishes in language education / by Roby Marlina.
Description: First edition. | New York, NY : Routledge, [2018] |
Series: Routledge studies in world Englishes ; 4 |
Includes bibliographical references and index.
Identifiers: LCCN 2017011726 | ISBN 9781138231184 (hardcover) |
ISBN 9781315315768 (ebook)
Subjects: LCSH: English language–Study and teaching–Foreign speakers. |
English language–Variation–English-speaking countries. | English language–
Globalization. | Communication, International. | Engish teachers–Training of.
Classification: LCC PE1128.A2 M3426 2018 | DDC 428.0071–dc23
LC record available at https://lccn.loc.gov/2017011726

ISBN: 978-1-138-23118-4 (hbk)
ISBN: 978-0-367-41078-0 (pbk)

Typeset in Galliard
by Out of House Publishing

Dedicated to:
My late grandmother, Marlina
My parents, Kamarullah and Lenggawaty
and
Ronny, Ricky, Kristinna, Jasmine, and Janice.

Contents

List of figures	viii
List of tables	x
List of boxes	xi

1	The need to teach EIL	1
2	Teaching EIL: calls to implement change	11
3	Studying teaching EIL	49
4	The journey to implement change: an autobiographical narrative	79
5	EIL teachers implementing change	104
6	Reviewing change: from teachers' perspectives	162
7	EIL students' responses to change	175
8	Reviewing change: from students' perspectives	215
9	Re-envisioning a program of ongoing inquiry	232

Appendices	247
References	260
Index	275

Figures

2.1	Kachru's concentric circles	13
4.1	An example of material from EIL1010, EIL-ex program 1	86
4.2	An example of material from EIL1010, EIL-ex program 2	86
4.3	An example of material from EIL1010, EIL-ex program 3	87
4.4	Questions set for end-of-semester EIL-ex final essay	88
4.5	Genre-based grammar exercise sheet	90
4.6	Objectives of the newly revised EIL1010	92
4.7	Oprah Winfrey show simulation exercise (adapted from Jenkins, 2003)	94
4.8	Food-for-thought for concluding week 2's lesson	95
4.9	Food-for-thought for concluding week 3's lesson	97
4.10	Student A's response to my discussion activity on writing	99
4.11	Student B's response to my discussion activity on writing	100
5.1	A text used in Indigo's lesson on speech act	119
5.2	A text used in Fatima's lesson on speech act	120
5.3	Email 1 used as teaching material	120
5.4	Email 2 used as teaching material	121
5.5	Email 3 used as teaching material	121
5.6	An article adapted from Garuda Indonesia Airways inflight magazine	122
5.7	An article adapted from *The Jakarta Post*	123
5.8	An article adapted from Vietnam Airlines inflight magazine	123
5.9	A newspaper article adapted from *The Straits Times*	124
5.10	A letter to the editor from an Australian newspaper	125
5.11	Language variation activity 1 in EIL1010	128
5.12	Language variation activity 2 in EIL1010	129
5.13	Activity on Internet English in EIL2120	130
5.14	Activity on metaphors across cultures in EIL3110	131
5.15	A text on intercultural misunderstanding of silence (adapted from Storti, 1994)	133
5.16	An intercultural miscommunication scenario	134
5.17	Questions for role-play observers	135
5.18	Real-life intercultural miscommunication scenarios	136

Figures ix

5.19	A discussion on big-P issues in EIL1020	139
5.20	Discussion questions on big-P issues in lesson on English, Globalisation, and Technology in EIL2120	140
5.21	Discussion questions on big-P issues in a lesson on Internet English in EIL2120	140
5.22	Discussion questions on big-P issues in a lesson on Englishes in the media 1 in EIL2120	141
5.23	Guiding questions for the Accents Debate lesson in EIL1010	143
5.24	Guiding questions for the Standard English lesson in EIL1010	143
5.25	Guiding questions for the Native and Non-Native Debates lesson in EIL1010	144
5.26	Ashish's debate activity for the Accents Debate lesson in EIL1010	144
5.27	Ashish's debate activity for the Standard English lesson in EIL1010	145
5.28	Fatima's discussion questions for the Native and Non-Native Debates lesson in EIL1010	146
5.29	Article 1 on ELT employment discussed in Indigo's class	147
5.30	Article 2 on ELT employment discussed in Indigo's class	147
5.31	Indigo's job vacancy simulation activity	148
5.32	Students' responses to Indigo's job vacancy simulation activity 1	153
5.33	Students' responses to Indigo's job vacancy simulation activity 2	154
7.1	Phil's email response	200

Tables

1.1	Forces of globalisation (Appadurai, 1990)	3
2.1	English as an International Language (EIL) pedagogical approaches recommended by Hino (2010)	32
2.2	Summary of previous studies on the effects of teaching English as an International Language or World Englishes (EIL/WE)	34
3.1	Summary of the knowledge claims	54
3.2	Characteristics of the case study in my project	59
3.3	Summary of the 'what', 'where/whom', and 'when' data generated for the project	65
4.1	Previous and revised programs for English as an International Language (EIL)	101

Boxes

7.1	Summary of Manida's views and experiences of learning English as an International Language (EIL)	177
7.2	Summary of Cheolsoo's views and experiences of learning EIL	182
7.3	Summary of Ogilvy's views and experiences of learning EIL	187
7.4	Summary of Phil's views and experiences of learning EIL	196
7.5	Summary of Tomoko's views and experiences of learning EIL	206

1 The need to teach EIL

1.0. (Teaching) English as an International Language

The concept of 'English as an International Language' (henceforth EIL) and the need to study/teach it were initially proposed almost four decades ago by Larry Smith (1976, 1978), to be followed up and re-emphasised over 25 years later by Sandra McKay (2002) in her book, *Teaching English as an International Language*. Smith and McKay's arguments about the need for a new paradigm of teaching and learning of English as an international language were prompted and motivated by observations and research that explicitly documented the changing sociolinguistic landscape of English as a result of its colonial and postcolonial expansion. This global spread of English, leading to the pluralisation of its users and forms, and its significant role in various international cultural and economic arenas, had seemingly given English the status of an international language. If English had acquired the status of an international language, then, Smith and McKay (and others) argued, it was no longer relevant to conceptualise it as a homogeneous language spoken only by so-called 'native-English speakers'. Pedagogically, the teaching and learning of an international language needed to move beyond the teaching and learning of a singular language and culture as written and spoken by a single group of speakers from a particular speech community. The literature I discuss below helps to explain why.

There is broad consensus in the EIL literature that one of the main factors contributing to the status of English as an international language is the changing demographic background of its users. Most researchers agree that the predominant users of English in the world today are bi-/multilingual speakers of English from, what Kachru (1986) termed, 'Outer-Circle' and 'Expanding-Circle' countries[1]. Statistically, there are approximately one billion reasonably competent speakers of English from those circles (Jenkins, 2009; McKay, 2012a). These speakers acquire English within their bi-/multilingual repertoires, use English and perhaps other languages in multilingual contexts, and use English to communicate predominantly with other bi-/multilingual speakers of English (Crystal, 1997; Graddol, 2006). Although it is difficult to determine the exact numbers of these speakers of English, it is clear that they exceeded the numbers of speakers from Inner-Circle countries long ago

2 The need to teach EIL

and are still increasing (Graddol, 1999; Jenkins, 2009; McKay, 2003). Thus, Graddol (2006) observes that nearly eighty percent of today's communication in English takes place between these speakers, and only between ten and twelve percent of communication in English takes place between speakers of English from Inner-Circle countries and Outer- and/or Expanding-Circle countries. These statistics are changing week by week, and if anything, the landscape of English language users is becoming more complex.

It would seem that the status of an international language has been 'bestowed' on English as a result of its pluralised forms. The global expansion of English and the increase in the numbers of bi-/multilingual speakers of English in the world have led to the emergence of several varieties of world Englishes (Graddol, 2001; Kachru, 1986). Journals such as *World Englishes, English Today*, and *English World Wide* have been publishing research for decades about the newly emerging and emergent Englishes in different parts of the world. These publications tend to illustrate that when the English language 'enters' a particular society, the language and associated cultural practices tend to be 'appropriated' (Canagarajah, 1999a) and 're-nationalised' (McKay, 2002) to project a new version of cultural and linguistic identities. With its pluralised forms, English can be seen as a vehicle for users of English to project their cultural identities and cultural conceptualisations (Sharifian, 2011) on those outside their local milieu. Users of English from Outer- and Expanding-Circle countries may not necessarily communicate in Inner-Circle varieties of English, and therefore communicate the worldviews, pragmatic norms, and cultural values of those countries. Rather, as bi-/multilingual speakers of English, these users of English are likely to develop their own language varieties in which their own cultural values, pragmatic norms, and worldviews are embedded within those that might be identifiable as the English language and cultural practices as spoken and enacted in Inner-Circle countries.

The various '-scapes' (Table 1.1) created by globalisation have further complicated the sociolinguistic landscape of English at local levels. The advancement of information and communication technology (the internet, online chatting, online networking sites, etc.) and increased human mobility around the globe have allowed citizens from different parts of the world to be in freer contact with each other both without stepping outside their national boundaries and by travelling more easily. In the case of the English language specifically, Clyne and Sharifian (2008) observe that world Englishes have not remained comfortable within the 'circles' that Kachru (1986) has proposed. Thanks to forces of globalisation, these Englishes have travelled across borders and settled in other countries, and at the same time they have enriched the sociolinguistic landscape of English in those countries. Australia is an example that well illustrates this global phenomenon. In addition to indigenous Australian cultures and Englishes, the growing numbers of international students, travellers, and migrants in Australia have provided its citizens with abundant exposures to people from diverse lingua-cultural backgrounds who are likely to speak their own varieties of English.

Table 1.1. Forces of globalisation (Appadurai, 1990)

The '-scapes'	Meaning	Examples
Ethnoscapes	Flows of people	Migrants, asylum seekers, exiles, tourists
Technoscapes	Flows of technology	Hardware components, technical know-how
Financescapes	Flows of money	National stock exchanges, commodity speculations
Mediascapes	Flows of information	Newspapers, magazines, satellite television channels, websites, the images and symbols they create and provide
Ideoscapes	Flows of ideas	Ideological discourses concerning freedom, democracy, human rights, environmentalism

These exposures are sometimes a remote-control switch away, as Australia has a television network – the Special Broadcasting Service (SBS) – that broadcasts news, shows, films, entertainment, etc. from many different countries and in different languages and world Englishes. Given this sociolinguistic landscape, Australia, considered by some to be "a microcosm of the world in its cultural diversity" (Clyne, 2005, p. 181), is a context in which communicative exchanges are often international and intercultural in nature. In other words, more than one variety of English is likely to be found in interactions that take place in a multicultural context such as Australia. Therefore, thanks to globalisation, the lingua-cultural backgrounds of interlocutors as well as the varieties of English they might be speaking are often unpredictable. As Xu (2002) and many others have observed, for English, as for any other language in the world, today's communicative exchanges are "characterised by variation in linguistic and cultural behaviour" (p. 231).

The changing '-scapes' of English shown in Table 1.1 have led many scholars (including Canagarajah, 2006; Matsuda, 2012a; McKay & Brown, 2016) to call for an urgent revision and reassessment of the current practices of teaching English and their underlying principles or ideologies. They argue that the practices of English language teaching that have been traditionally oriented toward the 'norms' of Inner-Circle countries need to be challenged and replaced with practices that reflect a different set of perspectives, which take into consideration and respond to the dynamic scapes of English and thus the new sociolinguistic practices of a truly international notion of the English language. This perspective is what McKay (2002) and Sharifian (2009) term the EIL paradigm. Based on the assumption that "English, with its many varieties, is a language of international and intercultural communication" (Sharifian, 2009, p. 2), and the varieties of English and lingua-cultural backgrounds of interlocutors that are often unpredictable in today's globalised communicative encounters, this EIL paradigm

4 *The need to teach EIL*

urges those who teach English in international contexts to professionally guide students from all Kachruvian circles to develop:

- a pluricentric view of the English language;
- a perception that all varieties of English should be equal and legitimately recognised; and
- an ability to negotiate and communicate respectfully across cultures and Englishes in today's communicative settings, which are international and intercultural in nature.

This knowledge and its associated perceptions and skills have been perceived as crucial attributes for graduates seeking employment, especially in the current context of postmodern globalisation. Globalisation and the -scapes described in Table 1.1 have altered the occupational landscape for university graduates, who are now required to demonstrate international/intercultural communication skills, familiarity with world Englishes, and international perspectives that can help them function competently in social and work environments that are international and intercultural in nature (Briguglio, 2006, 2007; Edwards, Crosling, Petrovic-Lazarovic, & O'Neill, 2003; Leask, 2008; Singh & Shrestha, 2008; Webb, 2005). For example, Briguglio's (2005) case study analysis of multinational companies in Malaysia and Hong Kong has shown that all graduates, regardless of the Kachruvian circles to which they belong, need to:

- expect and be able to deal with different varieties of English;
- show acceptance towards different accents in English; and
- develop accommodation strategies to deal with different accents and ways of speaking in English (where differences are perhaps more marked than in writing) (Briguglio, 2005, p. 180).

Therefore, a program, course, or curriculum that professionally develops graduates to demonstrate the above knowledge, perceptions, and skills is important and needed.

Despite numerous calls in the literature to implement some agreed principles of teaching EIL into everyday classroom practice, Matsuda (2012a; forthcoming) claims that the teaching of EIL still remains an abstract concept, and that there have not been many attempts from EIL-inspired scholars to illustrate how an EIL curriculum/program/course may look like (see also Brown, 2012). Teachers whose pedagogical practices have been critiqued for their lack of alignment with EIL principles have expressed some frustration (Matsuda, 2012a). They have stated that they do not have access to clear illustrations of EIL pedagogy that is explicitly informed by widely agreed principles for teaching EIL. Matsuda (2012a) believes that this may be because EIL educators are aware that pedagogical practices are contextually specific, and therefore they do not want to convey a message that their pedagogical practices are universally applicable. The problem is, however, that if this kind of practical knowledge is not shared, then those groups of frustrated teachers are going to feel even more frustrated and will continue to revert to habitual practices that promote the supremacy of varieties of English and cultures of Inner-Circle countries. This is one of the gaps in the literature that my book aims to fill.

There have already been some publications that briefly identify a set of principles of ethical EIL teaching and that illustrate how these principles should be implemented (e.g. Bayyurt & Altinmakas, 2012; D'Angelo, 2012; Lee, 2012; Matsuda, 2012a; forthcoming; McKay & Brown, 2016). However, in Wee's (2013) review of a recently published edited book on teaching EIL, he claims, supported by Qu (2016), that a set of principles about teaching EIL would be more effective if it "trigger[ed] debates about just how realistic it might be to try to implement particular suggestions" (p. 203) rather than just informing teachers what needs to be taught in EIL curricula and how it should be taught. This book project responds to Wee (2013) and Qu's (2016) concerns by exploring the benefits and challenges of teaching EIL in a particular institutional setting in Australia, a country where English is widely used as the national language. Research projects that provide more *in-depth* and *reflexive* accounts of the operationalisation of EIL principles in Inner-Circle countries are still relatively rare. This is also another gap that this book aims to fill. In providing accounts of EIL principles in action in a particular university teaching and learning setting in Australia, I do not wish to send a message that the practices and the outcomes I am reporting serve as the definitive account of how an EIL curriculum should be developed and taught. I acknowledge that this study is based on a single case of a single program in one particular institution in Australia and is not intended to be universally generalisable. Rather, I hope to provide a carefully theorised framework and some grounded reflexive accounts of EIL curriculum and practices that other EIL-inspired educators, especially those teaching in a similar context such as Australia, may engage with and use in examining and evaluating their own EIL or even traditional English language curriculum and pedagogical practices.

Furthermore, how realistic it might be to implement the principles advocated by the EIL paradigm I present in this book, it is also important to explore this through the eyes of another most important group of people involved in an EIL program, i.e. the students. As more studies emerge that advocate for the teaching of EIL, it is timely to understand how the main beneficiaries of these programs, i.e. the students, perceive, feel, or respond to what/how they have been taught. Brown (2012) agrees and argues that this is currently one of the gaps that needs to be empirically pursued. So far, a number of studies have only explored students' responses to the issues raised in an EIL lesson or the perspectives advocated by the EIL paradigm (Briguglio, 2006; Chang, 2014; Galloway & Rose, 2014; Kubota, 2001b; Rose & Galloway, forthcoming; Shin, 2004; Suzuki, 2011; Oxford & Jain, 2010). These studies have revealed that responses from students range from complete acceptance to hostile resistance towards the issues promoted by the EIL paradigm. Some studies attribute these mixed feelings to the short duration of the EIL lessons they conducted and reviewed for

6 The need to teach EIL

their study. They believe that more could be achieved if students have a longer exposure to or study more about EIL. However, there are no further attempts to explain in depth, particularly from the students' perspectives, what factors may have prompted them to agree with, challenge, or resist the perspectives and principles advocated by the EIL paradigm. A substantial component of my study explored these very questions through an extended research dialogue with some student-participants over a period of up to three years.

1.1. The key questions

To respond to Wee (2013) and Qu's (2016) call, the central research question that this book aims to address is:

> **How realistic might it be to implement the suggestions or principles of teaching EIL?**

To help tease out this central research question, this book addresses the following sub-questions:

- **How do EIL educators in one institution in Australia (Urban University) implement the values and beliefs advocated by the EIL paradigm?**
  - What curricula (materials and pedagogical strategies) have EIL educators developed/used to teach the perspectives advocated by the EIL paradigm?
  - What could be missing in the EIL curricula at Urban University? Why?
- **How do students in one institution in Australia (Urban University) respond to the perspectives offered and advocated by an EIL curriculum?**
  - Do students perceive any relevance, values, or benefits of learning about EIL? If so, in what ways?
  - What do students experience are the factors that have contributed to such perceptions?
  - Do students experience any challenges/dilemmas while learning about EIL or even after having learnt about EIL?
  - Why do students resist, struggle, or experience tension or conflict in learning to advocate the perspectives underlying the EIL curriculum?
- **What are other alternative pedagogical assumptions and approaches that EIL educators might like to consider in teaching in an EIL curriculum, lesson, or program?**

To investigate the research question and sub-questions, this study is framed as qualitative research, using a case study approach (Yin, 2009), employing a range of data collection methods. These methods include semi-structured interviews (Seidman, 2006), classroom observations (Sanger, 1996; Simons, 2009), artefact collection and analysis (Finnegan, 2006), and some critical autobiographical narrative writing (Doecke, 2004; Rosen, 1998), which helps to reflexively ground the other data collection methods. On the one hand, these methods allow me to observe how views advocated by the EIL paradigm are implemented into classroom practice and how students experience the values, relevance, or benefits of learning EIL. On the other hand, they allow me to uncover an additional important element that is still rather silent in the current discourses on teaching EIL, and that is illustrative of accounts of curriculum, course, and program implementation that have the potential to engage students to learn about and appreciate the diversification of English.

1.2. Significance and contribution to the professional community

This project and its outcomes may serve as one example of a program that genuinely attempts to execute and accomplish the goals of Urban University, and perhaps many other universities in the world, to become internationally known for excellence in providing international education. And yet, the story of my ten-year experience as a student at Urban University, followed by eight years of experience as a teacher, and my encounters with the university's strategic internationalisation initiative documents, does not constitute an unequivocal victory narrative for the principles of EIL education. Indeed, at the conclusion of this narrative, I must concede two things: (1) the provision of an ethical and comprehensive international education at this university, as at all universities, is still far from being realised; and (2) Urban University's view of international education, like that of most universities in the Western world, is still largely informed by a marketing and quality assurance paradigm whose main concern is maximising profit/income through increasing the number of recruited full-fee paying international students on campus. Informed by this paradigm, they view that having a large number of international students on university premises is a way to achieve internationalisation of education. This view is reported in a research inquiry into the nature of international education in Australian universities, which claims that "by seeing people from other backgrounds around on campus and in classes, Australian university students will gain an international perspective" (Universities Australia, 2009, p. 40). Therefore, in terms of higher education curriculum development and pedagogy, the typical Australian university appears to be still largely parochial, favouring an assimilationist approach to knowledge delivery. As Trevaskes, Eisenchlas, and Liddicoat (2003) claim, the curricula of some programs in Australian universities seem to be mostly governed by a "monocultural chauvinistic" worldview (p. 11). Specifically, national projects conducted by the Australian DAASH (Deans of Arts, Social Sciences and Humanities), which reviews the nature and roles of Bachelor of Arts (BA) degrees in contemporary Australia have further revealed that the curricula of many existing Australian BA programs fail to appreciate the importance of diversity in cultural and knowledge-based fields of endeavour (Gannaway & Trent, 2008; Gannaway & Sheppard, 2012). Therefore, it is hoped that this study and its outcomes can be used as an example of an undergraduate BA program that attempts to (1) contest the parochial and

8   *The need to teach EIL*

assimilationist approach to knowledge delivery, (2) genuinely reflect the rhetoric of plurality and interculturality, and (3) instil in students the necessary knowledge, attitudes, and skills for operating effectively in today's globalised world.

This book will also hopefully encourage EIL educators or other educators (such as from the disciplines of multicultural education or social justice education), who share a similar interest in inspiring their students to learn about and develop respectful views towards difference, to go beyond transmitting to their students a superficial list of the behavioural traits of people from different countries or simply teaching about cultural and linguistic differences (how are we all linguistically and culturally different from each other?). It is indeed a relief to witness the attempts of educators to urge their students to learn to understand and embrace people who are different from them, but 'difference' still needs to be pedagogically approached with 'extra care'. As Jenks, Lee, and Kanpol (2001) say, if extra care is not taken, differences could be viewed and constructed as deficits, which may further perpetuate the discriminatory practices that already exist in the society. Therefore, it is hoped that this project and its outcomes can inspire other EIL educators or educators from different fields of study who share a similar passion to provide a space and opportunity in their program, course, or curriculum to learn about difference *as well as* to recognise and inquire into practices and ideologies that implicitly marginalise one group and unjustly empower another.

1.3. Organisation of the book

In this introductory chapter, I have explained the background to my book project as well as what inspired me to conduct this study. I have also framed my study by outlining the central research questions, the ways in which I explore the experiences of teachers teaching and students learning EIL in Australia, and the significance of the outcomes of the study.

In Chapter 2, I review the current research conversations and/or discourses that are central to my study. In particular, I begin with a discussion of the sociolinguistic reality of English in today's globalising/globalised world, and in Australia where this book project was conducted. I then discuss two major frameworks for understanding the English language – World Englishes (WE) and English as an International Language (EIL) – and the pedagogical principles that have been developed to guide EIL-inspired teachers teach EIL. This is followed by a critical review of the empirical research that has been conducted so far to examine the instructional effects of teaching EIL. Thereafter, an alternative view of understanding teaching EIL drawn from the works of critical inquirers from several disciplines such as Critical Applied Linguistics, Critical Literacy Study, and Critical Multicultural Education, is discussed.

In Chapter 3, I present and discuss my research design, and explain the rationale for using case study as the framework of design for methodology. Additionally, I explain the context of my study (the setting and participants), the research instruments that I employed for data collection, the approaches that I used for processing and analysing my data, and finally how I sought to ensure the trustworthiness of my study.

In order to see how realistic it would be to teach EIL, this study sees the importance of incorporating the *voices of teachers*, to which Chapter 4, Chapter 5, and Chapter 6 are devoted. Specifically, they focus on the attempts as well as the journey of four EIL-inspired educators (my colleagues and I) to inspire students to learn about and appreciate the diversity of English through the curricula of our EIL program at Urban University. In Chapter 4, I present a critical autobiographical narrative which begins with my experiences of teaching in the previous EIL program and then moves on to record how I developed a new curriculum for one subject, which I believed to be genuinely based on the EIL paradigm (cf. McKay, 2002; Sharifian, 2009). I conclude Chapter 4 with some accounts of my teaching in a new EIL subject. Based on the principles of EIL teaching materials and pedagogy, Chapter 5 describes and analyses the materials and pedagogical practices that EIL educators at Urban University (my colleagues and I) developed and used to raise students' awareness of world Englishes and to inspire them to critically revisit their perceptions and attitudes towards different varieties of English and its speakers. The chapter also presents the theme that emerged from the data, namely the struggles, tensions, and challenges that my colleagues and I encountered in teaching EIL. Thereafter, in Chapter 6, I critically revisit, revise, and renew the frameworks – I propose an extended list of principles of EIL teaching syllabus materials and pedagogical practices, for which I drew on the theoretical discussions presented in Chapter 2 as well as my engagement with my own data.

In order to examine all the dimensions of developing, teaching, and reflecting on EIL curriculum, it is equally important to consider the voices of the key beneficiaries of the EIL curriculum, the students. Therefore, Chapter 7 and Chapter 8 are focused on the *students' voices*. In Chapter 7, I present and reflect on the students' experiences of learning EIL in the EIL program at Urban University described in Chapter 4 and Chapter 5. This involves some discussion and analysis of students' responses to the set of views and beliefs promoted and advocated by the EIL curricula. Based on this analysis, I develop an argument about the extent to which learning about these principles is relevant, valuable, and beneficial to the students. At the same time, I also present the specific materials and pedagogical practices that students believed had prompted them to feel and experience the values and benefits of learning about EIL. Similar to the EIL educators, these students also experienced struggle, tensions, and challenges in learning about EIL. Thereafter, Chapter 8 discusses the themes and issues which arose in the learners' experiences of being taught EIL in the light of the theoretical frameworks discussed in Chapter 2.

Chapter 9 highlights the overall key findings of this book project and proposes a variety of recommendations that my colleagues and I, as EIL teacher-participants in the EIL program at Urban University, and other EIL educators and scholars might consider in relation to the way in which the teaching of EIL is conceptualised and implemented at practice level. As part of this discussion, I also address Wee's (2013) question of the extent to which it might be feasible to teach EIL in university settings in the current ideological and political climate where diversity or difference is so often misunderstood, ignored, or feared.

Note

1 See Chapter 2 for a detailed explanation of the terms Inner Circle, Outer Circle, and Expanding Circle countries.

2 Teaching EIL
Calls to implement change

2.0. Introduction

This chapter provides a review of the theoretical and empirical literature on teaching EIL, including a more detailed review of issues concerning the globalisation and internationalisation of English, as well as its implications for curriculum and pedagogy, which I have briefly touched upon in Chapter 1. The review is divided into five sections: (1) the global spread of English; (2) two frameworks for understanding English Language education: World Englishes (WE) and English as an International Language (EIL); (3) teaching EIL; (4) previous studies on the effects of teaching of EIL; and finally (5) alternative views of understanding teaching EIL.

The first section presents the changing sociolinguistic landscape of the English language in the world today, which has been the main reason for a paradigm shift in the discipline. I will discuss the historical and sociocultural reasons for the spread of English and most importantly the outcomes of the global expansion, addressing the changing use of the language and the diversification of forms, users, and cultures of the language. I will also discuss the global complexity of English that has influenced the particular context in which I conduct this study, Australia. As more literature in the past three decades has acknowledged the complexity of English across the world, this has prompted a paradigm shift in the field of Applied Linguistics. In the second section, I draw on a wide range of this literature to conceptualise two frameworks for understanding English language education, situating EIL as a paradigm in relation to World Englishes (WE). The third section reviews theoretical discussions of the pedagogical implications of the global spread of English. I specifically explore some EIL/WE scholars' views on the pedagogical principles they believe should inform the teaching of EIL. These principles address questions such as: what should be taught in an EIL curriculum? how should EIL be taught? and, perhaps most importantly, why should EIL be taught this way? In the fourth section, I review a collection of empirical projects that investigate the effects of teaching EIL or world Englishes to students from different learning contexts and at different levels of study. In this section, I specifically discuss the 'desired' and 'undesired' effects of EIL/WE instructions on students, as well as their implications for teaching EIL. As these research studies

12 *Teaching EIL: calls to implement change*

on teaching EIL seem to have overlooked the importance of learning about 'difference' and responding to difference, the last section discusses the views of a number of critical inquirers from several disciplines on this subject. I use my discussion of their views to inform the significant claims I will make in this book, but in itself this discussion is presented as an additional contribution to scholarly knowledge on the teaching of EIL. I will close the chapter by highlighting some research gaps that this book attempts to address.

2.1. English 'going to strange shores' and its outcomes

2.1.1. *English in the world*

When Britain was the leading colonial nation and the leader of the Industrial Revolution in the late eighteenth and nineteenth centuries, the colonised peoples had to learn English to communicate with the coloniser. Others learnt English to understand new technological and scientific terminology, and to trade and communicate with the English-speaking inventors or manufacturers from Britain, and then later from America when it became a leading economic power in the late nineteenth century. Thus, English was considered to be the language exclusively 'owned' (or possessed) by the Britons and Americans. Learning and teaching English invariably meant learning about British or American English and cultural practices to communicate with British or Americans. However, in the second half of the twentieth century, the predominant view of English as an American/British language steadily eroded and was replaced with more complex notions about English, for example, as an Asian language and an African language, which, as Kachru (1986) asserts, has brought into realisation the linguistic vision of "1599 Samuel Daniel, a minor poet, who fantasised about the 'treasures of our language' going to 'the strange shores'" (p. 4). The global expansion of English to the 'strange shores', leading to the internationalisation and pluralisation of its use, users, forms, and cultures, has allowed English to be considered as the possession of everyone who uses it. This has contributed to the widely perceived understanding of English as an 'international language'.

Thanks to the new technologies bringing a wide range of new linguistic opportunities, Crystal (1997) argues, "English emerged as a first-rank language in industries which in turn affected all aspects of society – the press, advertising, broadcasting, motion pictures, sound recording, transport and communication" (p. 111). It became the dominant language in various economic and cultural arenas such as the language of international organisations, of the motion picture industry and popular music, of international travel, of publications, and of education (Crystal, 1997; Graddol, 1997; McKay & Brown, 2016). In fact, it is the non-English-mother-tongue countries that have been significantly active in using English, and that have enhanced its value in each of those arenas (Fishman, 1982). Taken together, it is these international roles or functions of English that have consolidated the sense of English being an international language.

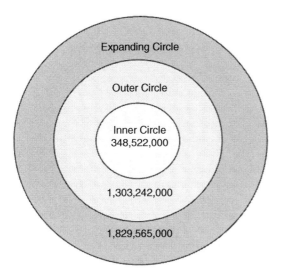

Figure 2.1 Kachru's concentric circles

The status of international language ascribed to English is also a result of the increasing numbers of countries in the world bestowing a special role or priority on English, either by making it an official language of the country or by requiring its study as a foreign language in schools and other institutions (Crystal, 1997; McKay & Brown, 2016). There are now over seventy countries in the world that give special status to English and approximately more than three billion speakers or users of English in the world today. In response to this, Braj Kachru (1986) has categorised these countries into three circles – Inner Circle, Outer Circle, and Expanding Circle (Figure 2.1) – on the basis of the types of spread, the patterns of acquisition, and the roles English serves in those circles.

Inner-Circle countries, Kachru argues, include Australia, Canada, New Zealand, the United States, the United Kingdom, and Ireland. These are countries where English is formally recognised as a national language, and they are traditionally regarded as 'the native English-speaking countries'. 'Outer-Circle' countries is the term used to describe former American and British colonies such as Singapore, India, the Philippines, and Nigeria. In these countries, English is used as an additional institutionalised language and in conjunction with other official local languages. The category of 'Expanding-Circle' countries includes Indonesia, South Korea, Japan, China, and some European countries where English does not have any official status and yet it is often mandated for study as a foreign language in school curricula.

However, many scholars argue that this model no longer reflects the contemporary situation of English in some of these countries (Jenkins, 2009; Park & Wee, 2009; Pennycook, 2003). They assert that the status or the use of English

14 *Teaching EIL: calls to implement change*

in those contemporary societies is not as simple as Kachru has described it. For example, Graddol (1997) and Jenkins (2009) point out that the status of English in Expanding-Circle countries has shifted and has almost become similar to Outer-Circle countries. Rather than simply learning English as a foreign language, English in Expanding-Circle countries such as in continental European countries and many Asian countries is increasingly chosen and used as one of the main mediums of communication in a variety of contexts ranging from kindergarten to secondary schools, and from universities to transnational corporations. In Inner-Circle countries such as Australia, not only is there a variety of Australian English spoken, but there are also locally developed varieties of English that are spoken by Indigenous Australians, i.e. Aboriginal Englishes, as well as other varieties of English spoken by migrants from diverse lingua-cultural backgrounds (Burridge, 2010; Marlina, 2010; Sharifian, 2014). I will discuss this further in a later section of this chapter. For the moment, it is sufficient to observe that, as an international language, English is now used by global citizens to communicate intranationally and internationally in multilingual and multicultural globalising societies (McKay & Brown, 2016; Smith, 1976, 1978). Although these concentric circles have been critiqued, they are still used by professional literature on World Englishes or EIL as a tool of inquiry. Park and Wee (2009) also state that these circles are still important reference points in many ways, especially for maintaining national identities of transnational communities when referring to these identities is an advantage, or pointing out "prevalent language ideologies that influentially shape and constrain local uses of English across many contexts around the world" (p. 393). Therefore, I use the terms Inner-, Outer-, and Expanding-Circle countries throughout this book.

Furthermore, the changing role and status of English in these circles have also suggested changes to the backgrounds of the users of English. This is another increasingly recognised phenomenon that gives English the status of an international language. The 'strange shores' to which English travels are not 'languageless'; the inhabitants of those shores already speak another language or languages, making English an additional language to their linguistic repertoire. Today's users of English are predominantly bi-/multi-/translingual users of English, who are fluent in English and in other languages, and who develop and use English in multilingual contexts (Crystal, 1997; McKay, 2012a; McKay & Bokhorst-Heng, 2008; Graddol 1999). Eighteen years ago, basing his figures on expected population changes, Graddol (1999) envisaged that "the number of people using English as their second/additional language will grow from 235 million to around 462 million during the next 50 years" (p. 62). Those figures had not yet included the numbers of people who had reasonable competence in English, who spoke English as their additional dialect, and who were pidgin or Creole speakers of English. Although it is difficult to determine the exact numbers of users/speakers of English, it is becoming clear that "the number of individuals who have some familiarity with the language today is vast and growing" (McKay, 2003, p. 11). Recent statistical analysis has calculated that nearly eighty percent of today's communication in English takes place between bi-/multilingual speakers of English

(Graddol, 2006), meaning that the so-called monolingual 'native-speakers' of English have more than likely become 'the minority' (Graddol, 1999; Jenkins, 2009; McKay & Brown, 2016). Thanks to the explosion of advanced information technologies in today's postmodern globalisation era, the cultural and linguistic backgrounds of the interlocutors with whom people communicate in English are often unknown. What is known is that today's communicative exchanges take place between speakers whose cultural and linguistic backgrounds are diverse and complex (Matsuda & Friedrich, 2012).

The global expansion of English and therefore the increasing number of the users of English, however, do not seem to be viewed positively by some (e.g. Phillipson, 1992, 2009). Using the notion of "linguistic imperialism", Phillipson (1992) argues that the spread of English is due primarily to the attempts of developed English-speaking countries such as the United Kingdom and the United States to maintain dominance over other developing countries through "the establishment and continuous reconstitution of structural and cultural inequalities between English and other languages" (p. 47). English language teaching enterprises located in developed English-speaking countries have allocated large sums of money to disseminate/promote English and support its use over another language. English learners in these enterprises are taught with the attitudes and pedagogic principles that favour monolingualism (Phillipson, 1992). Those who learn English from these teaching enterprises are likely to lose their mother tongue, speak the varieties of English promoted by those enterprises (either American or British English), and internalise the cultural norms of 'native' English-speaking countries. The more this happens, the more likely is the prospect that such practices will lead to language extinction and linguistic genocide.

However, this view is not entirely shared by other researchers (such as Brutt-Griffler, 2002; Bisong, 1995; Chew, 1999; Li, 1998). Bisong (1995) and Li (1998) have argued that Phillipson's theory underestimates learners' ability to judge what is in their best interests and overlooks parental expectations of their children operating with two or more linguistic codes in a multilingual and multicultural environment. More importantly, what has also been overlooked is the pluralised and pluralising forms of English emerging as a result of it being 'localised' in the country in which it lands. As Brutt-Griffler (2002) argues, the theory of linguistic imperialism denies the agency of learners and users of English to alter the language according to their needs; "it obscures the role of Africans, Asians, and other peoples of the world as active agents in the process of creation of world English" (p. 107). In other words, it ignores the very natural process or dynamics of languages in contact – the emergence of new different varieties of world Englishes and the increase in the bi-/multi-/translingual speakers of English (Graddol, 2001). When language and linguistic practices travel to and encounter the strange shores, they are not passively absorbed by the inhabitants. Rather, they are "nativised" (Kachru, 1986) and "appropriated" (Canagarajah, 1999a) to "suit the local tastebuds" (Marlina, 2010), to reflect local cultural pragmatic norms, and to project their local linguistic and cultural identities. Consequently, it is becoming more common to hear English being

16   *Teaching EIL: calls to implement change*

spoken of as 'Englishes' – a heterogeneous language with multiple grammars, vocabulary, accents, and pragmatic/discourse conventions (Canagarajah, 2006; Jenkins, 2009). A significant number of research studies, using a wide range of methodological approaches, explicitly document the newly emerged as well as the changing syntactical, lexical, semantic, pragmatic, and phonological features of English in all Kachruvian circles (see the journals *World Englishes* published by Wiley Blackwell, and *English Today* published by Cambridge University Press; see also Kachru, 1986; Kachru, Kachru, & Nelson, 2006; Kirkpatrick, 2010; Schneider, 1997a, 1997b). With its pluralised forms and its internationalised status, ownership of English has been de-nationalised (Smith, 1983) and "re-nationalised" (McKay, 2002). Scholars who approach these issues from this perspective, recognise that the new features and practices of English may not sound 'natural' to the ears of the so-called native-speakers from England or the United States, but they caution against those who seek to intervene or pass judgement, arguing that they have no authority to evaluate its appropriateness (Widdowson, 1994; Smith, 2003).

Finally, with its pluralised forms and its status as an international language, English is considered by some to be a vehicle for users of English to express their cultural conceptualisations (Sharifian, 2011) to those outside their local milieu. In other words, when bi-/multi-/translingual speakers of English from, for example Indonesia or South Korea, use English, they may not necessarily communicate the norms, thoughts, worldviews, and sociocultural realities of the so-called 'Western' English-speaking countries. Rather, they naturally draw on their own rich linguistic and cultural resources to express their perceptions of reality. Several empirical projects from the fields of cultural linguistics and cross-cultural linguistics (such as Frank, Dirven, Ziemke, & Bernandez, 2008; Sharifian, 2011; Sharifian & Palmer, 2007; Wierzbicka, 2006) have demonstrated how variations in the syntactical, lexical, semantic, and pragmatic features of English result from the sociocultural norms, values, beliefs, practices, and worldviews that bi-/multi-/translingual and bidialectal speakers of English bring into their use of English. Therefore, since the linguistic and cultural backgrounds of potential interlocutors with whom people will interact in English are often unknown and diverse, so is the variety of English that is being used and the sociocultural norms and cultural values it reflects (Xu, 2002).

To sum up, the following is a list of the outcomes of the global expansion of English and its emergence as an international language.

- English is perceived as one of the dominant languages in various international economic, technological, scientific, educational and cultural arenas.
- English is predominantly spoken and used in communications among bi-/ multilingual speakers of English, or the numbers of so-called 'non-native' English speakers whose numbers have exceeded the numbers of so-called 'native English speakers'.
- English is used by today's global citizens for international communication and intranational communication within multilingual societies.

- The worldwide spread of English has led to the emergence of different varieties of English, collectively called world Englishes. In its pluralised forms, English is a vehicle for communicating one's cultural identity, pragmatic norms, worldviews, and sociocultural practices. Therefore, English is a language with multiple identities and cultures.
- With its diversified forms, English is increasingly understood as belonging to everyone who speaks/uses it, and it is increasingly problematic for 'native English speakers' to claim exclusive ownership of the language.

2.1.2. Englishes in Australia: a multicultural country

The first diaspora of English that took place during the Renaissance and the eighteenth century led to the development of new 'mother-tongue' varieties of English in certain countries in the world – one of them was Australia. Based on the traditional Kachruvian concentric circles, Australia is classified as an Inner-Circle country where English is the primary national language. This classification suggests that only varieties of Australian English are spoken in Australia. This view, as well as the classifications of Inner- and Outer-Circle countries, has been problematised and widely contested by linguists in Australia for ignoring the diversity of English spoken in their country (Burridge, 2010; Collins & Blair, 1989; Clyne, 2005; Horvath, 1985; Kiesling, 2006; Malcolm, 2004a, 2004b). One view that these scholars unanimously share is as Clyne (2005) strongly asserts:

> Australia provides an opportunity to become exposed to many languages and cultures … [and] the languages and cultures that are represented on a daily basis in our housing estates, our shopping centres, our workplaces, and our schools are some of the ones on which worldwide communication in English as a lingua franca will increasingly be based.
>
> (p. 63)

One of the main factors having an influential role in diversifying the cultural and linguistic landscape of Australia is the mass migration that has been taking place since the 1850s. The gold-rushes and the influx of Chinese miners in the 1850s, as well as the immigration programs post World War II in the 1950s, led to the emergence of different varieties of English, based on the ethnicity of the language users (Burridge, 2010; Kiesling, 2006). Firstly, contacts between the English-speaking Anglo Australians and the Australian Aborigines, and therefore the assimilationist pressures of the past (Collins & Blair, 1989), have led to the decreolisation of Aboriginal pidgins and creoles, and the development of indigenised varieties of English, referred to as 'Aboriginal English/Englishes'. Even though some scholars claim that Aboriginal English is becoming progressively closer to "White Non-Standard Australian English" (Collins & Blair, 1989, p. 5), other studies have shown that Aboriginal English is phonologically (Malcolm, 2004a), syntactically (Malcolm, 2004b), morphologically (Dixon, Moore, Ramson, & Thomas, 1992; Malcolm, 2004b), and pragmatically (Eades, 1993, 2000; Sharifian, 2006,

18   *Teaching EIL: calls to implement change*

2011) different from Australian English. Even thirty years ago, urban Aboriginal Australians "pejoratively labelled the Standard Australian English as 'flash language', and viewed those members of the Aboriginal community who sp[oke] this language as attempting to raise themselves above the community" (Eagleson, Kaldor, & Malcolm, 1982, pp. 155–156). At around that time, as they still do today, many members of the Aboriginal communities preferred to retain some dimension of Aboriginality in the way they used English. As a result, they were often viewed as "linguistically and cognitively deficient, and [sent to] remedial programs to correct their putative shortcomings" (Collins & Blair, 1989, p. 6). These views and practices may still continue into the present day.

Secondly, contact between English-speaking Australians and post-war non-Anglo-Celtic migrants – such as Greeks and Italians – and various assimilationist pressures have led to the flourishing of ethnocultural varieties (migrant ethnolects) or what Kiesling (2006) terms, "New Australian English". Though these newly developed varieties of Australian English may share similarities with the more general Australian English, they also have their own distinctiveness (see Cox & Palethorpe, 2001). Second generations of these migrants are often bi-dialectally fluent, switching between general Australian English and their own migrant varieties, for example, for in-group/out-group (such as when parents meet with school teachers from other linguistic backgrounds) and identity projections (national identity vs non-Anglo ethnicity).

Finally, worldwide economic development and forces of globalisation such as mass migration and the rise of transnational corporations have enriched the sociolinguistic and sociocultural landscape of any so-called English-speaking nation. As Burridge (2010) observes, "massive flows of people, including tourists, migrants and refugees have produced an intermixing of people and cultures that is unprecedented" (p. 145). For example, Australia is currently one of the preferred study destinations for international students from Asia, and it is estimated that the number of these students will "increase sevenfold by 2025" (Ryan & Carroll, 2005, p. 4). Many of these students decide to settle permanently in Australia after completing their study. Not only does their arrival contribute to the nation's source of revenue, but it also provides Australian citizens exposure to diverse languages, cultures, and varieties of English. These languages, cultures, and varieties of English can be found and heard in some areas in, for example, Melbourne (refer to the list below of nationality and suburbs in Melbourne provided by Sharifian (2014, pp. 39–40):

Nationality	Suburbs
Italian	Carlton and Brunswick
Macedonian	Thomastown and St Albans
Indian	South Eastern Suburbs such as Hampton Park and Narre Warren, North Western Suburbs, and South Western Suburbs
Greek	Oakleigh, Northcote, Hughesdale, and interspersed in Northern and Eastern Suburbs

Sri Lankans	Dandenong, Endeavour Hills, Lynbrook, Hallam, South Eastern Suburbs, and North Western Suburbs
Vietnamese	Richmond, Springvale, Footscray, North Western Suburbs, and South Eastern Suburbs
Cambodian	Springvale South and Keysborough
Chinese	Glen Waverley and Box Hill
Jewish	North Caulfield, Caulfield, St Kilda East, and South Eastern Suburbs
Middle Eastern	Northern and South Western Suburbs
Maltese	Sunshine, Keilor, St Albans, and Airport West
Sub-Saharan African	Noble Park
North African	Flemington
Spanish	Fitzroy
Russian	Carnegie
Lebanese	Coburg
Bosnian, Serb and Croat	St Albans and Springvale
Filipino	Hoppers Crossing
Turkish	Broadmeadows

Furthermore, there has been an increase in the number of Australian corporations outsourcing jobs to countries such as India and Philippines (for example, call centres) where the labour costs are inexpensive and where English is spoken as one of the official languages. As a result, when people in Australia need customer service, they are likely to communicate with people from one of the aforementioned countries who may speak a different variety of English. One final source of exposure to different cultures, languages, and varieties of English in Australia is the range of new information communication technologies. Thanks to the advancement of these technologies, communication with people from different cultural backgrounds and therefore exposure to differences is only one 'mouse click' away. Apart from online forums and social networking sites such as Facebook and Twitter, the boom in MMORPG (massively multi-player online role playing games) such as World of Warcraft, Diablo, and League of Legends, where players are required to team up with other players whose identity and backgrounds are often unknown and can only be identified by their lingua-culturally unidentified nicknames such as 'n.0.0.b.i.e' or 'ch0pstix', has allowed gamers in Australia to interact with gamers from diverse lingua-cultural backgrounds in English.

To sum up, all of the above phenomena suggest convergence around the following views:

- Australia is "a microcosm of the world in its cultural diversity" (Clyne, 2005, p. 181).
- History and the effects of globalisation have made Australia a home to many varieties of English, languages, and cultures. In many cases, communicative

exchanges in English in Australia are likely to be intercultural and 'pluri-varietal' in nature and the trend for this seems to be increasing.

- There is a strong argument for teaching EIL in Australia.

Prior to discussing what teaching EIL involves, I will explore deeper conceptualisations of EIL. I will then move on to identify how this project understands and defines EIL as a concept and a broad set of practices.

2.2. EIL and WE: an anti-normative paradigm

As Thomas Kuhn (1962), a philosopher and historian observes, a paradigm shift or advance in knowledge takes place when "a series of peaceful interludes punctuated by intellectually violent revolutions in which one conceptual worldview is replaced by another" (p. 10). This view mirrors what has happened to the field of Applied Linguistics over the past three decades. The changing contemporary sociolinguistic reality of the English language, which I have discussed above, has led a growing number of linguists and/or applied linguists (e.g. Brutt-Griffler, 2002; Kachru, 1986; Kirkpatrick, 2011; McKay, 2002; Smith, 1976, 1978, 1981 to name a few) to develop different frameworks or academic approaches to discussing English language usage: English as an International Language (EIL) and World Englishes (WE). These two categories have variously prompted researchers, scholars, and educators in the field to reconsider the ways in which English is conceptualised, researched, taught, and learned. In sometimes similar and sometimes different ways, these frameworks have challenged the taken-for-granted or unquestioned superiority of notions such as 'the Queen's English', 'received pronunciation', or 'general American', and they have put forward a more liberal and democratic view. Kubota (2012) calls such frameworks the "anti-normative paradigm". These approaches also unanimously emphasise the importance of recognising the pluricentricity of English and the equal treatment given to all varieties of English and its speakers. Despite this, there have been terminological debates about WE, EIL, and English as lingua franca (ELF) (Matsuda & Friedrich, 2010), and therefore the ways in which they are conceptualised and interpreted have not been consistent. It is important to clarify how I interpret these terms and to propose which of them this book will adopt as a framework from here on.

The term 'English as an International Language' tends to be conceptualised differently by different scholars. It is variously conceptualised as "paradigms or perspectives" (McKay, 2002; Sharifian, 2009), "the functions or uses of English in international contexts" (Matsuda & Friedrich, 2010), or simply "a variety of English" (Tomlinson, 2003; Widdowson, 1997). However, I prefer to conceptualise 'EIL' as a paradigm, or as Sharifian (2009) puts it, "a paradigm for thinking, research, and practice" (p. 2). In other words, I see EIL as a linguistic and epistemological lens for researchers, scholars, and educators to 'put on' in order to critically:

- revisit and reconsider their ways of conceptualising English;
- reassess their analytical tools and the approaches they adopt in the Sociolinguistics of English and Teaching English to Speakers of Other Languages (TESOL) disciplines; and
- revise their pedagogical strategies for English language education in the light of the tremendous changes that English has undergone as a result of its global expansion in recent decades.

EIL recognises the international functions of English and its use in a variety of cultural and economic arenas by speakers of English from diverse lingua-cultural backgrounds who do not speak each other's mother tongues. However, this does not mean that there is a particular single variety of English called EIL – e.g. English for specific purposes ([ESP], Widdowson, 1997) – that is used specifically for international purposes such as English for international aviation or international business English. There are in fact cases where EIL is confused with or mistakenly referred to as 'International English' (see, e.g. Seidlhofer, 2003). As Sharifian (2009) argues, "the use of an adjective plus 'English' often suggests a particular variety (e.g. Australian English or Singaporean English) and 'International English' can suggest a particular variety of English … being selected as a lingua franca for international communication" (p. 2). Drawing on Sharifian (2009), my view is that the EIL paradigm rejects the notion of a single variety of English serving as the medium for international communication. "English, with its pluralised forms, is a language of international, and therefore intercultural communication" (Sharifian, 2009, p. 2). In international communicative encounters, speakers of different lingua-cultural backgrounds bring to their use of English a variety or varieties they are most familiar with. They are likely to employ various communicative strategies to engage collaboratively in meaning-making and to negotiate linguistic and other differences to achieve successful communication.

Because the EIL paradigm acknowledges diversification of English as a result of the global spread of the language, one of the central themes of EIL is its recognition of Kachruvian World Englishes, and its emphasis on the relevance of world Englishes in the teaching, learning, and thinking about English today (Matsuda, 2002, 2009; Matsuda & Friedrich, 2010; Sharifian, 2009). However, the notion of 'world Englishes' is also diversely interpreted and inconsistently used by researchers and scholars who have studied various aspects of different varieties of English in the world (Bolton, 2005). On the one hand, the Kachruvian school of thought conceptualises World Englishes (with capital letters) as a paradigm that "captures the dynamic nature of world-wide spread of the language" (Matsuda & Friedrich, 2010, p. 3). It calls for the equal recognition of the varieties of English from Outer- and Expanding-Circle countries, and argue for "the importance of inclusivity and pluricentricity in approaches to the linguistics of English worldwide" (Bolton, 2005, p. 204). On the other hand, world Englishes, as varieties of English, are often referred to either as *all* varieties of English in the world or only the 'new Englishes' in the Outer-Circle countries where English

22   *Teaching EIL: calls to implement change*

arrived as a colonial language and later became established as an additional language (Bolton, 2005). One of the criticisms that Pennycook (2003) and Saraceni (2009) offer about the WE paradigm is that it overlooks the diversity of English spoken within a single nation, i.e. regional varieties of English, sociolects, and idiolects. Saraceni (2009) argues that "the evolution of English is progressing in a complex manner which cuts across borders ... it evolves in ways that escape academic description ... and young users of English mix global and local norms freely" (p. 183). Canagarajah (1999a), supported by Park and Wee (2009), adds that Kachruvian WE tends to:

> ignore the ideological implications of the legitimating periphery Englishes. In his attempt to systematise the periphery variants, he has to standardise the language [which then valorises] the educated versions of local English, leaving out many eccentric, hybrid forms of local English as unsystematic.
>
> (p. 180)

In the light of this, I view the EIL paradigm as one that embraces/recognises all varieties of English at national, regional, social, and idiolectal levels in all circles as equal. According to this paradigm, differences should be neither viewed as fossil-ridden examples of interlanguages, which Vavrus (1991) terms, as the "deviational perspective". Nor should they be viewed from what Vavrus (1991) calls the "deficit perspective", through which differences are seen as inferior examples of incorrect speech or 'half-baked quackery' (Quirk, 1990). However, they are recognised as "sociolinguistically normal, necessary, and intrinsic to language varieties" (Tollefson, 2007, p. 30), which Vavrus (1991) calls the "dynamic perspective". By pluricentricity, I refer to the diversification of the varieties of English spoken in all circles, which is an outcome of the advancement of information and communication technologies and increased human mobility across the globe in today's postmodern globalisation era. As Clyne and Sharifian (2008) point out, "world Englishes have not remained comfortably within their traditional circles, but have travelled worldwide and have in many cases found new homes in other circles" (p. 6).

As the focus of this book is on the teaching of EIL, the following section reviews scholarly works that discuss the implications of the EIL paradigm for teaching EIL.

2.3. Teaching English as an International Language

The conceptualisation of WE in the 1960s until around the mid-1980s by Braj Kachru, and of EIL in the 1970s by Larry Smith, led to the emergence of a view of teaching and learning English that challenged the view of English as a static and monolithic language of the so-called 'native-speakers' of English. Since then, there has been a remarkably high level of interest in teaching EIL in the field of English Language Teaching (ELT). The topic of 'teaching EIL' has also established a clear and strong presence in numerous ELT-related journals, and conference themes, workshops, and sessions. One message that scholars, authors, and presenters almost unanimously voice is that "the teaching and learning of an international language must be based on an entirely different set of assumptions than the teaching and learning of any other second or foreign language" (McKay, 2002, p. 1). Awareness of the changing nature and sociolinguistic reality of the English language as a result of its global spread has prompted EIL scholars and educators to critique the irrelevance and inapplicability of the "mono-model" approach (Kachru, 1992) or the "native-speaker" model (Kirkpatrick, 2006) of ELT when discussing today's international communicative exchanges. In light of this, English language practitioners and teacher-educators have been suggested to reassess and reexamine their *teaching methodology* (Brown, 2006; Kumaravadivelu, 2003), *instructional variety and model* (Kirkpatrick, 2006; Matsuda & Friedrich, 2012), *curriculum and syllabus materials* (Brown, 2012; Gray, 2002; McKay, 2003, 2012b; Marlina & Ahn, 2011; Marlina & Giri, 2013; Matsuda, 2005, 2012b), *language testing* (Canagarajah, 2006; Hu, 2012; Jenkins, 2006b; Lowenberg, 2012), and *TESOL teacher-education program* (Dogancay-Aktuna, 2006; Dogancay-Aktuna & Hardman, 2012; Manara, 2012; Matsuda, forthcoming; Sifakis, 2007). Based on the EIL paradigm, EIL advocates have provided language practitioners and teacher-educators with various theoretical *principles* (Alsagoff, McKay, Hu, & Renandya, 2012; Brown, 2006; Hino, 2010; Matsuda, 2012a; McKay, 2012b; Smith, 1976, 1978) and *practices* (Baik & Shim, 2002; Bayyurt & Altinmakas, 2012; D'Angelo, 2012; Hino, 2010, 2012; Kubota, 2001a; Lee, 2012; Marlina, 2010; Matsuda, forthcoming; Matsuda & Duran, 2012; Sharifian & Marlina, 2012) for incorporating the pluricentricity of English into today's English language classrooms, and for instilling in students a sense of ownership and confidence in their own varieties of English (McKay & Brown, 2016). Since this book focuses on curriculum, I will discuss and review scholarly works on EIL syllabus materials and pedagogical practices, which I will use to detail the theoretical and analytical frameworks underpinning this book. However, prior to this, I define and explain how I propose to conceptualise and use the term 'curriculum' in this book.

2.3.1. Curriculum

Across a huge range of education literature, especially that generated by scholars in North American and British TESOL disciplines, the notion of English 'curriculum' is defined somewhat differently. For the purpose of this book, I conceptualise curriculum as planned approaches to teaching and learning that are informed by theoretical and philosophical beliefs about the kinds of knowledge that should be taught. From this perspective, a curriculum is not only *what* students have the opportunity to learn in a particular educational institution (Canagarajah, 1999a; Milner, 2010), but also *why* and *how* teachers provide their students with the opportunity to learn. Hence, a curriculum contains syllabus materials that teach specific content knowledge, pedagogical practices, and assessment strategies. However, both Eisner (1994) and Cochran-Smith (2000) postulate that a

24   *Teaching EIL: calls to implement change*

particular program of study has different forms of curriculum. The first form of curriculum is the explicit curriculum or text (Cochran-Smith, 2000), which concerns a sequence of what is overtly taught by teachers and how this is taught. It includes any public documents, policies, or guidelines that advertise or represent the goals of a given program. Another form of curriculum is the hidden curriculum or "subtexts, hidden texts, and intertexts" (Applebee, 1996; Barnes, 1992; Cochran-Smith, 2000), the covert, implicit messages, information, or knowledge that may be unavailable, and includes what is absent from the official syllabus materials and other publicly available documents, what themes are central and missing in the materials, or what learning activities are carried out the most and the least. According to Milner (2010), this hidden form of curriculum is the most powerful learning "because what students do not have the opportunity to learn or experience in learning is present in what students are learning" (p. 3). Or as Rosenberg (1997) explains it, the presence of an absence. Even if a particular topic is not covered and not available in learning, students may still be learning, for example, that the topic is possibly meaningless, unimportant, or irrelevant.

As EIL curriculum research is still in its infancy (Matsuda, 2009; McKay, 2012b), one important under-researched aspect is "what EIL syllabuses, learning sequences, textbooks, or curriculum projects already exist?" (Brown, 2012, p. 163). The project described in this book aims to investigate both forms of curriculum of a program that teaches EIL for two reasons. Firstly, English language educators and teacher-educators whose current practices have been critiqued for their inadequacy in preparing learners for using English in international contexts are not always offered clear and explicit guidelines as to how to incorporate EIL principles and practices into their classrooms. Most discussions of these issues seem to remain at a theoretical or abstract level (Matsuda, 2012a) and overlook the pragmatic dimensions of the curriculum. Matsuda and Friedrich (2011) further explain that "researchers have not engaged in profiling pedagogical ideas that are informed by research and at the same time specific enough to be useful in classroom" (p. 333). Consequently, there is a need to provide critical and detailed accounts of how EIL can be incorporated and enacted in a classroom; and to demonstrate how realistic it might be to implement the perspectives advocated or the principles (refer to the next paragraphs and sections) offered by EIL scholars (Wee, 2013). Secondly, there has not yet been an empirical project that critically examines the subtexts of an already-existing EIL curriculum, although recently a growing literature offers theoretical and practical aspects of teaching EIL. It is hoped that this project can contribute to these gaps in the literature.

The following section reviews the literature that considers some key principles that English language educators have been urged to take into account in developing their syllabus materials and pedagogical practices for EIL. However, I acknowledge that I have intentionally not included or reviewed some frameworks or principles because of the irrelevance of the context in which they are based and/or discussed. These unreviewed frameworks or principles are mostly related to the context of a General English language learning program/course (for example, Intensive General English program for learners of English as a

Second Language/English as Foreign Language [ESL/EFL]) as opposed to an academic-content program (which is the EIL program I focus on in this book).

2.3.2. EIL curriculum: syllabus materials

To provide educators with suggestions on how to introduce EIL paradigm into classrooms, some prior studies have discussed to some extent what should be included in EIL curriculum and syllabus materials (Baik & Shim, 2002; Brown, 1995; Crystal, 1999; Gray, 2002; Marlina, 2010; Marlina & Ahn, 2011; Marlina & Giri, 2013; Matsuda, 2002, 2005, 2012b; McKay, 2002, 2003, 2012b). Generally speaking, these studies propose that EIL syllabus materials need to provide students with knowledge, awareness, attitudes, and skills to use English competently in today's borderless world in which the communicative contexts are international, intercultural, and plurilingual in nature. To develop the knowledge, awareness, attitudes, and skills, EIL curriculum scholars and researchers (e.g. Baik & Shim, 2002; Brown, 1995; Crystal, 1999; Gray, 2002; Marlina & Ahn, 2011; Marlina & Giri, 2013; Matsuda, 2012b; McKay, 2012b) have proposed some EIL principles or, as Matsuda (2012b) terms, an EIL "framework" that language educators and researchers are encouraged to consider when evaluating, selecting, and developing EIL syllabus materials. In the following section, I identify and tease out from the work of the researchers I have mentioned here what I see as four of the key principles. To a large extent, these four principles inform and underpin the theoretical and analytical dimensions of the study on which this book is based:

- EIL syllabus materials should provide students with exposure to varieties of English;
- EIL syllabus materials should include representation of a variety of multilingual speakers of world Englishes and of interaction among them;
- EIL syllabus materials should include representation of and exposure to different cultural values; and
- EIL syllabus materials should provide students with skills to communicate across differences.

Later, I will propose an additional principle, which I will argue draws attention to an often under-appreciated dimension of EIL curriculum and practices. But let me first explicate what is entailed by these principles, one at a time.

2.3.2.1. EIL syllabus materials should provide students with exposure to varieties of English

If, as Crystal (1999) argues, "no one can avoid being part of the current of linguistic change or variation, and avoid bathing in the sea of linguistic variety" (p. 19), then it would appear that EIL syllabus materials should provide students with the opportunity to develop their meta-knowledge about English as

26 *Teaching EIL: calls to implement change*

a heterogeneous language by exposing them to different varieties of English. In order to support the ecological richness of this "sea of linguistic variety", this particular principle dictates that the materials also need to raise students' awareness of the ways in which the variety of English they speak, learn, use, or know is one of many Englishes, and it may be different from what their future interlocutors are likely to use. What is even more important is that this awareness should guide students to learn to view Englishes spoken by bi-/multilingual speakers from so-called 'non-native' English-speaking countries as "perfectly legitimate, in the same way as people in other 'native' English-speaking countries such as Ireland and Scotland take pride in their local varieties" (Li, 2007, p. 12). This is because, as Kubota and Austin (2007) argue, "teaching materials both construct and reflect discourses on what is worthy for learning ... or seen as the 'correct' knowledge to learn" (p. 76). With syllabus materials that adopt a monomodel approach to teaching or that presume that there is only one variety of English, students are likely to "feel confused with or resist different types of English uses; be shocked by different varieties of English and may view them as deficient (rather than different); and grow disrespectful to such varieties" (Matsuda, 2002, p. 438). Seargeant (2012) has suggested that teachers need to develop "interventions directed at people's behaviour" (p. 80). Teachers have been encouraged to use pre-packaged materials that already include multiple varieties of English or any supplementary materials that illustrate world Englishes (Baik & Shim, 2002; Kubota, 2001a; Marlina, 2010; Matsuda, 2012b). It is argued that these materials are likely to "abolish ethnocentrism" (Brown, 1995, p. 236) and native-speakerism (Holliday, 2005), both of which position native English speakers as the 'correct' source of knowledge of English and therefore the model for exclusively effective communication, teaching, and learning.

One important issue in regard to this principle, that both McKay (2012b) and Matsuda (2012b) have raised, is that the chosen varieties of English need to be relevant to the local contexts. If this is to be applied in the context of Australia, then it may mean that students studying in Australia need to learn only locally demarcated varieties of Australian English. The problem with this is that the porosity of regional and even local boundaries has led to the question regarding which variety(ies) of English is/are and will be locally relevant. As discussed previously, the increasing number of migrants in Australia and the advancements in communication technologies have allowed people in Australia to be exposed to varieties of English other than Australian Englishes. For instance, according to Singh, Kell, and Pandian (2002), the varieties of English spoken by the Malaysian population in Australia has challenged the predominant position of Standard Australian English and its teaching. Therefore, the variety(ies) of English to which learners need to be given exposures should be *glocal*ly relevant.

In exposing students to different varieties of English, there is another issue that has not been addressed clearly in the literature and has the potential to cause further confusion. While EIL scholars have been emphasising the importance of exposing students to different varieties of English, they themselves also argue that it is impossible and perhaps unnecessary for students to master all different varieties of English (Matsuda, 2012b). The question that has not been clearly addressed is: Where should an EIL curriculum in a university start? What do students need to read and engage with first in order to understand the notion of the varieties English and to view them from a dynamic perspective as opposed to a deviational or deficit perspective (Vavrus, 1991). It is hoped that the findings presented in this book can shed light on these questions.

2.3.2.2. EIL syllabus materials should include representation of a variety of multilingual speakers of world Englishes and of interaction among them

As previously discussed, the global expansion of English has brought dramatic changes to the demographics of users of English. However, some studies have revealed that some English language teaching materials still mainly use characters from Britain or America and frequently display interactions between so-called 'native-' and 'non-native-speakers' (Datta, 1939; Gray, 2002; Matsuda, 2002, 2005). Given that today's communicative exchanges predominantly take place between multilingual users of English who are mostly 'non-native' English speakers, this principle states that EIL syllabus materials should include representations of speakers from what Kachru referred to as Inner-, Outer-, and Expanding-circle countries (Matsuda, 2005, 2012b) and include more examples of interactions between these speakers in their own varieties of English and possibly in other languages (McKay, 2002, 2003, 2010, 2012b; Matsuda, 2012b). Not only do these representations provide students with a more realistic and accurate picture of the complexities of language described previously, but they also provide them the opportunity to develop a view that the category of users of English is not just restricted to those from Britain, America, or other 'native' English-speaking countries.

However, some research on this issue (Marlina & Ahn, 2011; Marlina & Giri, 2013) has revealed that although some teaching materials have included people/characters from diverse lingua-cultural backgrounds and interactions among 'non-native-speakers', these characters and their interactions are often portrayed from a deficit perspective. Characters who fall into the category of 'non-native-speakers' tend to be condescendingly represented as 'learners' of English as opposed to legitimate users and speakers of English. The conversations among these characters are often about how long they have been learning English, how to spell an English word, how important learning English is to them, and whether they can borrow an English dictionary. Even when the conversations are on a different topic, the pragmatic norms and the pronunciations are still based on so-called Inner-Circle varieties of English (Marlina & Ahn, 2011). I will explain this by offering a typical example, which could have been taken from a variety of textbooks or teaching materials.

A character (e.g. a businessman from Japan who is on a business trip in New York) is speaking English to a group of business people. Based on his profession and what he does – in this instance, we are told that he is on a business trip to New York – in the context of the scenario, this character might be regarded as

28 Teaching EIL: calls to implement change

a competent user of English. Yet, he is still condescendingly portrayed as a novice learner. In the listening exercise in which the character is asked to list what he brings in his briefcase to New York, he talks about not forgetting to bring his English dictionary and vocabulary notebook. These representations are likely to prompt "students to continue upholding native-speaker supremacy and at the same time develop an inferiority complex, believing that one is never going to graduate as a 'learner' of English unless he/she is from so-called 'native' English speaking countries" (Marlina & Giri, 2013, p. 92). It is important that the inclusion of speakers of world Englishes from 'non-native' English-speaking countries and representations of the interactions among them need to be done in a non-deficit way to provide students the opportunity to (1) expand their categorisation of legitimate speakers of English; and to (2) observe the effectiveness of a communicative exchange that takes place in a variety or varieties of English they may not have encountered before.

2.3.2.3. EIL syllabus materials should include representation of and exposure to different cultural values

There is wide agreement in EIL literature that language and culture are intimately interconnected (Kachru & Smith, 2008; Sharifian, 2011; Wierzbicka, 2006). The way people use language and the conventions of people using language appropriately are shaped by the cultural values and beliefs with which they have been socialised. Over 60 years ago, Krober and Kluckhohn (1952) observed that the notion of culture has almost 160 definitions because of its coinage and usage in different disciplines. The diversity of coinage and usage since that time has hardly diminished, making definitions very difficult to construct. Even though the notion of 'culture' is relatively difficult to define, EIL education specialists tend to agree that a study of culture should in some way be an essential component of English language curriculum (Araluce, 2008; Harumi, 2002; Stern, 1983; Tanaka, 2006) and that it "holds a legitimate space in language teaching and consequently in materials we teach with" (Matsuda, 2012b, p. 176).

The outcomes of the global expansion of English and the frequency of contact between people from different parts of the world due to globalisation have raised the importance of promoting multiculturalism and developing intercultural awareness in EIL teaching materials (Araluce, 2008; Baumgardner, 2006; Harumi, 2002; Marlina, 2011; Matsuda, 2012b; McKay, 2012b). The de-Anglicisation of English as a result of its spread does not mean that English has become de-culturalised. Rather it represents diverse sociocultural norms or conventions, cultural values, beliefs, and practices of speakers of English from different parts of the world, which they are likely to bring into any communicative encounters in which English is the medium of communication. With the rapid expansion of advanced communication technologies and increased human mobility across the globe in the context of postmodern globalisation, communicative encounters between speakers of English from different parts of the world are frequent and likely to result in exchanges of those norms, values, beliefs, and practices. Consequently, syllabus materials that are based on the "target culture" (Cortazzi & Jin, 1999, p. 204), or American or British cultures, are unlikely to be relevant in the changing social contexts.

Thus, in order to promote intercultural awareness and multiculturalism, the third principle argues that EIL syllabus materials need to reflect zero tolerance for parochialism and monocultural chauvinism (Trevaskes et al., 2003). Specifically, EIL and/or WE scholars and researchers (Baumgardner, 2006; Gray, 2002; Marlina, 2011; Marlina & Giri, 2013; Matsuda, 2012b; McKay, 2002, 2003, 2012a, 2012b; McKay & Bokhorst-Heng, 2008) have suggested that the cultural information taught in EIL syllabus materials needs to be based on what Cortazzi and Jin (1999) term, "source culture" and "international target culture" (pp. 204–205). As one's own culture is naturally embedded in the ways in which he/she uses English, students should firstly be provided opportunities to learn to develop skills in using English to describe and talk about their own community and culture with those outside their local milieu. Culture, however, should not be limited to traditional and often stereotypical notions such as 'kimchi' for Korea, 'sari' for India, or 'kung fu' for China. Any cultural values, norms, practices, and beliefs in which the students' experience is situated constitute local culture. They are the ones that EIL syllabus materials should include or use as the basis for classroom discussions. In addition to learning about or reflecting on one's own culture, English language students should also be exposed to culture(s) of their future interlocutors. Since potential future interlocutors are often unknown and diverse, and today's social communicative contexts are characterised by variations in cultural behaviour (Canagarajah, 2006; Xu, 2002), the materials need to provide students with a great variety of cultures from both 'native' and 'non-native' English-speaking countries. However, it would be almost impossible for teaching materials to cover every single country and culture within each country in the syllabus materials. Matsuda (2012b), in response to this challenge, suggests that teachers need to "strategically diversify the content to include countries and regions from various parts of the world in the teaching materials" (p. 177).

2.3.2.4. EIL syllabus materials should provide students with skills to communicate across differences

In the literature on EIL syllabus materials or curriculum development, the three principles I have discussed prior to this one seem to be the most commonly discussed. And they are the most commonly highlighted principles associated with selecting, evaluating, and developing EIL syllabus materials. Although it is crucial to raise students' awareness of how different varieties of English reflect cultural values and beliefs of users of English from diverse lingua-franca backgrounds, this fourth principle argues that it is still not enough if students are not given the opportunities to learn to employ strategies to communicate across those differences. There is no doubt that knowledge and awareness of linguistic and cultural diversity are basic requirements for developing strategies to deal with diversity. As Milner (2010) says, "once students *know* better, they are more likely

30 *Teaching EIL: calls to implement change*

to *do* better" (my emphasis, p. 45). However, knowing or being aware of differences does not always mean that one is automatically equipped with readiness or knowledge of how to respond to these differences. Thus, in addition to knowing why they are different and why others are different, EIL students should also have opportunities to develop knowledge of what to do when encountering differences (Brown, 2012). Drawing on the writings of Canagarajah (2006), Firth (1996), Higgins (2003), and Marlina (forthcoming), this principle requires that EIL syllabus materials need to provide students with the opportunity to learn how to negotiate across difference. In encountering different varieties of English, both Firth (1996) and Higgins (2003) argue that students should be given the opportunities to develop the following strategies and attributes:

- interpersonal strategies: i.e. repair, rephrase, clarify, gesture, change topic, seek consensus, and provide mutual support (Firth, 1996); and
- attitudinal resources: i.e. patience, tolerance, and humility to negotiate differences (Higgins, 2003).

One particular aspect of the notion of attitudinal resources that needs to be critically reconsidered is tolerance in negotiating difference. This is because the notion of tolerance or being tolerant does not have a particularly positive meaning: it can mean 'to put up with' and "oftentimes, one only tolerates people who are disliked for their differences" (Odora-Hoppers, 2009, p. 605). As Bredella (2003) says, "Tolerance is insufficient because tolerant persons prefer their own beliefs and values to those of the others" (p. 232). In the face of the diversity of Englishes and cultures in the world, and in countries such as Australia, this principle urges EIL educators to teach their students to better understand that differences are normal and necessary, and to enable their students to be metaculturally competent (Sharifian, 2011, 2014) in working with these differences. This metacultural competence involves the ability to demonstrate the following attributes (Sharifian, 2014).

- *Conceptual variation awareness*: i.e. awareness that one language can be used by different language users from diverse backgrounds to communicate different conceptualisations.
- *Conceptual explication strategy*: i.e. the ability to explain and interpret different conceptualisations.
- *Conceptual negotiation strategy*: i.e. the ability to seek clarification and negotiate different cultural meanings.

2.3.3. EIL curriculum: pedagogical practices

Another aspect of curriculum that is relevant to this book is the pedagogical practices of EIL or the 'how' of teaching EIL. In the TESOL discipline, a large number of English language pedagogical approaches have been proposed by language pedagogy specialists, such as the Grammar-Translation Method, the Direct

Method, Audiolingualism, The Silent-Way, Community Language Learning, Total Physical Response, the Language Experience Approach, the Natural Approach, the Communicative Language Teaching (CLT) Approach (see Celce-Murcia, 2001; Richards & Rodgers, 1985; Oller & Richard-Amato, 1983, for further discussions of the above approaches). However, the changing sociolinguistic landscape of English as a result of its global expansion and the changing communicative needs that globalisation has brought about have prompted scholars and researchers to critique the philosophical assumptions about teaching, learning, and communication underlying some of these approaches, particularly the CLT approach, which is "the generally accepted methodological norm in the field" (Brown, 1994, cited in McKay, 2002, p. 108).

CLT has been criticised for its implied or explicit promotion of Anglo-Saxon values, ideologies, attitudes, beliefs, philosophical assumptions about teaching and learning, and for its limited views of communication, which may not be applicable to other contexts of learning (Ellis, 1996; Holliday, 1994; Hu, 2002; Kramsch & Sullivan, 1996; McKay, 2002, 2003). Brown (2006) further argues that "socio-political variables, the notion that local conditions can affect varieties of language use, and the notion of ownership of English, played no role in CLT approach" (p. 685). As English has become both globalised *and* localised and therefore (at least potentially) *belongs* to its speakers, Kramsch and Sullivan (1996) believe that each pedagogical approach to teaching English needs to be localised. Local teachers need to be afforded the necessary authority to conceive, decide, implement, and develop a curriculum that is appropriate for their own contexts, one that encourages their students to "think globally; act locally" (Canagarajah, 1999b; Kramsch & Sullivan, 1996; Marlina, forthcoming; McKay, 2003). As advocated by Kumaravadivelu (2003, 2006), teachers should no longer conceptualise that they are in a Methods era, but rather a post-Methods era that is characterised by awareness of the fact that there is no one best or most effective teaching method that should be used and adopted as the 'norm'. Rather, teachers should take into account the local needs of their students and to use their local context as a base for developing their materials as well as their pedagogical approaches.

From my experience of sharing this knowledge with teachers in TESOL teacher-education programs and in ELT-related conferences in Australia, Indonesia, South Korea, and Vietnam, the offered view can be liberating but at the same time it can create further confusion in many teachers. On the one hand, teachers who adopt a relatively popular pedagogical practice in the field of ELT such as the CLT approach may be criticised for their failure to adequately prepare their learners for using English in international contexts and for the potential 'Western bias' embedded in their choices of practices. On the other hand, teachers are encouraged to refrain from seeking the 'best' model and urged to start developing their own pedagogical approaches, a practice that many of them still find abstract, vague, and unclear. Despite their theoretical interest in introducing EIL into their own classrooms, many teachers are on record as resorting to their usual and familiar ways of teaching because they find the suggestions to be vague and they are uncertain about what they can do to implement changes to their

32 *Teaching EIL: calls to implement change*

Table 2.1 English as an International Language (EIL) pedagogical approaches recommended by Hino (2010)

	Approach	Description
Type 1	Teaching about EIL	Raising awareness in the diversity of EIL by providing such knowledge to the students
Type 2	Exposure to varieties of English	Helping the students to become familiar with the linguistic and cultural diversity of EIL.
Type 3	Role-play as cross-cultural training	Learning to cope with cultural differences expected in the use of EIL
Type 4	Content-based approach to EIL	Learning EIL by learning content matters in EIL
Type 5	Participation in a community practice in EIL	Authentic, real-life experience in EIL
Type 6	Grammar-translation plus reading aloud	Approaches based on indigenous values that are compatible with local cultures
Type 7	Projecting the local teacher's own non-native English as a model	Attitude that considers the indigenous variety of English as legitimate

practice (Matsuda & Friedrich, 2011). If EIL scholars aim to encourage educators to implement the teaching of its paradigm, then they will need to provide a number of specific pedagogical practices that teachers can choose and adapt *not* as some kind of universal benchmark but as particular examples for exploring and practising the teaching of EIL.

Thus, Hino (2010) outlines seven different EIL pedagogical approaches that he believes have been effective in an actual classroom setting (Table 2.1).

In the following section, I review previous studies that have examined the effects of teaching EIL/WE on students in different educational contexts.

2.4. Previous studies on the effects of teaching EIL

For the past three decades, World Englishes and EIL scholars have extensively and widely published their empirical discoveries of new varieties of English. This has involved highlighting the irrelevance and inapplicability of using, learning, or teaching a single variety of so-called Inner-Circle English, and thus they have tended to propose principles that should inform classroom teaching and curriculum and/or syllabus materials development, selection, and evaluation. The question now is: then what? Applications and evaluations of EIL classroom pedagogy are still in their infancy (Briguglio, 2007; Matsuda, 2009; McKay, 2012a; Hino, 2010). Brown (2012) specifically highlights two research areas or questions that have not been pursued by many research studies, which I deal with in this book: (1) has the EIL curriculum been 'successful'? and (2) what are the effects of the curriculum on students who have been living in or who study in English-speaking countries?

Research studies examining the instructional effects of EIL/WE on students are relatively scarce. Bamgbose (2001) claims that "far too often we [World Englishes/EIL scholars] publish for the attention of our colleagues and to advance knowledge" (p. 361), but have overlooked the "treasure in our very own backyards: our students" (Soo Hoo, 1993, p. 390). Specifically, research studies in WE and English as a Lingua Franca (ELF) tend to be preoccupied with documenting, for example, the uniqueness or distinctiveness of the Englishes spoken by the so-called 'non-native-speakers' or the communicative strategies they employ within a controlled communicative context to achieve intelligibility and successful communication. Though it is crucial to build corpora of new varieties of English to promote the diversification of English and its relevance to everyday communication and classroom teaching, Li (2009) suggests that it is high time that researchers in the field "go beyond collecting strictly performance and experimental data" (p. 109) and begin to include voices, views, or reactions of both 'native-' and 'non-native-speakers' on a range of delicate and contentious issues that the fields of study have raised, promoted, and advocated. In the first part of this section, I review empirical studies that report on the instructional effects of EIL/WE on students in different educational contexts and at different levels of study – English for students at an American high school (Kubota, 2001b), business management major undergraduate students at an Australian university (Briguglio, 2006), a Global Englishes content courses for third- and fourth-year university students in Japan (Galloway & Rose, 2014; Rose & Galloway, forthcoming), a WE course for English major students in Taiwan (Chang, 2014), a Multicultural Education course for pre-service English teachers at a university in Japan (Suzuki, 2011), an Intercultural Communication course for in-service and pre-service EFL teachers at a Korean university (Shin, 2004), and a graduate course for students undertaking a master's degree in TESOL and PhD in International Education and Language Education at an American university (Oxford & Jain, 2010). (See Table 2.2 for a summary of these studies.) Although these empirical works have generated interesting insights, there are still some aspects that need to be critically reconsidered, which I discuss after presenting the findings of these different studies.

2.4.1. Desired instructional effects

All research studies I have consulted show that EIL lessons, workshops, and courses have, to some extent, prompted the student-participants to develop theoretical knowledge, attitudes, and skills that EIL and WE scholars desire learners of EIL/WE to acquire. These studies also reveal that the student-participants seem to become critically aware of their previously taken-for-granted perceptions and understandings of English and communication in English. The particular contexts in which student-participants (regardless of the so-called 'circles'

Table 2.2 Summary of previous studies on the effects of teaching English as an International Language or World Englishes (EIL/WE)

Study	Setting	Participants and L1	Duration of EIL/WE instructions	Data	Findings
Kubota (2001b)	High school English class (America)	17 college-bound high school students (L1 = American English)	8 sessions (55 minutes each)	Pre- and post-questionnaires and dictation tests, classroom observations, and post-study interviews	Quantitative data showed: • significant improvement in students' understanding of the difficulty of second language acquisition and perceived understanding of speech samples, *but* • increasing belief in the elimination of foreign accents, and positive attitudes towards the global spread of English. Qualitative data showed individual differences in attitudes and perceptions: • some showed positive attitudes towards linguistic and cultural diversity, eagerness to develop respectful strategies to communicate effectively with WE speakers, and respect for foreign languages, *but* • others showed xenophobic and ethnocentric attitudes, and attempted to avoid interaction with 'non-native-speakers' of English

| Shin (2004) | Intercultural communication course for EFL teachers (South Korea) | 25 pre-service English teachers (L1 = Korean) | 2 lessons (duration of each lesson = not stated) | Observations and exam responses | • Felt more confident about themselves as English teachers and as English speakers
• Challenged their status as non-native English teachers (NNESTs) compared to the native-speaker English teachers (NESTs) they encountered
• Critical views of the inequalities between NNESTs and NESTs, especially in relation to salary difference (NNESTs are underpaid despite their higher qualifications)
• Awareness of one major advantage of being NNESTs, i.e. awareness of their student learners' difficulties in learning English
• Critical views of the submissive attitudes Korean English teachers display in the presence of NESTs |
| Briguglio (2006) | International management: workshop on working in multinational teams (Australia) | 35 business management major students (from 12 nationalities, L1 = Australian English, Mandarin, Cantonese, Turkish, Bahasa Indonesia, Swedish, Bahasa Melayu (Malay), German, Thai, Croatian, Swahili, and American English | 2.5 hours workshop | Interviews, written progress reports, and a post-questionnaire | • Becoming culturally sensitive and showing the ability to operate successfully in multinational teams
• Confidence in written English and better understanding of people with accents
• More understanding and openness towards other cultures

However:

• some students displayed a deficit perspective of students from Outer- and Expanding-Circle countries (which the researcher does not mention, but is evident from the data) |

Table 2.2 (cont.)

Study	Setting	Participants and L1	Duration of EIL/WE instructions	Data	Findings
Oxford & Jain (2010)	A graduate course (title of the course not mentioned): a course that "had never been taught at our university" (p. 242)	8 MA (TESOL) students and 2 doctoral students in international education and English education (L1 = Mandarin, American English, African American English, Spanish, Hindi)	Not mentioned (presumably 1 semester)	Students' journal entries and course assignments.	Students' journal entries and assignments showed their changed previously taken-for-granted assumptions/beliefs on the following 'fallacies': • Native-speaker fallacy: native English varieties are valid forms of English and the speakers teach it best • Location fallacy: English proficiency is only gained in native English-speaking environment. • Standard English sufficiency fallacy: learning Standard English is enough for communication, not world Englishes • Legitimisation fallacy: native English speakers are the judges of what constitutes legitimate forms of English • Simplicity fallacy: Hegemony of English can be simply described

| Suzuki (2011) | Multicultural education in a language teacher education program (Japan) | 3 third-year student-teachers (L1 = Japanese) | 12 weeks (1 lecture, 100-minutes long) | Individual in-depth interviews and analysis of students' writing | • Broadened their perspectives of English and its users. However: • still reluctant to view established L2 varieties (such as Singaporean English) as equal to American or British English • still believed in universal intelligibility of American English and British English as a model for teaching and for international communication • Unsure of the significance of teaching multiple varieties of English to their future students • In their future classrooms, diversity would only be mentioned in passing but not taught |
| Chang (2014) | Elective course on World Englishes (Taiwan) | 22 English major students | A semester (once a week, 2 hours) | Students' reflection papers | Learning World Englishes made students: • more critically aware of the dominant power of English as a global language • more critical in their view of language learning and using • more open-minded about different varieties of English, and • more interested in finding ways to counter English hegemony |

Table 2.2 (*cont.*)

Study	Setting	Participants and L1	Duration of EIL/WE instructions	Data	Findings
Galloway and Rose (2014)	Global content courses (Japan)	108 third- and fourth-year English major students	4 semesters (13 weeks per semester)	Reflective listening journals and interviews	Reflective listening journals prompted students to: • develop interest in listening to and communicating with speakers of English from diverse lingua-cultural backgrounds • Challenge preconceived stereotypes and prejudices towards unfamiliar varieties of English However: • Englishes used by 'non-native' English speakers were still negatively perceived • Englishes used by 'native' English speakers (especially American) were largely favoured and viewed as the 'standard' and preferred yardstick
Rose and Galloway (forthcoming)	Global content courses (Japan)	108 third- and fourth-year English major students	4 semesters (13 weeks per semester)	Written Reflections on a debate of the controversial 'Speak Good English Movement' in Singapore.	Learning about the 'Speak Good English Movement' prompted students to: • Be aware of the diversity of the English language • Recognise Singlish as a legitimate variety of English • Be critical of the standard language ideology (in both English and Japanese)

L1, language 1; L2, language 2.

they 'belong' to) have learned about the diversity of English (its form, culture, and user in the world) include: a two and a half hour workshop (Briguglio, 2006), an eight-session 'educational intervention project' (Kubota, 2001b), a two-lesson sequence in a course on intercultural communication (Shin, 2004), one-semester course on WE (Oxford & Jain, 2010; Chang, 2014) and on multi-cultural education (Suzuki, 2011), and a four-semester Global Englishes content course (Galloway & Rose, 2014; Rose & Galloway, forthcoming). In all cases the student-participants seem to have gained awareness and broader understanding of the diversity of English. For example, the Japanese student-participants in Suzuki (2011), Galloway and Rose (2014), and Rose and Galloway (forthcoming) reported that their exposure to and inquiry into examples of English language variation prompted them to challenge their partial views of English and to develop awareness of (1) the existence of varieties of English other than the ones spoken by the so-called 'native English speakers', and (2) the different ways in which English is spoken by whoever speaks the language.

Based on the perspectives of 'non-native' English-speaking teachers in Korea, Shin's (2004) observations of her students' presentations, discussions, and written assignments revealed that her lessons on EIL and issues of 'native' and 'non-native' identity prompted students to develop critical views and attitudes towards ideologies and practices that promote inequality between 'native-' and 'non-native-speakers'/teachers. They seemed to begin gradually to perceive themselves as deserving equal status as 'native' English-speaking teachers. This view is also shared by the 'non-native' English-speaking student-participants in the study by Oxford and Jain (2010) as well as by Chang (2014). From the perspectives of 'native' English speakers in Australia and America, investigations of classroom discussions, written assignments, and interview transcripts indicate that EIL syllabus materials and pedagogical practices appear to have encouraged students to develop:

- respect, understanding, and open-mindedness towards cultural differences, diversity of English, and foreign languages (Briguglio, 2006; Kubota 2001b);
- critical attitudes towards the view that native English speakers speak the legitimate varieties of English and are the legitimate judges of what constitutes 'correct English' (Oxford & Jain, 2010); and
- critical attitudes towards ideology and practices advocating the view that learning 'Standard English' from 'native English speakers' in an environment where English is 'natively' spoken is the best means to become an effective speaker of English (Oxford & Jain, 2010).

In terms of skills, the studies also report that the EIL syllabus materials and pedagogical practices seem to have prompted student-participants to show the ability to operate effectively in a multicultural team and to communicate with people who speak English with unfamiliar accents (Briguglio, 2006). What needs to be further highlighted is that the syllabus materials and pedagogical practices also prompted 'non-native' English-speaking student-participants to feel more

40 Teaching EIL: calls to implement change

confident about their written proficiency in English (Briguglio, 2006) and about themselves as speakers and/or teachers of English (Shin, 2004). Although the data from which the researchers make these claims are sometimes unclear and, if mentioned, are merely anecdotal in relation to their own students, they have shown that EIL syllabus materials and pedagogical practices can encourage students to develop the knowledge, skills, and attitudes that are important for operating effectively in today's international and intercultural settings. However, what is still unclear are the pedagogical factors that guide students to develop those knowledge, skills, and attitudes.

2.4.2. Undesired instructional effects

Although the student-participants in the studies mentioned in Section 2.4.1 seem to have shown awareness of English language variation, the researchers, except Shin (2004) and Oxford and Jain (2010), noted that EIL/WE-oriented syllabus materials and pedagogical practices have not prompted the participants to entirely change their attitudes and views towards varieties of world Englishes from Outer- and Expanding-Circle countries and their speakers. For example, after the two and half hour workshop on EIL in Briguglio's study (2006), the student-participants still held a view of the supremacy of 'native' English speakers. Although Briguglio (2006) does not discuss this explicitly, the comments made by her student-participants, especially the 'native-speakers' of Australian English, revealed their deficit views of/about 'non-native-speakers' of English or, as labelled in the study, 'international' students (my emphasis, Briguglio, 2006, pp. 6–7):

> "for success in multinational teams, we have to be more *tolerant* of cultural differences"
>> "[we] have to understand that *others* have *language difficulties*"
>> "[we have to] accept that their *understanding of English may not be as good*"
>> "you have to *have patience*".

In another study, Kubota (2001b) clearly points out that despite a series of eight lessons on WE, some student-participants still believed that English should be spoken without a foreign accent. They displayed some level of negativity towards linguistic and cultural diversity, showing both "xenophobic and ethnocentric attitudes" (Kubota (2001b, p. 57). Some even claimed that they would avoid any interactions with 'non-native-speakers' of English. In the listening comprehension test where students were asked to listen (only once) to audio-recorded samples of speech of speakers from diverse English-speaking countries and to write down what they had heard, there was no sign of improvement especially from the students whom Kubota (2001b) describes as "less positive" (p. 59). She further reports that the students found it difficult to understand and appreciate problems and issues such as linguistic imperialism (Phillipson, 1992), the politics of the spread of English (Pennycook, 1994), and linguicism (Skutnabb-Kangas &

Phillipson, 1994). These negative attitudes and views were attributed to a lack of exposure to speakers of world Englishes in their daily life and their lack of interest in learning a foreign language.

Sharing rather similar findings but from the perspectives of Japanese pre-service English teachers and English major students, Suzuki (2011) and Galloway and Rose (2014) also discovered that their student-participants, to some extent, still believed in the supremacy and correctness of varieties of American and British English after a sustained teaching and learning period of thirteen weeks. Typically, the participating students used the following words to justify their beliefs: 'standard', 'norm', 'good', 'correct', 'major', 'prototype', 'authentic', 'normal', 'yardstick', 'perfect', 'clean', 'common', 'natural', 'smooth', 'easy', and 'orthodox'. Students in Suzuki's (2011) study did not believe that an established variety of English spoken by people in Singapore, India, or their own context (Japan) should stand equally alongside American and British English. As prospective English teachers, the student-participants claimed that they would only mention in their future classrooms these different varieties of English in passing, but would not teach about them because (1) they were unsure of the significance of teaching these multiple varieties of English, and (2) these Englishes were deemed to be "bad, peculiar, hard to catch, and not very comprehensible" (pp. 149–150) in international communication, unlike American and British English. The central reason for this, Suzuki (2011) believes, can be ascribed to their "deeply ingrained beliefs that American and British English is a single useful form of English for international communication" (p. 151). This also shows that there is an underlying, unchallenged belief that American and British English are homogeneous, and have no dialects or differences in pronunciation or grammars within their own countries. All of this has led Kubota (2001b) to question "whether educational interventions, such as her project, would reduce prejudices among students even if they were implemented under optimal pedagogical conditions" (p. 61). Affirming Kubota's (2001b) interpretation, Suzuki (2011) suggests that perhaps a "single-shot-intervention" in the diversity of English, even when this single shot lasts several weeks, may not be sufficient to bring students to "fully accept and appreciate" (p. 151) English language variation. Briguglio (2006) argues, confirmed and supported by Galloway and Rose (2014), that "much more could be achieved if the intervention were more sustained and over a longer period of time" (p. 7). However, it would be interesting to explore the extent to which longer and 'more-shot-interventions' guarantee that students will 'fully' accept and appreciate the diversity of English.

2.4.3. My critical reflections

Reflecting on the above studies, there are a number of gaps or limitations that I aim to highlight. Firstly, although most studies provide brief information about what was taught in their course/lessons/workshops, they did not seem to explore in depth what factors student-participants believed had prompted them to question their taken-for-granted views of English and its diverse users. Secondly, some

42 *Teaching EIL: calls to implement change*

of the data sources – such as students' written and oral assignments – used by Briguglio (2006), Chang (2014), Oxford and Jain (2010), and Shin (2004) can be critiqued as problematic. It is indeed a pleasant experience for EIL educators to read and listen to students' critiques of their misconceptions of English and of any bias/prejudices towards different varieties of English in their written and oral assignments. However, the views expressed in their assignments may not necessarily be valid and reliable because of the power imbalance within the nature of such assignments as exam responses (Shin 2004), written progress reports (Briguglio, 2006), and course written assignments (Chang, 2014; Oxford & Jain, 2010). Students are likely to write what the assessors desire to read and hear in order to receive a good grade. This Hawthorne effect (Evans, 1978) cannot be relied on (Diaper, 1990). Arguably, the results would have been more valid if the researchers had used other data and data collection techniques that would generate more valid and reliable data.

Thirdly, knowing that students had not 'fully' accepted and appreciated the diversity of English may trouble educators who are committed to EIL. However, there seem to be minimal attempts to investigate and explain further why students still held such views or beliefs after having engaged in an EIL curriculum. Rather than resisting or ignoring the data that suggest students hold various views, one would hope rigorous research would seek to query/question the students as to why they hold these views? It is surely significant for EIL educators and researchers to explore and inquire into what other important issues need to be addressed in EIL education.

Lastly, some of the underlying discourses of teaching and learning EIL/WE that were utilised by these researchers and some scholars may need to be reconsidered critically. The use of words such as 'interventions' and the underlying assumptions behind Briguglio (2006), Galloway and Rose (2014), and Suzuki's (2011) suggestions seem to imply a conceptualisation of teaching EIL as similar to administering medical injections to cure an 'illness' or, using Kachru's (1986) words, "attitudinal sins" (p. 101). Students seem to be expected to 'fully recover' from their 'deficiency', 'sins' or 'illness' (ethnocentric and less-positive attitudes towards different varieties of English) after an 'intervention'. If these 'symptoms' still persist, the implied strategy is that more 'EIL-shots' should be administered to 'abolish' them.

My continued intellectual discomfort with this kind of language in EIL classrooms and EIL debates drove my inquiry in the research presented in this book. I wonder, for instance, if students show those undesired attitudes, views, prejudices even after having learned an EIL curriculum for three years, at what point will this particular curriculum be considered as 'unsuccessful'. I wonder if an EIL curriculum will be considered as a 'successful' one when all learners have 'fully' accepted and appreciated the diversity of English, and have 'abolished' their ethnocentric manner. I wonder about the logic that suggests longer and more-shot interventions will eventually ensure that students 'fully' accept and appreciate the diversity of English. By posing these questions, I do not wish to imply that I am supportive of those who believe in and advocate for the supremacy of Englishes spoken by 'native-speakers'. However, I would like to highlight my concern at the outset of this chapter that the research studies summarised in Table 2.2 seem to me to have overlooked an important part of teaching and learning in a program or course that is informed by an anti-normative paradigm. The next section presents and discusses an alternative view of EIL teaching and learning that I present and evaluate in the pages of this book that follow.

2.5. Alternative views: struggles and tensions in diversity education

The above discourses of conceptualising teaching EIL as 'interventions' to 'abolish' persistent ethnocentric and native-speakerist perceptions and to 'fully accept' the principles advocated by the paradigm are consistent with more positivistic ways of understanding learning and they overlook the process of diversity education at a level of practice. It is indeed encouraging to read and observe the attempts of EIL scholars, researchers, and educators to propose syllabus materials and pedagogical practices that promote equality and acknowledge the legitimacy of different varieties of English. However, based on my own experiences of interacting with my university students at different levels of study, simply promoting differences and telling students that they should take pride in the varieties of English they speak, as suggested by McKay and Brown (2016), is less likely to achieve what EIL advocates aim to achieve. This view is also implicitly signalled by Canagarajah (1999a). By stating this, I do not mean to imply that there is no need to teach EIL and, that ethnocentrism and native-speakerism should be favoured and welcomed. Ethnocentric and native-speakerist practices and ideologies that have prompted students to experience tensions during their encounter with an anti-normative paradigm need to be recognised and, hence, pedagogically approached in a different way. If English language variation is argued as sociolinguistically normal and necessary, then the struggles and tensions that students/teachers are likely to experience in learning/teaching about language variation also need to be perceived as educationally necessary, and therefore brought to the foreground. This section discusses this alternative view by using works of a number of scholars whom I would classify as critical inquirers, from several disciplines such as Critical Applied Linguistics, Critical Literacy Study, and Critical Multicultural Education, and addresses why students experience tensions and struggle.

2.5.1. Struggle and tensions

Bakhtin's ability to "hear voices in everything and dialogue relations among them" (Min, 2001, p. 5) prompted him to observe that "human beings arrive in a verbal-ideological world that pre-exists them, a heteroglot world of competing discourses in which they must find their way" (Doecke & Kostogriz, 2008, p. 77). In the context of teaching and learning, when students engage in learning about a particular subject matter, they are, at the same time, cognitively engaging in dialogues with many other voices or discourses on that particular subject matter

44   *Teaching EIL: calls to implement change*

to which they have previously been exposed, and into which they have previously been socialised. As Canagarajah (1993) says, students do not leave behind them at the classroom door voices and discourses that they have heard and developed from their social relations, their rural/urban upbringings, or their relationships to their parents; instead, they bring them in with them. As they encounter different words/discourses or different ways of understanding the world, "words from the past that echo in our minds as we converse with one another, the routines that we follow in order to participate in institutional settings, the communities or social networks to which we belong" (Doecke & Kostogriz, 2008, p. 82) are used as referential frameworks to evaluate the extent to which these new discourses make sense, and are processed dialogically to form one's own ideology. In social environments where individuals encounter interactions of multiple competing and clashing discourses or voices, "humans inherently experience [tension and] struggle to assimilate discourses that they feel make sense" (Assaf & Dooley, 2006, p. 5). These struggles and tensions of learners to understand their own as well as others' ideological beliefs and assumptions are the stepping stone for individuals to develop their own. As Bakhtin (1981) sees it:

> the process of constructing the self involves the hearing and assimilating of the words and discourses of others – mother, father, relatives, friends, representative of religious, educational and political institutions, the mass media and so forth – all processed dialogically so that the words in a sense become half one's own words.
>
> (p. xvii)

For the sake of explanation, Bakhtin (1981) divides these multiple words, voices, or discourses into two distinct types of social discourse: authoritative and internally persuasive. Authoritative discourse, on the one hand, as Bakhtin argues, is "like the word of fathers, a prior discourse" (p. 342), whose authority has already been established and socially acknowledged, and that, therefore, demands our unconditional allegiance. An example of this is "the authority of religious dogma, or of acknowledged scientific truth, or of a currently fashionable book" (p. 342). On the other hand, internally persuasive discourses are the everyday discourses of the common people we encounter, which are not always backed by any authority and which influence the ways people think and contribute to forming what is ultimately persuasive to the individual (Freedman & Ball, 2004). As individuals interact in their social environments, they will experience moments in which the discourses that they encounter are different from their own internally persuasive discourses. It is during these moments that individuals undergo a process of negotiation and struggle between these diverse forms of discourses, especially learning in an "ideological environment" where one's internally persuasive discourses are in conflict with other discourses (Bakhtin & Medvedev, 1978, p. 14). Though this may be perceived as negative, Bakhtin believes that "the social interactions that are most effective in promoting learning are those that are filled with tension and conflict" (Freedman & Ball, 2004, p. 6). This would suggest that there needs to be a different pedagogical practice with respect to EIL teaching and learning that goes beyond McKay and Brown's (2016) suggestion on how to encourage students to develop a sense of ownership, and to confidently take pride in being and sounding different.

Informed by a similarly dialogic theorising of language, a number of critical applied linguists (such as Akbari, 2008; Canagarajah, 1999a, 1999b; Janks, 2010; Pennycook, 1990, 1999, 2000) and critical multicultural educators (Banks & Banks, 2006; Jenks et al., 2001; Milner, 2010; Nieto, 1999, 2004, 2010; Simon, 1992) have critiqued what some see as a liberal approach to the teaching of linguistic and cultural diversity that accentuates the need for learning to merely accept and recognise linguistic and cultural pluralism. According to Banks and Banks (2006), this approach or perspective tends to be overemphasised in many programs such as Applied Linguistics and TESOL teacher-education. As liberating as this approach may sound, Pennycook (1990) argues that it has failed to "deal adequately with the politics of difference and all too often declines into a romantic and anti-intellectual celebration of individual difference" (p. 308). For example, in response to the diversification of English presented in the materials, students could view this difference/variation as either 'diversity' or 'deficiency' – because it is different from the superior Inner-Circle Englishes. Jenks et al. (2001) concur and specifically assert that what they call a "'feel-good' approach that focuses on 'let's-get-to-know-each-other-better' is ignorant of the root causes of racism and inequality" (p. 93). This approach also overlooks how practices and ideologies in society implicitly influence students' learning about differences, and their attitudes towards differences. In relation to the teaching and learning of EIL/WE, Canagarajah (1999b) has highlighted the fact that the "apolitical stance of this paradigm buries our eyes ostrich-like to the political evils and ideological temptations outside" (p. 201). Therefore, he urges, language teaching in general or programs that specialise in teaching linguistic and cultural pluralism should not isolate themselves from sociopolitical questions (see also Pennycook, 1990, 1999, 2000) and should take into consideration the influence of sociopolitical contexts (Nieto, 1999, 2004, 2010) operating within a society and the schools in which students live and learn.

These kinds of argument suggest that in terms of the syllabus materials selection, development, and evaluation, political issues need to be taken into consideration. In order to organise the huge complexity of issues associated with politics and to clarify her own perspective, Janks (2010) divides the notion of politics into two: *Politics* (with a "big P") and *politics* (with a "little p"). By big-P *Politics*, she refers to "the big stuff, worldly concerns ... [such as] government and world trade agreements and the United Nations peace-keeping forces, ethnic or religious genocide, money laundering, and linguistic imperialism" (p. 40). Little-p *politics* refers to the "micro-politics of everyday life ... [such as] the minute-by-minute choices and decisions that make us who we are; it is about politics of identity and place such as how we treat people day-by-day" (p. 40). In relation to EIL, some scholars such as Matsuda (2003)

46 Teaching EIL: calls to implement change

and Kubota (2001b, 2012) emphasise the importance of incorporating these issues in a curriculum that teaches EIL. However, these issues are mainly what Janks would call big-P ones. For example, Matsuda (2003) asserts that an EIL curriculum "must address the politics of the language [such as] the colonial and possibly the postcolonial presence of the language and the power inequality associated with its history" (p. 722). Kubota (2001b, 2012), sharing a similar viewpoint, also argues the importance of learning about the value of multilingualism and about the global expansion of English as a potential threat to the multilingualism of a nation. However, discussions relating to little-p politics in an EIL curriculum have been relatively rare, such as how people are unjustly treated on the basis of their race or of speaking English without a 'native' English speaker's accent, or the relative respect or disrespect accorded to particular cultures, languages, and dialects. Such discussions, however, are even more important as these are the politics that students are most likely to encounter in their everyday lives. Some educators, according to Tollefson (2007), may see this as "not theoretically justified and not pedagogical but political" (p. 27), and thus believe they should be excluded. However, Janks (2010) believes that it is essential because "working with the politics of local enables us to effect small changes that make a difference in our everyday lives and those of the people around us" (cf. Janks, 2010, p. 41).

In terms of pedagogy, those who employ a so-called liberal approach to the teaching of linguistic and cultural diversity, and in this case EIL, offer unclear explanations as to whether students are given opportunities to voice the struggles and tensions that they experience during their exposure to unfamiliar and multiple anti-normative discourses, or whether they are invited to reflect critically on their experiences, views, beliefs, and ideologies in relation to the diversity of English. Based on certain philosophical principles, or informed by notions such as transformative pedagogy, scholars such as Doecke and Kostogriz (2008), Pennycook, (1999), and Simon (1992) argue that in dealing with differences or in engaging students with questions of difference, educators need to take on the role of "transformative intellectuals" who enable their students to "critically engage with the conditions of their lives and thereby achieve a better sense of their possibilities as human beings and members of a larger community" (Doecke & Kostogriz, 2008, p. 82). In order to do so, on the one hand, some educators (see Banks & Banks, 2006; Williams, 1996) propose approaching their teaching by bringing these issues and 'tough topics' into classroom discussions to raise their students' awareness of the tough political issues. As Williams (1996) asserts, to deal with conflicts/tensions, "we may need to study them" (p. 200). On the other hand, although it is important to talk about these tough issues, Freire (1970) and Pennycook (1999) believe that they can often become a rather tired set of social issues. Thus, these scholars have offered another mechanism for challenging oppression, by making visible and audible the underlying assumptions that produce and reproduce structures of domination. This, they believe, may prompt people firstly, to begin questioning (a) how they have come to be as they are and (b) how discourses have structured their lives, and secondly, to envisage versions of a more just world, or alternative possibilities for organising social life.

2.6. Filling in the research gaps

This chapter has shown how the changing sociolinguistic landscape of English as a result of its global expansion has led to a paradigm shift in the field of Applied Linguistics. This has prompted some scholars and researchers in this field and in TESOL to call for the revision of the way English is conceptualised, researched, taught, and learned. In areas of syllabus materials and pedagogy, several scholars have called for the incorporation of the EIL paradigm into the learning curriculum in which the pluricentricity of English is the focus of learning. They see this as crucial in any curriculum and pedagogy that hopes to inspire students to change their attitudes and perceptions towards different varieties of English and its speakers. I have shown how EIL scholars and researchers in the area of EIL syllabus materials and pedagogy have developed some EIL principles, which can be seen to have underpinned the development, selection, and evaluation of syllabus materials and in practising of EIL teaching. However, as a framework for effectively teaching EIL, I believe it remains under-developed and under-theorised at the moment. Principles that are often proposed in recent literature on the teaching of EIL (Alsagoff et al., 2012; Matsuda, 2012a) are not always based on an existing program that teaches EIL, and are not written from the perspectives of teachers who write about and research on their experiences of teaching EIL. This, therefore, has led Wee (2013), supported by Qu (2016), to question the extent to which these principles could be practically implemented. This is the **first gap** that this book project aims to address, which is by exploring how EIL educators in one university in Australia inspire their students to learn about and appreciate different varieties of English. It is also hoped that their experiences of teaching can help extend and contribute to the conversations about the theoretical and practical aspects of teaching EIL.

Another relatively under-researched area in the field that has been highlighted by a number of scholars, which is the **second gap** that this book project aims to fill, is the evaluation of the materials and pedagogy from the perspectives of students. In this chapter, I have reviewed a number of studies conducted by scholars in different contexts and who have attempted to evaluate the effectiveness of these materials. These empirical studies reveal a range of instructional effects, some of which are desired by scholars in the field and some of which are perhaps undesired. Researchers in these studies believe that there should be more 'interventions' in order to 'abolish' the undesired effects. However, apart from the sometimes problematic choices of methodological approaches, the implications of these research studies seem to conceptualise EIL education from a positivistic view (ethnocentrism + EIL = non-ethnocentrism), and in doing so they ignore the inevitable tensions and struggles that may occur during the process of learning about something that perhaps challenges students' existing assumptions, beliefs, and ideologies. Rather than stating that students *have* and *have*

48 *Teaching EIL: calls to implement change*

not achieved the objectives promoted by EIL education, it is important to start addressing questions such as:

- what have students learned from an EIL curriculum?
- what factors have prompted them to agree with the perspectives advocated by an EIL curriculum?
- what are they struggling with? and why?

And beyond these questions

- what then are the implications of this for the development of EIL syllabus materials and pedagogical practices.

The research by language theorists and critical inquirers that I have discussed in the last section of this chapter will be used as basis to help me formulate my claims. The next chapter discusses the methodological approaches that I employed and developed to investigate all these questions and more.

3 Studying teaching EIL

3.0. Introduction

> We know that you and some other scholars at this conference have been tell-
> ing us, ESL [English as a Second Language] teachers in Australia, to teach
> English as an International Language. But I think you all are making it sound
> so easy and simple. The problem is – and maybe it's just me – that you have
> no clear illustrations! What do you guys expect us language teachers to do
> in actual classrooms? What materials do you guys expect us to teach? Do
> you think it is feasible in an Australian context? Don't you think teachers
> may find teaching EIL in Australia challenging? To show that what you're
> suggesting [teaching EIL] is working, do you have any evidence of what stu-
> dents think about studying EIL? Do you think they would learn something
> out of it? I guess my students would probably feel confused, but that's only
> my opinion. At the moment, everything is so hazy[1]

This comment was made by a frustrated conference attendee in response to
my presentation on the lack of the quality of 'EIL-ness' usually found in typical ELICOS (English Language Intensive Course for Overseas Students) curricula currently offered by several ELICOS providers in Melbourne, Australia. The
comment led to a heated discussion between the attendee and a number of well-
established scholars in the field, who strongly urged him to familiarise himself
with the literature. Some of my colleagues advised me against taking his comment
too seriously whereas others told me that "It's one of those people who are not
open to new knowledge", and so I should simply ignore him. Although I was a
little frustrated at the comment the attendee made, I could not ignore it. Over
time, as I continued to reflect on it, I began to sense that there were certain issues
that were not, and still are not, adequately addressed in curriculum development
literature for English as an International Language (EIL). It is these sorts of issue
that are behind my interest in exploring in depth the experiences and feasibility of
teaching and learning EIL in Australia.

As I outlined in Chapter 1, the purpose of this book project is to explore the
feasibility of teaching/learning EIL by analysing how EIL educators in a tertiary

50 *Studying teaching EIL*

undergraduate program in a particular institution inspire their students to learn about and appreciate the diversity of English, and how this is experienced, felt, and/or responded to by students. Not only does this research aim to highlight the strengths and areas that need improvement in a program that teaches EIL, but it also provides an additional critical perspective and suggests several additional principles for developing and teaching EIL materials.

Since I am seeking to understand "what people (including the researchers themselves) see, feel, hear, [and do]" (Rossman & Rallis, 2012, p. 8) within a specific social setting, qualitative methodology is best suited to the background research project. To some extent, the type of qualitative research paradigm that is particularly suitable to describe this book project is, as Glesne and Peshkin (1992) term it, "backyard" (p. 21) research. This is because the specific social setting in which I conducted my research was an undergraduate EIL program in which I was teaching during the period of data collection. The participants for this study were students studying in the program (who had come from diverse lingua-cultural backgrounds), and my own colleagues. In-depth interviews, observations, and documents were the main methods of collecting qualitative data, due to their effectiveness in exploring people's perceptions, experiences, and understandings.

An important dimension of the project is the reflexivity through which I make explicit that all of my observations, analyses, and insights are culturally and linguistically mediated by my experiences as a learner and teacher of EIL, as well as by the educational, cultural, and institutional contexts within which I am conducting this research. This is perhaps most obvious in my critical autobiographical narrative, which constitutes Chapter 4. In that chapter I seek to better understand and make sense of how I, as an EIL advocate and educator, encourage students to learn about and appreciate the diversity of the English language as it is understood and spoken in different contexts. However, throughout this book there are some moments where I step back and reflect on the process of meaning-making that I am engaged in as a researcher and sometime participant in the project.

In this chapter, my discussion is organised into the five parts: (1) a framework for my research design, (2) context: setting and participants, (3) methods for data collection, (4) methods for data analysis, and (5) trustworthiness of the study.

3.1. A framework for the research design: qualitative approach

During the last three to four decades, researchers have stumbled on or even designed their own methodological approaches to guide them in undertaking and writing up their research projects. The approaches that researchers have used are shaped by how they conceptualise "the nature of reality, knowledge, and therefore the production of knowledge" (Merriam, 1998, p. 3). In presenting one's approach to doing research, a researcher needs to "be able to explain the basis for each decision in the conduct of a study and to document those decisions for others to understand, assess, review, and critique it" (Rossman & Rallis, 2012, p. 11).

This section explains and justifies a methodological framework that I have engaged with and used, and that has allowed me to learn about and better understand the researched issues.

As someone who is closely associated with the development of one particular iteration of an EIL program in the Faculty of Arts in the university where I lecture and teach (Urban University), I approached this study with aim to better understand the processes and experiences of teaching EIL within that particular program. I was also interested in investigating the responses, feelings, and/or perceptions that students within that particular setting developed during and after having engaged with the teaching; and I wished to explore some underlying causes of those responses, feelings, and/or perceptions. Considering the exploratory and descriptive nature of my study, and my valuing of "context, setting, and participants' frames of reference" (Marshall & Rossman, 2006, p. 54), I believe that a qualitative research method was the most appropriate.

The word 'qualitative' implies "an emphasis on the qualities, on entities, and on processes and meanings that are not experimentally examined or measured (if measured at all) in terms of quantity, amount, intensity, or frequency" (Denzin & Lincoln, 2005, p. 10). A qualitative research approach is a type of approach that allows researchers to study people's words and actions, and the uniqueness of things or situations (Creswell, 2007; Denzin & Lincoln, 2011; Holliday, 2007; Rossman & Rallis, 2012) by asking the following important questions (Patton, 1985, p. 1):

- What does the world look like in that particular setting?
- What do those things mean for participants in that setting?
- What are their lives like?
- What is going on for them and what are their meanings?

Another important question for me as a qualitative researcher to ask is what I aim to learn about what participants (including myself) see, do, feel, and hear in a social setting in which they (we) operate. I want to emphasise, from the outset, what Rossman and Rallis (2012) argue about the connections between qualitative researching and learning. "Qualitative researchers", they say, "are learners whose purpose of doing research is to learn about some facet of the social world" (p. 5). In order to do this, qualitative researchers need to get closer to the participants' perspectives and actions, as much as is ethically possible to 'enter their world' to make sense of their everyday worlds, thoughts, perceptions, experiences, and feelings through interactions, and at the same time, to critically reflect on their own world, perceptions, thoughts, and experiences.

One concern or critique expressed by positivist researchers such as Phillips and Burbules (2000) regarding the issue of getting closer to or knowing the participants well – such as a close work relationship that I have with my colleagues – and working in one's own 'backyard' is that the study will not be able to provide objective perspectives and analysis of the participants, which they refer to as a crucial aspect of 'competent' inquiry. There is an assumption in this line

52 *Studying teaching EIL*

of critique that my position in the program and my work relationship with the participants were likely to cloud my perceptions, and to make it difficult for me to separate myself from my participants' perceptions. The interactions that I have with my participants may be

> shaped and guided by the core aspects of the researcher's experience and not the participant's ... [which will unduly] affect the analysis, leading to an emphasis on shared factors between the researcher and the participants and a de-emphasis on factors that are discrepant, or vice versa.
>
> Dwyer and Buckle (2009, p. 58)

Had I adopted a positivist approach to this research, I would have been required to generate a workable and ethical design by devising ways to collect a range of data that would allow me to create an objective account of the actions and words of my participants as they went about their everyday work as students or educators. In the process of collecting this/these data, it would have been essential for me to minimise the extent to which my presence as collector and observer of data would be obtruding into to the 'everyday' of their practices.

However, in a qualitative study such as I designed, I was conscious that one cannot utterly separate oneself from the lives and experiences of one's participants (Dwyer & Buckle, 2009). This is because of the deeply relational nature of qualitative research in which the trustworthiness of the study, unlike a quantitative approach, is not centred on the notions of 'scientific' objectivity.

> The process of qualitative research is very different from that of quantitative research. As qualitative researchers, we are not separate from the study, with limited contact with our participants. Instead, we are firmly in all aspects of the research process and essential to it. The stories of participants are immediate and real to us; individual voices are not lost in a pool of numbers. We carry these individuals with us as we work with the transcripts. The words, representing experiences, are clear and lasting. We cannot retreat to a distant 'researcher' role. Just as our personhood affects the analysis, so, too, the analysis affects our personhood. The intimacy of qualitative research no longer allows us to remain true outsiders to the experience under study and, because of our role as researchers, it does not qualify us as complete insiders. We now occupy the space between, with the costs and benefits this status affords.
>
> Dwyer and Buckle (2009, p. 61)

As with Dwyer and Buckle's (2009) explanation, my position in this study as researcher of the program at the same time as being a co-worker with my colleagues, a member of the team teaching the very program I was researching, need not have negatively influenced the research process. In undertaking this research, I was interested in listening to participants' stories or voices about the contexts and/or settings in which they and I operate, and constructing a complex detailed

Studying teaching EIL   53

understanding of the researched issue through engaging with the participants' stories. Since I was also aware that my presence as a researcher could not be wished away as being of no consequence, I aimed to be critical and reflective of my role or 'presence' in their stories and how much we share these stories. Dwyer and Buckle (2009) contend that the core ingredient of doing this kind of research is

> not insider or outsider status but an ability to be reflective on the subject-ive research process; and to be open, authentic, honest, deeply interested in the experience of one's research participants, and committed to adequately representing their experiences.

(p. 59)

It is within this "hyphen of insider-outsider" (Adlher & Adler, 1994, cited in Dwyer & Buckle, 2009, p. 60) that I was shuttling between the roles of researcher and participant in doing my research.

Rossman and Rallis (2012, pp. 8–11) claimed the following to be the characteristics of quality qualitative research. Qualitative researchers:

- get to know or know their participants, on some level, in order to understand their everyday worlds;
- understand people through engaging with them in multiple modes: talk with them; watch and listen as they go about their everyday tasks; read documents and records etc.;
- value and focus on the context and the messiness of the lived world;
- do not subscribe to the principle of inductive logic as this oversimplifies and trivialises the complexity of a qualitative research project. Rather, they begin with a well-thought out conceptual framework that focuses and shapes their decisions, and at the same time reminds them that this framework is flexible;
- do not control and predict, but rather focus on description, analysis, and interpretation;
- recognise the importance of reflecting on who they are, and therefore value their unique perspective as a source of understanding rather than something to be cleansed from the study; and
- raise sufficient discussion to interrogate established views rather than to generalise.

Applying these characteristics to my study allowed me to critically scrutinise the complexity of the teaching of EIL, and to consider what EIL educators, including myself, need to be aware of and to do to engage their/our students to learn about and appreciate the diversity of English, especially when teaching something that is 'against the grain' or contrary to the common sense understandings that students bring with them into their study of this EIL program.

In addition to explaining and justifying how a particular research approach was suitable for my study, as Creswell (2003) asserts, I need to address three important

54　*Studying teaching EIL*

elements of inquiry, namely: knowledge claims, strategies, and methods. The following sections answer three important questions which I adapted from Crotty (1998) and Creswell (2003), and which were central to the research design.

- What knowledge claims did I bring to the study?
- Which strategies of inquiry associated with qualitative methods governed my research procedures?
- What methods did I believe to be suitable to collect and analyse my data? (This will be discussed in Section 3.3 and Section 3.4.)

3.1.1. Knowledge claims: social constructivism

Any researcher brings their own worldview or paradigm to the research project and uses them to inform the conduct of their study. "Good research makes these [their worldviews/paradigms] explicit in the writing of a study" (Holliday, 2010, p. 15). In the broad field of qualitative research, methodologists suggest there are four different research paradigms or epistemological perspectives to which qualitative researchers typically refer in showing their understanding of the nature of the society in which the observed actions take place and to inform the way they conduct their study. Table 3.1 provides a summary of the perspectives that

Table 3.1 Summary of the knowledge claims

	Positivistic/ post-positivistic	*Interpretive/social constructivist*	*Advocacy/ participatory*	*Postmodern/ poststructural*
Purpose	Predict, control, generalise	Describe, learn, understand, explain, and interpret	Change, debate, emancipate, and empower	Deconstruct, problematise, question, and interrupt
Types	Experiment/ quasi-experiment, causal modelling, cost-benefit analysis, survey	Case study, ethnography, phenomenology, grounded theory, narrative inquiry	Critical race theory, disability inquiry, feminist perspectives	Postcolonial, queer theory, poststructural
Reality	Objective reality, 'out there', laws govern the world, absolute truth	Varied, multiple and complex, context-specific	Multiple and complex realities are situated in social, political, and cultural contexts (realities are conflictual and oppressive)	Questions assumptions that there is a place where reality resides

I have adapted from a range of writers, including Creswell (2007), LeCompte and Schensul (1999), Merriam (2009) and Rossman and Rallis (2012).

The conduct of this study was informed and shaped by the social constructivism paradigm. Social constructivists or researchers who work within this paradigm appreciate the importance of gaining an understanding of the social contexts in which people live and/or work and/or operate (Creswell, 2003; Lincoln & Guba, 2000; Newman, 2000; Schwandt, 2000). They believe that what people know and understand about the world is constructed, is situated within a particular context, and that this knowledge and understanding can be altered as these people interact with one another over a period of time within those specific social settings (Creswell, 2003, 2007; LeCompte & Schensul, 1999). In other words, how individuals think, believe, and present themselves is "affected by [the] social, political, cultural, economic, ethnic, age, gender, or other contextual characteristics of those who espouse them" (LeCompte & Schensul, 1999, p. 49). Researchers whose work can be categorised by this paradigm tend to "rely as much as possible on the participants' views of the situation" (Creswell, 2007, p. 20). The more that participants' particular views of a situation are valued (as opposed to checking whether they are accurate or correct or not), the more that the methods for generating or collecting data tend to involve "face-to-face interactions, whether in the form of in-depth interviews or extended observations or some combination" (Rossman & Rallis, 2012, p. 44). My study can clearly be situated within this paradigm, in that I aimed to learn more about and better understand the world in which I and my colleagues live and work, specifically the 'world' of the newly revised EIL curriculum.

But I was also keen to investigate the various *worlds* of different university classrooms where this course is being taught. I wanted to observe and critically reflect on what the teachers (including myself) are doing in these classrooms, and I wanted to inquire into the various (and sometimes shared) aims as we taught this program. Of particular interest to me are the ways in which teachers in this one newly revised EIL curriculum seek to engage their students in learning EIL (through their production and selection of materials and pedagogical strategies). In addition, I aimed to learn and understand how students respond to what they learn, and why they have responded in particular ways. I was interested in investigating what factors prompted them to develop particular responses or perceptions.

Therefore, over a semester, I invited student-participants to participate in one-on-one interviews to share their views about the various aspects of this particular EIL program and their understandings and perceptions of the ideas and theories underpinning it. When educator-participants were willing, I observed their classes (three of them over two semesters). This enabled me to note the students interactions with their classmates and their responses to the teaching and the teaching materials that were made available to them. All this was done to make sense or to interpret the meanings others have about the world to gain knowledge about the world, all of which is in line with broad understandings of a social constructivist paradigm of research.

56 *Studying teaching EIL*

One last aspect of social constructivist inquiry involves generating or inductively developing a theory for making meaning from the data collected in the field as opposed to starting with a theory. This latter understanding of theory suggests that it exists in some reified form, such as what Creswell (2003, 2007) argues researchers in the post-positivism paradigm tend to believe. Through closely examining the materials that EIL educators used and scrutinising the pedagogical practices they employed to engage students in learning about and appreciating the diversity of English, I aimed to develop a situated theory which would help me to make sense of the variety (and the commonalities) of what I had seen. In a similar way, through critically engaging with the range of students' views, responses, or feelings towards their learning, I hoped to affirm existing principles or frameworks for teaching EIL and/or develop new ones. However, as Rossman and Rallis (2012) have argued, in approaching my research in this way, I ran the risk of overlooking some of the complexity of the intellectual work of qualitative research. As a researcher, I could not and did not enter a particular research site with no theoretical framework in mind – a completely clean slate, as it were. Rossman and Rallis (2012) argue that a researcher enters an inquiry space with some kind of personal perspective and/or an emerging conceptual framework that to some extent focuses, guides, and shapes his/her decisions. They further argue that, based on the views of Aristotle and Plato, "all inquiry proceeds through a complex, nonlinear process of induction, deduction, reflection, inspiration and just plain old hard thinking" (Rossman & Rallis (2012, p. 10). Clearly, there was a sense in which I gradually developed a conceptual framework that drew on my reading of a range of relevant literature by scholars in the field. However, I did not perceive this framework as static, but rather as an emerging and flexible guideline. The range of meanings that I constructed through the course of the study was always responsive to the particular experiences and observations that I encountered on my research journey. I tended to move back-and-forth between my emerging framework (how this framework allowed me to understand/interpret my data and the teaching of EIL) and what I was hearing and seeing during my interactions with the participants and their voices and their stories (and what these voices and stories allowed me to understand about the teaching of EIL in this setting). It was through this journey that I gained a different understanding of the teaching of EIL and of how my colleagues and I (as EIL educators and advocates) can further improve the way we inspire our students to learn about EIL.

3.1.2. *Strategies of inquiry: case study*

In the previous section, I explained why it was appropriate to describe my research design and paradigm using qualitative methodology, and how it is best to categorise the study as operating within a social constructivist paradigm. Even though qualitative social constructivist inquirers may share similar research objectives and views of realities, they are likely to follow different specific directions for procedures in a research design. Since the 1990s, qualitative researchers have encountered and carried out research projects that are guided by one or more of the following inquiry strategies or research genres.

- *Narrative inquiry* (e.g. Chase, 2005; Clandinin & Connelly, 2000; Riessman, 1993): this strategy seeks to understand the biographical particulars narrated by the one who lives them.
- *Phenomenology* (e.g. Moustakas, 1994; Nieswiadomy, 1993): this strategy seeks to explore the meanings of an individual's lived experience and how he/she talks about the experience.
- *Ethnography* (e.g. Crang & Cook, 2007; Heath, Street, & Mills, 2008; LeCompte & Schensul, 1999): this strategy seeks to understand the culture, actions, and interactions of individuals and social groups.
- *Grounded theory* (e.g. Strauss & Corbin, 1990, 1998): this strategy seeks to develop increasingly abstract ideas about research participants' meanings, actions, and worlds.
- *Case study* (e.g. Merriam, 1998; Stake, 2005; Yin, 2009): this strategy explores in depth a particular program, an event, an activity, a process, or one or more individuals in order to understand a larger phenomenon.

For my project, I employed a form of case study methodology due to its emphasis on a bounded site of inquiry. I felt that a case study would be a suitable and helpful strategy to assist me in understanding what remained a complex and multifaceted problem. As explained by Marshall and Rossman (2006), "studies focussing on how things work in a group, a program, or an organisation typically espouse some form of case study as a strategy" (p. 55). In particular, I believe that the case study approach allowed me to explore the ways educators in the EIL program inspired their students to learn about EIL and appreciate the diversity of English, as well as the strengths and limitations of the EIL syllabus materials and pedagogical practices from students' perspectives. In fact, case studies are often spoken about as suitable for researchers who aim to highlight the innovative nature of a program and to evaluate its effectiveness (e.g. Bassey, 2003; Casanave, 2010; Guba & Lincoln, 1981; Kenny & Grotelueschen, 1980; Merriam, 1998; Simons, 2009; Yin, 2009).

Moreover, case study has a rather elastic meaning; it means different things to different scholars from different disciplines (Bassey, 2003; MacDonald & Walker, 1975; Merriam, 1998; Stake, 2005; Simons, 2009; Yin, 2009). Yin's (2009) definition puts the emphasis on case study as a *process* of investigating a contemporary phenomenon within its real-life context. Stake (2005), on the other hand, stresses the need to focus on the actual *unit of study* or the case. Merriam (1998) defines case study in terms of its *end product*: a rich description and analysis of a single entity, phenomenon, or social unit. In this research project, my approach concurs with Casanave (2010), who refers to the case study as both the process of doing a study on a particular case within a particular context and the final report that it generates. More specifically, I view case study as an in-depth exploration of the particularity or uniqueness of particular bounded phenomena – an individual

58 *Studying teaching EIL*

or individuals, policy, institution, or program – in their everyday social situations from which one can learn about and develop an understanding of a particular larger phenomenon.

The case study approach allowed me sufficient scope to explore in greater depth some research questions that have been proposed before, but which I felt deserved closer scrutiny. These questions included: what EIL syllabuses, learning sequences, textbooks, or curriculum projects already exist? what do students think about these? It also affords me the space to present a complex and rich picture of the particular taught EIL program at Urban University. Within this picture is incorporated a closer focus on: the overall objectives of the program; the syllabus materials and pedagogical practices teachers chose to engage students with in learning about EIL and learning to appreciate the diversity of English; the teachers' experiences of teaching EIL; and the students' experiences and views of learning EIL. The nature of in-depth exploration of a particular social unit or phenomenon, and the freedom to choose a wide variety of research instruments in case study research further allowed me to uncover and learn about the subtexts or hidden texts (Cochran-Smith, 2000) of the program through my reflections on my own teaching; observations of my colleagues' classrooms; focused professional conversations with my colleagues about their experiences of teaching EIL; and conversations with my students about their experiences of learning about EIL over a period of time. Through a focused analysis of the data generated in this range of situations, case study provides a structure for me (1) to generate knowledge and critically inquire the propositions offered by a range of key theorists that I have critically reviewed in Chapter 2 (Bassey, 2003; Simons, 2009; Yin, 2009), i.e. conceptual aspects of teaching EIL; and (2) to "inform action" (Simons, 2009, p. 21) or the "judgements and decisions of practitioners" (Bassey, 2003, p. 117), i.e. practical aspects of teaching EIL.

Table 3.2 provides a summary of the key characteristics of the model of case study research I undertook in my study. The characteristics are drawn, to varying extents, from the work of Bassey (2003), Casanave (2010), Merriam (1998) and Yin (2009).

Even though I claim that case study is a research methodology that helped me conduct this project, it does not necessarily mean that other research methodologies such as ethnography, or, as suggested by Jenkins (2004), action research methodology, are not suitable to conduct a similar research study. I would also like to acknowledge that some approaches that I used had an action research as well as an ethnographic dimension. McNiff and Whitehead (2011) point out that action research generates "living theories [here is my explanation for what I am doing] while other social science research generates propositional theories [here is explanation for what other people are doing]" (p. 49). This book project generates theoretical principles that are reflective of both, as I explained and critically inquired into my own pedagogical practices as well as those of others. Moreover, according to mainstream sociologists, ethnography is the direct observation of the activity of members of a particular social group, the description of the activity, and the evaluation of such activity from the perspectives of

Table 3.2 Characteristics of the case study in my project

Characteristics of the case study	Explanation	My project
Particularistic	• Focusing on a particular program, situation, event, an individual or individuals, a phenomenon.	• I focus on the curricula of a particular program and phenomenon – the curricula of the newly revised program at Urban University and the teaching of English as an international language (EIL)
Descriptive	• Using a wide range of techniques to provide a rich and detailed description of the phenomenon under study: describing, eliciting images, and analysing situations	I use interviews, observations, and document collection/analysis to: • investigate and analyse how teachers in this newly revised EIL program teach EIL (the explicit and hidden curriculum) • investigate how students respond to the teaching of EIL
Heuristic	• Illuminating the reader's understanding of the phenomenon under study • Aiming to extend the reader's experience or confirming what is known	• I explain the strengths and challenges of teaching and learning EIL • I explain the factors behind students' responses to the teaching of EIL: • What pedagogical factors have prompted students to see the value of learning about EIL? • Why do students experience struggles/tensions in learning about EIL? • I discuss an alternative way of conceptualising and practising the teaching of EIL

participants (Luders, 2004; White, Drew, & Hay, 2009), which are very similar to my aims for this book. Hence, while case studies and ethnography are different particularly in terms of their genesis, Willis (2007) suggests that "case studies are much more similar to ethnography than dissimilar" (p. 240).

3.2. Context: setting and participants

Most methodology literature about case study takes as its starting point that a case is a single unit, a bounded system. In order to assess the boundedness of this system, one needs to ask how "finite" (Merriam, 1998, p. 27) the data collection would be: is there a limit to the number of people I am studying? If there is no limit, then, in Merriam's view, it cannot be called case study research. Since my

60 *Studying teaching EIL*

case study data were generated "from a limited number of people and settings" (Casanave, 2010, p. 70), I need in this section to explain the context of my study. I include here a description of the specific *setting* in which I carried out my research (i.e. the undergraduate EIL program), and some demographic details of the *participants* who volunteered to participate in this study (i.e. three teachers from the program and five students enrolled in the program – three first-year and two final-year EIL major students).

My overall rationale for choosing the setting and participants was based on Patton's (2002) view of "purposeful sampling" (p. 169). It suited the purpose of my research because I did not intend to generalise the results of my study from the relatively small sample that I had chosen to the broader population. Rather, I wanted to "discover, understand, and gain insight and therefore [had to] select a sample from which the most [could] be learned" (Merriam, 1998, p. 61). Qualitative methodology scholars have further divided purposeful sampling into four common types such as unique, maximum variation, convenience, and snowball or chain sampling (Creswell, 2007; Patton, 2002). I chose to gather together a unique sample: that is, "a sample that is unique, atypical, or perhaps a rare occurrence of phenomenon of interest" (Merriam, 1998, p. 62). The reason for claiming that the setting and participants were unique is explained below.

3.2.1. *The setting*

In order to help me inquire into some of what Dorothy Smith (1987, 2005) calls "problematics" of the research enterprise – "a territory to be discovered, not a question that is concluded in its answer" (p. 41) – I explained in Chapter 2 that I used the revised undergraduate EIL program in which I taught as the setting for this case study. In this section, I provide a brief narrative-based account (cf. Doecke & Parr, 2009) of the recent history of the program at Urban University, describe the revised program, and justify the reason for choosing this program.

The program was formerly known as EIU (English in Use) and was established in the 1990s. In the early 1990s, EIU was a part of Urban University's English language centre and offered two subjects that aimed to equip non-English-speaking background (NESB) international students with knowledge of academic English and academic oral/written skills prior to studying at the university. The program leader at the time, who was employed to teach at the university, developed a full three-year academic program using systemic functional linguistics (Halliday, 1985) as the dominant paradigm for teaching academic English and oral/written skills to NESB international students only. As an NESB international student who was interested in learning languages, I chose to study in the program without realising the values and perspectives embedded in the program and promoted in the teaching.

In 2004, after I had graduated, there were approximately thirty students in first-year subjects, fifteen in second-year subjects, and six in third-year subjects. As a result of the decreasing number of student enrolments, the program was reviewed by the university and was on the verge of closure. At that time, the faculty appointed a new academic staff member who then reviewed the existing curriculum offerings and subsequently proposed what was described as a 'name change' in the unit, one which suggested the course of study would be underpinned by an EIL paradigm to replace the existing one that was based on EIU and systemic functional linguistics. A year after the name change, I was employed to teach in this 'new' course. Surprisingly, even though the program had acquired a new name, it soon became apparent to me that the materials were still similar to the ones that I studied before. After a number of incidents, such as student complaints and a lack of interest observed during the lessons, it was my understanding that I was being brought in to revise the curriculum based on the EIL paradigm in order to reflect the name of the program.

The revised undergraduate EIL program was established in 2009 and was offered in the Department of Languages and Linguistics (pseudonym) in the Faculty of Arts at Urban University. The program has continued since that time, but (unlike the program described in D'Angelo, 2012) it has not been teaching General English to NESB students based on EIL perspectives. At the time the data for this research were collected, it was a three-year academic content-program[2] that claimed to teach all students, both 'native-' or 'non-native-speakers', about EIL, intercultural communication, World Englishes and its implications for researching, teaching, and learning, and using English. Further detailed descriptions and analyses of what this program teaches are discussed in Chapter 4 and Chapter 5.

One main reason I decided to choose this program as the context for this case study research was because of its uniqueness. It was 'unique' in that it claimed to be the first program that specialised in teaching EIL to undergraduate students from different backgrounds in Australia (Doan, 2011). There were (and still are), in fact, a number of programs in Australia that also use(d) the same label. However, the analysis of published artefacts, the subjects offered, and admission requirements revealed that the programs were designed to improve general English language proficiency of NESB international students (Doan, 2011; Sharifian & Marlina, 2012).

3.2.2. Selecting the 'treasures in the backyard'

Karavas-Doukas (1998) argues that data on program implementation and evaluation should be obtained from those who are directly involved in the program: "students, teachers, and perhaps other relevant stakeholders" (p. 27). For this study, I selected two groups of participants who played a major contributory role in helping me achieve the objectives of my study and in shedding light on the problematics. One group of participants consisted of lecturers from the undergraduate EIL program, and the other group were undergraduate students who studied EIL with the lecturers. Most importantly, they were the "key protagonists in classroom transactions or in translating principles into practices, and the 'lived experiences' of the program that need to be documented and studied for a case

62 *Studying teaching EIL*

study research to be educative" (Simons, 2009, p. 71). The full profiles of the participants are described in detailed in Chapter 4 and Chapter 5.

As coordinator of this newly revised EIL program, I had some sense of what was being taught and how it was being taught. However, in order to learn more and to understand better how EIL was taught in the program, I invited three lecturers from the undergraduate program of EIL who were my colleagues and the only lecturers in charge of teaching the undergraduate students. They came from diverse lingua-cultural backgrounds and had been teaching with me since the first year the newly revised program had been established. As coordinator of the undergraduate program, I have always involved these three lecturers in working collaboratively, for example, in lesson planning, material selection, activity development, and this collaboration was not significantly affected by my research or the decisions of my colleagues to accept my invitation to participate in the research. Indeed it is fair to say that these ongoing collaborations between myself and my EIL teaching colleagues prompted the development of trust and openness in our collegial relationship, which Dwyer and Buckle (2009) perceive as an important element in a relationship between researcher and participant or interviewer and interviewee (see also Ellis, 2004; Seidman, 2006). Prior to undertaking this research, there had already been a number of professional conversations and interactions in which we exchanged and critiqued each others' ideas and views related to EIL material selection, writing EIL subject guides, assessing EIL assignments, and teaching/learning EIL. Hence, it is fair to state that this research benefitted from interviewing my colleagues as the research interactions/ conversations with them were always intended for us to learn from each other about the teaching of EIL and to enhance the quality of the program.

In terms of their educational backgrounds, my colleague-participants (Ashish, Fatima, and Indigo, pseudonyms) were sufficiently qualified to teach in the program and to participate in the present study. At the time of data collection, Ashish was a PhD graduate whose area of research was in language policy and language variation, Fatima was also a doctoral student, whose area of research was in Teaching English to Speakers of Other Languages (TESOL)-teacher education and EIL, and Indigo was pursuing a master's degree in EIL. In fact, at the time I was conducting this book project, Indigo was writing her master's dissertation on rapport-building and EIL, so there was a degree of scholarly dialogue operating at many levels of the collaboration. These educator-participants' university-level teaching experiences ranged from one to fifteen years. Prior to teaching in the EIL program, all three had taught mainly General English and/or Teaching Methodology in a TESOL teacher-education program in their respective home countries. Although they had become familiar with the principles underpinning generic notions of the EIL paradigm through their studies, they had not had any experience of teaching EIL, which is worth exploring. By saying this, I do not wish to imply that I am necessarily more experienced than my colleagues in this field. I still need to engage in critical reflections on my own teaching.

To explore the teaching of EIL, merely observing my colleagues' classrooms would not have been sufficient because they were only in charge of the first-year sequence of EIL (due to teaching load restrictions for part-time casual lecturers). My analysis of their classrooms would only have shown how EIL was taught at the first-year level rather than as a program. To provide a more comprehensive picture of how the perspectives offered and advocated by EIL scholars were implemented in the program, I included myself as one of the participants in the study. In fact, "in a case study, the researcher can be seen as one of the participants" (Casanave, 2010, p. 70). Subsequently, my experiences of teaching second- and third-year EIL subjects, which I detailed as written reflections in my research journal, became a key part of the data for the whole study.

In addition to investigating how EIL teachers engage their students to learn about EIL and to appreciate different world Englishes, I was also curious to know the extent to which learning about EIL was important in the eyes of the students. I, therefore, chose to involve the most important 'treasures' in my very own research backyard, i.e. students enrolled in the undergraduate EIL units. These students typically included both domestic and international students from a wide range of cultural and linguistic backgrounds. Having students from eight to twelve different nationalities in one class was not rare. Since the program was offered within the Faculty of Arts, students were often from languages/linguistics disciplines and humanities/social sciences disciplines (Media, Sociology, Politics, International Studies, and others). In addition, the program also attracted students from other faculties such as Business and Economics, Information Technology, Education, Sciences, and Engineering, who chose to study EIL as part of their degree. Students from any disciplines can study EIL at any level without any prerequisites. For example, students who were in their second year of their Information Technology degree could choose to study a third-year EIL subject without having to complete a first- or second-year sequence. Apart from having students from diverse nationalities and disciplines in one class, a first-year EIL class, for example, could have students who were in their first, second, and final year of their degree.

For this book project, in order to explore how and if a longer exposure to EIL was likely to make difference, I had hoped to be working with a balanced number of students from the first, second, and final years of the course. However, at the time of inviting the participants, the program was still in its 'infancy' and therefore did not have a large number of students. The numbers of Australian-born English-speaking students were relatively low (approximately three per class), as were the numbers of students who chose to specialise in EIL. Thus, I did not have the luxury of a balanced number of students from relatively similar backgrounds in this study, and this is reflected in the limited diversity among the student-participants. I received expressions of interest from six first-year students, none from second-year students, and two graduates of the EIL program. I could only select three students from first year because they had already completed the first-year sequence subject, but I have data from both graduate students because (at the time of data collection) they had graduated with a major in EIL. The reason for choosing students who had completed a sequence (two first-year subjects) or a major in EIL was that I believed they would provide a richer account

64 *Studying teaching EIL*

of their views on and experiences of learning about EIL in the program than the excluded participants. Thus finally, five undergraduate students participated in the study: three first -year students and two students who had already graduated with a major in EIL. One student, Ogilvy (pseudonym), was born in Australia and had an Anglo-European background; another student, Phil (pseudonym), was born overseas but called himself an "ABC" (Australian Born Chinese) because he came to Australia at a very young age; and the rest (Manida, Cheolsoo, and Tomoko, pseudonyms) were born overseas (Laos, South Korea, and Japan, respectively) and came to Australia under an international student visa. Two first-year students were from the Faculty of Business and Economics whereas the others were from the Faculty of Arts (Department of Languages and Linguistics). Despite the limited number, the input from these interested participants provided me with rich and nuanced data to address the questions and 'problematics' I had provisionally identified.

For ethical reasons, I was not permitted by the Ethics Committee at Urban University to invite my own students to participate in the study unless they had already graduated. For first-year students, I chose to invite my colleagues' students in order to avoid power imbalances and even the appearance of possible coercion. Because of my role as the coordinating lecturer for first-year subjects, this power imbalance could not be entirely removed because these students were technically still my students, in the sense that they attended my lectures. However, the imbalance was minimised because I was not responsible for assessing and grading their academic performance. Therefore, to invite them to participate in the study, I presented the aims of my study and what it involved to the students at the beginning of the lessons. I assured them that their participation was not at all related to their grades and was entirely on a voluntary basis. I also stressed that they would not be identifiable, and whatever they shared during the research would remain confidential. However, preserving the anonymity of the teachers and students has been relatively difficult because, as Casanave (2010) explains: "As [a case] study becomes more and more particularised, it becomes difficult to protect participants' identities and to separate private issues from those that can be written about without risk" (p. 72). With awareness of the need to preserve anonymity, I carried out the following steps: (1) both lecturers and students who agreed to participate in the study were given an explanatory statement which outlined what was expected in terms of their participation in the study, and which stated very clearly that they had the right to withdraw from the study at any time; (2) prior to collecting the data, I had a conversation with them again about the project and asked if they had any questions about the study and were still interested in participating in the study; (3) upon agreement, I gave them a consent form to sign; and (4) after I had collected, transcribed, and described the data, I shared the data with the professional colleagues and students alike to check whether they wanted any materials excluded for privacy and confidentiality reasons (Creswell, 2007).

3.3. Methods for data collection

The overall purposes of the case study were to provide a multifaceted picture of the newly revised EIL undergraduate program and to investigate, through the eyes of the participants, its strengths and areas that needed improvement. In order to achieve these purposes, and obtain trustworthy and reliable data, case study researchers have the freedom to choose from a range of research instruments, and therefore, they often use multiple instruments and present the researched case from different angles (see Bassey, 2003; Casanave, 2010; Creswell, 2007; Merriam, 1998; Simons, 2009; Stake, 2005; Yin, 2009). Case study research data are mostly drawn from

> observations, which are combined with information from conversations, interviews, and where appropriate, documentary sources to produce rounded picture ... or qualitative descriptions of human behaviour, which places the perspectives of group members at its heart and the richness and complexity of their social world.
>
> Foster (2006, p. 72)

Therefore, following recommendations by Casanave (2010), I generated my data through a combination of: *artefacts collection* (e.g. teaching and learning materials: subject outline; textbooks; observation notes; reflective journal notes), *observations, in-depth interviews*, and *critical autobiographical narratives* of my experiences of revising the curriculum and teaching in the program. Table 3.3 shows the summary of the data that were collected, and where/whom the data were collected from.

Table 3.3 Summary of the 'what', and 'where/whom', and 'when' data generated for the project

Data	Source
Observations	First-year EIL lessons and first-year students
Artefacts collection	Classroom activities, handouts, lecture PowerPoint presentation notes, email exchanges, students' classroom written responses, and subject outline
In-depth interviews 1 + follow up	Teachers
In-depth interviews 2 + follow up	First-year students
In-depth interviews 3 + follow up	EIL graduates
Narratives	My experience of revising the former EIL program, my experience of teaching in the newly developed EIL subject; and my teaching experiences in second- and third-year classrooms.

66 *Studying teaching EIL*

3.3.1. Observations

The approach to observation in qualitative research is fundamentally important (Rossman & Rallis, 2012). In case study research, observation can be a "powerful tool for understanding and eliciting the nuances of incidents and relationships in the 'lived experience' of people in particular situations and contexts" (Simons, 2009, p. 62).

To gain better understanding of the teaching of EIL in this program and to explore its strengths as well as the areas that needed improvement, I arranged a series of observations of my colleagues' first-year EIL classrooms (mainly first-year EIL subjects) for two semesters (one year), and of the first-year students in the second semester. To understand the strengths and challenges of teaching and/or learning EIL, I did not want to establish an intrusive formal assessment mechanism such as written or oral tests of students' (and even teachers') knowledge of EIL. As Stake (2005 asserts, in qualitative case study research, researchers should "try to observe the workings of the case in its ordinary activities and places, and minimise intrusion [by] avoiding special tests and assignments of survey or laboratory study" (Stake, 2005, p. 134). It was through observations of the participants, the activities and interactions, and the conversations between the participants that I was able to "see patterns people may not see themselves and may not want to talk about, and move beyond the selective perceptions of both [myself] and the participants" (Rossman & Rallis, 2012, pp. 192–193). I conducted observations of (1) teachers' teaching practices (including my own), (2) students' reactions and behaviours, (3) classroom conversations, and (4) daily conversations between my colleagues and myself. I also kept a research journal that contained extensive reflective notes. Through this combination of methods, not only was I able to explore the official curriculum documents and texts but also the subtexts which it became apparent were not always consistent with the official curriculum texts. This prompted me to see the need to develop a critical view of the conceptual and practical aspects of teaching EIL.

In entering the site of observation (i.e. the classroom), I always took with me a checklist of what to observe, which I used as a particular lens/framework to observe the workings of the case (Simons, 2009). I used my knowledge of the particular EIL paradigm at Urban University and the four principles of EIL teaching materials and pedagogical practices I discussed in Chapter 2 as the framework/s to guide my observations of the teaching and learning of EIL in the program. However, during the observations, I tried to keep myself open to other unexpected things that were observable because I was very aware of the fact that "looking through a familiar lens can prevent [me] observing what is there and revealing what is significant" (Simons, 2009, p. 58). Therefore, I was constantly reminding myself to be conscious of what guided my selection of what to observe, and at the same time recognising that

> there is a place for recording the free-floating, apparently random observations [case study researchers] make in particular settings which may provide a

basis for later examining different theoretical precepts [researchers] hold that are built into [their] observations.

Simons (2009, p. 56)

In other words, observing these 'free-floatings' encouraged me to be receptive to "stories [I] do not know [I] can tell and provide a stimulus for further understanding" (Sanger, 1996, p. 4). My decision to be open to the 'unexpected' allowed me to observe practices and behaviours that prompted me to further develop a critical view of the way we (my colleagues and I) engaged our students in learning about and appreciating different varieties of English.

One main issue that case study scholars often highlight in undertaking observations is the impact of the presence of the researchers on participants' behaviours and practices. Participants who know that they are being observed are more likely to behave in socially acceptable ways and to present themselves in a manner that (they imagine) fits into the researcher's expectations (Foster, 2006; Merriam, 1998). However, studies have shown that "the extent to which an observer changes the situation studied is not at all clear" (Merriam, 1998, p. 104). I had hoped that the impact of my presence in the classroom would be minimal, because of my role as a participant-observer who had been accustomed to teaching alongside other lecturers in the program while acting a researcher. I was already known to my colleagues and my students, and therefore was able to be less obtrusive in the classroom when observing and taking the notes needed for the study.

On the one hand, Foster (2006) believes that "because the researcher is a participant, subjects forget that he or she is doing research and behave in the way they usually behave as a result" (p. 74). On the other hand, Dwyer and Buckle (2009) reminded me that it was still important to "not hide behind the wall of professional distancing … [and to] honour the consequences of acting with genuineness by highlighting the importance of remaining reflexive" (p. 60). Thus, throughout my observations, and in my writing about them, I remained conscious of the ways in which my role as a researcher invariably mediated the research dynamic. During the observations and data-processing stages, I still attempted to be sensitive to the effects my presence in a classroom might have had on the situation and I tried to account for those effects in interpreting the data. Another way for me to minimise the effects was, as suggested by Foster (2006), to apply the technique of triangulation, i.e. using other research instruments to cross-check my observed data, and to use respondent validation (discussed in Section 3.5). The other research instruments that I used to collect my data are discussed next.

3.3.2. Artefacts

Sociocultural theorists would argue that the insights gained from a series of classroom observations are only meaningful in terms of the curriculum, institutional, and policy contexts in which they take place (Lantolf, 2000). For this reason, I also consulted and analysed important policy and curriculum artefacts to gain

68   Studying teaching EIL

in-depth understanding of how students engaged in learning about EIL in the newly revised program, and, in some cases, how students responded to learning EIL. In other projects, these artefacts can range from official curriculum documents to lesson plans and to website texts that describe the higher education faculty within which a program is being taught (see Finnegan, 2006, for a comprehensive list of artefacts used as documentary sources in research). In my project, I collected the following artefacts.

- *Subject outlines* of all former and newly revised undergraduate EIL subjects: consisting of the synopsis of the subject, the objectives, the topics covered in the subject, the readings for the chosen topics, and the assessment tasks.
- *Teaching materials*: photocopied handouts, lecture and seminar notes (PowerPoint presentations).
- *Students' written responses* to the in-class learning activities (permission to use these for research had been obtained): I did not refer to the assignments that the students had to submit to receive a grade/score (unlike the ones used by previous studies I reviewed in Chapter 2). Rather, these were students' written responses to the activities given by teachers in the class for the purpose of classroom discussions.
- *Email conversations* between my students and myself (permission to use these for research had been obtained).

Another artefact that I also used to provide a richer picture of the way EIL educators in this program engaged and inspired students to learn about and appreciate different varieties of English was my research journal, which Parr (2007) labels as an " 'other text' – that is [a text that is] generated in and around [a] project but which does not necessarily become public" (p. 25). A research journal, according to Merriam (1998), is a personal and reflective research-generated text that the researcher prepares after the research has begun, which contains "first-person narrative that describes an individual's actions, experiences, and beliefs" (Bogdan & Biklen, 1992, p. 132). In this study, my research journals included (1) the reflective notes I made about any dialogues that I had with my colleagues and scholars about the teaching of EIL; and, most importantly, (2) some critical autobiographical narrative accounts, such as those that described my experiences of revising the former EIL program and (critical reflections on) the ways in which I engaged my second- and third-year students in learning about and appreciating different varieties of English. I will discuss these further in Section 3.3.4.

The reasons for including this journal artefact were: (1) as a qualitative researcher undertaking research in my own 'backyard', I could not exclude myself from being a participant in the program as I mentioned previously; (2) I could only observe first-year EIL subjects, which only presented a partial picture of how teachers in this program engaged students in learning about EIL. Consequently, I relied on my own written observations and critical reflections of my own classrooms – autobiographical narratives – and my interactions with EIL colleagues to help me generate a richer and multi-perspective picture to understand the teaching of EIL. I was aware that these texts were potentially subjective in the sense that I was the one selecting what was considered as important to record and how it should be recorded. However, understanding a particular phenomenon from the perspectives of individuals is what qualitative researchers are seeking, and these individuals are not just the research participants, but also the researchers themselves (cf. Burgess, 1982; Casanave, 2010; Merriam, 1998; Rossman & Rallis, 2012). Not only did this artefact contain a description of what I did and/or heard, but also a critical reflexive account of my practices as an educator in my own classrooms. Such critical autobiographical narratives help to generate and support the intellectual rigour and the trustworthiness of my research.

Some qualitative scholars (such as Finnegan, 2006; Marshall & Rossman, 2006) claim that what they call "documentary" sources and artefacts have lesser value or, as they maintain, they are "supplemental" to the central research endeavour. Dorothy Smith (1987), for one, shows how powerful such texts can be in supporting or mediating the work of educators and researchers. For my study, I argue that artefacts (both public and personal) can be powerful sources of data in the sense that they provide a richer picture of the teaching practices of this program and of the changing ideological standpoint that the program valued. Through these documents, I could also learn about the lived experiences of the participants in the program. Moreover, many qualitative scholars, including those who regard documentary sources as supplemental (Finnegan, 2006; Marshall & Rossman, 2006; Merriam, 1998; Simons, 2009), claim that the documentary data are objective sources of data as they are 'unobtrusive'. In other words, the presence of the investigator does not have any effects at all on what is being written/stated in the collected artefacts (except the personal documents I mentioned earlier) unlike data gathered from observations and interviews. Therefore, it was through all of these artefacts that I was able to add an additional layer of description and explanation in the ways I addressed the research gaps highlighted in Chapter 2.

3.3.3. Interviews

Sometime into the data-generating phase of this study, after I had observed classes and collected the range of documents and artefacts discussed in Section 3.3.2, I believed that I still needed more information and perspectives to gain a deeper understanding of the lived experience of the program. The classroom observations and the materials only provided me with what Schutz (1967) terms, "observational understanding". What I, as an observer, understood as a result of the observations might not necessarily be consistent with how my participants understood, thought, or perceived. As a case study researcher, I wanted to have access to their "subjective understanding" (Schutz, 1967) – the meanings they made of their experiences – by exploring and asking more 'hows' and 'whys' (which I could not do in the observations or document analysis) of their learning

70 *Studying teaching EIL*

and teaching experiences. For example, I wanted to know *how* the student-participants felt about or viewed a particular phenomenon before/during/after the class and *why* did the student-participants and educator-participants do and/or say the things that I had just observed? In-depth semi-structured interviews with individuals (educators and students) enabled me to further explore these questions. As Seidman (2006) states, "if the researcher is interested in what it is like for students [or teachers] to be in the classroom, what their experience is, and what meaning they make out of that experience, ... interviewing, in most cases, may be the best avenue of inquiry" (p. 11).

Due to the hectic and diverse schedules of the EIL teachers, in-depth interviews with them had to be conducted at the end of both semesters 1 and 2. For first-year students, I conducted the interviews at the beginning, middle, and end of semester 2. The reason I observed and interviewed students in semester 2 as opposed to semester 1 was because I wanted to recruit and interview students who had already completed a semester 1 EIL subject and had chosen to continue studying the EIL stream of units in semester 2. For the final-year students who were my own students, interviews could be conducted only at the end of the semester after all assessment had been finalised and after the official release of their scores and grades, to avoid the potential for researcher coercion and to minimise bias (if students responded to my questions in ways that might be deemed to be pleasing their lecturer).

In case study research, interviews are widely recognised as the most important sources for collecting information and diverse perspectives on a phenomenon, because they allow researchers to listen to participants' stories through which they gain insights into their thinking about the world or the contexts in which they operate (Creswell, 2007; Rossman & Rallis, 2012; Seidman, 2006; Simons, 2009). Since my case study research aimed to construct a complex and detailed understanding of the participants' experiences of teaching and learning in EIL subjects, I considered that both semi-structured and open-ended forms of interviews were most likely to allow for probing interviews and to encourage in-depth insights and stories on the part of the interviewees (Minichiello, Aroni, Timewell, & Alexander, 1995). In the end, both forms of interview were utilised to help me "listen carefully to what people say or do [or think about] in their life setting" (Creswell, 2007, p. 21). I was encouraged by Yin's (2009) argument about the ways that open-ended interviews were relatively common in case study research interviews. I believe this form of interviewing was suitable also because of its flexibility and its effectiveness in (1) helping me understand in greater depth what was in and on the teachers and students' minds; and (2) giving me "potential for uncovering and representing unobserved feeling and events that cannot be observed" (Simons, 2009, p. 43). The latter was very important for this study as my observations showed that the participants, particularly the students, did not usually share in the class their feelings about what they learned in detail, especially because they knew they were learning something that was 'anti-normative'. In the case of the teachers, since it was their first time teaching a curriculum built on EIL principles and philosophies, I assumed that there would be frequent inner-self-conversations in their minds when they were teaching, which I was not able to observe.

Encouraged by the potential of semi-structured in-depth interviews, I developed interview questions around a list of broad topics "without fixed wording or fixed ordering of questions" (Minichiello et al., 1995, p. 65) based on what I intended to ask before and after observations. This allowed me a great deal of flexibility, control, and freedom to allow participants to elaborate further on aspects of the questions or to ask further questions in response to any interesting comments that they had made. In many instances, participants' reflections and responses moved beyond the structured questions and so enriched the data.

Taking full advantage of the flexibility that comes from conducting interviews in a conversational and relaxed manner, I hoped to be able to minimise the potential for inequality between the researcher and the interviewer (Minichiello et al., 1995; see also Simons, 2009). Through this relationship, I sought to build a closer rapport with the participants, knowing that the more comfortable they were in the conversations the more likely they would be to share their experiences openly. This was even more crucial when I was interviewing the students, because they knew that I was one of the lecturers in the program and might suspect that they would offend me if they said something that was critical of the program and/or the lecturers who taught in it. To reduce any anxiety the students might have been feeling and hopefully to generate 'honest' data, I emphasised at the start of the interview my interest in *their* opinions/views even though they might be different from the ones advocated by the program. Through these efforts I sought to obtain rich and honest descriptions of the interviewees' ideas and thoughts. In the end, I believe some of this 'honesty' from the students can be seen in their critiques of my teaching. However, this still reminded me that I needed to maintain a reflexive stance during the interviews and data analysis, and to resist the assumption that I could generate 'honest' data simply by saying to a participant that "I'm interested to hear about what *you* say".

To clarify further and to probe ideas and thoughts that the participants had shared, I conducted several follow-up interviews with both students and teachers. Such follow-up interviews usually involved my sending the participants the transcripts from previous interviews and inviting them to add and further comment on areas that were not clear on the day the follow-up interviews were conducted. As well as reassuring the participants that their views and perspectives were appreciated at all stages of the research, I had hoped that such follow-up interviews would also help to take the interview to "a deeper level by asking for more detail" (Ulin, Robinson, Tolley, & McNeill, 2002, p. 86). For students, follow-up interviews took place during the semester break in order to give them more time to read and process the transcripts that I sent them. This also applied to the teachers. However, there was another form of follow-up interview that I conducted with the teachers, which Brown and Durrheim (2009) term "mobile interviewing" – interviewing while researchers are "on the move" (p. 911). The nature of this follow-up interview was very informal (like a casual chat) as it could take place "when I hang around the setting" (Rossman and Rallis, 2012, p. 177).

72 *Studying teaching EIL*

For example, some mobile interviewing took place when a colleague and I were walking together to a class or returning to our office after the class, taking a bus together to another campus, having coffee in a staff-room, during a short program meeting, or having lunch together in the university canteen. Notes were usually taken immediately after this chat. Although such interviews may have lasted only fifteen to twenty minutes, I was able to gather intriguing insights and record them in my research journal, to be considered and analysed later.

3.3.4. Narrative

As mentioned previously, much of this research was conducted in my own 'back-yard', as it were, in order to learn and understand more about close and familiar territory and the lived experiences of people in that territory. Since I could not separate myself entirely from the undergraduate program because of my roles as the curriculum-'reviser' or developer, and a lecturer in the program, I decided to include a written narrative or, specifically an autobiographical narrative, of my experiences of revising, redeveloping, and teaching the undergraduate EIL program as an additional research instrument and research data. In fact, this research instrument and type of data suited (1) my choice of a case study design as well as (2) the general aims of my study. Casanave (2010) argues that in a case study, the researcher can be one of the participants … and [therefore a] case study report includes quite a bit of narrative … [which] includes the writer's roles in class or programme" (p. 71). Beyond this, Parr (2010) observes that narrative modes have been increasingly used by many education researchers "when inquiring into the program and practices they have been working with … and when critically evaluating their own programs, practices" (p. 49). Prior to explaining the contributions my narrative made, I first explain my particular perspective on the nature and role of narrative in my study.

For several decades now, narrative has been used as a mode of inquiry in diverse disciplines such as in Literary Criticism (e.g. Mitchell, 1981), History (e.g. Carr, 1986), Psychology (e.g. Polkinghorne, 1988), Education (e.g. Bell, 1997; Clandinin & Connelly, 2000), and TESOL education (e.g. Casanave & Schecter, 1997; Holliday, 2005; Lam, 2000). Narrative or narrative-based inquiry, according to Bell (2002) and Gannon (2009), is more than just stories or the act of telling stories. Rather, "narrative is the shaping or ordering of past experience; a way of understanding one's own and others' actions, of organising events and objects into a meaningful whole, and of connecting and seeing the consequences of actions and events over time" (Chase, 2005, p. 656). In the context of teaching, narratives of teachers can "capture, more than scores or mathematical formulae ever can, the richness and indeterminacy of our experiences as teachers, our understandings of what teaching is, and how others can be prepared to engage in this profession" (Carter, 1993, p. 5).

In writing my autobiographical narrative, especially based on my experience of revising and redeveloping the undergraduate EIL program, I was conscious of keying into Carter's (1993) basic three elements of narrative: "(1) a situation

Studying teaching EIL   73

involving some predicament, conflict, or struggle; (2) an animate protagonist who engages in the situation for a purpose; and (3) a sequence with implied causality (i.e. a plot) during which the predicament is resolved in some fashion" (p. 6). For example, my autobiographical narrative includes the struggle that I had when teaching in the former EIL program and my attempts to resolve this struggle by replacing existing objectives with different learning objectives, assessment tasks, and syllabus materials that were better aligned with EIL principles and perspectives.

In writing this particular narrative, I had to ensure that it was not read and constructed as a "victory" narrative (Lather, 1994, cited in Parr, 2010, p. 52) in which I was positioned and perceived as "the hero of my own tale" (Parr, 2010, p. 52). Though there are several 'scenes' in the autobiographical narrative where I narrate my 'success' in replacing the former EIL program with a new program, I also reflexively question my own experiences, the pedagogical practices that I have adopted, and the learning materials that I use. In fact, through this process, I could experience and realise several roles that narrative played in contributing to my study.

- Exploring a narrative perspective, as a complement to the other scholarly writing I was doing in more conventionally analytic prose, allowed me to better understand the impact of the experience itself, and to develop a different way of understanding EIL teaching (Bell, 2002; Carter, 1993; Doecke & Parr, 2009).
- Narrative prompted me to bring some of my deeply hidden assumptions to the surface, such as any assumptions about the goals, purposes, and methods of my teaching – the implicit curriculum, as it were – that I previously had not recognised in myself as an EIL educator (Bell, 2002; Simons, 2009). One example to support this is Holliday's (2007) reflexive narrative of his own teaching that had provided him with a way to develop an insight into some aspects from his teaching that he thought could be considered as chauvinistic.
- The rich and thick narrative descriptions of my lived experience of developing and teaching an EIL curriculum constitute another form of knowledge or knowing (Fenstermacher, 1994) about the issues I am investigating in this book. They offer other researchers, scholars, and lecturers in the field an opportunity to grapple with, and perhaps to vicariously experience, what happened in a program or a classroom that engaged students in learning about EIL and in appreciating different varieties of English.

3.4. Methods for data analysis

In this book project, I found it helpful to consider data that I as a researcher have generated (e.g. in transcribed interviews, notes from observations, documents, and narratives) as initially existing in 'raw' forms which "constitute the undigested complexity of reality" (Patton, 2002, p. 463). Before I begin to analyse and interpret raw data, I have always sought to 'process' it in some ways. Huberman and Miles (1994, cited in Creswell, 2007) talk about the need for raw data to be

74 *Studying teaching EIL*

"revised and choreographed" (p. 150). Other researchers working in different qualitative paradigms have developed their own approaches to processing and 'choreographing' the data (Creswell, 2003; Rossman & Rallis, 2012). Case study researchers, in particular, begin their data processing and choreographing by looking closely at the "physical surroundings, time and place, actions, events, words, people, and interactions on the scene" (Rossman & Rallis, 2012, p. 270) to obtain a thick description of the settings or individuals, and then analyse them for themes or issues (Creswell, 2003; Stake, 2005; Wolcott, 1994). In analysing and making sense of large chunks of data gathered from different sources such as interviews, observations, and documents (including my own written notes and narrative writing in my own research journal), I mainly adopted a *thematic analysis* approach. Such an approach has often provided case study researchers with a "tactic for reducing and managing large volumes of data without losing the context, for getting close to or immersing oneself in the data, for organising and summarising, and for focusing the interpretation" (Wiebe, Durepos, & Mills, 2010, p. 927). It also helped me deepen my understanding of the data that I had gathered.

In applying this analytical approach to making sense of my data, I used the strategy of *coding* in which I carefully read and re-read the interview transcripts, observation notes, and collected documents, in order to (1) familiarise myself with the data, and (2) "look for recurrent themes, topics, or relationships, and by marking similar passages with a code or label to categorise them for later retrieval and theory-building" (Wiebe et al., 2010, p. 927). Boyatzis (1998) suggests three different approaches to developing themes and codes.

- *Theory-driven approach*: in this approach researchers use an existing set of theoretical concepts that they want to 'test' to see if they are useful in making sense of the researched issue, situation, or phenomenon, or whether they have to be modified to provide alternative ways of understanding the issue, situation, or phenomenon. In practice, researchers usually begin with 'a priori' themes and look for these themes in their data.
- *Prior-research-driven approach*: this is similar to the previous approach. But rather than using readymade theoretical concepts, researchers use findings from prior research studies as themes.
- *Data-driven approach*: in this approach, researchers try to avoid starting with any pre-formed, pre-determined theoretical ideas, and remain as open-minded as possible as they look for ideas and issues within the data, as it were. Themes emerge from and are 'grounded' in the data.

My approach to analysing the data and developing the themes for this book project tended to draw on all three of these suggested approaches. Using only one approach for thematic code development suggests a simplistic view of doing qualitative research study. As I previously argued, I moved back-and-forth between the theoretical concepts and the participants in order to understand the researched phenomenon. The theoretical framework of my study and the research findings from previous studies helped me, as a case study researcher, to stipulate the broad focus more closely and to suggest directions for potential codes and themes. To analyse how EIL educators engaged students in learning about EIL and appreciating different varieties of English, I used the principles of EIL syllabus materials and pedagogical practices, and the desired and undesired instructional effects discussed in Chapter 2 as both analytical frameworks as well as a priori themes. However, I was also fully aware that by relying on these frameworks I would run the risk of remaining blind to the uniqueness of the setting or the participants' experiences and/or even from understanding the researched phenomenon from the participants' perspectives. As Holliday (2010) asserts, good research depends on the principle of "submission, which requires researchers to submit to the data in such a way that the unexpected is allowed to emerge" (p. 100). Guided by this advice, I often applied the data-driven approach (sometimes called 'grounded theory'), which allowed me to recognise or uncover the silenced voices or perspectives buried in the data (Boyatzis, 1998) and to obtain a richer portrait of the setting and the participants. Most importantly, I was able to generate additional themes from the data such as: *challenges of teaching and learning EIL* and *reasons behind the factors*, which were not present in my research questions at the early stage of my study.

3.5. Trustworthiness of the study

In previous sections, I described my methods for data collection and data analysis. Even though I have attempted to carefully reconstruct my research design, the question that I, as a qualitative researcher, must now address is: how might one's study be untrustworthy? Or, as Casanave (2010) puts it: "why should we believe what you have said about your case?" (p. 73). This section discusses my approach to ensure the *internal trustworthiness* of my study, which is a claimed strength of a qualitative study (Creswell, 2003; Merriam, 1998). The irrelevance of the *external trustworthiness* (the generalisability) to my case study project will also be addressed by highlighting its "minor role in qualitative inquiry" (Creswell, 2003, p. 195), and its ability to "seriously hinder the overall trustworthiness of a qualitative study" (Hammersley, 1987, p. 74).

One of the assumptions underlying qualitative methodology is that "reality is holistic, multidimensional, and ever changing; it is not a single, fixed, objective phenomenon waiting to be discovered, observed, and measured as in quantitative research" (Merriam, 1998, p. 203). Therefore, my task as a case study researcher is not to claim that there is pure truth to be known or found out there in the real world, but to represent experiences, events, understandings within a rigorously reflexive paradigm of seeking for truth. In order to enhance the *internal trustworthiness* of the case study program that I studied, I employed several strategies.

- *Triangulation of data*: this strategy means using different data sources of information or employing a variety of methods to collect and examine information from different perspectives. As evidenced and discussed in Section 3.3, I used multiple research instruments such as artefacts analysis, observations, interviews, and narratives to provide my researchers with a rich and

76 *Studying teaching EIL*

thick description of the case study program. Not only did this enhance the internal trustworthiness of the data, but it also enhanced the credibility of my findings and interpretations.

- *Respondent validation or member-checking:* throughout the process of collecting and analysing data, I provided my participants with the transcripts and extracts of the data and invited them to check that the ways I represented or talked about them were consistent with what they thought and felt at the time of observations and interviews (Schwandt, 2007). I had also emailed to the student-participants a journal article that I wrote that concerned their participation in the study (Marlina, 2013a). I encouraged them to read it critically and to inform me whether they agreed with my descriptions, analyses, and interpretations of their experiences.
- *Peer briefing:* during the analysing and interpreting process, I discussed my project with my colleagues from the School of Languages, Cultures, and Linguistics (not my participants) who were kind enough to review and question my study so that "the account [would] resonate with people other than the researcher" (Creswell, 2003, p. 196).
- *External auditor:* in the course of working on this project, I gave two presentations of my research at international conferences (Marlina, 2011, 2012) and published two articles (Marlina, 2013a, 2013b) in international journals on the data that I collected. Through these processes, several critical readers (through double-blind peer-reviewing and in other contexts), who were new to the project, could assess and comment on the project. This strategy was, in fact, discussed nearly sixty years ago by Foreman (1948), who viewed it as an effective way to "establish trustworthiness through pooled judgment" (p. 413).
- Spending *prolonged time* in the field: this is one of the strategies that Creswell (2003) suggests qualitative researchers employ to ensure that the gathered data are internally trustworthy. I had been fortunate enough to teach in and research on the undergraduate EIL program. With this, I was able to develop an in-depth conceptual and practical understanding of the phenomenon I studied (i.e. the teaching of EIL) and to convey detailed information about the site. Chapter 4 provides detailed information about how I revised the program and how we, as collaborative EIL lecturers in this program, engaged our students in learning about and appreciating different varieties of English. It was through these data that I was able to hone the objectives of the program, develop the strengths of the program (the teaching of EIL), and identify those areas that EIL educators would need to work on or think about.
- *Clarifying bias:* in qualitative research, "we cannot eliminate bias or the influence of researchers on participants and settings, but we can openly acknowledge that bias" (Casanave, 2010, p. 73). Therefore, in order to do so, I reflexively addressed, as suggested by Casanave (2010), Creswell (2003), Dwyer and Buckle (2009), and Gannon (2009) my role as the researcher in this research. This is why I included, as previously explained, my critical autobiographical narrative as a research instrument. Not only did I include this as

Studying teaching EIL   77

data, but I also made explicit and as transparent as possible my role in the context, the biases I brought to the study, and my attempt to study them critically.

The generalisability of the results of a research study (Merriam, 1998) or _external trustworthiness_ of the study, I believe, was not relevant to the project. Firstly, the reason why I had chosen case study research and selected a single case of small non-random sample was "precisely because qualitative researchers wish to understand the particular in depth, not to find out what is generally true of the many" (Merriam, 1998, p. 208). Secondly, as an EIL advocate (and not just an implementer of other people's ideas), I hope that the knowledge generated through my research may be instructive and perhaps productively provocative for educators working in other contexts. However, I cannot claim that what people do, see, hear, and feel in my particular social, cultural, academic, and institutional context may be generally applicable to other contexts. Every context or institution has its own social, linguistic, cultural, political, economic, and educational uniqueness; each has its own 'stories' to tell or 'issues' to grapple with. Therefore, as a case study researcher, my task was to provide a rich and robust description of the case under study and leave a critical space for the readers to consider the ways my case can be applied to their circumstances. As Walker (1980) has claimed, in the process of engaging with the findings from case study research, "it is the reader who has to ask, what is there in this study that I can apply to my own situation, and what clearly does not apply" (p. 34).

Lastly, although some researchers (such as Merriam, 1998; Stake, 2005) have advocated multisite designs, investigating several sites or situations to diversify the phenomenon of interest and to enhance generalisability, I believe that this would not have been possible for this book project (even if it had been desirable). As previously mentioned, at the time of undertaking this study, there were no other similar EIL programs established in Australian higher education (Doan, 2011) that I could study and use for comparison. And as I have previously stated, my aim in conducting this case study as part of qualitative research was not to generate the ultimate or definitive EIL curriculum or pedagogical model of EIL teaching. Nor do I wish to provide 'the definitive truth' of participants' experiences of teaching and learning in the program under critical consideration. Rather, I seek to "generate ideas which are sufficient to make us think again about what is going on in the world" (Holliday, 2010, pp. 101–102). I hope that in the next chapters, the analyses of the experiences of EIL educators teaching EIL (Chapter 4, Chapter 5, and Chapter 6) and of EIL students learning EIL in the undergraduate program of EIL at Urban University (Chapter 7 and Chapter 8) will prompt researchers and educators to rethink or maybe 'speak back' (Parr, 2010) to the current discourses on teaching English as an International Language.

3.6. Chapter summary

This chapter began by explaining and justifying my view of qualitative methodology as the most suitable framework for this study; social-constructivism as the

78 *Studying teaching EIL*

philosophical belief or assumption of knowledge search; and case study as the strategy of inquiry for my study. Informed by these, I then explained and justified my choice of the context, the institutional setting (the newly revised undergraduate EIL program) and the participants (EIL educators and students enrolled in EIL classes). In order to provide a theoretically grounded understanding of how I sought to learn about what people did and experienced in the chosen setting, I explained the multiple research instruments that I used: observations, artefacts collection and analysis, interviews, and narratives. Thereafter, I explained the strategy I employed to process and analyse the raw data gathered through those instruments in order to address the research questions. The chapter then concluded with the steps that I, as a case study qualitative researcher, took to ensure that those processed data could be regarded as trustworthy in the eyes of readers of research, and would allow interested readers to think about the possibilities and challenges of applying the findings presented in this book to their own contexts. In the next chapter, I employ some of the methodological methods and arguments discussed here to present an autobiographical narrative of my journey of developing and teaching an EIL curriculum.

Notes

1 These were not the exact words of the conference attendee, but a re-creation based on the notes that I wrote (after the conference) in my research journal.
2 In the Department of Languages and Linguistics at Urban University, the study programs were divided into two types: language-program and content-program. The former term was used to refer to a program that equipped students with knowledge of and proficiency in a particular language (e.g. Korean, Indonesian, Spanish, etc.). The latter term – which should not be confused with a language program that adopts a content-based teaching methodology – was used to refer to a program that equipped students with content knowledge of a particular field of language-related study (e.g. linguistics/applied linguistics – includes English as an International Language, European Studies, Asian Studies, etc.). The lessons in the content-program are conducted predominantly in English whereas the lessons in the former are conducted in, depending on the linguistic proficiency level, both English and the learned language.

4 The journey to implement change
An autobiographical narrative

4.0. Introduction

In this chapter, I present some historical institutional background, explaining how and why the undergraduate EIL program at Urban University was developed. In order to do this, I present a critical autobiographical narrative based on my experiences of teaching in an earlier 'version' of the EIL program (formerly known as EIU). I make explicit my role in developing and revising the program as the newly appointed undergraduate program coordinator. In this respect, I am following the advice of Casanave (2010), who argues that a case study report should include "quite a bit of narrative … [on] the writer's roles in class or programme" (p. 17).

In this narrative, I also address my own experiences of how a particular undergraduate program of EIL was developed from one that looked more like a traditional English as a Second Language (ESL) curriculum, albeit with some occasional gestures to EIL discourses, to one that was more responsive to recent research and developments in regard to EIL, and to the principles of EIL syllabus materials and pedagogy. Drawing on extensive entries in my journal describing my day-to-day experiences and conversations with students and colleagues during that time, some syllabus materials and teaching artefacts, and also my memories of that period (cf. Haug's [2008] notion of 'memory work'), I present an extended autobiographical narrative (cf. Doecke, 2004; Rosen, 1998) of my journey of teaching in and revising the earlier version of the EIL program. Consistent with Haug's notion of memory work, this narrative is not based on 'everything' that I remember, but rather a number of important and major encounters, exchanges, and actions, which highlight (1) my stance and belief as an EIL advocate; (2) my attempt as an EIL educator to incorporate a more coherent understanding of EIL paradigm into the existing program; and (3) my intention to foreground and critically reflect on any assumptions about my teaching (see also Gannon, 2008).

By including an autobiographical account of this period, I do not imagine I am securing a definitive insider's view of the events in one institution. Indeed, one important and yet problematic aspect that I would like to acknowledge through this account is the multiple roles (narrator, curriculum/program developer, lecturer, colleague, and researcher/analyst) that I have played in writing this account

80 *The journey to implement change*

and (re)presenting the voices or views of those who are involved. Mason (2002) from the field of Mathematics education advises that an autobiographical account such as this needs to be written "as impartially as possible by minimising emotive terms, evaluations, judgements, and explanation" (p. 40). However, contesting the positivistic assumption embedded in this view, Erdinast-Vulcan (2008) argues that the notion of impartiality in writing a narrative is problematic because the boundary between "the living subject and a character in a work of fiction is often unstable" (p. 3). Removing myself entirely from my role as an actor in and a writer of this narrative is impossible. This is not my aim. Rather, as a critical narrator, analyst, and an actor in the events I relate, I endeavour to give voice to a range of views, voices and perspectives, so that there is no danger of seeing this account as reflecting just one of the multiple positions I occupy as educator, curriculum-developer, author, and researcher in writing it. I am aware of the tensions that I experience between my desire to achieve a degree of objectivity in viewing the situations within the account and the unavoidable subjectivity with which I approach the writing. Since this narrative also involves my reactions/responses to what I have experienced in my journey of revising the earlier EIL program, there are times when I record some interpersonal tensions with some individuals with whom I interacted during the journey. It would be an incomplete and possibly disingenuous account were I not to acknowledge some of these interpersonal tensions. However, I endeavour to ensure that my reactions/responses are less an account of personal differences with individuals and more a multiperspectival, scholarly critique of the practices of and beliefs underpinning the program. Additionally, I also would like to acknowledge that I am not a totally neutral participant in some kind of pseudo-scientific laboratory exercise where all potential for bias is extracted from the site. My role in developing the new EIL course was driven by my belief in and advocacy for EIL curriculum and pedagogy. This is my standpoint, and I do not seek to hide or disguise it, under some methodological cloak of assumed objectivity. Having stated this, I also seek to scrutinise and, where appropriate, critique my own practices and any assumptions/values that were reflected in my teaching.

My autobiographical narrative begins early in 2007 in my time as a postgraduate student, when I was developing my understandings of the issues and debates associated with the concept of 'English as an International Language'.

4.1. An autobiographical narrative: from EIU to EIL

While undertaking a postgraduate degree in TESOL, I had been looking for EIL- or World Englishes (WE)-related conferences that I could attend to learn more about the field. There did not seem to be much information about this for postgraduate TESOL students, but one day I suddenly remembered my undergraduate lecturer from the EIU program (Lorna – pseudonym) whom I regarded as my mentor. Perhaps Lorna would be able to advise me which conferences would suit my professional interest as a teacher of EIL and my research agenda in this area. As she was the only lecturer in the program, she was not available to

The journey to implement change 81

'catch up' at that time, but she invited me to attend a conference entitled 'English as an International Language of Professional Communication'. The conference had been organised by 20 final-year EIU students, as a part of the assessment for the subject they were undertaking, at the very university where I was doing my master's of TESOL. Fascinated by the theme of the conference, I quickly jotted down the time, date, and venue and even set up a reminder on Google calendar, making sure that I did not miss it. I was astonished to see that there had been a change of the program's name: from English-in-Use to English as an International Language. So, just when I finally had been thinking that nothing of that type existed in Australia or elsewhere in the world, in my own backyard I had stumbled upon a fully established and internationally oriented program that both taught and researched EIL. In order to convey my excitement of this time in my academic life, but also the uncertainty and disquiet I felt in some significant episodes following the EIL conference, I will narrate the next section of the autobiography in present tense.

4.1.1. EIL *is only the* 'exterior'

Arriving at the conference venue, I pick up the conference booklet, find myself a seat, and scan the abstracts of the papers. I see there are six abstracts. They all have one aspect in common: *the difficulties encountered by multilingual speakers of English in using or learning to use English in professional communication.* I proceed to read the abstracts, feeling a little strange. They are not what I am expecting. I was under the impression that since this is an 'EIL' conference, there would be discussions on the contributions of multilingual speakers of English to the variation of the use of English in professional contexts, not just a focus on their 'difficulties'. But I manage to stop myself from making any judgements. After all, these are just the abstracts I am reading.

While waiting for other conference attendees to arrive, I meet Lorna. The conference is about to start, so there is not much time for us to catch up. But before she walks to the lectern to give her welcome speech, she tells me how grateful and appreciative she and the students are for my attendance. *Most importantly* (Lorna's emphasis) she is interested in any comments/feedback that I might have. Of course I will not make any comments if these students are presenting what I *think* they will be presenting. Time will tell if this is the case …

… as it turns out, yes, it *is* the case. So at the end of every paper, I do not make any comments.

Midway through one of the opening sessions, Lorna seems to have noticed my silence and she suddenly throws a question at me. She asks me to suggest some strategies to 'help' multilingual students overcome those difficulties. I feel cornered. I am quite uncomfortable with the assumptions underlying the question! So many questions are echoing in my mind: But are they really *difficulties*? Why is a multilingual speaker's rich linguistic repertoire regarded as an 'impediment' to their use and their learning of English for professional communication? And why should they need 'help'?

82   *The journey to implement change*

I don't want to Lorna to lose face, so I share my thoughts with some discomfort. I begin by telling Lorna (and the audience) what I think she wants to hear: "Maybe multilingual students may need to familiarise themselves with or learn the expected genres in that professional community". While I am speaking, Lorna keeps smiling and nodding. Having noticed that, I become curious and I wonder: what do her smiling and nodding mean? Is she impressed? By what? But the last point that I make is that I believe one should take pride in one's multilingual linguistic repertoire. I notice that this comment prompts a smile in the presenters' faces. Again, I wonder, what is behind those smiles?

As I am about to leave the venue after the closing session of the conference, Lorna quickly grabs me and asks if I would be interested in teaching as a part-time instructor in the program next semester. I am stunned, surprised. Surely, my comment earlier in the conference suggested to her that I hold a different set of beliefs about EIL compared with those presented by her students. I nervously tell her (without looking at her in the eyes) that I am not too sure if I am knowledgeable and qualified enough to teach in the program. Lorna rebuts this with confidence, asserting that I know the EIL 'stuff', that I am the program's 'successful' student, and that I am the role model for other students. She feels I am more than qualified!

I walk away from that conversation and from the conference working through the hidden meanings and problematic constructions behind this conversation and all that I have observed I am also relatively touched by Lorna's acknowledgement. If I am honest with myself, I am indeed looking forward to teaching in the program and sharing my passions and enthusiasm with the students. I have a lot of 'maybes' going through my mind … Maybe Lorna has been impressed by my last comment and the beliefs that underpin it. Maybe she has revised the whole curriculum to reflect the name of the conference program and to reflect its claim as an internationalised program. Maybe the papers I have heard today are not indicative of the direction she wants to take the program. Maybe, since the program's name changed only some months ago, it would have been difficult to ask students who have been learning the 'old EIU belief' for the past three years to suddenly present a paper based on a new EIL paradigm just because of the name change.

Five months later, the semester starts! As I am a new instructor for the program, Lorna asks me to attend her first lecture in which I will be introduced to the students. It feels so odd being in this lecture as the instructor especially when I still have a lot of the above 'maybes' echoing in my mind. She starts her lecture by praising the students for having chosen the 'right' course to learn about the English language. Then she introduces me to the students as the instructor of the program. She mentions that I am a former student, and, much to my chagrin, informs the students that "Roby used to study in this program, and he is our program's most successful student". I am more than a little embarrassed, but after having listened to this acknowledgement again, my fire of enthusiasm to teach in the program keeps burning and burning.

The journey to implement change 83

* * * * *

Three weeks into the semester, I remember feeling that that the burning flame of enthusiasm that I had at the beginning of the semester was entirely extinguished. After having observed the way in which students were admitted into the program, I had proceeded to teach with the program's syllabus materials, I had read my students' writings, and observed their attitudes towards the curricula. And I had begun to question the message that the students received at the beginning of the semester: was this program really the 'right' course for students to learn about the English language? I also began to question whether the name of the program (EIL) was only a mask.

Four months into the program, I had done a lot more reading and observing. I had participated in hours and hours of conversations with students. And my reflections on all of these had prompted me to view this program, despite the change of the name from EIU to EIL, and despite its claim to be a program that taught English as an 'international' language, with some scepticism. It still seemed to be what Trevaskes et al. (2003) call a "monocultural-chauvinistic" program (p. 11). It was as if the program had been designed to bring 'foreigners-up-to-speed', and as a learning space for 'NESB international students' to (figuratively) seek refuge, to learn about their deficiency, and to investigate ways to remedy this deficiency[1]. The exterior rhetoric for this program was EIL, but the entire interior discourses were EIU (henceforth, 'EIL-ex' will be used to refer to this program). It taught students about various spoken and written genres based on the discourses of systemic functional grammar. And it assumed a single variety of English and single homogeneous view of culture in Australia.

4.1.2. Prerequisites for studying in EIL-ex

The more I looked into the program, the more I was concerned by what I found. I was greatly disturbed by the process by which students were admitted or perhaps (to put it very bluntly) 'filtered' into the course. This was definitely not reflective of the principles of teaching EIL, as I understood them. EIL surely needed to be studied by all speakers of English regardless of which Kachruvian circle they belonged to (Smith, 1983). An EIL program should be open for all students. However, one day when I was reading the program's website carefully, I noticed the following: "the prerequisite for undertaking this subject is that students must meet the 'Faculty of Arts second language entry criteria'". Did this mean that all students must undertake a second language study or that they must have both studied *and* already be speakers of a second language? My curiosity leads me to consult the faculty's student advisor …

I began by asking about the requirements of students who wanted to enrol in the EIL-ex course. An unhappy-looking woman in her mid-forties was already answering 'NO' even before I had finished asking my question! She took out a thick book from her cabinet, put on her glasses, and wet her finger to find the

84   *The journey to implement change*

page where the requirements were listed. Then she read to me: "Students who are permitted to enrol in this program (1) must be on an international-student visa; and (2) must speak English as their second language". OK, so there it was in black and white. Those who did not fit into the stated criteria, i.e. those who were not second language speakers and on an international student visa, were 'thoroughly screened' to assess their intention for undertaking this program. Those who were brought up in Australia, who were citizens of Australia, who had completed primary and secondary schooling in Australia, and even those who had 'Anglo-European' names and surnames were not permitted to study in the EIU program. It was about that time that I remembered there was an occasion where a Caucasian student with an Anglo-European name and a 'domestic' status on his attendance record was informed about the faculty's policy, and was politely requested to leave and change to a different subject.

My suspicions having been confirmed, I decided to pay a visit to Lorna's office. I would politely explain to her that I did not believe students should be excluded from learning about the use of English in various discourse communities on the basis of their backgrounds. Even within a particular discourse community, I would suggest, the use of English can be different depending on the lingua-cultural background of the speaker. So, I would point out, it was important for students to learn and exchange these differences.

If my memory of the ensuing conversation serves me well, what I said was regarded as a 'stupid idea'. It was 'stupid' because I was seen to be ignorant of the fact that Anglo-Australian students were only looking for 'easy marks'. Their presence would not be 'safe' for international students to advance their knowledge of 'the' English language. Needless to say, I disagreed heartily with the line of argument. I thought (although I did not feel I could say this out loud): if there was a concern that excluded students would create an 'unsafe' (whatever that may mean) learning environment, then shouldn't it be the role of educators to address that head on by providing them with necessary knowledge, beliefs, and skills to make each other feel 'safe'? Did separating out one group of students from another group ensure a 'safe' learning environment or could it give birth to more animosity, mutual misunderstandings, and ignorance?

After my perspective was labelled as 'ignorant' and 'stupid', I remember that I became more determined to fathom what I was fast coming to see. Factually and philosophically, from my reading of the literature, I was becoming convinced that the exclusionary practice and the objectives and synopsis of the subjects offered in the name of EIL were not consistent with what the literature described as being an EIL paradigm. This was nowhere more apparent than in the repeated emphasis on 'second language speakers' in every subject's objective (see Appendix 1). There did not seem to be any recognition of the pluralisation of English or of world Englishes in the curriculum documents. The language of the objectives of all of the subjects offered in the program was instructive in itself. All objectives were framed in ways "to offer the second language speaker of English knowledge of *the* English language" (my emphasis), as if there was only one variety of English. From my observation of lectures and classes, there were

The journey to implement change 85

no opportunities for students to learn about the differences in the way people from different cultural backgrounds use English. There was no forum to open up a dialogue about these differences.

4.1.3. Description and analysis of EIL-ex syllabus materials

Apart from the practice of filtering students, as detailed above, my observations and readings of the week-to-week learning assessment tasks and students' responses to those tasks, on the one hand, led me to lose interest in teaching this would-be 'EIL' curriculum. On the other hand, it prompted me to develop the view that there was an urgent need for changing and revising the entire program's curriculum. However, as Waugh and Punch (1987) argue, change cannot be implemented when there is resistance from many personnel, not to mention a variety of institutional and curriculum constraints. Here, I will show some samples of 'EIL-ex' syllabus documents that were used in two first-year subjects (EIL1010 and EIL1020) that I was employed to teach. I will evaluate their values/relevance from widely agreed EIL perspectives and the four principles of EIL syllabus materials and pedagogy I outlined in Section 2.3.2.

The teaching materials that were set to teach often included neatly cut newspaper articles and printed advertisements, from which students were expected to identify various linguistic features, and on the basis on such identification, they were expected to analyse those texts. This kind of activity was repeated throughout a whole semester. In a sense, learning about textual analysis or how to analyse texts was useful and helpful. However, when I would be reading the articles that I was instructed to teach each week (see Figure 4.1, Figure 4.2, and Figure 4.3) in EIL1010, I did not feel comfortable using and teaching them because they were predominantly based on a single cultural context. I did not even feel confident talking about the materials because the knowledge that I myself had of the issues in these materials was rather limited.

During the lessons in which the texts (shown in Figure 4.1, Figure 4.2, and Figure 4.3) were used, I encountered several challenges from students as I attempted to explain these documents. Not only this, I also observed that most students in my class did not seem to be interested in listening to my explanations of the texts. Some students were drawing cartoons on the material. Some were texting, some were passing notes to each other, and only a few students appeared interested. When I asked questions, nobody responded and the class became very quiet.

As I reflect on this experience now, I do not want to assert that these materials were unimportant and not worth teaching. But, if a program claimed to teach English as an *International* Language, then the 'International' needed to be reflected in the teaching materials. Rarely did any of the lesson materials use newspapers articles or any texts written by international writers. Experiencing this situation prompted me to better understand the arguments put forward by many scholars (Briguglio, 2007; Hayward, 2000; Stella & Liston, 2008; Stier, 2004; Trevaskes et al., 2003) that although programs/universities make claims about

In answering these questions consider how the language of the advertisement suggests a particular way in which people relate to each other and how diffent people are perceived in terms of age, relationship and communication.

FOR SALE

OPEN FOR INSPECTION SATURDAY 9TH NOVEMBER 2-4 PM.

Superb new apartment in Melboune's garden suburbs.
Close to the city but also far enough to be away from the grime and clatter
This beautifully spacious apartment has rooms for every member of the family to have their own space.

A sewing room, a study and a huge deck suitable for a friendly, relaxed BBQ on a hot Melbourne night.
A point of special interest are the separate bedrooms (at the opposite end of the house) that will keep all the children happy.
This wonderfully planned apartment also includes a small guest room for those in-laws and relatives that have to be accommmodated when they come and stay overnight.

A great living space, wonderful views of the Bay and a manned security entrance this apartment building also includes a fully maintained garden setting and undercover parking.

Interested buyers contact
Sam Henshaw
D'Odgee Brothers Real Estate

(mobile) 04 2781 02 009
(e-mail) dodgebros@di.smartmail.org.au

Figure 4.1 An example of material from EIL1010, EIL-ex program 1 (see text for abbreviations)

Full Bench announces decision on BLF today

By MATTHEW MOORE, Industrial Reporter

MELBOURNE: A Full Bench of the Arbitration Commission will this morning bring down its decision in the deregistration case against the Builders Labourers' Federation.

The three-member Bench, headed by Justice Terry Ludeke, will hand down its decision at 10 am, just two weeks after it finished hearing evidence in the case, which began seven months ago.

It is considered almost certain that the decision will grant the Federal Government its application, enabling it to deregister the union federally.

A large police contingent is certain to be on hand in case of any demonstration by BLF members, although the union's general secretary, Mr Norm Gallagher, said no security would be necessary as no demonstration was planned.

"They're too busy working and getting the 3.8 [per cent]," he said, maintaining his claim that BLF members have not been disadvantaged by the commission's refusal to pass on last November's national wage increase.

Mr Gallagher said no officials would be present although the BLF's legal advisers would attend.

"Why should I go?" he said. "I've got work to do. I have had these decisions before. This thing has been going on longer than *Blue Hills*."

If the Federal Government gets its decision as expected, it will then be able to cancel the union's Federal registration, which will trigger Victorian legislation cancelling the registration in Mr Gallagher's home State.

The BLF has already been deregistered as a State organisation in NSW.

Until the Federal Government acts, the BLF will remain a registered body and the complicated business of trying to carve up the union and distribute its members to other unions will not get under way.

The Victorian Government has already released a draft plan for breaking up the union and it is believed the Federal Government has virtually finalised its own actions.

Figure 4.2 An example of material from EIL1010, EIL-ex program 2 (see text for abbreviations)

> **1:** After reading the following text examples suggest a possible context for each example. Justify your choice by reference to the language of the text.
>
> Example a:
>
> ### Tankers need more checking says Minister
>
> Melbourne
> Wednesday afternoon
> The petrol tanker which caused the delay in peak traffic yesterday when it overturned on the highway outside of Sale has now been moved. Although no one was injured in the accident the delay closed the main Gippsland Highway for four hours. The police spokes person at the scene reported that the tanker had been filled beyond its safety level.
>
> "The uneven distribution of weight had contributed to the accident", he said. The Minister for Transport was questioned in Parliament today as to the way in which the safety regulations were enforced as this was the sixth accident in similar circumstances in the last three months.

Figure 4.3 An example of material from EIL1010, EIL-ex program 3 (see text for abbreviations)

providing an internationalised curriculum/education, often the rhetoric does not match the actual practices.

One day, I found a newspaper article in which a Singaporean journalist was discussing the debates on Lunar New Year routines. It was a text that spoke more directly to the cultures and educational landscape with which my students were familiar. It had only recently been published in *The Straits Times* (an English-based national newspaper from Singapore). I thought this would be a perfect resource for teaching the use of English to reflect a person's or a community worldview, and of course for teaching EIL! So, I took this article to Lorna and asked her if she would be interested in reading this article. She put on her glasses and began to read it. After she finished, we exchanged views about the New Year. I remember that it was a genuinely interesting conversation for both of us. Feeling somewhat encouraged, I seized the moment to ask her, diplomatic-ally (I hoped), if she felt this could be a good teaching material for the week on worldview that was coming up. Her reply was 'Maybe next time'.

When I later received the teaching materials for that week, there was no men-tion of Singapore or Singaporeans or any Chinese issues or events. Instead, there was a collection of newspaper articles about the Australian troops in Iraq. And students would be required to write a letter to the editor expressing their views on this issue of Australian troops in Iraq.

* * * * *

In May, several weeks after the meeting I described above, the time was approach-ing when students would be expected to submit their major assignments. It was my responsibility, as the seminar instructor, to clarify the essay questions for the students and to answer any questions they have. Prior to this, I had to ensure that I myself understood the questions (see Figure 4.4). Thus, as I read the exam questions, I kept asking myself: Why is this program called 'EIL'? Had I really been teaching in an EIL program? What was wrong with my students (and myself)

88 *The journey to implement change*

EIL1010 – Communication

- The genre of essays is one of the most recognisable genres in this academic discourse community. However, it is a genre that causes many *multilingual students* a great deal of *difficulties*. What do you believe are the main *reasons for these difficulties*? (My emphasis.)

- *First language speakers share what is understood as conventional or community meaning.* What effect does connotative meaning have on the way in which a message is understood? What makes this aspect of textual comprehension *difficult for the second language speaker,* both in the general use of language and in this discourse community in particular? (My emphasis.)

Figure 4.4 Questions set for end-of-semester EIL-ex final essay

being multilingual speakers of English? The wording of the questions confirmed my view that the 'EIL' program I had been teaching in was a place to learn to accept and confess that to have a multilingual speaker of English *identity* was to be culturally and linguistically deficient. And the *condition* of being a multilingual speaker of English needed to be remedied by learning the 'mainstream' cultural values and linguistic conventions.

Since I was only assigned to teach first-year subjects, I was under the impression that this question might only be given to first-year students. Later, my readings of the essay topics from first- to third-year subjects proved me wrong (see Appendix 2).

Critically observing and reading the selection of essay questions shown in Appendix 2, it can be seen that students had been required (from first year through to third year) to identify with what was framed as the *difficulties* or *problems* they had as multilingual speakers (that there was something wrong with being multilingual speakers) in understanding the use of English in various discourse communities in Australia. The intention seemed to have also been to assess the extent to which each student had successfully learnt the mainstream conventions and, as Kubota and Lehner (2004) argue, whether they could operate effectively within a single particular culture as opposed to flexibly across cultures. In other words, students had been evaluated on the basis of their awareness and knowledge of what they (as multilingual speakers of English) needed to be 'helped' with, why they needed 'help', how they could be 'helped', and whether or not they had been 'helped'.

The day after the assignment submission deadline, I received an email from the administrators that my students' assignments had already been put in my pigeonhole. I recall an uneasy feeling as I walked towards the pigeonhole to collect the assignments. My gut feeling was that marking the assignments was definitely going to be a struggle, that their assignments would be filled with apologies and self-blaming or self-devaluing statements.

The journey to implement change 89

And it was indeed the case. When I was reading the essays, they sounded like letters of apology from students to me – apologising for coming from a different cultural background, for having different cultural values, for having English as their additional language. All of these were, needless to say, detrimental to their understanding of the mainstream linguistic and cultural values and linguistic conventions, and therefore barriers to their success in operating effectively in the mainstream community. The program had 'helped' them realise this and had provided them with knowledge of what they needed in order to 'fit in' to the mainstream. It was a struggle for me to grade these essays.

Experiences such as these prompted me to begin to critically question again my position as the instructor of the 'EIL' program. I wondered, once again as I had during that first EIL conference, what Lorna meant when she said that I knew the *stuff*, that I was the program's *successful* student, and a *role model* for other students. This accumulation of experiences extinguished my enthusiasm for teaching in the EIL-ex program. Yet, at the same time, these experiences and especially my observations of my students' reactions to this program provided me with a valuable opportunity to scrutinise and critique an existing program, which in turn helped me to revise the program the following teaching semester.

4.1.4. Teaching EIL1020 in Semester 2

Semester 2 arrived, but I saw nothing substantially new in the subject that I was in charge of teaching (EIL1020). Though the content this time had a slightly different focus from the previous semester, the message was still the same: my teaching needed to show how multilingual speakers (such as my students) have difficulties and problems, and explain what they can do to overcome these difficulties and problems!

As a student in my own undergraduate and graduate studies, the first week of a new semester had always been 'fun'. Despite my despondency at the end of the previous semester, the start of this new semester of EIL was also fun. It was an introductory week where we did not delve straight into the content of the subject, a week where I could get to know my students and explain the overview of the semester. In the second week though, I would experience something deeply unpleasant. Once again, in order to convey some of the immediacy and discomfort of this experience, I will narrate it in present tense.

* * * * *

Week 2's topic is exploring the basic patterns of text through genre-based grammar. Thirty minutes before the lesson begins, I have my lesson plan thoroughly prepared based on Lorna's lectures) and my activity sheet photocopied (as given to me by Lorna – see Figure 4.5).

I arrive at the classroom ten minutes early to make sure that the computer, data projector, and overhead projector are working. No one else has arrived as yet in this small cosy classroom. The students are all still in the lecture. Fifteen minutes later, my students begin to arrive. None of them looks happy. While they are

90 *The journey to implement change*

> **EIL1020 – English as an International Language: Form and Function**
> **Week 2**
> **Genre-Based Grammar**
> **Activity Sheet**
>
> Question 1:
>
> Write an instruction of how to tie shoelaces and identify its linguistic features.
>
> Question 2:
>
> Why is genre-based grammar important for multilingual speakers of English, especially in order for them to have access to the academic discourse community in Australia? Discuss with your partner.

Figure 4.5 Genre-based grammar exercise sheet

---

finding their seats, I quickly write the main concepts of the week on the board. As I am writing, I overhear students whispering to each other. Surprisingly, some students are talking about the lecture, but it is not very clear. Judging by the tone, they do not sound pleased. Above the murmuring, I hear the occasional expletive. Other students are whispering loudly to each other in their own mother tongue (in Mandarin, Cantonese, and Korean) about the lecture. This time, I can hear it very clearly and I understand what they are saying. (At this stage, my students do not know that I have learnt and can speak those languages.) They are complaining about what they experienced in the lecture. Some are planning to discontinue the subject.

What is happening? My heart is beating very fast and my palms are sweating and becoming cold. Before I start, I quickly drink a glass of water to calm myself down. Then I begin the lesson ...

As I am summarising the weekly topic and the main concepts of the week, I notice that virtually none of the students are paying attention. Some of them are passing notes to each other, some are looking at the window with their cheek resting on their hands, and some are drawing pictures on their notebooks. I press on and hand out the activity sheet, hoping that they will respond to the questions on this sheet.

Some minutes after I have distributed the sheet, two students sigh, pack their bags, leave the activity sheet on the table (unattempted), and walk out of the classroom. An eerie silence descends upon the classroom. Once again students start whispering to each other. I quickly move to redirect their attention to a new activity and instruct them to complete it in 10 minutes. Once again, there is no interest in the activity. All students seem to be off-task. As a teacher I weigh up the questions that are echoing in my ears: should I force them to do the activity? should I blame these students for not showing any interest in the activity?

By taking a line of least resistance, I somehow manage to make it through the end of the lesson.

After the class, I return to my office, still trying to figure out the key to the problem, searching in my professional repertoire as a teacher for ways to resolve this situation. Should I talk to the students about this when I see them next week? (Will they return to class at all next week?) If action is not taken, then the program will lose a large number of students. If things get worse, then perhaps it will be required by the university to close down. Once more, I resolve to speak to Lorna about my concerns.

But before I go to Lorna's office to inform her of this incident, I receive an email from one of the students who packed their bags and left the class. In the email, the student offers her apology to me and an explanation for leaving class. She says she is frustrated by the patronising nature of the teaching materials she had been exposed to in EIL1010 and EIL1020. People from different cultural backgrounds, according to the student, are being asked to declare that being multilingual and coming from a different cultural background are "problematic". She says she is finding this very difficult to deal with.

Reading this email strangely makes me feel a bit relieved. At least I am not the only person with this view on the program. However, I don't know how I should reply to the student's email? Should I inform her that she and I are on the same wavelength? Rather than respond to the email, I print it and take it with me to show Lorna that the program is not teaching what the students want to learn.

When I walk into Lorna's office, she is in the middle of a conversation with another lecturer in the program, Ali (pseudonym), who is in charge of a post-graduate program and other undergraduate subjects. I judge this to be a perfect time to bring up this issue so that it could be dealt with at a program level. I show them both the email. While reading it, Ali looks shocked and Lorna puts both her hands on her head and lets her jaw fall, leaving her mouth agape in an expression reminiscent of Edward Munch's 'The Scream'.

Summoning up my courage, I ask both Ali and Lorna if there is anything that can be done especially about the *program*. The subsequent conversation will show that Ali, Lorna, and myself are not going to agree on the need to revise the program. However, a decision is made to employ a research assistant to assess both EIL1010 and EIL1020 from the students' perspectives. A week later, when students' surveys and interviews results are revealed and the extent of student dissatisfaction is out in the open, an agreement is reached for me to change the content, but only for one first-year subject (EIL1010).

* * * * *

In the following section, I present a number of vignettes of my experiences of engaging my students in learning about EIL/WE in this newly revised subject;

92 *The journey to implement change*

and of developing an EIL program based on the EIL paradigm, principles of EIL syllabus materials, and what I learned from teaching in the EIL-ex program.

4.1.5. First trial: An EIL subject for first-year students ...

Based on my previous experience of teaching in the EIL-ex program and on my knowledge of the EIL literature from across the word, I had learned that it was important for all speakers of English from any geographical context to have knowledge of differences in the way people from diverse lingua-cultural backgrounds use English. Informed by this view and belief, an official request was submitted to remove 'the Faculty of Arts second language entry criteria' as the prerequisite for undertaking this subject to allow any students regardless of their linguistic backgrounds to enrol in the subject. The removal in fact allowed me to interact with students from diverse backgrounds who were either monolingual or multilingual speakers of English, and who spoke English as their first, second, or third language.

Since it was the first and only subject in the program that was developed with a genuine focus on EIL, I aimed (somewhat optimistically) to teach 'everything' about EIL/WE to the first-year students. My hope was that the 'new' approach would mean that the unit would have a better chance of achieving a range of objectives (see Figure 4.6.), which reflected the rhetoric of linguistic plurality and interculturality as opposed to ones that indicated elements of monocultural-chauvinism.

Rather than focusing on '*the*' English language from a single community, my experience of teaching in the EIL-ex program encouraged me to develop this newly revised subject with a focus on understanding 'English*es*' and how they reflect diverse cultural practices, and developing intercultural communication skills. As opposed to prompting 'second language speakers' to disclose difficulties or problems they would have in understanding the 'mainstream' culture and language, my experience of reading students' essays in the EIL-ex program and the email from the student who walked out of the class, led me to revise EIL1010 with an aim to encourage students to critically challenge this discourse. These experiences and encounters had also driven me to design new topics, readings, and assessment tasks (see Appendix 3) in a hope that they could engage

---

Upon completion of this subject, students will be able to demonstrate:

- advanced knowledge of the recent/current status of English and the implications of its development as an international language or world Englishes;
- broader understanding of international/intercultural communication and the skills to communicate across cultures; and
- critical reflections and attitudes towards issues and/or assumptions on 'accent' and being a 'native' or 'non-native' speaker of the language.

Figure 4.6 Objectives of the newly revised EIL1010

The journey to implement change   93

and inspire students to learn to see and understand that being a multilingual speaker of English or being/sounding 'different' from so-called 'native-speakers' of English is not something that students need to feel apologetic for. In fact, with this awareness of the diversity of English, I hoped that students would develop a respectful perception towards themselves and other users of English. However, my experience in teaching in this new subject showed me that it was not all as 'neat and tidy' as I had hoped it would be.

In Section 4.1.6, Section 4.1.7, and Section 4.1.8 I will present an account of three lessons (weeks 2, 3, and 9) from across the semester. In this account, I illustrate how I attempted to translate my emerging understanding of an EIL paradigm (McKay, 2002; Sharifian, 2009) and the principles of teaching EIL into practice, how my students responded to the teaching, and how I responded to their responses.

My approach will be to present each lesson in present tense accounts, which will not only give a sense of the teaching plans and materials I brought to the lesson, but also some sense of the unfolding nature of the experience of teaching the lessons. After the narrative account of each lesson, I provide some reflections on my plans, the lesson materials/texts and activities and the students' responses to these materials and activities. In one place, I present (with permission from the ethics committee) samples of students' writing to illustrate the nature of the students' responses and as a focus for some of my reflection and analysis.

4.1.6. Lesson in week 2: What is language variation?

In week 2, I aim to introduce students to the nature of variation: why language varies and in what ways it varies. I want to give students the opportunities to 'look around you' and to observe why they speak differently from other people: friends, classmates, parents, grandparents, and people from different genders, age groups, socioeconomic backgrounds, ethnic backgrounds, suburbs, regions, states, and countries.

In the scheduled three-hour lesson, I spend approximately an hour in lecture mode, explaining a large number of basic sociolinguistic concepts that illustrate the idea of language variation: difference between language and dialect, variety, sociolects, idiolects, pidgins and creoles, accents, register and style, standardisation of language and its politics, and mutual intelligibility (which is determined by a person's exposure to the language and motivation to communicate as opposed to the language varieties). I use different resources such as YouTube clips, recordings, and movies that provide students with ample examples of language variation.

To engage students in learning those concepts, I divide them into four groups and invite them to reflect on their daily interactive exchanges in English and come up with their own examples of regional dialects, sociolects, idiolects, creoles, register and styles. While students are discussing examples of these concepts, I walk around the class and listen to the examples they share with their group members – very interesting examples indeed! When the whole class share their

94 *The journey to implement change*

examples, I am impressed. One group shares examples of African American English as an example of ethnolect. Another group talks about the frequent use of 'like' as an example of teens' language. A third group shares words that Australians in different regions use to describe a 'swimming costume'. And the final group talks about how the word 'elder' is understood by the students who come from South Korea, Sudan, and Adelaide. What a fascinating example, I think. Students seem to have shown awareness of variation in English. But what I am curious to know is how they respond to this variation. So, I conduct another activity, which I call an 'Oprah Winfrey' show.

Still working with the same groupings I made earlier, I hand out a printed conversation to every student (Figure 4.7). As I am handing out this activity, I tell them: "In 20 minutes, we are going to have a show, a live Oprah Winfrey show! So, what I would like you to do is imagine if you were Oprah, how would you have responded to the comment made by the second caller?" When students are reading the conversation, I can hear them giggling, scoffing, and shaking their heads. They seem genuinely engaged.

In what seems like no time at all, twenty minutes are over! I invite students to select one spokesperson per group to share what they have discussed. To my surprise, all four spokespersons unanimously believe that there needs to be one Standard English that everybody needs to speak in order to sound right and to know 'that's what they are saying'. I cannot believe what I have just heard. So, I ask the whole class: "Is that even possible? Haven't we just talked about language variation? Haven't we just discovered that there are differences in even one language? Haven't we just talked about the idea of mutual intelligibility lying in a

---

Conversation

2nd caller:	Hi, Oprah?
Winfrey:	Yes.
2nd caller:	I guess what I'd like to say is that what makes me feel that blacks tend to be ignorant is that they fail to see that the word is spelled A-S-K, not A-X. And when they say asked, it gives the sentence an entirely different meaning. And this is what I feel holds blacks back.
Winfrey:	Why does it give it a different meaning if you know that's what they're saying?
2nd caller:	But you don't always know that's what they are saying.

(quoted in Milroy and Milroy, 1999, p. 152–3)

If you were Oprah Winfrey, how would you have responded to the 2nd caller?

Figure 4.7 Oprah Winfrey show simulation exercise (adapted from Jenkins, 2003)

Source: Jenkins (2003)

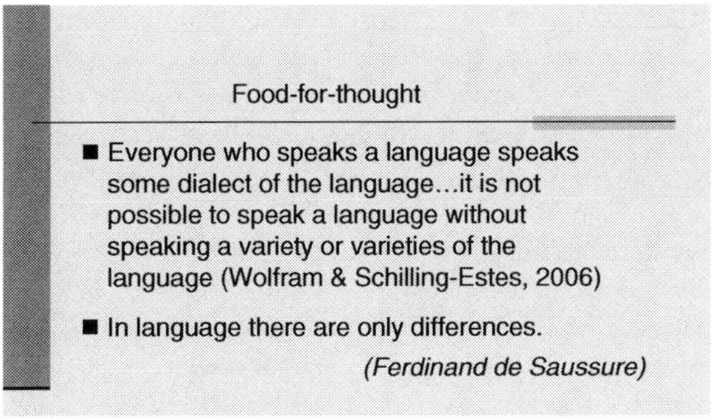

The *journey to implement change* 95

> **Food-for-thought**
>
> ■ Everyone who speaks a language speaks some dialect of the language…it is not possible to speak a language without speaking a variety or varieties of the language (Wolfram & Schilling-Estes, 2006)
>
> ■ In language there are only differences.
>
> *(Ferdinand de Saussure)*

Figure 4.8 Food-for-thought for concluding week 2's lesson

person's exposure to language and motivation to communicate? Why do you still believe in the Standard English?"

The questions are met with silence. Since there is not enough time for further discussions and for me to probe their views more deeply, I conclude the lesson with quotes from two sociolinguists which highlight that variation in language is 'normal' and which I hope students will take away and think about. I also inform students that the slide with these quotes (Figure 4.8) is available online for them to refer to, think about and reflect on.

* * * * *

Reflecting back on my teaching approaches in that week, I revisited some of the many questions I kept asking myself in the days following that lesson. Why did my students respond to my questions at the end of the lesson with silence? What was behind that silence? One explanation for this silence was that I was being too dogmatic in the way I taught students about language variation and, in the way I encouraged them to appreciate variation. Was that an 'appropriate' way to *inspire* students to learn to appreciate differences? Was it fair for students to be asked those questions in that way in just their second week of a subject and their first class on language variation? Was it appropriate for me to adopt what Tudor (2003) calls a "technological" approach to teaching – in effect, bombarding them with numerous concepts and examples of language variation – and then expecting them to change their attitudes towards language variation in their first class on language? I wonder if, during the conversations with students about their responses, I had overlooked and silenced a very important element in the process of inspiring students to learn about language variation and to appreciate differences.

4.1.7. Lesson in week 3: English in Singapore (Singaporean English)

This week is intended to be a continuation of last week's conversation about language variation. When selecting materials and examples to discuss, I specifically

96 *The journey to implement change*

choose Singapore and its varieties of English as examples to illustrate the concepts of pidgins and creoles (as these concepts seemed to have been the most important, yet difficult ones for students to grasp). When I first began to design this syllabus, Ali (the third person who had been present in the significant conversation with Lorna when I raised my concerns about the previous EIL-ex syllabus) had encouraged me to use Australia as a case study to teach those concepts. But I choose Singapore because I want to encourage students to 'get out of their comfort zone' to develop an internationalised perspective. I want them to learn about a variety of English with which they may not be familiar.

During the opening lecture part of the lesson, I present the sociolinguistic landscape of English in Singapore, which includes some historical facts about Singapore's colonisation by the British and its influence on language development. Before I move on to talk about the linguistic features of English in Singapore, I show the students a five-minute episode of a Singaporean television sit-com drama, *Phua Chu Kang*, without subtitles, and I ask if they can 'pick up anything'. While watching the sit-com drama, I do a quick scan of the classroom and I can see students scratching their heads, frowning, and laughing (perhaps because they find the actors' English 'funny'). When the episode ends, I ask students if they have 'picked up anything'. Half of the class shakes their heads and one of them says that "the actors spoke so fast, so I didn't catch anything". The other half of the class understands the gist of the episode. In response to this, I ask them: "Why did some of you 'catch' something whereas the others did not? How can we relate this to last week's concepts – mutual intelligibility and the role of exposures and experiences?"

Those who understood the gist of the episode say that they have travelled to Singapore and Malaysia, have friends and lecturers from these countries, and therefore are "used to it". Those who did not 'catch' anything say that this was the first time for them to listen to the English spoken by Singaporeans, and they found it "different from what we learned before and funny". After this discussion, I play the episode again and this time I direct them to "pay attention to the choices of vocabulary, grammar, pronunciation, and any linguistic features that are different from the ones you know". When the show ends, students share their observations with the whole class, and explain in what way these features are different from American, Australian, and British Englishes. Most examples are phonological and lexical features because these features are the most noticeable ones.

After this activity, I discuss some syntactical, morphological, phonological, and socio-pragmatic features, and the lectal continuum (Platt, 1977) – basilectal, mesolectal, and acrolectal – of Singaporean English. I can see that students are quite impressed with the continuum and how speakers of English from Singapore can switch from one continuum to the other depending on the context. I then raise the issue of the process of de-creolisation in Singapore, which is the government's attempt to stop Singaporean citizens speaking Singlish and to learn 'proper' Standard English (American English) through the 'Speak Good English Movement' campaign. When I discuss this with students, some of them show sympathy for Singaporeans and others, especially those who 'didn't catch anything', show full support for the government campaign because, after listening to the English spoken by the actors in the sit-com, "their English is incomprehensible and not native anyway". One of the students asks me, "Do you want your kids or students to speak like Singaporeans?" Hearing these comments and this question increases my frustration. I'm conscious that there are Singaporeans in my class. Students who are making these comments do not seem to have taken this into consideration. And they do not seem to have been able to link to the materials and ideas that I talked about in Week 2. Indeed, this comment upsets me and leads me to launch into a series of questions for the whole class: "What is Proper English? What is Standard English? Whose Standard are you referring to? Do you think this is fair? How do you feel if I ask you to stop speaking the language that you have been speaking for so many years? And what's wrong with sounding like Singaporeans? If I do not want my students to sound like an Australian or an American, I believe there is nothing wrong with that, right? And if my students want to learn to sound like Indians, I don't think there is anything wrong with that, right?"

Again these questions are met with silence. As I stand and listen to the silence, I feel that I need to think about more ways in future to 'prevent' them from developing that attitude and view. As we are about to run out of time, to conclude the lesson, I include again some quotes, a question, and a diagram (that shows the relationship between language, culture, and identity: "food for thought", Figure 4.9). I hope these will prompt students, especially those supporters of

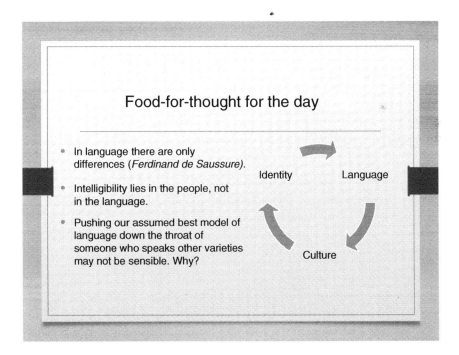

Figure 4.9 Food-for-thought for concluding week 3's lesson

98 *The journey to implement change*

the Singaporean campaign to 'speak good English', to critically re-examine their views/attitudes.

* * * * *

When I look back on my account of this week's lesson, I am encouraged by the students' interest in the YouTube video, but I am disturbed by the conclusion of the lesson. Why did I choose to get 'upset' at the groups of students who supported the 'Speak Good English Movement'? Why did I not try to encourage students to tell me more about their thoughts for me to further inquire into and dialogue about what had prompted them to make such comments? By getting upset and asking so many questions at once in a way that could be interpreted like an 'attack', had I not silenced and overlooked something very important? I could also observe how problematic the underlying assumptions of my future approaches to teaching EIL was: "I need to think about more ways in future to *'prevent'* them from *developing that attitude and view*". The underlined words indicate my ignorance of the complexity of the process of making sense of or learning about something that was 'against the current'.

4.1.8. *Lesson in week 9: Writing in international communication contexts*

In week 9, just a few weeks before the end of the semester, I begin again in lecture mode. I introduce the students to the diversification of written discourse conventions in English. I argue that this diversification is a result of difference in cultural values and in conceptualising the notion of politeness in writing. I present examples of written texts from an academic and professional contexts (e.g. essay and business letters) written by writers from diverse lingua-cultural backgrounds, and highlight how their macrostructure and microstructure are reflections of the cultural values and beliefs that the writers bring to their writing. In response to this, some students comment and raise interesting questions: "How should *we* write then?" "We cannot bring our flavour into our writing and we need to stick to standard!" "We will fail!" Inspired by the work of Canagarajah (2002), I discuss the notions of negotiation and re-appropriation of writing. Most of them again show their confusion in a range of facial expressions. Some are clearly annoyed. In the next activity, where I invite students to write their response to the question: "How has EIL changed your view about academic writing?", some students (see Figure 4.10 and Figure 4.11) criticise the EIL view of writing and my view as being too utopian. They display a strong belief in the correct way of writing, and believe that, as Student B (Figure 4.11) wrote, 'bowing down' to their superiors as they are lower ranks is not a negative thing.

Reflecting on those responses brings me back again to the feeling that I had when I was teaching the EIL-ex subjects. In relation to my teaching, what should I do? Why were students still adamant about having those deficit and problematic views even after weeks and weeks of activities and lessons on EIL? I thought my lesson on language variation was clear enough to show them that differences are normal. But was I expecting too much? Something seemed to be missing!

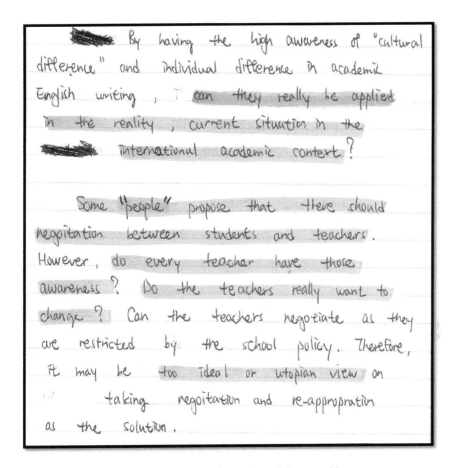

Figure 4.10 Student A's response to my discussion activity on writing

4.1.9. End of the semester

When the semester was over, I was still not satisfied with my teaching and with the responses I had seen in the students. I was encouraged in some respects: students were often more engaged than they had been in my EIL-ex teaching. And yet, ultimately, I had not achieved what I had planned to achieve. I had not seen what I wanted to see in my students. Although they seemed to be aware of what the new EIL subject was promoting, the questions that they asked and the comments they made during classroom discussions still showed that 'it is not a negative thing to bow to the power of the superiors'. It still showed a firm belief in the 'wrong'-ness of sounding and using English differently from the glorified 'native' English speakers from so-called Inner-Circle countries. So, maybe Kubota (2001b) is right when she expresses her doubts about changing students'

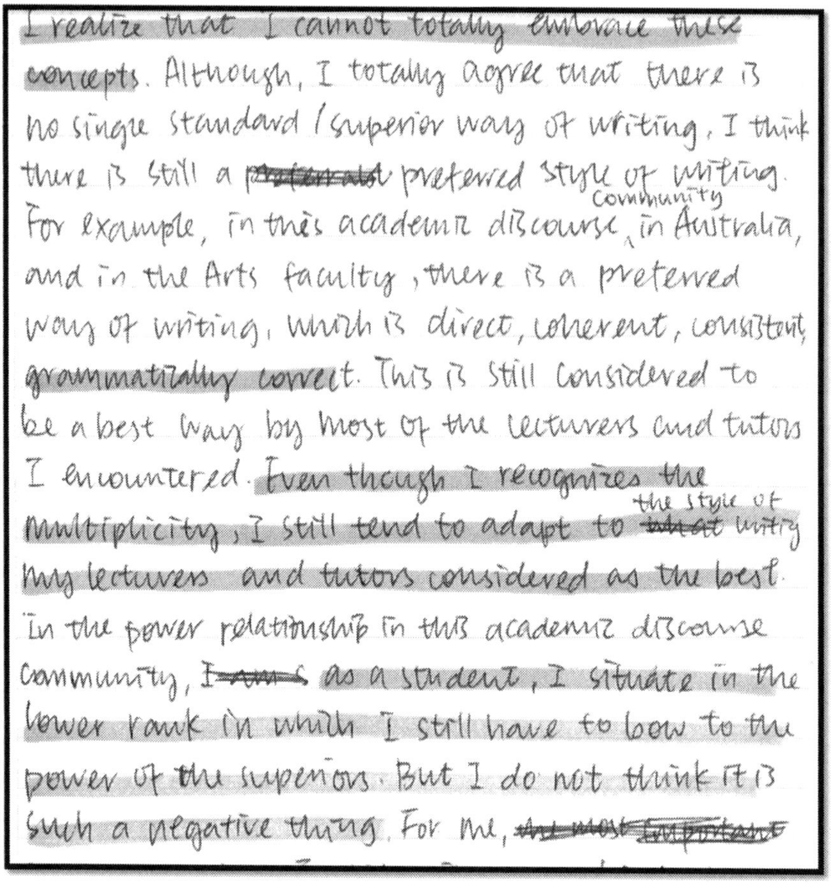

> I realize that I cannot totally embrace these ~~concepts~~. Although, I totally agree that there is no single standard / superior way of writing, I think there is still a ~~preferred~~ preferred style of writing. For example, in this academic discourse Community, in Australia, and in the Arts faculty, there is a preferred way of writing, which is direct, coherent, consistent, ~~grammatically~~ correct. This is still considered to be a best way by most of the lecturers and tutors I encountered. ~~Even though I recognizes the~~ multiplicity, I still tend to adapt to ~~that~~ the style of writing my lecturers and tutors considered as the best. In the power relationship in this academic discourse Community, ~~I am a~~ as a student, I situate in the lower rank in which I still have to bow to the power of the superiors. But I do not think it is such a negative thing. For me, ~~the most important~~

Figure 4.11 Student B's response to my discussion activity on writing

native-speakerist perceptions/beliefs even if the "educational interventions were implemented under optimal pedagogical conditions" (p. 61).

Despite this, I remember that a week after the end of the semester, I received an email from one of the students (Hyun, pseudonym) in my class who informed me that my teaching had allowed him to gain 'self-confidence' and 'self-esteem'. The new EIL class had encouraged him to view himself as a 'wonderful person'. My experiences of teaching in this new subject, Hyun's email, and Briguglio's (2005) and Suzuki's (2011) research papers, convinced me to believe that greater exposure to and engagement in the field might give me the results that I wanted and hoped for. So, one single subject in just one semester was not enough. Perhaps a longer period, may be a whole program would need to be developed to make a real difference in students other than Hyun.

4.1.10. From a single subject to a program

Not long after the trial semester was over, Lorna retired and I was appointed by the department to coordinate, revise, and teach in the program. My experience of teaching in my very first EIL subject and my reading of the literature of EIL, including the recommendations for syllabus materials and pedagogy, led me to develop a full three-year undergraduate program that specialised in teaching EIL and intercultural communication. I suspect that I was still hoping that I could 'completely prevent' students from having the 'deficit' views of language variations and their speakers, and from glorifying the varieties of Inner-Circle English.

In proposing a newly revised EIL program to the faculty, I argued that the program comprised an academic-content program, which provided students with knowledge of English language variation and its implications for communication in English, teaching and learning English, and researching English in a variety of intra/international contexts. To establish that this was not an English language learning program, I argued for the second language prerequisite entry criteria to be changed. Most importantly, in the curriculum materials, I aimed to ensure that expressions such as "second language speaker", "increase language skills", "correct and appropriate form or use of English" were completely removed. The names of almost all of the EIL-ex subjects were changed to ones that echoed the values and my understandings of what constituted an EIL paradigm (see Table 4.1).

Driven by my unhappy experience of observing how linguistic and cultural diversity were regarded as a 'problem' in previous EIL-ex program, the new program situated cultural and linguistic difference (pluricentricity of English and multilingualism) as core to the program's curriculum. Informed by this core and

Table 4.1 Previous and revised programs for English as an International Language (EIL)

EIL-ex program subjects	EIL program subjects
First Year	
EIL1010: Communication	English Language, Society, and Communication
EIL1020: Form and Structure	International Communication
Second Year	
EIL2110: Form and Function: English in Context	Researching English as an International Communication
EIL2120: The Language of Spoken English	Language and Globalisation
Third Year	
EIL3102 – Professional Communication	World Englishes
EIL3110 – Language and Culture	Language and Culture
EIL3130 – Making Sense of the Environment: English as a Language of Action and Reflection	Language and Education (Teaching English as an International Language)
EIL3210 – The Language of Written English	Writing Across Cultures

102   *The journey to implement change*

by my readings of the principles of teaching EIL in the literature, the main general objectives of the EIL program became:

- to guide students to develop knowledge of English language variation;
- to foster the beliefs, attitudes, and skills to communicate effectively with speakers of Englishes from diverse lingua-cultural backgrounds in a variety of intra/international contexts; and
- (for those who might see themselves as future English teachers) to develop understanding of the complexity of today's English language pedagogy, and the ability to teach English in the light of the changing sociolinguistic reality of English.

To achieve the above objectives, I developed eight subjects for EIL students at different levels of study. Although each subject had its own focus reflected in the names of the subject, I endeavoured to make sure that each subject aimed to teach students about cultural and linguistic differences, to understand a "multifaceted and potentially confusing linguistic world" (Crystal, 1999, p. 97), and to be open-minded and respectful towards linguistic and cultural differences. This can be observed in the objectives of each subject: the emphasis on gaining knowledge of and appreciation for world Englishes; understanding the implications of English for using/learning/teaching English; and critiquing problematic ideologies, practices, and policies in societies that are socially, racially, and linguistically unjust (see Appendix 5).

To help and work with me in achieving those objectives, three new staff members were employed (Ashish, Fatima, and Indigo, whom I will introduce in Chapter 5). I was keen to learn from them and also to see if they would encounter similar scenarios as I had done in the trial semester. If their experiences and their values vis-à-vis EIL teaching were at all similar to mine, then I was also keen to observe their teaching approaches and to learn from this observation. The journey of our collaborative effort in teaching EIL and inspiring students to learn to appreciate diversity begins in the next chapter.

4.2. Chapter summary

In this chapter, I have, through an autobiographical narrative, provided a thick description of the historical background of how and why the EIL program at Urban University was developed. In this narrative of my first effort to teach an EIL subject and to develop an EIL program, not only do I foreground my role in the development of the program (Casanave, 2010), but I also begin to articulate some of the fundamental beliefs and principles of teaching language that I hold as an EIL advocate and EIL educator. I show how these emerging beliefs and principles played a significant role in my revision of the original EIL-ex program. Most importantly, writing this narrative prompted me to question and reflect critically on my first practices as an EIL educator and some underlying assumptions, of which I was, at the time of these experiences, only partly aware. However, the accounts and the reflection I present in this chapter are not sufficient to illustrate the pragmatic dimension of teaching EIL as they are only based on the curriculum of a single subject and one person's experience of teaching in this subject. In the next chapter, I present and analyse how my colleagues and I inspired our students to learn about and to appreciate the diversity of English based on the principles of EIL teaching materials and pedagogy as frameworks. Discussions on the data from this chapter and next chapter in the light of the theoretical frameworks are presented in Chapter 6.

Note

1 This was not very clear when I was a student until I was exposed to literature on EIL and Internationalisation of Education.

5 EIL teachers implementing change

5.0. Introduction

Recently published books on the teaching and learning of English as an International Language (EIL) (Alsagoff et al., 2012; Matsuda, 2012a; McKay & Brown, 2016) have reviewed and critiqued some traditional principles and practices of teaching English across a range of international settings. Contributors to these books have offered new perspectives on English language teaching in the light of the complexity of the sociolinguistic reality of English, and called for these new perspectives to be implemented. However, as discussed in Chapter 2, both Matsuda (2012a) and Brown (2012) argue that discussions on the teaching and learning of EIL mostly remain at a theoretical/abstract level, i.e. there is some distance or even disconnection between these discussions and actual classroom practices and professional experiences. Brown (2012), in particular, highlights that there has not been any research that addresses this gap or the question: "what EIL syllabuses, learning sequences, textbooks, or curriculum projects already exist?" (p. 163). If EIL educators aim to engage their students in reflecting critically on and perhaps modifying their perceptions and attitudes towards different varieties of world Englishes, changes or revision must occur at three levels: "(1) teaching materials or syllabi; (2) techniques, approaches or activities; and (3) beliefs and principles underlying the materials and approaches" (Karavas-Doukas, 1998, p. 28). In addition, although there have been some publications explicating and advocating EIL principles, programs, and pedagogical ideas, the pragmatic dimensions of the curricula (syllabus materials and pedagogical practices) tend to be inadequately addressed or overlooked altogether. Having reviewed this recently published literature, Wee (2013) takes a similar line and argues that the research literature about the teaching of EIL needs to incorporate more pragmatic discussion, including considerations of how realistic it might be to implement suggested principles. This chapter addresses the above gaps and extends the journey from the previous chapter by presenting more voices and discussing the 'live experiences' of all the EIL educators teaching in the undergraduate EIL program at Urban University.

I begin this chapter by introducing my three colleagues who were employed to collaborate with me in teaching the newly revised undergraduate EIL program.

Thereafter, I present the materials and pedagogical activities that my colleagues and I selected and used to inspire our students to learn about EIL and appreciate different varieties of English. In doing so, I draw upon the principles of EIL teaching materials and pedagogical practices discussed in Chapter 2. I use these principles as a framework for presenting and discussing my classroom observation notes, my analyses of the collected learning materials, my own teaching reflections (my journal), and the transcripts of interviews with my colleagues. Last, I also discuss another theme that emerged from my data analysis: namely our engagement with the politics of differences and the challenge my colleagues experienced in doing so, and which were reflected and evidenced in the interactions that they engaged in the least.

This approach to case study research aims to provide a thick description of the EIL program at Urban University, i.e. what and how EIL-inspired educators taught EIL in the period of this study, as well as the ups and downs of teaching EIL in a real-life setting. It is through this description that this book project intends to discuss what else these EIL-inspired educators could consider incorporating in teaching an EIL curriculum, lesson, or program in the future. A more detailed discussion of this question in the light of the experiences of EIL teachers (Chapter 5) and students (Chapter 7), however, will take place in the conclusions and recommendations chapter (Chapter 9).

5.1. Profile of EIL educators at Urban University

In this section, I provide descriptions of and insights into the profiles of the three lecturers who worked with me as the seminar lecturers (lecturers who are in charge of seminars as opposed to lectures) for the first-year EIL program following the establishment of the new program. These three lecturers came from different lingua-cultural and educational backgrounds: Ashish (Nepal), Fatima (Indonesia), and Indigo (Australia). In presenting their profiles, I also discuss a range of their encounters and engagement with the EIL paradigm. I start with Ashish who was the most senior of the participants.

5.1.1. Ashish

Ashish was from Nepal, which Kachru (1986) categorises as an Expanding-Circle country, i.e. a country where English is used as a foreign language. However, in his research on the sociolinguistic context of Nepal, Ashish had discovered that the sociolinguistic characteristics of Nepal are not much different from its neighbouring country, India. Therefore, if he had to situate himself with respect to Kachru's model, he preferred to be viewed as a user of English from an Outer-Circle country. He spoke fluent Nepali, Hindi, and English (his own educated variety of English, which he described as "a mixture of all these: Nepali English, Indian English, American English, and British English". He had a Bachelor of Education (with a major in English Education) and a Master of Education

106   *EIL teachers implementing change*

(Teaching English as a Foreign Language) from a university in Nepal. Not long after he had completed his postgraduate degree in Nepal, he won the prestigious Fulbright Scholarship and pursued a Master of Applied Linguistics (English Education) at a university in the United States. At the time he was employed to teach in the EIL program at Urban University, he had just completed his PhD from a university in Melbourne in the field of English Language education and policy.

At the time that began our collaboration, Ashish had been in Australia for nearly a decade. Prior to coming to Australia, he had taught undergraduate and postgraduate programs in English Language Teaching and Applied Linguistics at a university in Nepal for 12 years, which had earned him the title and status of reader. Apart from teaching in universities and schools, he had also worked with the British Council in Nepal on a project in which he and his colleagues collected educational resources such as English books, English magazines, and English newspapers to establish an English-language learning and teaching resource centre for the nation. In the undergraduate EIL program at Urban University, he was in charge of teaching the seminars for the first-year program (EIL1010 and EIL1020).

The EIL paradigm was not something with which Ashish was familiar when he had been a student (in Nepal and the United States) and later a lecturer (in Nepal). However, he reported that throughout his life he had encountered many different varieties of English.

> When I was a student [in school], the Nepali government prescribed the British English, so I was taught the British English by Indians, because we did not have enough English language teachers in Nepal, so we had Indians, the British English taught by Indians. I was also exposed to Indian English and a variety of English spoken with a Nepali accent. When I was in the States, I had a lot of exposure to different American Englishes. But at the university where I studied my master's, I did not study anything about EIL or World Englishes, so the focus was still on the traditional ESL paradigm, teaching American English to non-native-speakers.

In spite of his experience with a varieties of Englishes, Ashish claimed that he did not have a positive attitude towards certain varieties of English.

> I hated Indian English because I thought that that's not the standard, to be very honest, and if someone was speaking with an accent, Nepali accent, then I would say that he wasn't speaking Standard English. American English of course, but when I went to America, actually my affection on for British English grew in a sense, because I couldn't connect with the American variety of English. I didn't accept the American variety of English, I don't know why, I cannot explain. Maybe in some form, I had this love for the British variety, so I couldn't converse in or assimilate with this [American] variety of English.

EIL teachers implementing change 107

Therefore, he explained, in the English classes he had taught in Nepal, he used "the Queen's or King's English model".

Ashish's first encounter with a similar conception of English as the EIL paradigm (one that appreciates and respects linguistic diversity) was during his doctoral studies in Australia. Initially, he had, as he described, "an elitist approach" to his research, which was to explore the role of English in Nepal and how its status and role could be elevated in Nepal.

> I had this view that English should be the most important language in Nepal and if that means replacing, elimination of other languages, so be it. So, I believed in it actually. I believed that English had a very prominent role to play in bringing development in Nepal, to be very honest, and being a tourist country, we have to connect with the people of the world and English is or was the medium to do.

However, as Ashish progressed, he told me he was "encouraged by his supervisor to go beyond that superficial or elite vision approach and to look at other languages in Nepal because one cannot talk about one language in isolation". When he discovered through his research that considerable resources had been invested into the teaching and learning of English in Nepal – to the extent that this highly-sought-after and 'elite' language could potentially devalue the national language and threaten other local languages – he pinpointed this as the moment when he "started to shift [his] paradigm". In fact, it was his awareness of the extinction, and the threat of extinction, of local languages spoken by some of the indigenous Nepali people that prompted him to change his way of thinking towards a "more inclusive approach to language".

> I remember I grew up in the village, and my house was surrounded by indigenous people called Tharus, they're like the Aboriginal in Australia, they're the indigenous, tribes and I started to think about their situation. If we don't consider the fact that they have a language, they love their language, they want to have their identity, then we must do something to help them do that … but if we say, OK you can't have your language, meaning you cannot have your identity, that's denying their identity right? So, if I say their languages should be replaced, meaning their identity should be replaced by fake identity.

5.1.2. *Fatima*

Fatima was from Indonesia (interestingly also deemed by Kachru as an Expanding-Circle country) and she had a Chinese background. She spoke fluent Bahasa Indonesia, two ethnolects spoken in Indonesia (Javanese in Java island and Palembangnese in Sumatra island), and a "variety of English which is influenced by my multilingual repertoire and multicultural background". Despite acknowledging her Chinese background, Fatima did not speak Chinese and was not familiar with Chinese culture because she had not been brought up with

108 *EIL teachers implementing change*

the language and culture due to the racial and ethnic tensions between Chinese Indonesians and other ethnic groups in the environment where she grew up. Thus, her Chinese identity was hidden from her as a child and was revealed to her by her family only in her late adulthood. She had a Bachelor of English Language Teaching (ELT) from a university in Indonesia and a Master of Arts (ELT) from a university in Thailand. At the time she was interviewed for my project, she had already been in Australia for two years and was undertaking her doctoral studies in the field of English Language teacher education at a university in Melbourne.

Prior to coming to Australia, Fatima was a senior lecturer in her university in Salatiga (one of the most ethnically diverse cities in Indonesia). She was in charge of teaching a Methodology course, Literature in EFL classrooms, General English, and Academic Writing. One year after she had completed her postgraduate degree in Thailand, she went to work in Singapore as a researcher at a southeast Asian organisation for English language teaching, called RELC (Regional English Language Centre). One year after she arrived in Australia, she, like Ashish, was recruited to teach in the first-year EIL program at Urban University (EIL1010 and EIL1020).

Her encounter with the beliefs and values advocated by the EIL paradigm was slightly different from Ashish's. While she was undertaking her undergraduate degree in the 1990s in Indonesia, she reported that the BA (ELT) program was predominantly informed by a paradigm that advocated the primacy of native-speakerism (Holliday, 2005) and monolingualism. She reported that British or American English was promoted as the 'correct' model for learning and communication, which she was required to choose and emulate.

> I still remember ummm … my education at that time, the orientation is only on two Englishes so either you study American English or British English, and you have to imitate *precisely* [Fatima's emphasis] like that … so you have to choose if you want sound like American, you stick with that, if you want to sound like British, you stick to that one, don't mix, and at first I thought – that's how you learnt English.

This system, she believed, led her to develop an American accent and to teach her students American English. However, it started to change after going through "a number of phases or maybe encounters" with the EIL paradigm.

Fatima's first encounter with the paradigm was through her colleague when she was in Indonesia. In an interview with me, Fatima explained that the beliefs and values promoted by the EIL paradigm were introduced to her by her colleague (a lecturer working at the same university as her in Indonesia). This colleague shared (and continued to share) some interesting readings about EIL and reflections on how she had been prompted by these ideas to think about herself as a speaker of English:

> [my colleague] loves to share everything she learnt with me and … actually the first time I really know about EIL is from her. She asked me, 'Do you get

that feeling when the teachers are correcting, you feel so bad?' And I said, 'Yeah'! and we start sharing about this thing and we are trying to understand. I think the first, my first reaction was relief in a way. I feel better about myself, so liberating. I was like 'Are you serious that we can be ourselves? Is that so?' and she said: 'Yeah'. From there, I learned a little bit more about EIL ... and the thinking as well, but it's not intensive, but at least I have the awareness, but I couldn't really understand it in a whole.

Fatima reported that "everything became quite clear" when she left for Thailand to pursue her postgraduate study in English Language teaching.

We were introduced to this concept EIL but it's not on the first year, it's introduced not explicitly, but umm ... it's sort of being modified in a way. So we were studying like the theory and practice of reading, e.g. they did teach the theory, but rather than teaching us the concept of EIL, they taught us the theory that was informed by the EIL paradigm. When they talk about reading materials, they start talking about how to incorporate English in other parts of the world ... you know ... this new developing Englishes ... and at first we didn't understand but then after I think on the second semester, we have a course called EIL, in that course, we start talking lots of these issues, native-speakerism, linguicism, world Englishes, and so on.

While this course clearly stimulated Fatima's thinking, prompting her to reflect on many of her existing assumptions and practices, Fatima told me she believed that she "became more aware of EIL perspective" when she encountered an American classmate who, during a classroom discussion, asked her about her claim, "My English is my variety":

I become more aware of that when we have lively discussions between native-speaker students and the non-native-speaker students in a class on EIL. I remember I was arguing with this American, and we were talking, we were talking about Englishes and, you know, that your English is your variety and I was ... I was struck with that and I thought huh ... so I could really ... so it's OK to have your own variety of English. And this American classmate was against that and said that was silly. So, I said why is that silly? and then this person suddenly also asked me a question that actually keep ringing in my head and then try to, try to ummm ... talk back to me and said, 'Oh come on, [Fatima], look at yourself, look at your accent, you have an American accent, and you call that *your* English'. And I was struck and I was like, 'Hmm ... how should I respond to that?' And I was like, 'Oh ... I didn't realise that, but I thought it's just that, well, OK, maybe I have an American accent, but it's just an accent, doesn't, but the way I use my English is my English, yeah, it's my variety of English' ... I thought you know, but then I kept on, you know ... this thing, umm ... that question actually become a struggle for me, so I'm still struggling with that ... I mean at that class.

110 *EIL teachers implementing change*

The comment by Fatima's American classmate further prompted Fatima to realise, understand, and believe in the need to project one's identity through the way one uses English, which is a view advocated by EIL scholars. To project a more authentic sense of her identity, she attempted to replace her American English accent with a Malaysian English accent.

> I don't want people to consider me as an imitator of a certain native English. I want people to see me as an Indonesian, a Sumatranese, and Chinese background, but who speaks English, who uses English. And I thought how should I project this identity? OK, if people judge me based on my accent, maybe I need to change my accent. I have a lot of exposure to Malaysian English, maybe I adopt Malaysian English, Malaysian accent, at least people know that I'm Asian [laughter]. But at least the first impression is they know that I'm an Asian, so I used Malaysian accent to help me project my Asian identity at least.

On her return to Indonesia, Fatima reported that her effort to project her multilingual and multicultural identity through the adoption of a Malaysian English accent was not appreciated by her students. Her students told her that "before [she] left for Thailand [she] sounded so 'native', now [her] English is different and it's weird".

> My effort of having an identity, a multilingual and multicultural identity is not very welcomed in Indonesia and even when my students sometimes felt that err ... accent shows your intelligence. If you have a native-speaker's accent, you would immediately be considered as intelligent. I have some colleagues who have a very strong Indonesian accent, Javanese accent I mean, but they're brilliant people, brilliant lecturers, and I don't understand why this student don't want to take their classes. Then I realised that because they have a Javanese accent and that's why students see them as not intelligent. Oh my god, it is not right!

However, this situation did not prevent Fatima from continuing her effort to "phase out the American accent bit by bit and project an Indonesian identity by speaking a little bit of Javanese accent to see how students react". She explained that she did this to show students that "there is nothing wrong with not having a native-speaker's accent, what is important is how you show who you are through your use of English". In fact, she claimed that her effort to "mix different varieties of English and the national language, Bahasa Indonesia" produced an unexpectedly positive outcome:

> I somehow I felt I get closer to my students. I'm doing this Javanese accent, so because most of them are Javanese students. I thought if I do with my American accent English all the time, there will be a distance between me and my students. So I felt that when I'm doing this mixing thing, combining

my language with their language, their way of speaking. I'm trying to relate to them, and I have become approachable to students. They trust you as a teacher and they come to me when they need explanation or anything or help with their study and I felt that it is working ... I mean it's my relating with them and they're ... like opening the door, not being a total stranger, keeping distance to myself.

That is, by not attempting to so acutely differentiate her own accent from the culture that she and her students shared, she found that she developed stronger rapport and a palpable sense of solidarity with her students. This journey, she shared, is what she "aim[s] to share with [her] current and prospective students" so that her students can learn to "see and understand the value of being 'themselves' rather than 'someone else', which is one of the things that EIL paradigm values".

5.1.3. Indigo

Indigo was from Melbourne, Australia (an Inner-Circle country, according to Kachru). In my interview with Indigo, she described the English that she spoke as "my variety of English – a bit of Australian and a bit of American" and some German. She had a Bachelor of Arts (majoring in German Linguistics and Indigenous Australian Studies). She had also completed a 120-hour online short course on TEFL (Teaching English as a Foreign Language). At the time of our interview, she was undertaking her postgraduate degree in EIL at the same university and was writing her dissertation on rapport-building in Australian ESL classrooms from an EIL perspective.

Prior to her appointment in the undergraduate EIL program, Indigo had taught English for nearly five years. She had been a private English and German tutor for secondary school and university students for several years. On completion of her TEFL certificate short course, she worked as an ESL instructor in Vietnam and Laos for several months, and as a volunteer on Christmas Island for five weeks, teaching English to a group of refugees. After Indigo had completed one semester of her postgraduate degree in EIL, she was recruited to work with Ashish, Fatima, and myself to teach the first-year students in the EIL program at Urban University (EIL1010 and EIL1020).

In terms of her familiarity with the EIL paradigm, Indigo claimed that "its relevance to language teaching, learning, and communication definitely" was something that she had never thought about before and had not been taught in the TEFL short course. However, the "thinking and what the paradigm promotes" was not new to her and was in fact in line with her belief and "[her] ideology" that she believed she had developed as a result of her undergraduate major in Indigenous Australian Studies.

The things that I learn in EIL is very much related to my zero tolerance for racism, cultural erosion, and assimilation, especially growing up as an Aussie observing the way the [Australian] Aborigines are being unfairly treated, like

112 *EIL teachers implementing change*

how their language and culture were stripped off. That's why I have studied Australian Indigenous Studies before to learn about this and how we can put a stop to this, so EIL is not different from the indigenous study where you have to learn to appreciate differences.

Therefore, the native-speaker-oriented TEFL short course that she had undertaken, she claimed, did not make her feel comfortable at all. Indigo was genuinely surprised that it was

> still very native-speaker-oriented and they were really like getting to you about how you're the native-speaker, so, you're better so you're not gonna have any problems getting jobs and you don't need to worry ... you're gonna be amazing because you have this short course. I am not comfortable with some position of power purely from where I was born, the type of English I speak. I'm not comfortable with that. I've never been comfortable with that, which is as I said before, that's why I've studied Australian Indigenous Studies. So, it's very uncomfortable having to present a class that explains how you do things as a native-speaker or how you do things in Australian English.

During her postgraduate study, though, Indigo found her encounter with EIL "challenging, but a positive thing or a positive challenge". In a sense, she felt that it was challenging her to make the extra effort to learn about and engage with differences, and "simply, to be a better person".

> I want to put myself in a position where I am working with the ... mutually working ... and learning is a two-way process ... that's what I'm interested in ... so this native-speaker ... learning about native-speaker fallacy is very interesting to me because it's a nice way of going ... OK, good, we should not have this position of power, so let's put effort into really mutually engaging with other people and other people's ways of doing things. So, to me, it's great ... let's look at how other people do things and let me learn about them ... I know my version of English, I know my version of pragmatics, how great would it be to learn about everyone else's. I also feel that native-speakers have to work harder being good teachers, communicators. You can't take that position of power just because you're just native-speaker, then you have to put effort into the whole learning process, and have to have the right attitude.

In summary, Indigo's understanding of EIL, she believed, was not just restricted to "bringing something to teaching how others do things and think about things differently", but also about "social justice, teaching people how to respect and appreciate differences".

5.2. EIL in classrooms

This section presents an account of how the EIL educators at Urban University implemented their particular perspective on English as an International Language

(McKay, 2002; Sharifian, 2009) in an attempt to engage and hopefully inspire their undergraduate first-, second-, and third-year students to learn about different varieties of English, to examine arguments about the need to see all varieties of English as equal, and to develop the ability to communicate across cultures. This account will present not only what I have observed in classes and what I have heard from a majority of students and their teachers, but I also report on minority views, and show how sometimes it is these minority views that prevail most powerfully. The following discussion is based on the analyses of the collected learning materials, classroom-observation notes, transcripts of interviews with my colleagues, and my own reflective research journal.

5.2.1. Raising awareness of the diversity of English, its users, and culture

As a way to achieve the main objectives of the EIL program at Urban University outlined before, one most noticeable aspect of all EIL curricula was the emphasis on developing awareness, understanding, and appreciation of the diversity of English (world Englishes), the changing demography of English language users, and the different cultural values and norms different users of English incorporate in their use of English. The following statements (taken from interviews with me) by my teaching colleagues in the EIL course provide a good overview of the philosophical, curriculum and pedagogical concerns we shared as teachers in that program.

> What we mostly strongly promote through our teaching is understanding different cultures and understand that people are different linguistically and culturally. We've got this core part of going … you do this for your politeness, but I do this for my politeness norms. Wow! we do it differently … now we live in a multicultural society and now we work internationally.
>
> (Indigo)

> As a program, we mostly teach students to become aware of different ways of doing, different ways of writing, different ways of speaking, and different ways of reading. Being aware of this different Englishes like OK, so I come with one different and you come with a different English. And because there are so many Englishes, there are so many cultural differences, this is what we all have promote in the way we teach.
>
> (Ashish)

> Our teaching or classroom is all about promoting the diversity, respecting your own variety of English and other people's varieties of English and understanding why this English is different from this English and that English. Learning to understand, not to judge why people speak differently. To understand English is being used to promote your background, your culture, your linguistic knowledge and everything. So different people speak different English because they have their own history or their own reasons.
>
> (Fatima)

114   *EIL teachers implementing change*

These philosophies, and curriculum and pedagogical ideas can be observed in the choices of topics, prescribed reading materials, and pedagogical activities that featured in the EIL course at Urban University. I want now to explain some of the particular thinking that underpinned these dimensions, beginning with our shared vision with respect to 'topics and readings'.

5.2.1.1. *EIL topics and readings*

As each subject in the EIL program had its own focus (e.g. writing, language education, globalisation, and research), my colleagues and I during the time of this study attempted to ensure that the diversification of the form, user, and culture of English were reflected in the choices of topics covered in every subject. We also attempted to ensure that those topics were adequately addressed by the 'authoritative voices' from the selected prescribed reading materials. Firstly, as can be seen in the list of topics covered in every subject I have summarised in the list of EIL subjects, topics, and prescribed reading materials (see Appendix 6), the discourses associated with linguistic plurality and interculturality are prevalent. This is particularly evident in the language such as "variation", "Englishes", "cultures", "English as an International Language", "international communication", and "intercultural communication". The kind of plurality that students were exposed to, and engaged with in their learning, varied across subjects depending on the level and the focus of the subject. Learning from my previous EIL trial of one first-year subject when I 'overloaded' my students with a large number of concepts of language variation and with different varieties of English in two two-hour sessions, my colleagues and I took a slightly different approach in the newly developed course. When I discussed with them what I did in my trial subject, they were rather taken aback. They unanimously agreed that this was too much and/or too early to have expected this degree of complexity in the first year of the course.

> I feel it is way too early for students at first year level if we give them different examples of world Englishes or to study in detail about variation of English language at phonological, lexical, syntactical, and pragmatic level.
>
> (Ashish)

> It may be quite confusing because I remember when I was doing my master's degree in Thailand, my lecturers talked to us about different varieties of English. It was great for me to know about it, but hard for me to kind of process it.
>
> (Fatima)

> I believe it will be too hard, complicated to throw them with multiple world Englishes like how Singaporeans and Australians use their grammar, vocabulary, pronunciation differently from each other.
>
> (Indigo)

We agreed, though, that it was important for students to know about and to be exposed to different varieties of world Englishes fairly early in their study of EIL. Thus, my colleagues and I redesigned and sequenced the first-year EIL subjects such that first-year students would need to understand, firstly, the nature of English language variation (EIL1010), and, then secondly, the nature of international/intercultural communication in the next semester (EIL1020). As Fatima asserted, "Before we introduce different world Englishes, they need to know in advance in what ways we all naturally sound and use language differently from each other". Otherwise, Indigo added, "they will be like, OK! Singaporean English, hmmm ... so what? It's wrong anyway". In EIL1010, all four of us lecturers attempted to raise our students' awareness of the diversity of English and its users by exploring for over six weeks the metaphor of language as a dialect with an army and navy, and by introducing important basic sociolinguistics concepts such as: variety, dialects (national dialects, regional dialects, sociolects, ethnolects, register, and idiolects), pidgins, and creoles. Authoritative voices of several sociolinguists (including Hudson, 1996; Stockwell, 2007; Wardhaugh, 1993; Yule, 1996) were included to provide students with conceptual tools to learn about and understand the nature of language variation. Having taught about the nature of English language variation in EIL1010, my three colleagues and I decided to incorporate topics in EIL1020 (i.e. in the following semester) that could inspire students to understand the nature of international communication, and to view communication in English as a 'two-way street'. Hence, in studying this subject in semester 2, students would be exposed to differences in pragmatic discourse conventions, speech acts, cultural schemas and scripts, politeness, and writing in English. At this stage we introduced them to the writing and research of some pioneers of EIL and World Englishes (e.g. Kachru & Smith, 2008; McKay, 2002), and the students continued to engage with the work of these pioneers in an ongoing dialogue for almost three-quarters of the semester.

At second-year level, we moved on to expose students to the notion of the pluricentricity of English, predominantly in EIL2120 (Language and Globalisation). The significant voices in this unit included scholars such as Bhatia (2006), Crystal (2006, 2008) and Martin (2006), and we used texts written by them as the basis for learning and dialogues. The students in this subject would be given opportunities to explore and would be exposed to another form of English language variation or potentially emerging dialect of English as a result of the influence of advancement in information communication technology (internet English, texting English); and another variation in media and popular culture (Englishes in the media, music, and advertisements). In EIL2110, students would not have much exposure to the pluricentricity of English through the teaching and prescribed reading materials as the topics were mainly teaching students how to conduct an empirical project (see Appendix 6). Even though there was a topic on "English as an International Language: State-of-the-Art", it was only intended to introduce students to the paradigm of EIL and how this had been used as a paradigm to inform research studies in the field. However, we planned the assessment tasks – i.e. the research proposal and research project that students were

116 EIL teachers implementing change

required to complete – such that doing these tasks would either directly or indirectly provide students with opportunities to explore and therefore be exposed to the diversification of the forms, users, and cultures of English. This is because they were required to conduct a small-scale research project on any issues that reflected the main focus of the program (EIL) and that addressed the following main theme: the globalisation and internationalisation of English, and its implications for using, learning, and teaching English. As supporting evidence, the following is a list of some research projects that the EIL2110 students[1] eventually undertook:

- Exploring the 'Koreanness' in the variety of English spoken by Korean *jogi-yuhaksaeng* (early-study-abroad-students) living in Melbourne.
- How 'Thai' is the English used by Thai-pop singers in rapping?
- Death = taboo? Investigating how 'death' is conceptualised by speakers of English from mainland China and from Australia.
- Investigating the use and function of "like" in speakers of English from Singapore who are currently studying in Australia.
- Do we have 'Indonesian English'? From the perspectives and experiences of Indonesian students in Australia.
- Exploring how Inner-Mongolian students respond to compliments in English, and the factors behind their response.
- Comparing the pragmatic strategies used by Japanese and Singaporean students to request for an assignment-deadline-extension through email.

At third-year level, the chosen topics and the very names of the subjects suggest that students would be more exposed to, and engage in depth with learning about, the pluricentricity of the form, users, and culture of English. For example, EIL3102 (World Englishes) would provide students with a semester-long exposure to the plurality of the English language, its users, and its cultures through topics on Englishes from Inner-Circle, Outer-Circle, and Expanding-Circle countries, and readings by eminent scholars in those countries. Our belief in the importance of this notion of the plurality of English and its cultures can also be observed in other third-year subjects that would devote nearly three-quarters of a semester to the study of how English is used as a medium by different users of English from different lingua-cultural backgrounds to communicate their own cultural values, norms, and beliefs. This is evident in a more general way in EIL3110 (Language and Culture), and students would begin to explore more specificities, e.g. in their study of English language writing in EIL3210 (Writing Across Cultures). In EIL3130 (Language and Education), though, students would be less exposed to the notion of the plurality of English, and more concerned with exploring alternative perspectives of the teaching and learning of English in the light of the contemporary sociolinguistic reality of English. These perspectives, as seen in the EIL list of subjects, topics, and reading materials in Appendix 6, were voiced through the writing of EIL and World Englishes scholars who had been strongly advocating for the incorporation of a pluricentric view of English into English language teaching (e.g. Brown, 2006; Hino, 2010; Kachru, 1992; Matsuda, 2002; McKay, 2003). By engaging with these writings, students would have the opportunities to be exposed to both English language variation and other different perspectives on English language education as the implications for English language teaching discussed in these writings are predominantly based on the authors' observations and research studies on the pluralisation of English language, its users, and cultures.

In addition to exposing students to ideas associated with the diversity of English and Englishes across the world, my colleagues and I believed it was important to encourage students to examine the potential reasons behind the differences in using English. We wanted them to appreciate that no one uses language differently without a reason. In this, as in so many aspects of the new EIL curriculum we were developing, we expressed our views slightly differently, but there was strong commonality in the underpinning principle:

> [students] have to learn to understand that there are meanings behind these different use of English.
>
> (Ashish)

> I think this is important because if we only raise awareness of different varieties of English, they would only be like: OK, that's just a mistake made by non-native-speakers of English. They have to go beyond this view.
>
> (Indigo)

> [a]s I said before, people speak English differently because they have their own history or their own reasons or their stories to tell. It is important for them to understand this.
>
> (Fatima)

Therefore, in some subjects such as EIL1010 (English, Society, and Communication), EIL3110 (Language and Culture), and EIL3210 (Writing Across Cultures), it can be seen that students in those units would be required to read about and explore how language variation is a reflection of various identities, worldviews, and norms. Students in the EIL program would be encouraged not only to be aware of English language variation but also to reflect on and understand the reasons behind this variation. Fatima introduced the idea to her students in the class in the following way:

> How do the different ways you all communicate in English reflect who you are, who you want to be as well as your understanding of the world, your cultural values, beliefs, and practices?

Informed by our shared belief in the importance of inspiring students to gain understanding of the underlying reasons or factors behind English language variation, the three lecturers and I strongly agreed on the importance of writings – such

118   *EIL teachers implementing change*

as those by Kramsch (1998), Rubin (1997), and Thornborrow (1999) – that drew connections between language and identity and identity formation. Ashish explained his own reasons for wanting to emphasise this with his students:

> [s]tudents come [to this course] with a particular attitude that may see differences as a bad thing, or the reason behind this 'deviation' if you like is because of poor language proficiency or that it has something to do with them being a non-native-speaker. So, encouraging students to understand how we use language reflects who we are and what we think is I believe one way of approaching that kind of attitude.

Although these writings or topics were not necessarily seen in other subjects of the course, opportunities were still provided by the four of us to examine and discuss the potential reasons or factors underlying English language variation. This will be presented and discussed in the next section on pedagogical activities.

5.2.1.2. Pedagogical activities

In the previous section, I presented something of the scope and sequence of the revised EIL course, using the voices of different teachers to explain the reasons behind our decisions. I detailed the topics and prescribed reading-materials my colleagues and I designed to raise students' awareness of the diversification of the form, users, and culture of English, and to engage students in learning to appreciate this diversity. To teach those topics and the content of those reading-materials, my classroom observation notes and analysis of materials revealed my colleagues devised a number of pedagogical activities or tasks for students to experience and have more exposure to the diversity of English, its users, and cultures. Rather than comprehensively describing all these pedagogical activities and tasks, I have categorised them based on the sources from where students could access to the diversity of English.

5.2.1.2.1. TEACHERS' OWN COLLECTION OF TEXTS

In addition to using and presenting examples of different varieties of English from the prescribed readings, novels (*My Boyhood in Siam* by Chandruang, 1970; and *The Kite Runner* by Hosseini, 2013), a folk tale ('Chung hyo ye' by Diamond Sutra Recitation Group, 2007), a journal article ('Soul and style' by Geneva Smitherman, 1974), my colleagues and I often used our collections of texts written in different varieties of English to expose students to world Englishes, and to encourage them to analyse and understand these Englishes. These collections were predominantly from our encounters with texts written in different world Englishes "in our everyday life in Australia" (Indigo) as well as "when we were overseas on a conference trip" (Fatima). For example, in a lesson on interaction as cooperation in EIL1020 (International Communication), Indigo used her experience of observing a conversation between her friends from Malaysia and Thailand (Figure 5.1)

Conversation: a Malaysian (M) and a
Thai (T) students

- M: Hey T, where you going ah?
- T: Hi M, just walking around. Are you well?
- M: Yeah, like that lah! as usual! You?
- T: same same (laughter)
- M: Ok, I go first, see you later!
- T: OK, ok, see you!

Figure 5.1 A text used in Indigo's lesson on speech act

as a way to expose her students to a different use of speech act in English across cultures. As a speaker of a variety of Australian English, she shared with students her feeling of confusion when listening to this conversation and that:

> I wanted all of us [Indigo and her students] to work together to try to make sense of their use of greeting, response to greeting, and leave-taking, and see how different this might be with the ones that you are familiar with, and I am familiar with.

Similarly, Fatima also provided her students with an 'authentic intercultural conversation' which was based on her own experience of being one of the participants in an intercultural exchange (Figure 5.2). Coming from the same background as one of the participants in that exchange, she informed her students that H's response surprised her. Students were then instructed to work together with her "to analyse this intercultural miscommunication scenario ... to interpret H's response and the intended meanings behind G's use of 'I'm OK' in this context".

Other real-life texts written in different varieties of English that Ashish and I also used to expose our students to world Englishes included email exchanges that we had had with speakers of English from diverse lingua-cultural backgrounds. The emails shown in Figure 5.3, Figure 5.4, and Figure 5.5 were used in our lessons on 'register and style' (in EIL1010: English, Society, and Communication), 'contexts': cultural scripts and schemas (in EIL1020: International Communication), 'online intercultural communication' (in EIL2120: Language and Globalisation), 'world Englishes and culture' (in EIL3110: Language and Culture), and contrastive rhetoric (in EIL3210: Writing Across Cultures) as a way to expose students to a different way of writing in a variety of English or Englishes. In Ashish's lesson on cultural scripts and schemas, for example, he cut up one of the emails (see Figure 5.5) into strips of sentences and instructed students to reassemble it according to how they thought it should be ordered. Then the students were

120 EIL teachers implementing change

> *The following is data from a real intercultural conversation.*
>
> **H:** Hussein (Bangladesh) & **G:** Gary (Indonesian)
>
> Context: At the dinner table, Hussein is offering Gary more food.
>
> ---
> **H:** Do you want me to give more?
>
> **G:** I'm good, thank you!
>
> **H:** (Baffled) Okay……here take some more.
>
> *Hussein then puts more food on Gary's plate*
>
> ---
> What is going on here?
> - Has there been a miscommunication?
> - What did G mean?
> - What was G's intended speech act?
> - How did H interpret G's response?
> - Why was H baffled by G's response?

Figure 5.2 A text used in Fatima's lesson on speech act

encouraged to explain why they sequenced it in the way they did, and link this explanation to their own scripts and schemas of email writing. It was in this explanation that students shared with their classmates and teacher the discourse conventions they had learned and had been practising. Finally, Ashish showed the actual email and highlighted in the ways it was different from his students' and

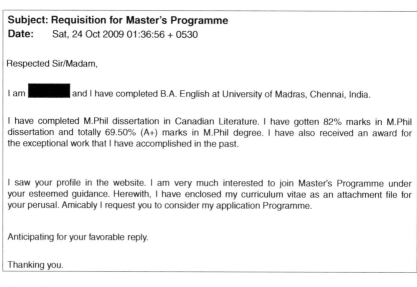

Figure 5.3 Email 1 used as teaching material

EIL teachers implementing change 121

> **Subject: (no subject)**
> **Date:**   26 February 2011 12:35:32+0410
>
> Dear Sir,
>
> Please take my thousands of my salutations to your lotus feet. I have completed my one year post graduate degree in English writing, having English language teaching methods in higher secondary level in Bangladesh which is fully related to your offering subject.
>
> So would you give me a chance please to complete my post graduate degree under you?
>
> May God bless you

Figure 5.4 Email 2 used as teaching material

explained the scripts/schemas with which the email sender would have operated. With a slightly different focus, I used one of the emails in a lesson on online intercultural communication (EIL2120: Language and Globalisation), in which I instructed students to analyse the distinctive lexical, syntactical, and pragmatic

> **Subject: Requesting a copy of your thesis**
> **Date:**   Fri, 7 Aug 2009 12:03:34 + 0330
>
> Dear Marlina Teacher,
>
> I am immensely delighted and profoundly honoured to send you this letter. My name is ███████ and I am a PhD student from the Faculty of Letters (American culture studies) at the University of Tokyo, Japan. I am also a lecturer in the Faculty of Education in the field of English Education. I hope that you have been physically well and that your teaching at the university in Australia has been running as smoothly as silk.
>
> I am currently doing research on international students studying in Japan and their experiences of coping with a new tertiary environment. I have been informaed that your have done a research study on international students in Australia and have had experiences teaching international students. As a matter of fact, it is ███ Teacher from the department of Japanese studies at ███ university, who used to be my colleague, has referred me to you. So, I'm very interested to hear about your viewpoints on this issue.
>
> I am writing to ask if you could kindly email me a copy·of your thesis. Please take as much time as you wish, because it is not an urgent matter. I beg for your forgiveness if I have caused you any great inconvenience and I'm deeply grateful to you for each second you have so graciously spent reading my email. Should you need any assistance from me in future, please do not hesitate to contact me as soon as possible.
>
> Please do accept my deepest thanks for your gracious attention and consideration, and my most genuinely sincere wishes of constant happiness, success, peace, prosperity, now and in the future.
>
> I look forward to hearing from you soon.
>
> Yours truly,

Figure 5.5 Email 3 used as teaching material

122 EIL teachers implementing change

> **W**ell-known for hosting Chinese New Year or Capgome celebrations, pagoda temples all over Indonesia also play a part in traditional Sejit Kongco celebrations, which are essentially birthday parties for the gods that guard the temples. Last October, the Bio Fat Cu Kung temple, which is located in Petak Sembilan in the West Jakarta district of Glodok, hosted one of these supernatural parties.
>
> The celebration was named, Sejit Kongco: the Honourable Kongco Fat Cu Kung, and a unique story lies behind the merriment. "We will have to *so-pue* first," said Nico, this year's party committee chairman, referring to a process of asking the gods for permission to hold the celebration. While prayers were being recited, the committee threw two pieces of red wood, which were convex and ovular in shape, into the air. If both fell on the ground in the same position, it would mean that the gods gave their approval for the Sijit Kongco celebrations. If not, then the whole party would be off.

Figure 5.6 An article adapted from Garuda Indonesia Airways inflight magazine

features of the email, to interpret the intended meanings, and to discuss the underlying sociocultural factors behind this distinctiveness.

It was important to us that the collections of texts written in different varieties of English that we used in our lessons came from everyday published materials that we collected while we were travelling, such as airline magazines and newspapers. For example, in EIL3102 (World Englishes), I used articles on 'Chinese New Year celebrations in Indonesia' (Figure 5.6) and 'a ritual of a particular ethnic group in Indonesia (Figure 5.7) to engage students in learning about English used in an Expanding-Circle country. Students were required to analyse and interpret the lexical items and syntax of these texts as well as how these features communicate local cultural values/practices. More than this, we urged them to discuss the implications of their interpretations or understanding of these texts for using, learning, and teaching English.

Similarly, in teaching a lesson on 'language and worldview' (in EIL1010: English, Society, and Communication), both Indigo and Fatima used articles which they collected from a Vietnam Airlines magazine (Figure 5.8) and from *The Straits Times*, a Singaporean newspaper (Figure 5.9). In engaging students in learning how world Englishes reflect different sociocultural realities, students in Indigo's class were engaged in discussing the different types of market mentioned in Figure 5.8: "brocade market", "love market", "forge market". As she instructed:

> I want you to discuss with the person next to you the following questions: (1) Have you heard of these markets? (2) What do you think they 'sell' in each of those markets? (3) How is market conceptualised here? In other words, how do people in Vietnam conceptualise the function of market?

Protecting against evil in a Sasak Ritual

Panca Nugraha
(THE JAKARTA POST/EAST LOMBOK/WEST NUSA TENGGARA)

The Sasak ethnic group in Pringgabaya, East Lombok, has conducted a ritual to protect against an evil called *Rebo Buntung* on Tanjung Menangis Beach for centuries.

The annual ritual is held on the last Wednesday of the month of Safar in the Muslim calendar. Sasak people believe the date is a day of tribulation, when men are likely to be subjected to maladies and natural disasters.

Apart from warding off the time-honored tradition is also meant as an expression of gratitude to God and bears a message to harmonize humans' relationships with their environment.

On Wednesday morning, the shore of Tanjung Menangis south of Pringgabaya and 65 kilometers east of Mataram was packed with thousands of people of all ages who came to witness the event.

"On the last Wednesday of Safar, 144 evil things are believed to fill the earth, so we have to leave our homes until sunset to avoid them. We call the ritual *Rebo Buntung*, meaning fortunate Wednesday", said Surpriadi, 40, a Pringgabaya resident who observed the ceremony along with his wife and four children.

According to Supriadi, people can choose to go out farming, fishing or do other work as long as they are outside, but most prefer to be part of the *Rebo Buntung* crowd while enjoying the beach.

As in previous years, at 10 a.m. Pringgabaya's communal elders led local Sasaks in the ritual by carrying out *Tetulaq Tetampar*, or presenting offerings to the sea made up of crops, traditional snacks and a black buffalo head.

Figure 5.7 An article adapted from *The Jakarta Post*

In discussing this text, Indigo asked a number of her Vietnamese students to "share [their] interpretations and teach everyone else about these markets". At first, she and the students from other countries discussed and shared their interpretations and their conceptualisations of the market. Then the Vietnamese

---

Market is a place of liking exchange

People come to the fair not only to exchange products and seek essential products, but also to meet and exchange information and show affection. We often think about love markets of hilly ethnic minorities in the North. Bac Ha Market is regarded as one the 10 most attractive markets of Southeast Asia due to this unique characteristic probably.

When Lao Cai province was established, the Bac Ha market was also formed in Chau Bac Ha. Since then, Bac Ha market is always held one session every Sunday, it is more a place of cultural exchange between ethnic groups in the Northwest, than the one of buying and selling like other markets. Bac Ha Market is where the locals barter goods with the outside of province, it is divided into smaller markets (or sections) with identifiable characteristics such as brocade market, cuisine market, horse market, poultry market, food market, bird market, forge market.... Each market brings rich and diverse local ethnic colors.

Figure 5.8 An article adapted from Vietnam Airlines inflight magazine

Figure 5.9 A newspaper article adapted from *The Straits Times*

students were asked to "to take over [her] role, and tell us if we shared similar interpretations and conceptualisations". She later explained her reason for doing this:

> I want students to see that even though I am the so-called native-speaker of English, I don't know everything. Even though I was the one who chose the text, doesn't mean I comprehend it entirely. My knowledge of Englishes is quite limited, I'm happy to learn and to expand my knowledge. And that we should learn about Englishes and cultures from each other.

Similarly, in discussing a Singaporean newspaper article (Figure 5.9), students in Fatima's class were asked to discuss their own use and conceptualisation of 'aunt', and to interpret the notion of 'aunt' as used by the author of the article.

> Discuss what other meanings or worldviews are embedded within the use of aunt in Singaporean community. And also justify your answer with examples of language use in this article.

Although Fatima was relatively familiar with the concept of 'aunt' in Singapore, as she had worked there before, she still asked her Singaporean students to lead the class and shared with their classmates the way 'aunt' was conceptualised in their country, and the contexts in which it was used. As she justified:

> I want these Singaporean students to be the knowledge providers to the class or to give insights into their local cultures, and I also want students to see

I'm a Western Desert woman and I want to be heard

I refer to your article "Racist children part of men's business" (16/5).

I challenge, in the strongest terms possible, any suggestion that Aboriginal culture is to blame for endemic levels of sexual violence against children in Central Australia. It puts down the cultural values that I grew up with.

I'm a 70-year-old Western Desert woman. As a child, I was indeed promised to a husband older than myself, but I never experienced the aberrant abuse described in your article.

I would like to make the following points:

- Men's business was conducted under strict laws over a prolonged period of time. Men who'd been dealt with under those laws remained under the authority and control of the elders. Any violation of the strict code of proper behaviour was immediately punishable by spearing or worse.
- Sexual relationships were strictly regulated and could only occur only in the context of prescribed kinship and generational relations. There never was a sexual free-for-all whereby initiated men could abuse or molest women, much less children and infants.

- A major difference in men's business nowadays is that the effective control of initiates by older men has largely broken down. The authority of older men has been undermined since European contact.
- The situation is made worse when young men go through law in an area other than their own and return to their country with no effective controls in place. They may then indeed feel they are a law unto themselves.
- The whole fabric of Aboriginal society on the lands has been challenged from within and from without. Substance abuse and pornographic and violent videos and TV have challenged the authority of elders and led to the disempowerment of women, contributing to the dysfunction in some communities.

We may well suffer from 'tragedy fatigue', but this does not mean that our voices are muted. We challenge the Government to hear and listen to our voices.

Mona Ngitji Ngitji Tur
Croydon, SA

Figure 5.10 A letter to the editor from an Australian newspaper

that not only they can learn or should learn from me, but also from their classmates as well. Everybody has knowledge to share.

On the other hand, Ashish taught a similar topic by using a local text – a letter to the editor written by an indigenous Australian woman, published in an Australian newspaper (Figure 5.10). Students were asked to read and discuss two questions that would require them to analyse how the writer's use of English reflects her worldview: "How does this letter reflect the writer's conceptualisation or worldview of 'Age' and 'Law'? And can you provide linguistic evidence?". Even though Ashish was not an indigenous Australian and was less familiar with their cultural values and practices, he still decided to use this text and to collaborate with students in interpreting and understanding a variety of English and cultures that nobody in the class was familiar with. This, Ashish said, "is what learning Englishes is about". When we were having a conversation about his choice of text and his activity on our way back to the office after his class, he further justified his choice of this text in the presence of Indigo:

126 *EIL teachers implementing change*

I don't want my students to know that reading a newspaper or a text in Australia means that you're reading a variety of Australian English, but also other varieties of English as well like a variety of Aboriginal English with their cultural values and worldviews embedded in it.

Indigo supported his view:

yes, yes, yes, yes, I agree! Thank you for saying that. I think as an Australian, I would not want our students to view Australia as this sort of 'white' Australian-English-speaking country and operating with a particular culture. That is a big misconception and myth. There are many texts written in different Englishes, which include Aboriginal Australian English and languages which act as a way to promote their cultures. It is in out there and therefore must be made visible in language teaching materials.

5.2.1.2.2. MOVIES AND ONLINE RESOURCES

My classroom observation notes and analysis of the teaching materials showed that my colleagues and I also used movies and online materials (e.g. websites, YouTube clips) as a way to expose students to different varieties of English. These movies and websites presented and exposed students to intercultural stories/issues and examples of the use of different varieties of world Englishes. Not only were the movies used to show examples, but they were also analysed by students using the theoretical concepts/issues discussed in the relevant subject as their conceptual and analytical tools. We used the following movies and websites:

Movies

- *Bend It Like Beckham* (2002)
- *Bride and Prejudice* (2004)
- *Bringing Down the House* (2003)
- *Crocodile Dundee in Los Angeles* (2001)
- *Gung Ho* (1986)
- *Japanese Story* (2003)
- *Marci X* (2003)
- *My Big Fat Greek Wedding* (2002)
- *Outsourced* (2006)
- *Phua Chu Kang Pte Ltd* (1996)
- *Sweet Home Alabama* (2002)
- *The Joy Luck Club* (1993)
- *The Kite Runner* (2007)
- *The Namesake* (2006)
- *The Other End of the Line* (2008)
- *Under One Roof* (1994)

Websites

- www.bbc.co.uk/voices – varieties of English in the UK
- http://sounds.bl.uk/Accents-and-dialects – varieties of English in the UK
- www.ncsu.edu/linguistics/download.php – varieties of English spoken in North Carolina (United States)
- http://web.ku.edu/idea – international archive of different world Englishes

5.2.1.2.3. OTHER 'LIVE' AUTHORITATIVE VOICES

Although movies and online resources (such as YouTube clips) exposed the students to different varieties of English, my colleagues believed that the exposure was "quite limited and restrictive" (Indigo) and "less interactive" (Ashish) because there would be "minimal or no opportunities for students to ask questions if they don't understand" (Fatima). Hence, another pedagogical approach that we all unanimously agreed to use to engage students in learning about English language variation was to invite colleagues in the department who had expertise in a particular variety of English. It was through this approach we believed that students would be able to listen to 'live' authoritative voices about different varieties of English, to interact with these experts, and to "gain insights into these varieties of English" (Ashish). This was mostly observed in EIL3102 (World Englishes).

Depending on which 'circle' of countries was the focus of the week, I invited either an academic staff member or a doctoral student who had expertise in, or who had undertaken research on, the English language from the 'circle of the week' to come to the class as a guest lecturer and share their knowledge and research. However, this does not mean that students from other subjects and from other levels of study were not provided this opportunity. For instance, in EIL1020 (International Communication) a lecturer who had published extensively on communicative strategies employed by Aboriginal Australians was invited to give a lecture on speech acts and politeness across cultures in which examples from his own research were shared. In EIL2120 (Language and Globalisation), I invited a doctoral student whose dissertation focused on the online use of English by Chinese learners of English to give a talk about online intercultural communication. In EIL3130 (Language and Education), a lecturer who had completed a large-scale national project on English language teaching materials in Vietnam was invited to share her experiences and engage students in learning about the development of EIL teaching materials.

5.2.1.2.4. STUDENTS' OWN EXPERIENCES AND OBSERVATIONS

Another important source to which students were frequently urged to refer was their own experiences of using English as well as their observations of others' use of English. As Fatima justified, "their experiences are important 'places' because those are the starting point for discussing differences or perhaps uniqueness in using English" (Fatima). My observations of my colleagues' lessons and my

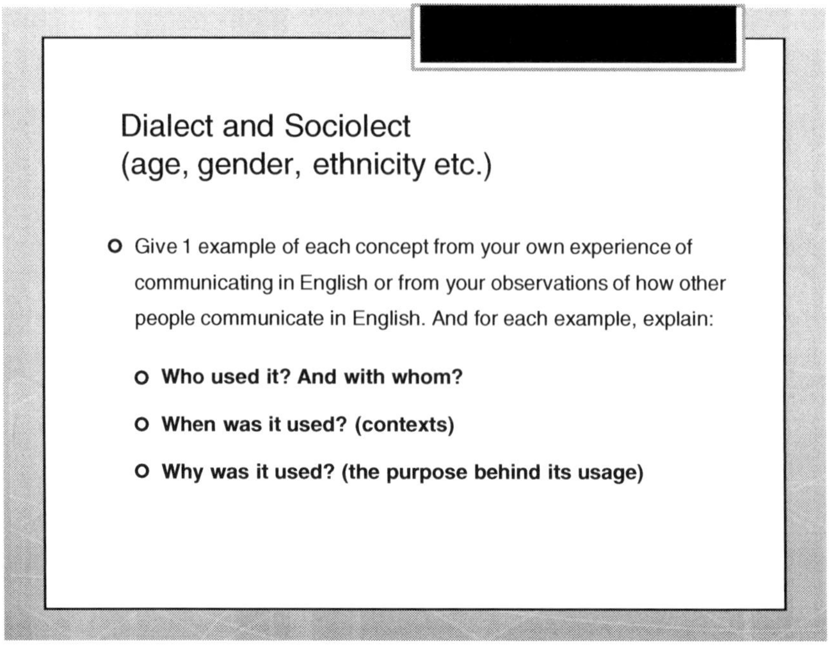

> ## Dialect and Sociolect
> ## (age, gender, ethnicity etc.)
>
> O Give 1 example of each concept from your own experience of
>   communicating in English or from your observations of how other
>   people communicate in English. And for each example, explain:
>
>   O **Who used it? And with whom?**
>
>   O **When was it used? (contexts)**
>
>   O **Why was it used? (the purpose behind its usage)**

Figure 5.11 Language variation activity 1 in EIL1010

reflections on my own teaching reveal that the classroom learning activities were often designed to prompt students to continuously reflect on, observe, and share their cultural and linguistic knowledge in order to enlighten their lecturers as well as classmates about themselves, their language(s), their use of English, and their cultural values and norms. Students were also provided with opportunities to observe and learn to study about other peoples' use of English and how this different usage reflects different cultural norms or values. For instance, in a series of lessons that explored English language variation (dialect and sociolect) in EIL1010 (English, Society, and Communication), my colleagues asked their students to provide examples based on their own experiences of using language or their observations of how other people use English in their surroundings (see Figure 5.11 and Figure 5.12).

In another lesson, on writing across cultures in EIL1020 (International Communication), students were given a scenario in which they were asked to write a professional letter responding to a customer's complaint. Monolingual English speakers responded in English, whereas bi-/multilingual students wrote initially in their own mother tongue or other language(s) they knew and then translated this into English. When students were required to share their analyses of the macro- and micro-structure of their letters and explain the underlying reasons behind those structures, they shared their own individual cultural values,

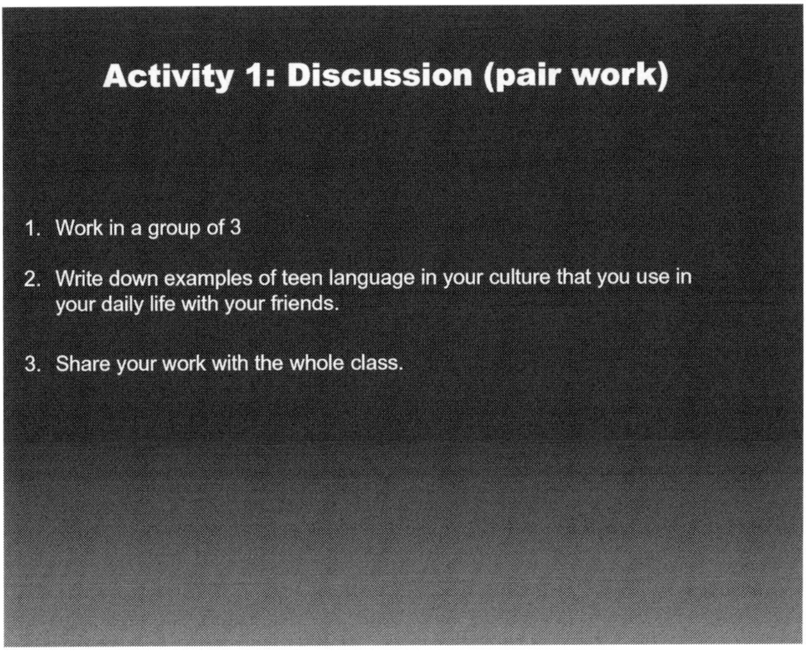

Activity 1: Discussion (pair work)

1. Work in a group of 3

2. Write down examples of teen language in your culture that you use in your daily life with your friends.

3. Share your work with the whole class.

Figure 5.12 Language variation activity 2 in EIL1010

worldviews, and pragmatic norms, and how these were embedded within their letters. Based on her teaching experiences, Indigo believed that this activity provided her students with

> opportunities to learn how to communicate their cultures in English to those who are unfamiliar with them; and to teach everyone in the class the potential reasons behind the use of English which we might not be familiar with.

At second-year level, in EIL2120 (Language and Globalisation), to encourage students to explore the influence of technology on English, they were asked to collect samples of their own or others' online use of English from different social networking sites (Figure 5.13), and then present their analyses of those samples.

Similarly, third-year students were also required to use their experiences of using English, and/or encountering varieties of English other than the ones they were familiar with, for understanding variations in English language. For instance, as almost every week of EIL3102 (World Englishes) focused on different varieties of English in different Kachruvian circles, students were required to collect, analyse, and present 'authentic' examples of these Englishes either from their own contexts (if they were from the 'circle of the week') or others' such as classmates, friends, relatives, or even strangers. Similarly, in a lesson in EIL3110 (Language

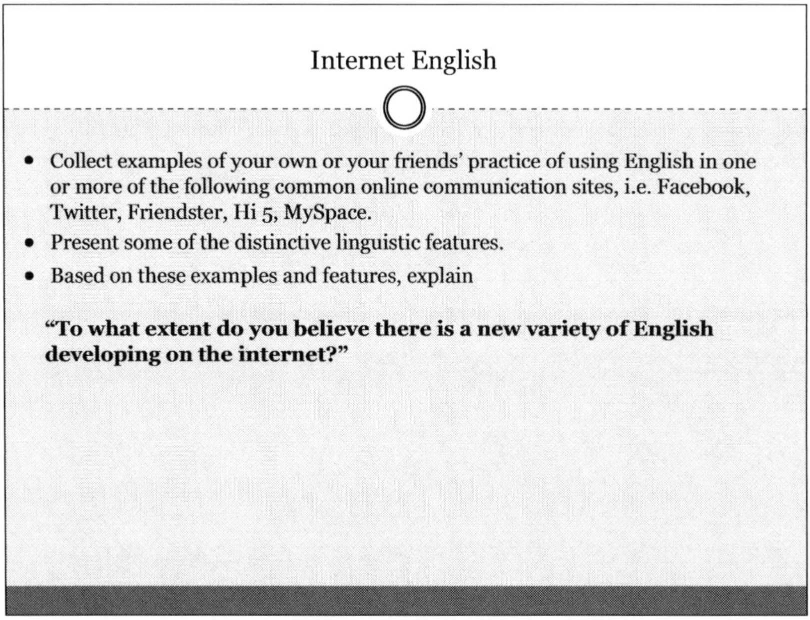

130 *EIL teachers implementing change*

Internet English

- Collect examples of your own or your friends' practice of using English in one or more of the following common online communication sites, i.e. Facebook, Twitter, Friendster, Hi 5, MySpace.
- Present some of the distinctive linguistic features.
- Based on these examples and features, explain

  "To what extent do you believe there is a new variety of English developing on the internet?"

Figure 5.13 Activity on Internet English in EIL2120

and Culture) on figurative language and its cultural meanings, students were asked to discuss examples of figurative language, metaphors, and idioms from their own language and explain their underlying cultural meanings (Figure 5.14).

When I was conversing with my colleagues about the purpose behind encouraging our students to reflect on and analyse their own experiences of using English during one of our bus trips to another campus, Fatima asked me to read the following quote from a book by a sociolinguist, which she said would summarise our underpinning principle:

> We may deplore this or that bit of variation, but at the same time we are not even aware of considerable variation elsewhere and even participate – generally unconsciously but sometimes quite consciously – in actually promoting variation
>
> Wardhaugh (1993, p. 167)

My colleagues further asserted that encouraging students to observe other people's use of English in their surroundings, e.g. in "a classroom or outside the classroom like on a train or at the café in front of our house" (Fatima), was "a good way for our students to know that differences might just be sitting next to them, or in front of their house, or in the suburb where they are living" (Indigo). Ashish agreed:

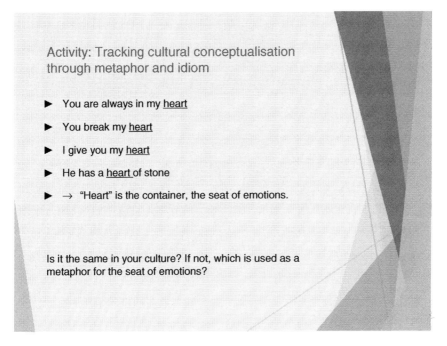

Figure 5.14 Activity on metaphors across cultures in EIL3110

> Where else would you find the best place to raise their awareness of English variation other than your own classrooms where you have students from like ten countries? And even like Australian students, they are all different depending on their backgrounds and sound different to me. So, I have to take advantage of these great resources.

Indigo, born in Australia, further confirmed and concurred with Fatima's observation of Englishes "in front of our house or in a suburb where they are living" (Fatima). She believed in the effectiveness of the pedagogical approach that used students' experiences and observations in raising their awareness of the diversity of English in their own learning context.

> [T]he Australia that I see today is different from the Australia that I saw back in the old days. I think Australia is the best location to teach students about Englishes or to have courses on world Englishes because you don't only hear people using only Australian English. You go to the market for example, you see Chinese, Africans, Greek, Fijian, Italian, Indian, Korean, who do not necessarily speak English I speak. Even the Australian English itself is so complex because, apart from the regional variation of Australia English, you can also hear and talk to Aboriginal Australians who sound Australian but they don't

132 EIL teachers implementing change

speak the stereotypical Australian English. And I don't have that stereotypical Aussie English because I have travelled to so many different countries which have changed the way I use English. Some of my Aussie friends said that I sounded more Canadian than Australian [laughter]. So, Australia is truly an international meeting point and only being able to communicate and understand one single variety won't be enough, which students should learn and know that.

5.2.2. Working with differences

In addition to raising students' awareness of the diversification of English language, users, and cultures, my observations and reflections of syllabus materials in EIL1020 (International Communication), EIL3110 (Language and Culture), EIL3210 (Writing Across Cultures), and EIL3130 (Language and Education) showed that students were also provided opportunities to learn to work with differences[2]. Rather than prescribing reading materials on 'how to work with differences', my colleagues and I devised a number of pedagogical tasks in which students encountered different uses of English and different cultural practices, and then learned to develop strategies to communicate (mostly observed in EIL1020, EIL3110, and EIL3210) or to teach (mostly observed in EIL3130) across differences.

My observations of the lessons and analyses of the materials of EIL1020, EIL3110, EIL3210, and EIL3130 showed that intercultural learning role-plays and participation in a community of practice in EIL (Hino, 2010) were common learning activities that my colleagues designed to furnish their students with strategies to communicate effectively in unfamiliar intercultural situations or to develop metacultural competence (Sharifian, 2011). In EIL1020 (International Communication) where Kachru and Smith's (2008) notion of "interaction as cooperation" was the main focus, my colleagues provided several examples of intercultural miscommunication scenarios in which students were required to, as Indigo instructed, "describe, interpret, evaluate, and repair" those given scenarios. For example, in Indigo's lesson on 'speech acts', students were asked to read an intercultural misunderstanding of 'silence' (Figure 5.15). They were then asked to:

> describe what this miscommunication was about. Interpret why Janet was not very satisfied ... you know, why she's not happy. What could possibly be the intention or meaning behind Maruoka's silence. And evaluate Janet's response to Maruoka's silence.

After guiding students to interpret and understand this conversation, she talked about how people in different societies performed actions through silence, and highlighted the value of silence embedded in the proverbs or sayings found in different societies such as: "With time and patience, the mulberry leaf becomes a silk gown", "Speech is silver, silence is golden", "It's the empty can that makes the

EIL teachers implementing change 133

62.Negotiations

MARTHA: How did the negotiations go?

JANET: Not so well. We were taken.

MARTHA: What happened?

JANET: Well, I proposed our starting price, and Maruoka didn't say anything.

MARTHA: Nothing?

JANET: He just sat there, looking very serious. So then I brought the price down.

MARTHA: And?

JANET: Still nothing. But he looked a little surprised. So I brought it down to our last offer and just waited. I couldn't go any lower.

MARTHA: What did he say?

JANET: Well, he was quiet for about a minute, and then he agreed.

MARTHA: Well, at least we've got a deal. You should be pleased.

JANET: I guess so. But later I learned that he thought our first price was very generous.

Figure 5.15 A text on intercultural misunderstanding of silence (adapted from Storti, 1994)

Source: Storti (1994)

most noise", and "Learn from paddy, the more rice grain a stalk of paddy has, the more it will bow". With this knowledge of silence, students were then asked to 'revise' the conversations (see Figure 5.15) through role-play. As she instructed:

> now that you know the function of silence, right? How people from different societies interpret silence and use silence. Now, I want you to repair this miscommunication. So, pair up with the person next to you. Choose who is gonna be Janet and who is Maruoka. And then show me how you would, the Janet, respond to Maruoka's silence or like what we talked about, work cooperatively with Maruoka to ensure that this intercultural communication is successful.

In addition to using texts or conversations from published materials, my colleagues in EIL1020 designed an intercultural role-play activity in which students had the opportunity to experience and learn to negotiate different pragmatic discourse conventions that are available in the multicultural classroom, which Hino (2010) terms, "participation in a community of practice in EIL" (p. 4). For example, after having discussed the concepts of cultural scripts and schemas in a lesson on politeness in international communication, Fatima asked her students to form groups based on their nationality (Chinese, Australian, Indian, South Korean, and Malaysian) and read through the scenario shown in Figure 5.16. After they had read and discussed the scenario, the students were instructed to

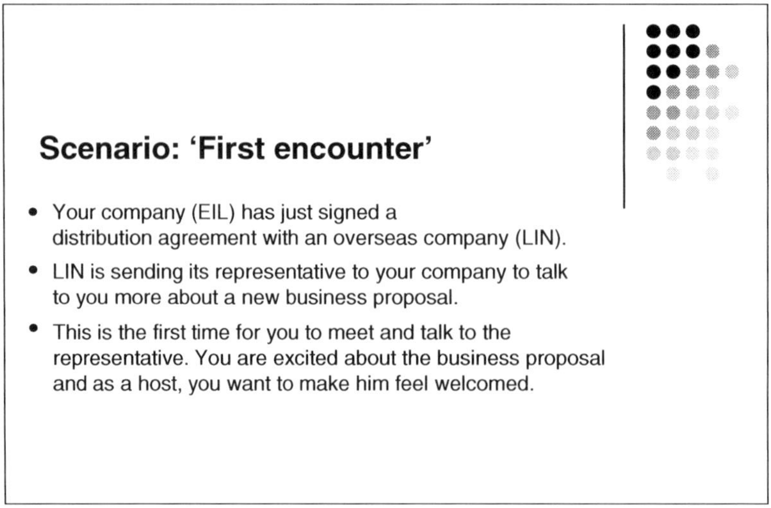

Scenario: 'First encounter'

- Your company (EIL) has just signed a distribution agreement with an overseas company (LIN).
- LIN is sending its representative to your company to talk to you more about a new business proposal.
- This is the first time for you to meet and talk to the representative. You are excited about the business proposal and as a host, you want to make him feel welcomed.

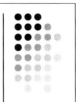

Figure 5.16 An intercultural miscommunication scenario

discuss with their fellow group members: "What would be a polite script for a first business encounter according to [their] cultural group?"

To allow students to view, experience, and negotiate different cultural scripts, each group selected one from the rest of the cultural groups as the culture they would like to visit. Each group then assigned one person as their LIN manager, who would visit the other cultural group (e.g. an Indian manager visiting the South Korean group or a Australian manager visiting the Malaysian group). Once this decision had been made, group members from one cultural group acted out the script that they had discussed earlier when the group was visited by the LIN manager. While the students in one group were role-playing, the other cultural groups were asked to answer some questions (see Figure 5.17).

I observed that the managers seemed rather baffled during the role-play, particularly when encountering scripts that were different from their own, and were searching for ways of working with those differences. At the debriefing session, Fatima invited each group to share the different scripts they had observed, their critiques of the managers' strategies of handling different scripts, and their proposed strategies. It was during this session that students learned to negotiate their ideas with classmates whose proposed strategies were different from their own.

At the third-year level, I also adopted pedagogical practices such as the above. I used real-life examples or scenarios of intercultural (mis)communication as the basis for guiding students to develop strategies to communicate across differences or to teach in a diverse classroom (EIL3130). For example, in a lesson on contrastive rhetoric in EIL3210, I shared and encouraged students to analyse the emails (refer to the emails I presented in Section 5.2.1.2.1).

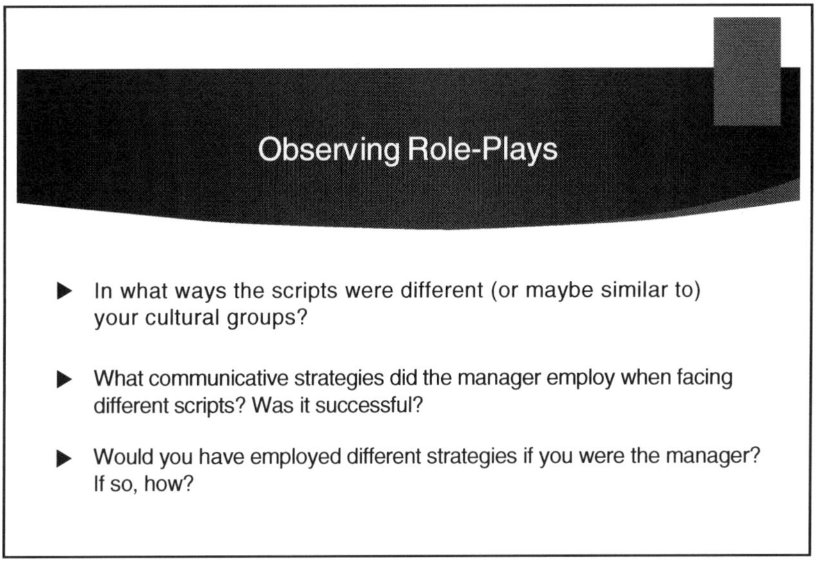

> ## Observing Role-Plays
>
> ▶ In what ways the scripts were different (or maybe similar to) your cultural groups?
>
> ▶ What communicative strategies did the manager employ when facing different scripts? Was it successful?
>
> ▶ Would you have employed different strategies if you were the manager? If so, how?

Figure 5.17 Questions for role-play observers

To explore the notion of contrastive rhetoric in this week, I am using emails that Ashish and I have been collecting as the main texts for classroom activity. As soon as I finish my lecture on Ulla Connor's notion Contrastive Rhetoric, I put students into groups, hand out these emails, and ask students to read those emails before I give further instructions. I can see some students are laughing at the emails. After five minutes of reading, I inform students that I want to see two things: (1) analysis of the micro- and macro-structure of the emails – unpacking meanings or reasons behind those structures; and (2) their reply to these emails based on their understanding of what's behind the structures, and of course their justification of their own choices of macro- and micro-structure.

(My reflective journal)

In EIL3110 (Language and culture), I also provided my students with several real-life scenarios I had experienced myself or had heard from my friends or colleagues (see Figure 5.18), which could attract diverse interpretations. Since I had students in my tutorial group from four different countries (Australia, China, Singapore, and South Korea), they were grouped based on their nationalities, and were instructed to describe and interpret the given scenarios. Thereafter, based on their interpretations, they were required to role-play how they responded to the scenarios and then justify their responses. During the acting out of students' responses to the scenarios, there were critiques and disagreements from their peers from other nationalities about their responses. Although those who were critiqued did not seem pleased at all, I managed to minimise this tension by

136 *EIL teachers implementing change*

DIFFERENCES AT WORK

- Your co-worker notices that you have been eating sandwiches for your lunch. So, she says to you: you stupid, why do you eat sandwiches everyday for your lunch?

- Your supervisor consistently corrects you, but never tells you when you are doing a good job.

- Your manager gives you an assignment with no specific information about how to accomplish it.

- You have led a team that has completed a very important project and your manager tells you it is brilliant and she will be presenting it at a major conference. You attend the conference with her and listen to her report about the project during which she makes no mention of your critical role in its completion.

- You notice that one of your employees has done an outstanding job, and you have decided to award him. When you inform him your decision, he says "I don't think I deserve this, please give to others as well'.

Figure 5.18 Real-life intercultural miscommunication scenarios

highlighting how these interactions that involved critiques and disagreements tended to be indicative of a clash of different worldviews, values, and norms. I encouraged them to learn to work with this clashing of worldviews.

In EIL3130, which focuses on the practices of teaching EIL, I also used real-life teaching scenarios in which students were required to understand and develop strategies to respond to differences that they were likely to encounter as a future teacher of English. For example, in a lesson on teaching writing from an EIL perspective:

> I start the class with different perspectives of teaching writing: one that is based on the traditional TESOL view of teaching writing and one based on an EIL perspective. Since I want to make it practical, I hand out a number of essays (about three pages long) written by my former students, which were written in a reader-responsible and a slightly 'non-linear' style of writing. I then ask my students to imagine if they were the teachers, what mark/score they would give these essays and justify their decision.
>
> During debriefing sessions, there are a lot of disagreements. Some groups say that this should be given a high score whereas the others refuse to do so because these essays have not been written in the so-called 'Standard' style. Then I introduce a little bit of theoretical discussion on writing and identity by Donald Rubin (1997), whose work I also use in EIL3210; and academic writing and culture by Phan Le Ha (2001). With this theory in mind, I encourage them to work in groups to brainstorm what strategies they, as future teachers, can use to guide their prospective students develop the ability to write in the so-called 'Standard' way but not at the expense of their

own culturally preferred style of writing. Reflecting on this session, I wondered if I should have let those students who refused to give a low score a chance to talk more about their evaluation. Introducing them to the writings by Rubin (1997) and Phan (2001) might not have been appropriate.

(My reflective journal)

After the end of the semester, I received some anonymous written evaluative feedback from the students on my preference of using real-life scenarios and examples:

I really like how the teacher use examples from your everyday life, cos it will show us that it is out there, it's happening out there and we must prepare ourselves for that.

Thank you for sharing your stories and examples. You make it so clear that things are not as what we expected it to be. So, I have learned about different strategies when I face a different way of doing things.

Those real-life stories like the interesting emails showed in class have prepared me for my future workplace in Malaysia.

5.2.3. Challenges in engaging with the politics of differences

The reflections on my own teaching, analyses of materials, interviews with colleagues, as well as my encounters with the unexpected 'free-floatings' (Simons, 2009) for which the theoretical framework of EIL teaching materials and pedagogy in Chapter 2 had not prepared me, led to the emergence of an additional theme in my research: the importance of engaging with the politics of differences in the EIL curricula. In particular, the data allowed me to identify: (1) how EIL educators at Urban University addressed these 'tough topics' or engaged their students in learning these topics, and (2) the challenges they faced in doing so, which were rather similar to what I had experienced myself.

5.2.3.1. Addressing the politics of difference in the curricula

The EIL subjects, topics, and reading materials listed in Appendix 6 clearly show that there were attempts to incorporate topics and authoritative voices from the prescribed reading materials that aimed to raise students' awareness of, and engage them in learning about, the big-P '*Political*' and the little-p '*political*' (or micro-political) issues (Janks, 2010). The big-P issues were observed in the lesson on Globalisation and English: Threats? in EIL3110. The prescribed reading materials for and my lesson on this topic covered and discussed concepts and issues such as "linguicism"; "linguistic imperialism"; "linguistic nationism"; "creative destruction"; "the positive and negative spread of English in the world"; "linguistic genocide (English as a Killer Language?)"; and "competing languages in the world". As the following narrative reveals, to raise my students' awareness of these concepts and issues, I attempted to show them how these concepts/issues could be observed in everyday life practices.

138 *EIL teachers implementing change*

The lesson for this week focused on the concept of Linguicism and Linguistic Nationism. Since these concepts were very abstract, I wanted to give students an opportunity to see how they could be observed in some occasions in our everyday life. And this is how the lesson proceeded.

To help students understand the notion of Linguicism and Linguistic Nationism, I ask my students to share with their classmates their experiences or observations of their chosen contexts where some certain groups of people are privileged, are given privileged treatment, or have access to material power based on the language they speak.

To give them an example of linguicism, I talk about a scenario of how my Cambodian colleague who completed a master's in TESOL from a prestigious university in Thailand was employed by an international school in Cambodia to work as a 'baby-sitter', 'toilet trainer', and 'language-assistant' in an English class taught by a 'native' English-speaking teacher from America, who was a backpacker and had no university degree in TESOL. Some students frown, some raise their eyebrows, some shake their heads perhaps because they have encountered a similar scenario in their own contexts. And one of them, an Anglo-Australian student, utters with a loud voice: that's ridiculous! For Linguistic Nationism, I share an example of one of the countries in the African continent where the local/national language was replaced with English because the language was perceived to have a very powerful value. As soon as I finish sharing my examples and invite students to share theirs, the class turns into a market.

Most students illustrate the concept of linguicism by sharing how English language competency in their countries is used as the criteria to determine who gets employed and who does not. One student from South Korea shares the craze for achieving a full score in an English language test called TOEIC in order to be employed. Another South Korean student shares his observation of how English language competency is associated with social strata in the society and how this is portrayed by media such as in Korean dramas (in which the main protagonists are the ones who are affluent and speak English fluently with an American accent).

Focusing on Linguistic Nationism, one student from a Cantonese-speaking province in China argues that English is not just the only killer language. She shares an example of the competing local languages in China: Cantonese and Mandarin. In particular, she talks about how Mandarin is proposed to replace the use of Cantonese in, for example, newspapers, television news, entertainment, film, education, and law in Cantonese-speaking provinces (Guangzhou, Shenzhen, and Hong Kong). She asserts quite strongly: 'I am proud to be a Cantonese speaker. Cantonese is a language, not a dialect, it is our identity and should not be replaced'. This is responded by her classmates with a big round of applause.

(My reflective journal)

Although the list in Appendix 6 shows that the big-P issues were covered only in EIL3110 (Language and Culture), the issue of the hegemonic spread of English

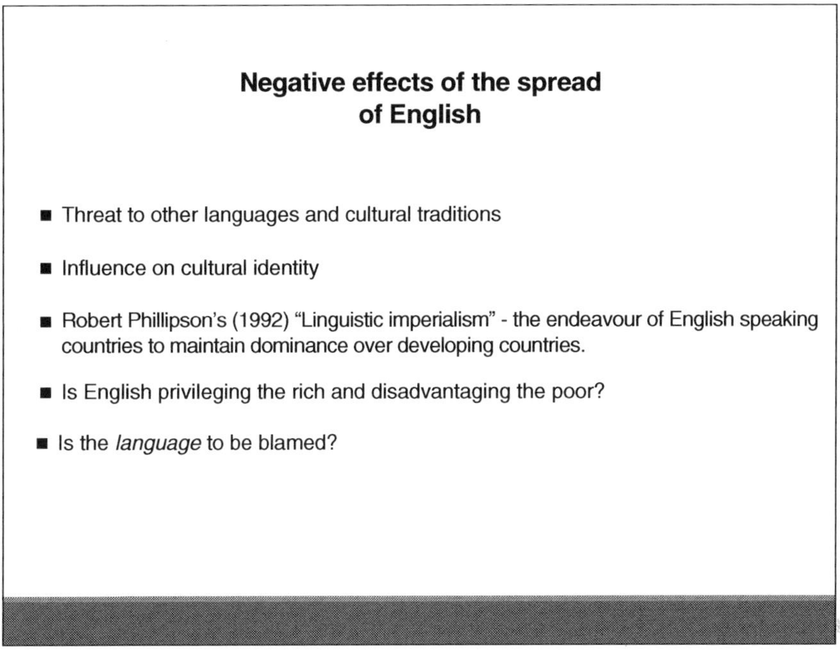

> ## Negative effects of the spread of English
>
> - Threat to other languages and cultural traditions
>
> - Influence on cultural identity
>
> - Robert Phillipson's (1992) "Linguistic imperialism" - the endeavour of English speaking countries to maintain dominance over developing countries.
>
> - Is English privileging the rich and disadvantaging the poor?
>
> - Is the *language* to be blamed?

Figure 5.19 A discussion on big-P issues in EIL1020

and it being a potential killer language was also covered in EIL1020 (International Communication) as well as in EIL2120 (Language and Globalisation). The notion of linguistic imperialism (Figure 5.19) was introduced in EIL1020 and briefly discussed in the lesson on English as an International Language to highlight the potential negative consequences of English acquiring the status of an international language, and being chosen as one of the languages for international communication. In EIL2120 (Language and Globalisation), students were also engaged in thinking about and discussing the big-P issues in lessons on English, Globalisation, and Technology (Figure 5.20), Internet English (Figure 5.21), and Englishes in the Media (Figure 5.22). Although the main focus of EIL2120 was on variation of English as a result of technology and media, these big-P issues were discussed in the prescribed readings, were largely relevant to the topics, and were therefore inquired into in class.

Furthermore, the analyses of the curricula allowed me to observe the attempts of EIL educators at Urban University to spark and/or incorporate classroom discussions on issues that could be categorised as little-p issues or issues around the "micro-politics of everyday life" (Janks, 2010, p. 40). These discussions could be predominantly observed in the lessons on Accent Debates, Standard English Debates, and Native and Non-Native Debates in EIL1010 (English, Society, and Communication). All of my colleagues believed in the importance of discussing controversial issues and the educational outcomes this discussion may bring:

IMAGINED COMMUNITIES: DISCUSSION

In the context of globalisation:

- What do speakers/learners of English believe they will gain access to if they know English?
- In your home countries, what were the narratives about the 'imagined community' of English speakers you would join if you could speak English? (i.e. In terms of the global world/technology: what would you have access to? Who would you connect with? What benefits would you obtain?)
- To what extent have you found these communities/ideas to be real?

Figure 5.20 Discussion questions on big-P issues in lesson on English, Globalisation, and Technology in EIL2120

Spread of Netspeak (Discussion)

- Has internet language (predominantly in English) had an impact on other languages in the world?

- Do you view the impact/influence of Netspeak on languages as positive or negative? Explain.

Figure 5.21 Discussion questions on big-P issues in a lesson on Internet English in EIL2120

EIL teachers implementing change 141

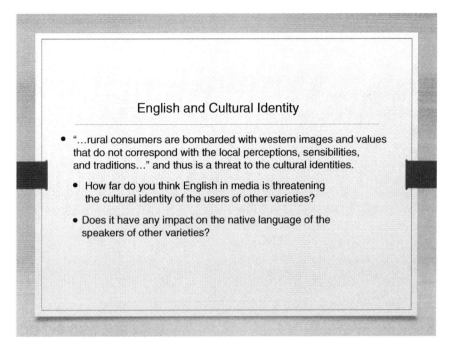

Figure 5.22 Discussion questions on big-P issues in a lesson on Englishes in the media 1 in EIL2120

if I don't present controversial issues, I won't be promoting differences, cultural differences. Because I always deal with cultural and linguistic differences, I have to be controversial, I have to raise controversial issues. And it is through these controversial issues that we are questioning and approaching our students' attitudes to variations.

(Ashish)

EIL is considered as controversial topics, and of course we have to be controversial and teach these topics because you are dealing with something quite sensitive, something that requires people to change their attitudes, change their ways of thinking.

(Fatima)

I'm very strong into social justice and I think that … education and linguistic issues are to do with social justice. So, I think as my position of the teacher, I have this smaller opportunity to influence the minds of young people. So, I need to talk about these political issues with my students. It's important because these issues make you to stop and hold on a second, look at yourself, and see that maybe your positions or others' are also more privileged, and

142 *EIL teachers implementing change*

> to question 'Is that fair'? So, by engaging students with these issues, we ask them to think about how we can create a society or world that is more equal in opportunity.
>
> (Indigo)

Motivated by this as well as by my encounters with EIL-ex students' negative responses to being positioned in deficit ways, my colleagues and I agreed that not only would we intend to discuss variations in accents and in the use of Standard English, as well as the anachronism of the 'traditional' classification of 'native-' and 'non-native-speakers' of English, but we would also seek to engage students in problematising the existing practices and ideologies that unfairly empower certain individuals and marginalise others. Therefore, during our weekly lesson planning meetings, we agreed to begin our lessons on 'accents', 'Standard English', and 'non/non-native' by "showing students and unpacking what these basic notions such as accent, Standard English, and native and non-native mean" (Ashish) and after that "the complexity and diversity of accents, the way people use Standard English, and the way people classify native and non-native" (Indigo) prior to raising these controversial issues. This is because, as Fatima succinctly said:

> our students often come to the class with misconceptions of what accent or Standard English is, and a lack of understanding of these notions is actually the first step of building up the negative attitudes.

After raising students' awareness of the pluralistic nature and complexity of accents, Standard English, and the notions of native/non-native, we unanimously agreed to "then proceed to highlighting the discriminatory practices or perspectives that exist in our or their everyday life, or that they do/have" (Indigo). Informed by this perspective, my colleagues and I designed a number of questions (Figure 5.23, Figure 5.24, and Figure 5.25), which were then used as the guiding frame/structure for conducting my lectures and their seminars.

In engaging students in learning these topics with an aim to "help students become a better person or communicator meaning changing attitudes, changing styles, changing behaviours, changing strategy" (Ashish), pedagogical activities such as classroom debate, reflective questions, and real-life scenario-based discussions, were developed to link the topics with the micro-political issues encountered and experienced in everyday life. For example, in a lesson on Accent Debates, Ashish organised a classroom debate in which students were divided into six groups and, as he instructed

> discuss in groups whether you agree or disagree with these statements [Figure 5.26] that I [Ashish] often come across from my students and the underlying assumptions. And then justify your point of view.

A classroom debate was also conducted by Ashish in his lesson on Standard English Debates. After having shown the competing views on Standard English

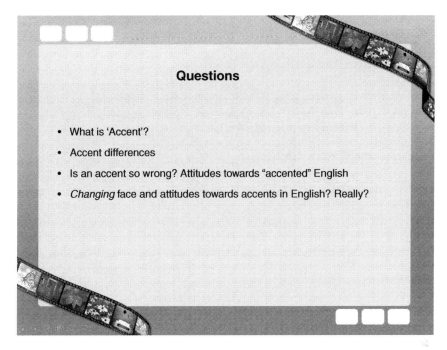

Figure 5.23 Guiding questions for the Accents Debate lesson in EIL1010

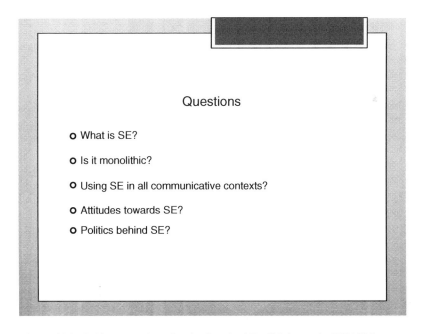

Figure 5.24 Guiding questions for the Standard English lesson in EIL1010

- 'NS (Native Speaker) or 'NNS' (Non-Native Speaker)?
- Criteria for classifying 'NS' and 'NNS'?
- Are these criteria problematic? and still applicable today?

Figure 5.25 Guiding questions for the Native and Non-Native Debates lesson in EIL1010

The Accent debate

- **Group work:**
- **Group A:** Are you sorry for your accent? Why? Why not?
- **Group B:** You are not as good as the native speakers because you speak English with an accent.
- **Group C:** You are different from all others who speak English with an accent because you are a native speaker.
- **Group D:** You are more intelligent than others because you speak with the 'standard' accent.
- **Group E:** You belong to a higher social status than other because you speak with a standard accent.
- **Group F:** The 'native' accent is the best accent. The non-native speakers must acquire the accent.

Figure 5.26 Ashish's debate activity for the Accents Debate lesson in EIL1010

Two views on Standard English

The Quirk (1990) view	The Kachru (1991) view
☐ Standard English applies only to Standard British and American English.	☐ Many New Englishes are now developing in parts of the world → each has its own standard.
☐ Only learn/teach standard Am/BrEnglish	
☐ Non-native teachers should keep in constant touch with this Standard.	☐ These new Standards are easier, quicker and cheaper for people in those countries to learn.
☐ Differences from this Standard that appear in their writing should be corrected.	☐ They should be taught in schools by local teachers, and should be respected as Emerging Standards.

Figure 5.27 Ashish's debate activity for the Standard English lesson in EIL1010

by Randolph Quirk (1990) and Braj Kachru (1992) (Figure 5.27), the students were instructed to:

> choose whose views you agree with the most. If you choose Quirk's view, please form a group and sit on a left side of the room, and if you choose Kachru's, please sit on a right side of the room. Prepare your arguments and justifications for the debates in fifteen minutes.

Fatima employed the same approach and led the same activity in her class on Standard English Debates. However, in her lessons on Accent Debates and Native and Non-Native Debates, she chose to engage her students in learning about the issues with questions that prompted them to reflect on their experiences and their perspectives in relation to the issues (Figure 5.28). As Fatima explained,

> in order to teach controversial topics, I have to come up with something that really really makes them think about … probably things that they take it for granted and want them to break away that misconception, really to problematise what they thought as normal and what the society thought as normal or what normal really is. And I want them to be critical … that's why I always come up with questions. I try to find questions that are related to their daily life ….

Similar to Fatima and Ashish's lesson on Standard English Debates, Indigo also chose to conduct the same classroom debate on the competing views offered by Quirk (1990) and Kachru (1992). However, for her lessons on Accent Debates

146 *EIL teachers implementing change*

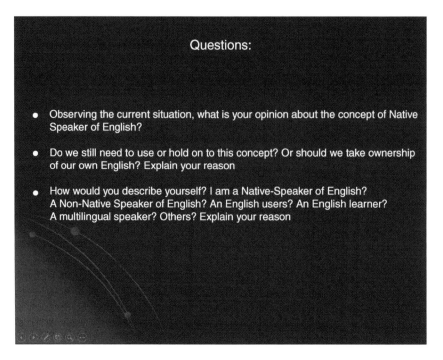

Figure 5.28 Fatima's discussion questions for the Native and Non-Native Debates lesson in EIL1010

and Native and Non-Native Debates, she chose to conduct classroom discussions based on controversial real-life scenarios to engage students in observing and discussing the micro-political issues she had encountered.

> As a social justice person, I have to make sure that my students know what's going on out there. I would use very, very controversial issues or scenarios, that really strike, that really get students' attention. I am certainly feeling uncomfortable if I don't talk about these issues. The more controversial it is, the better, so that they know the consequences of having perspectives that marginalise others or discriminate others on the basis of their language etc.
> (Indigo)

For example, for her lesson Native and Non-Native Debates, she used an online newspaper article (Figure 5.29 and Figure 5.30) that reported on the discriminatory practice of hiring English language teachers, and conveyed a message that:

> the only teacher who is employed and qualified to teach English is someone who looks like me, white Anglo who speaks English as their first language regardless of your qualification! Hmm … what do we think class?
> (Indigo)

The hiring practices

Classified advertisement for private English tutors and cram school instructors in Taipei's English-language dailies routinely call for "Western-looking applicants," "no ABCs [American Born Chinese] please" and "native foreigners only."

Those who don't fit the descriptions will sometimes be offered positions – but for lower wages. And many schools are unapologetic about their practices, saying a white face is needed to placate parents' demands "If they're not white, they're not American".

"Nobody really said anything direct but there was always an uncomfortable pause after I tell them that I'm Chinese American," Liu says of her phone interviews. "It's like 'Oh, you're not really American.' It's unsettling that my background often cuts out my credibility."

Figure 5.29 Article 1 on ELT employment discussed in Indigo's class

After having the read the above articles and problematised the underlying assumptions of how Native and Non-Native speakers were traditionally classified, Indigo conducted a simulation activity (Figure 5.31) in which students were grouped and then asked to design an advertisement for hiring English language teachers in the light of this lesson's discussions.

Another pedagogical activity that I conducted in my lecture on Accent Debates was called 'linguistic-identity-switching'. This is where students were required to speak in an accent of a variety of English they did not grow up with,

Becker, who was born in Spain but raised in the US since the age of three, has Malaysian, Thai, English, Polish and German ancestries. Since she began teaching last August, several parents of her students have complained that their child was not receiving the "full, foreign experience" because Becker did not look white, she says.

Cecilia Wan, born in England to Chinese parents, says the preference for white English teachers extends beyond Taiwan to other Asian cities and countries. While living in Hong Kong two summer ago, she applied for a job that required a "native English speaker" and was quickly dismissed. "They blatantly told me 'You're Chinese, not Caucasian. You can't teach our kids,'" Wan says.

"My personal experiences interviewing are one thing, but just to see ads in papers asking for 'native foreign speakers' infuriates me. I mean, what do they mean by 'native'? I'm native, but I know that someone like me is not who they're looking for," Liu says.

Figure 5.30 Article 2 on ELT employment discussed in Indigo's class

148 *EIL teachers implementing change*

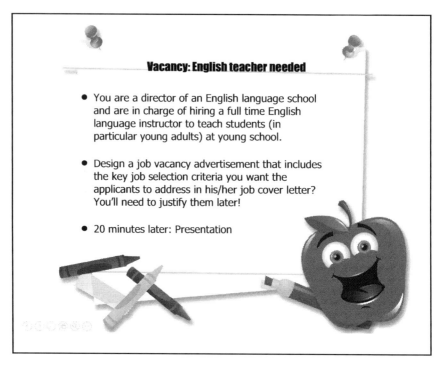

Figure 5.31 Indigo's job vacancy simulation activity

and were penalised for deviation. Indigo believed that this activity had allowed her students to experience "the politics of difference, meaning how it felt like to be in the shoes of those whose varieties of English were suppressed and who were pressured to emulate the 'voices' of the dominant mainstream group". My recollection of the lesson with my class was as follows.

> This morning's lesson focused on 'accent debate'. Instead of 'telling' students that it was not OK to discriminate others on the basis of one's accent or that changing one's accent was the same as changing identity, I decided to do an activity called the linguistic-identity-switching identity. The following is how the lesson proceeded.
> "Ok, to allow you to experience what it is like to be in the position of people who are pressured or required to change the way they sound, I'm going to experience it". Some students frown in response to that, and I can hear one of them say: "Oh oh! This is not gonna be good!" (laughter), to which I respond "Yes, it's not good indeed" (the whole class laughs).
> Then I give the following instructions with an Indonesian accent: "The activity is quite simple. Here is a short passage and I want you to read this passage out loud" Before I finish this, one of the student interrupts

and says: "How difficult is that"? I smile and say: "I haven't finished what I wanted to say! I want you to read this passage out loud in the accent that I am currently putting on (and the whole class gave me a long 'Ooooh nooo!'). And if you don't read this passage like the way I sound, you are going to be penalised, maybe you will lose your participation mark".

I hand out the passage and ask the students to listen to the way I read it. "If you want to write down the phonetics, it is entirely up to you!" I read the passage out loud twice. As I'm reading the passage, some students scratch their heads, some shake their heads, and others laugh. I then give them about five minutes to practise.

Five minutes later, I ask a couple of students to read out the passage. I continuously correct them, and asked them to repeat after me! One of them gives up, and with a frustrated facial expression and tone, he says: "I can't do this man! It's hard! I've been speaking English with my accent for nearly two decades now, and now you're asking me to change! It's ridiculous!" "WOW! thank you!", I responded, "this is what I want to see and hear!" That student looks at me with a surprised face!

"Now we all know what it feels like to have one's accent changed! Not comfortable at all. Why? Imagine when you are correcting someone! You know how they feel now, right? So, when you have this intention to correct the way someone speaks, think about this activity! Put yourself in the shoes of the person you intend to correct, and how do you feel? Something for us to think about, right guys?" A few students; many sigh! Then I use this activity to discuss the relationship between accent and identity. But once again I am prompted to reflect on the responses from students. Why did they sigh? Had I been ignorant? Could there have been something missing?

(My reflective journal)

5.2.3.2. Not as smooth as we had planned!

I have taken some time and space to represent a wide cross-section of activities, teaching resources, and classroom tasks. I have woven in among these representations, a range of the ways we four teachers in this study observed, reflected upon, and dialogued with each other about the ways in which the above activities were conducted. This allowed me to observe and capture the 'free-floating' (Simons, 2009) dimensions of our teaching that my presentation of the EIL paradigm and the theoretical framework for EIL teaching materials and pedagogical practices discussed in Chapter 2 did not allow me to do.

Although my colleagues claimed the importance of engaging students in learning about the politics of difference by incorporating controversial issues or tough topics, it is clear that they experienced some challenges in engaging their students in the above debates as well as in discussions on the controversial issues. When they encountered students who challenged the EIL perspectives they advocated, the choices of approaches that were mostly adopted by my colleagues in this encounter often culminated in silence as opposed to further inquiries or dialogues

150   EIL teachers implementing change

on the issues. While I was observing these, I also realised that these scenarios were not much different from those of my own (see autobiographical accounts in both Chapter 4 and this chapter). All of this allowed me to uncover the 'hidden text' (Cochran-Smith, 2000) or assumptions/values that might have informed the approaches we adopted to teach EIL and that might have been unintentionally conveyed to the students. This 'hidden text' will be discussed in Chapter 6.

The classroom debate activity that Ashish conducted on different statements about accent differences was shorter and less 'heated' than I had expected. During this activity, I noticed the struggle that Ashish experienced in discussing these tough issues with his students. This was particularly evident in his response to those who vocally asserted their support for the idea that speaking English with a native English accent is the best and makes one look more intelligent. Once again, I will try to capture the immediacy of the drama and the sense of unfolding events by narrating this in the present tense.

* * * * *

The debate on the statements starts. One group of students strongly claim that they believe that having an accent is not a big deal whether it is a native and a non-native accent as long as people can understand each other. One of them (Student A) points at Ashish and says, "You have an accent of a non-native-speaker, we can understand you and that's it, right!"

Ashish smiles and responds: "Thank you! That is an excellent point. See! As long as we can understand each other, why do we have to make a big fuss about it? That is what all we need – a need and willingness to understand regardless of how you sound!"

Another group of students disagrees. They strongly claim that people, especially non-native-speakers, still have to speak English like native-speakers. One of them (Student B) claims: "That's the accent that gets us jobs. Who wants to listen to you if you don't sound clearly. This is the reality that we are facing at the moment. Nobody wants to talk to you if you don't have a native-speaker's accent. Like an English teacher, if he or she does not have a native-speaker's accent, I don't think he will be employed to teach English right?" Other students in that student's group nod.

Ashish utters: "Hmm!", and pauses for a long time, showing his uncertainty in how to respond to this. This leads him to direct the comment and question to the whole class: "So, what do we all think about what Student B just said?"

Students from other groups agree and one student (Student C) says: "I'm a non-native-speaker of English, and I'm ashamed of the way I sound. So, I am not confident with my English if I don't sound like Australian." Ashish looks a little worried and responds to Student C: "Look, there's nothing wrong with your English, you sound fine because there are different Englishes and different sounds." Student C looks away when he was giving his comments. Then returning to what Student B said: "Look (pause) I understand what you're saying. I am not saying that you are wrong, but you need to look at another different perspective and consider another view too because accent is changing and there are so many different Englishes. I know it's your view, and it's up to you if you don't want to change." Student B does not say anything and looks at her mobile phone. The class goes silent. In response to this silence, Ashish proceeds to the summary of what he wants his students to learn from this lesson, explaining it is impossible for people not to speak English without an accent, the monolithic nature of a standard accent, and that the attitudes towards accent are changing. After this, the class is dismissed.

* * * * *

After this episode, Ashish and I discussed what had just happened. He expressed his disappointment and dissatisfaction at the students' performance because "they were still praising and favouring the native-speakers' accent". He also commented on the poor performance of a presentation from a group of students prior to the debate activity, which I missed because I was observing another colleague's class. As he said (with a big frown on his face):

> you know [Students X, Y, and Z] from Singapore, Malaysia, and Brunei. They were doing the presentation on Accent before you came to the class. I wasn't happy with it at all. They said that they wanted to speak or change their English to sound like people from England because that's a prestigious accent, and that's how they have been taught. They are OK with that. I mean we have already taught them English variation and still they have that perspective. Hmm … I'm quite disappointed!

I asked him if he posed any follow-up questions to explore what might have caused students to make such comment. Rather than posing follow-up questions, he reported that he "just made comments on the presentation saying that they should think more about other perspectives, consider other Englishes, and their English accent is fine". Having listened to this, I began to wonder if a different approach could have been employed.

In our further conversations about how Ashish approached what he labelled as "anti-EIL" comments, he claimed that the reason for his long pause and his decision to direct the comment to the whole class was because:

> it was a challenge for me! A big challenge because I was not really sure about how to deal with students who favour and glorify one particular model. My aim is to help them become more accommodative, more inclusive, more tolerant, not hate any particular accent, not discard or disrespect any particular accent. And this has been a challenge for me. I wouldn't say that I have always been successful because towards the end of the subject, I have talked to my students and some still have not got this inclusive attitude, so to break this deadlock, to break this hard-line approach, it has been my real challenge.

Ashish claimed that he knew why it was difficult for him to successfully 'break this deadlock'.

152 *EIL teachers implementing change*

> I know and can clearly see where these attitudes came from … like for example their previous English language education that only taught them that American English or British English was the best English, and others are bad. I came exactly from the same backgrounds as them. And I also know as they said that when they go outside the classrooms, that's the, for example, accent or English they had to have … hmm, it's confusing, isn't it?

To overcome this challenge, what Ashish proposed to do and what he had done most of the time in his class was to provide students with as much exposure as possible to different perspectives. He would let the students decide which perspective they choose to adopt.

> As an EIL teacher, I still have to present different ways of looking at things. I would still say look, the only person who want to change or not to change is you. And this will depend on a lot of things right, first of all, do you feel the need of change? Do you think it is appropriate to change? So it's only you can decide. Yeah, probably I'll also say that 'Look [pause] the only decision appropriate in that context is what you think you should do. There's no prescription and the teachers cannot prescribe anything in that context. I can't say that that person is wrong and you're right. There are only differences, and you need to learn to appreciate different views.

This again prompted me to wonder if his approach might further confuse students, which I could see from their facial expressions.

I also stumbled on a rather similar scenario in Indigo's lesson on Native and Non-Native Debates, especially during the discussion with her students on the job advertisements that they had designed. Indigo also struggled to respond to her students who showed a strong preference for hiring native English-speaking teachers with Anglo-European backgrounds. I pick up the story of Indigo's class from the moment when she was inviting two groups to present their advertisement to the whole class.

* * * * *

"Ok, can Butterfly English school group present their job advertisement please?", Indigo instructs. Three students walk to the front of the class and present their job advertisement using a PowerPoint presentation (Figure 5.32).

The students claim that they do not care about the nationality of the teachers as long as they know how to teach, have a high proficiency in English, are open to different cultures, and can speak different languages. Most importantly, "These teachers should have studied EIL or know about world Englishes so that they can teach students to not to be ashamed of their own English". Indigo looks very impressed and happy, and comments: "Excellent! Let's give them a big round of applause. Thank you! The next group is the International English Language Centre group!"

EIL teachers implementing change 153

Figure 5.32 Students' responses to Indigo's job vacancy simulation activity 1

Four students walk to the front of the class and show their job advertisement also using a PowerPoint presentation (Figure 5.33). They explain that they are looking for Anglo-European background teachers from Inner-Circle countries to teach English at their school, like "our tutor here, Indigo". They continue: "The reasons are because they speak better English, have a clearer accent than people from Outer- or Expanding-Circle countries. Parents want this and want their children to speak like native. You learn best with people who don't know how to speak your language, that's all".

Indigo does not look very impressed this time. She responds: "Okay, but what's wrong with people from Outer- and Expanding-Circles? They speak English too and can connect better with maybe students from your own countries. Who are native-speakers? We have problematised these notions already, right? And how can we call it an "international" centre if you only employ people from Inner-Circle countries?" One of the students from the group responds: "But that's not what the parents want! And do you want your kids, for example, who want to study English and end up speaking English with Chinese accent or like an Indian?". Indigo looks at me and sighs. She then replies to the students: "Look, I don't have an answer for you! We don't have an answer to everything because there has not been an answer yet. But what I want you guys to think about is this new EIL perspective and to think about how you can incorporate this perspective. And are you saying it is okay for people to discriminate against others and

154 *EIL teachers implementing change*

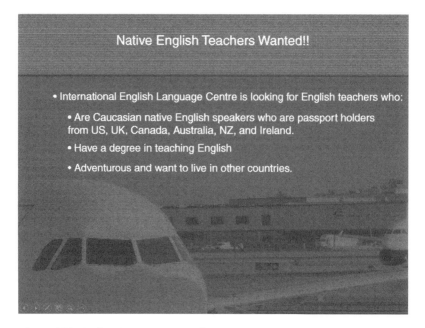

Figure 5.33 Students' responses to Indigo's job vacancy simulation activity 2

that you're supporting the article we talked about before? (The class and the students are silent) Okay, think about it! And we can talk about it later!".

As she is giving her comments, I notice that several students in the group are looking down and not paying attention.

* * * * *

When we sat down to discuss this class, Indigo expressed her disappointment at the students who still "glorified and believed in the supremacy of native-speakerism". She was aware that her approach "where [she] asked the student if they were okay with discriminatory hiring practices was a little harsh", and she claimed that she had no choice but to do so because

> if someone doesn't make you aware of it, you can go through your entire life and having no idea what impact you're having, how detrimental it will be. Someone has to help you peel back the layers of the onion you are actually a racist or whatever.

Having a similar thought when I was interviewing Ashish, I began to wonder if being 'harsh' with students who resisted or challenged the perspectives we advocated was pedagogically sensible or even ethical. Further conversations about the students' presentations also revealed her disappointment at the students from the Butterfly group, whose essays she had just marked prior to coming to the interview with me. She reported that the standpoint that the students took in their essays was different from the ones they showed during the presentation.

> Sometimes you could see in class that little glimpse from the Butterfly group students where they did start to self-reflect and that they have got it. They seem like they are nodding … nodding … nodding! But when I read their essays before I came here, it's just shut down again. It says 'No EIL, this is a bullshit, we should stick to native-speakers norms and these norms are really amazing! And we have to do what the system asks us to do'. I don't know what to say … it's so arrrgghh …. So, it's quite different from what they presented in class! I thought my students have come further than this, but they are still in that native-speakerism world where native-speakers are the best English speakers and teachers. It's frustrating!

When we were having a further chat more about why the students were showing different points of view, she claimed that she was aware of the struggle that these students had to go through. She too experienced these struggles in teaching these EIL subjects. She was aware of the pressure to conform to the dominant conventions of "the Australian system" within which they all operated. Indeed, she remarked that her own postgraduate study in EIL had not equipped her with sufficient confidence to handle such struggles.

> Very difficult … I don't think it's just them. That's something that I am myself battling with. It's to do with the world … the problem is that they've come into Australia, and so they do need to be following an Australian system, umm … it's difficult. I need to, on the one hand, to teach them to embrace different cultures and also I'm sorry, but the system doesn't appreciate different Englishes. So, that's why I don't know how to sort of … communicate this to students. That's why I tell my students that I don't have answer for you. You need to think about it yourself. And I don't think EIL has really prepared me for dealing with this, which makes me think that EIL can still sometimes be a bit idealistic. It's telling that us that we should teach world Englishes blah blah blah, but OK, I understand! Fabulous! But how to actually deal with this pressure? And because we don't have answers to that or … I don't feel that I have yet got concrete answers to that, because no one is writing about it. And I know that students can see that I'm being honest that I don't have an answer for that.

Therefore, in dealing with this, Indigo proposed to me what she would do and had done a few times in her class when encountering a similar scenario. She would "make them [students] just realise that people do things differently in the world, which is enough" and she would urge the students 'to try their best' to incorporate world Englishes perspectives.

> So, there are differences in doing things! Because the world is changing! And then ask them to think about how they would go about this. Then

156   *EIL teachers implementing change*

look for what works, what might not work, what would be offensive, what wouldn't be offensive! You should no longer think in your old ways like native-speakers are the best English speakers or whatever because the world has now changed with English being an international language. If the world Englishes stuff has not gone deep enough ... uumm ... I guess they're just not really having realised that this is going to be an issue if they don't understand world Englishes. Well, I just said do your best, umm ... try you know, maybe it's uncomfortable, difficult, and that maybe this is not great for you, but it's going to be interesting for the rest of us, so for our and your benefit.

Fatima also encountered a similar scenario during the debate that she conducted in her lesson on Standard English Debates. She reported that she was struggling to respond to students who were adamant about their view of the need to avoid speaking different varieties of English and to speak this "glorified mythical and imaginary thing named Proper Standard Native English" (Fatima). Since I did not have the opportunity to observe her class, she provided me with a very clear scenario during our interview. What had startled me was her decision to choose an 'avoidance strategy' when facing those students who challenged her or who, as she said, "[had] any complaints" about the EIL perspectives she advocated. This strategy, Fatima claimed, was aimed to let students think more about her questions.

> When I tried to talk about or when we are talking about 'Standard English' and varieties of English and I remember there's this Chinese student and she says: 'I'm a teacher, but these [world Englishes] are wrong, you only need to learn one English either American or British English, this is wrong, and you cannot give wrong examples to students'.
>
> And I was shocked and I was really numb at that time, because I don't know what to say to her and or react to her. Hmm ... how should I say this without judging her? And I don't want to judge her. So, I say: Ok, why do you think it's important for your students to know Standard English ... because 'Standard English' is there and everything is there and you just use the books. And do you think people speak like the book?
>
> She is like: 'No, but who cares'
>
> When I hear that, I ask myself what I should do next, and say, right, let me ask you a question. Do you think you speak Standard English?
>
> She stopped and says: 'Yes, for most part of it.'
>
> And I say: OK, do you think all people here speak Standard English?
>
> She: '[pauses for a long time] Maybe.'
>
> I say let's think about this. And then I come to conclusion and tell her that: What we are doing here is we want you to be critical with Standard English, so please be critical about Standard English. I just explain to you what or how people have problematised this idea. But if you think it's still difficult, not impossible, to be implemented in your culture or in your teaching context, how do you think? What would be the best thing to do? A better

thing to do? OK, you want Standard English, what about Englishes? Would you like to introduce Englishes or would you choose to ignore it? Let's just not answer that right away?

Because if I let this person keep continue, it will never stop, so I just let this person think about this in their mind and say: just think about it, you don't have to answer it right now. If you decide not to introduce other varieties, explain it to me why? You can write it to me. Think about it!

I try to avoid direct argument. I think it's difficult once a person always has his/her mind set on one thing and just continue the conversation. It's useless, it would go nowhere. At least just let this question play in his/her minds. So that's usually my avoidance strategy. I wouldn't like to use the word 'avoidance', but in reality that's how and what I did.

As soon as I finish with this Chinese girl, there's this Indian girl starts challenging me and talking about: 'What's wrong with Standard English?'

Then I say: No I didn't say this is right or wrong! This is what Standard English perspective suggests. This is the implicit erm … meaning that is being set through Standard English discourse. Now you have these other Englishes, even you speak your own English.

And I just go and point at that person and then say, just think about it and if you have any complaints, why don't you write it down in your journal?

And this is the best way for me … I do it this way, it makes them think and to conclude the lesson, I want students to think about the importance of their identity in using language

As Fatima and I continued to discuss the above class episode, she reported that teaching EIL at Urban University was often filled with "tensions, dilemmas, and contradictions" and was therefore a challenge for her. During the time of this book project, she experienced some unpleasant interactions in her daily life as a student and a foreigner in Melbourne. She felt she was treated as a deficit learner of English, someone who did not have the ability to speak and write well in English. These interactions had undermined her self-confidence as a user and teacher of English. Thus, she questioned how possible it was for her to inspire students to learn to be advocates for EIL while she was not confident herself. Fatima reported that she could not reveal this feeling to her students because she still held a traditionalist belief that as a teacher, one should be firm, 'know everything', and should not display the struggle she had had:

I personally think that teaching EIL is a challenge and self-confidence is the thing. Right now, I'm the tutor. So my understanding is that the tutors need to be firm with this concept of EIL or the perspective it upholds. By firm, I meant, you know, how to answer everything. I know I'm still a traditionalist as well. I myself am still trying to understand how these EIL ideas exist in my life. So, how am I supposed to teach this to my students when I am still struggling myself? I cannot appear to be struggling as a tutor. I need to be confident and firm about this concept. But it's hard for me in a way that because I still get same treatment as what my students experience in a sense that being treated as non-native.

When I came here to Australia, I repeatedly experience several incidents where they first look at me as a non-native instead of as a person or as an individual. When taking a bus, the bus driver talks to me as if I don't know English. In my academic life, my thesis supervisor, who is a non-native-speaker, commented on my English instead of the content. What strike me the most is they didn't treat me as a professional. I see myself as a teacher, a lecturer who is learning in an academic institution. I'm not a total learner, I'm also a professional. The way they communicate with me, they treated me like I'm a learner, an elementary student. When my supervisor and I start talking about what I have written, she was always going back to the language. I thought, what is wrong with my language? Is it really not readable? What's the problem? How about the content? I expect to see a supervisor not a language teacher. Because I'm being treated like this all the time, I become so self-conscious about my English ability. It ruins this self-confidence of mine. I try to fight it and I shouldn't let this experience ruin myself. When I teach EIL, these experiences keep popping up in my mind. But I don't want my students to know about how I also struggle with this, cos I'm their teacher.

In response to the challenging episode where Fatima encountered students who displayed a strong resistance to the EIL perspective she advocated, unlike Ashish and Indigo, Fatima claimed that students needed to be given more time to discuss and think about their ideas. She observed that spaces given to topics in which little-p issues could be further discussed were still the minorities in the EIL curricula at Urban University.

Sometimes I felt that there's so little time to touch upon these topics. With a topic like native-speakerism, or Standard English, I think it needs more time. It needs to have two meetings, not just one meeting, because once I am involved with my students, especially when we start arguing with each other and discussing about this, I felt it's like, there's not enough time for discussions. Because at first I have to at least introduce the theory first and that already takes a lot of time. It's hard to put or cram these issues about Standard English into just one meeting and then expect students to discuss about it and really have an opinion or have their own opinions about that.

Lastly, encountering and dealing with students who did not support or who resisted the perspectives advocated by the EIL curricula at Urban University was also something that I had experienced since I first started teaching EIL (see my autobiographical narrative in Chapter 4). I assumed that I would not encounter a similar scenario at the third-year level, but my experience of teaching in EIL3130 (Language and Education) proved I was wrong. Since this subject focused on the ways in which an EIL paradigm could be implemented into the context of teaching, most of my lessons could potentially become 'political' as students were encouraged to critique the existing practices and ideology of English language teaching. Although most of the lessons were not as 'heated' and challenging as my colleagues' had been, the lesson on Assessing and Testing EIL was very difficult. I pick up the story of that lesson at the point when I invited students to look critically at the current English language tests that were administered worldwide and used to serve different purposes such as TOEFL (Test of English as a Foreign Language) and IELTS (International English Language Testing System).

Today's class focused on testing from an EIL perspective. To let students experience assessing learners' English language competency, I decided to play a video recording of two IELTS candidates undertaking the speaking test. While watching this video, students would assess the candidates' spoken English competency based on the IELTS marking scale. This is a short snippet of the lesson.

* * * * *

As students are watching the video, I can see that some of them are laughing, possibly at the way the candidates are speaking. And I am right, because I can hear those students imitate the way the candidates are speaking. When the recording finishes, I firstly ask students to rate the candidates for five minutes. Then I divide them into groups with whom they share their rating and their justifications. Again, I can hear laughter from the same group of students.

Sharing time! "Okay, guys! What I would like you to do is to share with the class how you have rated these two candidates and justify your rating". Several students believe that these candidates deserve a high score because, as they list, "it was understandable and quite clear; had very few odd syntactical constructions and lexical choices which did not hinder the meanings". One student (Student A) raises his hand and says that "native-speakers make those odd grammatical constructions too". Another student (Student B) critiques the IELTS marking scale and claims that "it is too superficial, and it has a lot problematic underlying assumptions". Having listened to this, I am quite impressed especially at Student B's critique.

Those students who were laughing do not seem to be happy with Student A and B's comments. One of them (Student C) raises her hand and says: "I don't really agree with you guys. But would you seriously pass that? They are not even speaking English like native-speakers". Some of the students from Student C's group nod. She further explains that if these candidates are given a high score, "we are not doing them any justice. It is OK for them to speak English that is not clear to native-speakers since they are doing this test to stay in English-speaking countries". Student B, a monolingual speaker of English from Australia, responds: "But it is understandable to me! Big deal!" Student C replies: "Yes B! It is a big deal! You can't just pass someone who doesn't sound clear to native-speakers! They will be discriminated out there for sounding funny!" Student A replies: "Wow, that's an exaggeration!"

After listening to this and sensing the tension in the room, I step in and ask everyone, especially Student C and those who agree with her: "So, how do you understand 'clear' or comprehensibility? Let's think about Kachru and Smith's

160   *EIL teachers implementing change*

(2008) notion again of Comprehensibility! Who are 'native-speakers'? Whom do they interact with in English-speaking countries? Have you thought about the changing sociolinguistic reality of English? I thought we have already been through these questions so many times! And you have an accent as well which is different from these candidates and everybody else, and it's comprehensible to us".

I can see that Student C is frustrated and she ignores my comments. But I still want to know what she thinks: "Student C, what do you think?", to which she unhappily replies: "I have already said what I wanted to say". The class suddenly becomes quiet. Student C has a point, but it's still very superficial.

* * * * *

This again prompted me to reflect on this lesson. I still did not understand why students such as Student C still had that perception even though a lot of them had studied in a number of subjects with me. Had I approached it 'appropriately'? Had I been too dogmatic again?

(My reflective journal)

It was relatively evident in the above scenarios that all EIL educators at Urban University were rather uncomfortable with students who resisted the perspectives and beliefs that the EIL curricula advocated. Experiencing and talking with my colleagues about this feeling of discomfort and the silence in class (after particular input from us as teachers) eventually prompted me to see the need for all EIL educators, including myself, at Urban University to reconceptualise the way we taught EIL and the way we approach students such as Student C.

5.3. Chapter summary

In this chapter, I have attempted to respond to two main questions that Brown (2012) regards as under-researched, and that Wee (2013) claims as lacking in the current literature on teaching EIL. They urge researchers in the area of EIL teaching to illustrate "what EIL syllabuses, learning sequences, textbooks, or curriculum projects already exist" (Brown, 2012, p. 163), and to explain how realistic it would be to teach EIL in an actual classroom setting (Wee, 2013). I have endeavoured to address these questions by presenting the collaborative effort of four EIL educators (including myself) to engage students in learning about and learning to appreciate the diversity of English; and by illustrating the pragmatic dimensions of teaching EIL through the voices and experiences of my colleagues. Specifically, this chapter presents a thick description of the syllabus materials and pedagogical practices that my colleagues and I collaboratively developed, based on our emerging understandings of the principles of teaching English as a pluricentric language. I have also shown how my colleagues and I sequenced the way we engaged students in learning about the diversifying forms, users, and cultures of English; and the way we sought to inspire our students to appreciate and develop respectful perceptions of this diversity.

In addition to engaging students in learning about and learning to work with linguistic and cultural differences, my colleagues and I also engaged our students in discussing controversial (big-P and little-p) political issues that might arise as a result of differences. However, the experiences of my colleagues have shown that discussing those controversial issues or teaching EIL in general can be a challenge, a struggle, and filled with tensions. Although all of us as educators were aware of the tensions, the 'inner battle', and the struggle we and our students experienced in advocating the EIL paradigm due to the clash of multiple discourses from EIL and those that they had encountered in the past and brought with them to the classrooms, this awareness sometimes did not seem to translate into classroom practice. There seemed to be more (perhaps too much) emphasis and insistence placed on inculcating the values and beliefs of the EIL paradigm, and less emphasis on the importance of inquiries and dialogues into those clashing discourses. In the following chapter, I will discuss the data presented in this chapter as well as Chapter 4 in the light of the theoretical frameworks discussed in Chapter 2.

Notes

1 Consistent with the ethics approval I received, I sought and obtained consent from students enrolled in the course to publish the titles of their projects.
2 These were not observed in EIL1010, EIL2110, EIL2120, and EIL3102 as their focus is predominantly on raising students' awareness of differences (EIL1010, EIL2120, and EIL3102), and on learning about research (EIL2110).

6 Reviewing change
From teachers' perspectives

6.0. Introduction

In this chapter, the EIL curricula and the teachers' experiences of teaching EIL at Urban University which I presented in Chapter 4 and Chapter 5 will be discussed in the light of the theoretical framework I presented in Chapter 2. To help organise this discussion, I use the principles of EIL teaching materials and pedagogy listed below. The principles are articulated here in the form of a series of questions, question '5' having been added to this initial list as it is based on a theme that emerged from my engagement with the data. Have the curricula of the EIL program at Urban University:

(1) provided exposure to world Englishes?
(2) included a variety of speakers of world Englishes and interaction among them?
(3) provided exposure to different cultural values?
(4) provided opportunities to develop skills to communicate across differences?
(5) adequately addressed sociopolitical concerns or questions?

6.1. Have the curricula provided exposure to world Englishes?

There is strong convergence in the literature that any EIL curriculum must provide opportunities for students to develop metaknowledge of English as a heterogeneous language by exposing them to different varieties of world Englishes (Matsuda, 2012b; McKay, 2012b). Unlike the previous program at Urban University (EIL-ex), which focused on only a single variety of Australian English or 'the' English language, my analyses of the curricula, and the accounts of those teaching and learning in the newly revised EIL program at Urban University, revealed numerous ways in which the program exposed students to English language variation in every subject. Although different subjects had their own focus or discussed different issues such as 'politeness', 'writing', 'online communication', 'English language education' and so on, all EIL educators at Urban University ensured that the issues were discussed in the light of the pluricentricity of English, and that samples of different varieties of English were included to promote discussion of those issues. Since there were no pre-packaged learning materials that already included multiple varieties of English (a suggestion offered by Matsuda (2012b) in Chapter 2), my colleagues and I collected and disseminated different varieties of English from a wide range of sources to expose students to, and engage them in, learning about multiple varieties of English. The first category of resources included a variety of writings by respected EIL and World Englishes scholars (to name a few: Crystal, 2006; Kachru, Kachru, & Nelson, 2006; Kachru & Smith, 2008; Kirkpatrick, 2007, 2010; McKay, 2002; Sharifian, 2009; Smith, 1983, 1987). Also, scholarly articles from journals such as *English Today, World Englishes*, and *Asian Englishes* were prescribed as reading materials, exposing students to world Englishes and providing them with theoretical and analytical frameworks or tools to help frame their learning about different varieties of English. However, the examples provided by these readings were sometimes limited, and my colleagues and I felt that relying only on these scholarly reading materials would limit students' exposures to world Englishes. Therefore, to maximise exposure to different varieties of English, my colleagues and I used a variety of contemporary online resources (such as websites containing different varieties of English), video clips from popular culture movies, and our own collections of authentic 'public' and private texts, such as international newspapers written by users of different varieties of English, email exchanges with speakers/ writers of different world Englishes, and even airline magazines. All these helped the students engage in the process of learning about world Englishes.

The analyses of the materials, pedagogical activities, and interviews with my colleagues, also revealed the inclusion of 'live' examples of world Englishes in action. Students could listen to or read live texts, they could enter into dialogue with those who generated the texts and thus participate in or negotiate meaning making, and study about world Englishes. In the view of Ashish, Fatima, Indigo, and myself, the students were being encouraged to, as Hino (2010) puts it, participate in a community of practice in EIL. The first authentic and 'live' examples of such resources that students encountered tended to come from guest lecturers who were invited to present a talk and interact with the students about the varieties of English they spoke and/or they had researched intensively. The second category of authentic and 'live' examples of world Englishes, which has not yet been discussed in the literature of teaching EIL, were contributed by the students themselves. It must be remembered that the student cohort at Urban University hailed from diverse lingua-cultural backgrounds. Some of them spoke English as their dominant language; others spoke English as an additional language (unlike the EIL-ex program where so-called 'native-speakers' were excluded, and 'second English language speakers' were judged to be the only legitimate student-participants in the program). As can be seen from the curricula, students' cultural and linguistic capital (Bourdieu, 1991) or more specifically their experiences of using or communicating in English, were used as sources of information for learning about English language variation in this program's curricula. In addition, their observations and analyses of how their peers and other people used and communicated in English in their surroundings were also used as resources for learning about English language variation.

164　*Reviewing change: teachers' perspectives*

Pedagogically, students were continuously required during classroom discussions and in their written/spoken assessment tasks from first- to third-year level to reflect on, analyse, share, and dialogue about the way they or others used and communicated in English. They had to consider how their English might be *different* (but not deficiently) from others or from themselves. All EIL educators agreed that, at a base level we devised this pedagogical approach as a way to raise student awareness of differences in the way English is used. However, we also wanted (1) to prompt students to consider the fact that they themselves were in a position – subconsciously or consciously – to promote and contribute to the diversification of English (Wardhaugh, 1993); and (2) to raise their awareness of the fact that the diversity of English language can be observed "in their classrooms sitting next to them, on a train, at a market" (Fatima), in "the café in front of their house, or in the suburb where they are living" (Indigo).

Another distinctive element of the EIL curricula at Urban University relates to the concept of curriculum progression (or sequencing) in cognitively engaging students in learning about world Englishes. This has been an under-researched element in previous studies of EIL curricula (Brown, 2012). To encourage students to develop a "dynamic perspective" (Vavrus, 1991) of different varieties of English, my autobiographical narrative of trialling an EIL curriculum, and my interviews with my colleagues, has illustrated that engaging students in learning about world Englishes needs to begin with instilling in them knowledge of the nature of language variation and change, or as Fatima said, "in what ways we all naturally sound and use language differently from each other". I have learned from my own narrative, and this was affirmed in conversation with my colleagues: that giving students examples of different world Englishes at the beginning or early stage of learning about EIL is more likely to overwhelm and confuse them, and may subsequently prompt them to perceive different varieties of English as "so what? it's wrong anyway" (Indigo). Minimal awareness or understanding of the fact that language naturally changes and therefore varies – even within the so-called Inner-Circle countries – might help to consolidate deficit and deviational perspectives (Vavrus, 1991) on English language use. In response to this, at the early level of the EIL program at Urban University, my colleagues and I agreed to spend nearly three-quarters of the time in the first two EIL subjects that students study allowing them to develop some understanding of the ways in which people naturally use and communicate in English differently from each other, and most importantly to develop a view that nobody uses language differently without a reason. Equipped with this knowledge and understanding, then at the second- and third-year levels, students tended to embark on further and in-depth explorations of different varieties of world Englishes and consider the implications of their earlier learnings. In the light of all of this, the answer to the question for this section, 'Have the curricula provided exposure to world Englishes?' is an unequivocal 'yes'.

6.2. Have the curricula included a variety of speakers of world Englishes and interaction among them?

The second principle of teaching EIL in an EIL curriculum that I am proposing in this book project states that the curriculum must include representation of a variety of speakers of world Englishes and of interactions among them (Matsuda, 2012b; McKay, 2012b) from a non-deficit perspective (Marlina & Giri, 2013). Since the curricula of the EIL program at Urban University endeavoured to expose their students to, and engage them in, learning about different varieties of world Englishes, students were also exposed to users of those varieties of English, and were able to observe interactions among them. Firstly, the prescribed reading materials (see Appendix 6) included a wide variety of 'authoritative voices' of scholarly speakers of different world Englishes from different Kachruvian circles, who wrote about the varieties of English they speak fluently and about which they are knowledgeable. In addition to these written voices, a range of world Englishes could also be observed in the 'live' voices of scholars who were invited as guest lecturers to talk about the varieties of English they spoke and/or they had researched intensively.

Secondly, the representation of a variety of speakers of world Englishes and interactions among these speakers can also be seen in the choices of popular culture video materials featuring actors and actresses from different lingua-cultural backgrounds and speak different Englishes. For example:

- *Bend It Like Beckham* (2002): speakers of varieties of Irish English, British English, and Indian English;
- *Bride and Prejudice* (2004): speakers of varieties of Indian English, British English, and American English;
- *Crocodile Dundee in Los Angeles* (2001): speakers of varieties of Australian English and American English;
- *Gung Ho* (1986): speakers of varieties of Japanese English and American English;
- *Outsourced* (2006): speakers of varieties of Indian English, and American English;
- *Phua Chu Kang Pte Ltd* (1996): speakers of varieties of Singaporean English;
- *Sweet Home Alabama* (2002): speakers of varieties of American English;
- *The Kite Runner* (2007): speakers of varieties of American English and Middle-Eastern Englishes; and
- *The Namesake* (2006): speakers of varieties of Indian English, and American English.

Thirdly, the representation of a variety of speakers of world Englishes and the interactions among them could also be observed in the teachers' collections of texts from various intra-/international contexts, which they used either as examples of world Englishes or as the main text for a classroom learning activity. The novels *My Boyhood in Siam* and *The Kite Runner* were written by speakers

166 *Reviewing change: teachers' perspectives*

and writers of English from Thailand (Chandruang, 1970) and Afghanistan (Hosseini, 2013), respectively. The folk tale, *Chung Hyo Ye*, was written by speakers and writers of English from South Korea (Diamond Sutra Recitation Group, 2007). These novels and the folk tale are written in different varieties of English, and they contain lexical, syntactical, and socio-pragmatic features that reflect the sociocultural realities, values, and discourse-conventions of the authors' countries of origin. The journal article, 'Soul and style', written by an African American scholar Geneva Smitherman (1974) is a variety of African American English (Black English Vernacular).

Furthermore, the authentic or real-life texts that all the EIL educator-participants had collected, such as emails exchanges, newspapers, dialogues, and articles from airline magazines also allowed students to see the richness of the lingua-cultural backgrounds of today's users of English. For example, rather than displaying and using interactions between so-called 'native-' and 'non-native-speakers' of English, the conversational data that Indigo and Fatima used to teach the topic of 'speech acts' involved interactions between speakers of English from diverse lingua-cultural backgrounds, including (1) a Malaysian and a Thai student in Indigo's class (Figure 5.1), and (2) a Bangladeshi and an Indonesian at a dinner table in Fatima's class (Figure 5.2). The emails that Ashish and I had used to teach in lessons on 'register and style', 'cultural scripts and schemas', 'world Englishes and culture', and 'contrastive rhetoric' were sent by postgraduate students from Bangladesh and India (Outer-Circle countries: Figure 5.3 and Figure 5.4), and a colleague from Japan (an Expanding-Circle country: Figure 5.5). The articles from newspapers (*The Jakarta Post* [Figure 5.7] and *The Straits Times* [Figure 5.9]) and from the airline magazines (Garuda Indonesia Airways [Figure 5.6] and Vietnam Airlines [Figure 5.8]) that were used to teach language and worldview (EIL1010: English, Society, and Communication) and English in Expanding-Circle countries (EIL3102: World Englishes) were written by authors from Indonesia (from different ethnic backgrounds), Singapore, and Vietnam. Although Ashish chose to use an article from a local Australian newspaper (Figure 5.10), the writer of the article was indigenous Australian. This was intended to show students that Australia is not always "this sort of 'white' Australian English-speaking country" (Indigo).

Lastly, the second principle states that these variety of speakers of world Englishes should not be portrayed condescendingly as novice learners of English, but as legitimate speakers of English, whom students should eventually learn to categorise themselves (Marlina & Giri, 2013; McKay & Bokhorst-Heng, 2008). This principle was observed in the ways students from different lingua-cultural backgrounds were involved in the learning and teaching of EIL. As Ashish justified very well, "where else would you find the best place to raise their awareness of English variation other than your own classrooms where you have students from like ten countries?". Unlike the EIL-ex program in which students from diverse lingua-cultural backgrounds were required to admit their deficiency by continuously explaining the difficulties they had as multilingual speakers of English, students in this newly revised EIL program were invited to take ownership of their own use of English by reflecting on, analysing, and justifying how their use of English was uniquely different, but not deficiently different. To allow students to learn to recognise themselves as legitimate speakers of English, EIL educators at Urban University invited students to take the role of a teacher and to become knowledge providers when the learning activities used the texts written by authors or were spoken by conversation-participants from similar lingua-cultural backgrounds as the students. It was through this pedagogical approach that my colleagues and I aimed to instil in our students confidence to perceive themselves as legitimate speakers of a particular variety of English, which was not based on one's 'nativeness' to English. In the light of this discussion, 'yes' is also an answer to this section's question.

6.3. Have the curricula provided exposure to different cultural values?

The third in this amended set of principles of teaching in an EIL curriculum I am proposing states that the curriculum should aim to develop intercultural awareness by exposing students to diverse cultural values, beliefs, and norms (Matsuda, 2012b; McKay, 2012b). However, as highlighted in the literature, one main concern for this principle is its practicality because it is virtually impossible to cover cultural values, beliefs, and norms of all countries in the world in a single course. Matsuda's (2012b) suggestion of strategically diversifying content to include *all* countries and cultures in the world did not seem concrete enough to the EIL teachers at Urban University. The question that still remained was 'how strategic'? Including cultures of some countries in the world may also have run the risk of crude generalisations and cultural stereotyping.

Rather than implementing Matsuda's (2012b) recommendations, once again the EIL educators at Urban University chose to take advantage of the richness of the lingua-cultural backgrounds of their students by designing pedagogical activities in which the students themselves became the main sources for generating information about different cultural values, norms, and beliefs. Unlike the EIL-ex program in which students only learned a cultural value, norm, and discourse convention of a particular group in a particular community and were required to explain again and again how coming from a different culture presented them with difficulties in operating in that community, the newly revised EIL program designed its topics and pedagogical activities so that students had opportunities to: (1) share their own cultural values, beliefs, norms, and practices; (2) unapologetically explain how these factors shaped the way they communicated in English; and, at the same time, (3) listen to those of others whose values and norms may or may not be different from their own. The EIL educators at Urban University ensured that the topics covered in the subjects (such as 'worldview', 'politeness', 'figurative language', 'writing') were sufficiently broad and general enough to invite multiple perspectives and interpretations. Invariably, these would be shaped by individuals' cultural norms, values, beliefs, and practices, which was celebrated. Even in a subject such as EIL3102 that focused specifically on world Englishes, students had ample opportunities to learn about cultures of different

168 *Reviewing change: teachers' perspectives*

Inner-, Outer-, and Expanding Circle countries, and also to compare/contrast with the cultural norms, values, and beliefs within which the students themselves operated in order to avoid cultural stereotyping and crude generalisations. This is why it was crucial for the new program to remove the prerequisite of the EIL-ex program that only allowed a group of students from certain lingua-cultural backgrounds to study in the program.

Another approach that EIL educators devised to expose their students to different cultural values could be observed in the classroom learning activities in which the role of lecturers as the knowledge-providers was muted, and students were put in charge of using their 'cultural' and 'linguistic' capital (Bourdieu, 1991) to educate their lecturers as well as their classmates about their cultures. In this way, not only were the students exposed to diverse cultural values, but they were also given the opportunity to learn to communicate their own cultural practices, norms, beliefs, values, and sociocultural realities to those outside their local milieu, and to understand how those factors contributed to the pluralisation of English and its users (including the students themselves). This is in line with the aim of teaching English as a pluricentric language (McKay, 2002, 2003, 2010). In the light of this, a 'yes' is again an answer to this section's question.

6.4. Have the curricula provided opportunities to develop skills to communicate across differences?

In addition to knowledge and awareness of linguistic and cultural diversity, another principle of teaching EIL states that students should also be given opportunities to develop the ability to work across Englishes and cultures (Brown, 2012), as encounters with linguistic and cultural differences are characteristic of social contexts in today's postmodern globalisation era (Canagarajah, 2006; Xu, 2002). This principle could be observed in the way my colleagues and I used scenario-based activities, where students were assigned to work with real-life scenarios or cases that consisted of issues that arose from cultural and linguistic differences with which they might or might not be familiar. I found that through these scenarios, students were provided with multiple opportunities to learn to be metaculturally competent (Sharifian, 2014) in the following ways.

- *Conceptual variation awareness:* including opportunities to understand different ways of understanding silence (EIL1020), different schemas/scripts of 'a first business encounter' (EIL1020), different cultural values/norms behind different behaviours (EIL3110), and different ways of structuring writing (EIL3210 and EIL3130).
- *Conceptual explication strategies:* students were encouraged to explain and interpret others' understanding of silence, a first encounter, cultural values/ norms, and rhetorical style.
- *Conceptual negotiation strategies:* based on their knowledge and awareness of variation, students were asked to demonstrate and justify their choices of

linguistic, behavioural, and attitudinal strategies they employed or proposed to employ in working with these differences.

However, the opportunity to communicate and negotiate across differences was available not only during a particular scenario-based activity but also after the activity when students were considering and critiquing each other's strategies. In fact this kind of session provided students a more authentic and real-life opportunity to learn to justify what had informed their choices of strategies, and to employ necessary communicative strategies and attitudes to negotiate across differences. These pedagogical activities have shown that 'yes' is again the answer to this section's question.

6.5. Have the curricula adequately addressed sociopolitical concerns or questions?

Another important element that has not yet been discussed in the framework for EIL teaching materials and pedagogical practices but emerged from the data presented here, and which I propose as an additional principle, is the inclusion of teaching materials and pedagogical activities that address sociopolitical concerns/ questions. In particular, this additional principle relates to engagement with the big-P (*Political*) and the little-p (*political*) issues (Janks, 2010), and to efforts to grapple critically with the politics of difference (Pennycook, 1999). My analyses of the EIL curricula at Urban University revealed several effective attempts by the educators to address both big-P and little-p issues in their teaching. In line with Matsuda (2003) and Kubota's (2012) suggestions, it was relatively clear that there were several lessons in a number of EIL subjects (EIL1020, EIL2120, and EIL3110) that engaged students in learning and discussing big-P concepts and issues such as 'competition among local languages', 'linguistic imperialism', 'linguicism', and 'linguistic nationism'. In discussing these concepts, students were encouraged to reflect on and analyse the extent to which such concepts and issues could be observed in their everyday life. This, once again, illustrates the value placed on drawing on, or in the case of this topic, critically reflecting on students' everyday life experiences in learning about EIL in the EIL program at Urban University.

Furthermore, driven by a belief in social justice and encounters with students' responses to the deficit-approach curriculum of the former EIL-ex program that problematised that program, all EIL educators at Urban University also recognised the importance of incorporating and discussing little-p issues/concerns or controversial and tough issues in students' own everyday life that were related to the politics of difference in an EIL curriculum. As learning about and learning to respect cultural and linguistic diversity were at the core of the EIL curricula at Urban University, EIL educators believed that being controversial or engaging in controversial discussions was unavoidable. For instance, in order to encourage students "to think about how we can create a society or world that is more equal in opportunity" (Indigo), all the EIL lecturer-participants set aside time to

170   Reviewing change: teachers' perspectives

discuss the diversifying forms, users, and cultures of English *as well as* to engage students in discussing linguistic inequality or how difference is discursively constructed and treated. Thus, examples of discriminatory practices and ideologies from everyday life (e.g. articles on tongue surgery in South Korea and China and racial discrimination in the hiring practices of English language teachers) were used as a basis for classroom discussion after having exposed students to the diversifying forms, cultures, and users of English. Similarly, I also designed a linguistic-identity-switching activity that provided students with a first-hand experience of discovering the feeling of being pressured to conform to or emulate a particular accent that they did not grow up with, and which was spoken by someone in power. Classroom debates (e.g. Quirk vs Kachru's view on Standard English [Figure 5.27], an Oprah Winfrey-style show [Figure 4.7]), questions that prompted students to be self-reflective, and a simulation activity (e.g. job advertisement activity [Figure 5.31]) were developed in a way that aimed to prompt students to be critical of and to challenge beliefs, attitudes, or practices that could unjustly promote the supremacy of certain individuals or cultures and marginalise others. In light of all of this, a 'yes' *might* be a response to this section's question. That is, I am hesitant to confidently respond with a 'yes' because further analyses of the data revealed that these sociopolitical concerns, especially the little-p concerns were not, and at the time of writing still have not, yet been addressed *adequately.*

Al the EIL educator-participants (including myself) at Urban University aimed to inspire students to be critical of existing linguistically unjust practices and ideologies as well as to learn to advocate for the perspectives or beliefs underlying the EIL curricula, by engaging them in controversial little-p issues. However, our experiences revealed that teaching EIL was not as 'simple' and 'stress/challenge-free' as has often been presented by some scholars in the field. Some of the challenges of teaching in this environment were evident in the scenarios in which all the EIL educator-participants encountered a group of students who (1) verbally challenged or questioned what were seen as 'EIL perspectives' advocated in the curricula during classroom activities; (2) did not see any problem with 'situating [themselves] in a lower rank and bowing to the power of the superiors'; and (3) were "nodding ... nodding ... nodding ... in class" and yet wrote in submitted assignments: "No, EIL is bullshit and …. Native-speakers are amazing!". My EIL colleagues and I agreed that teaching EIL was filled with "challenges" (Ashish) and "tensions, dilemmas, and contradictions" (Fatima). Indeed, these challenges prompted Indigo – who was still undertaking her postgraduate study in EIL at the time of the study – to assert that EIL "can still sometimes be a bit idealistic". She felt that it did not prepare her (as well as other EIL educators) with principles and pedagogical approaches for working or dealing with those few students whose resistance to EIL principles was sometimes vigorous. In fact, the interviews with my colleagues revealed that they were fully aware of where "[their students'] attitudes came from" (Ashish), because my colleagues themselves were also "battling with" (Indigo) or "struggling with" (Fatima) the beliefs they advocated in class.

Echoing the contentions of several scholars (Bakhtin, 1981; Canagarajah, 1993; Doecke & Kostogriz, 2008), my colleagues shared with me their encounters with past voices, discourses, or practices from a range of sources. Ashish mentioned his previous English language education experiences. Indigo pointed to a system that did not appreciate different varieties of English. And Fatima spoke of people in daily life such as bus drivers and PhD supervisors who repeatedly treated and constructed her as an incompetent user of English. Indeed, Fatima said, these thoughts "kept popping up in [her] mind" as she was teaching EIL and therefore prompting her to experience 'inner battles', tensions, or struggle. All of my colleagues expressed some uncertainty as to whether it was appropriate for them to reveal and share with students their own inner battles and tensions with the discourses or voices they had also brought with them to their teaching in this course. In Indigo's view, this uncertainty had been driven by a lack of guiding theoretical principles that could give her the confidence to communicate to the students her own inner battles. For Fatima, a traditionalist view of a teacher would constantly be telling her that when teaching she should not be struggling with the perspectives and values one advocates.

It is interesting to speculate what might have happened had Indigo's and Fatima's views been shared and dialogued with students or had any of the EIL educators given students who challenged the EIL perspectives the opportunity to inquire more into the underlying assumptions or 'stories' behind their attempts. Perhaps there may have been more conversations and lively exchanges rather than silence and sighs from some students. However, the pedagogical approaches that my colleagues and I had used to respond to students who challenged or questioned what we advocated (see my autobiographical narratives in Chapter 4 and Chapter 5) seem to have conveyed a particular 'hidden message' or 'text' that students might have learned. I shall explain this in the light of the alternative theoretical perspectives offered by critical inquirers whose works I discussed in Chapter 2.

Rather than prompting students to dialogue and inquire further into the factors or ideological discourses that might have subconsciously prompted them to challenge and question the perspectives we advocated, the EIL educators in this book project adopted the following strategies in the classrooms. We persistently and frustratingly raised questions that problematised students' views to the extent that it sounded confrontational and dogmatic. We also insisted that our students consider other views that we offered by showing that 'there are different views out there' and 'that the world has changed'. At moments of acute tension, we stopped students from dialoguing 'out loud' and requested them to write their views down, especially if they had any further 'complaints'. Additionally, we asked students to 'try their best' and think of a resolution to the dilemma or tension themselves.

Informed by the alternative theoretical perspectives, these approaches have shown that my colleagues and I, as EIL educators at Urban University, may have overlooked or perhaps failed to fully recognise that tensions and struggles are in fact natural outcomes of or reactions to learning a new discourse and learning

172 *Reviewing change: teachers' perspectives*

in a heteroglot world of competing multiple discourses (Assaf & Dooley, 2006; Bakhtin, 1981; Doecke & Kostogriz, 2008; Gleeson & Davison, 2016) or in a complex ideological environment (Bakhtin & Medvedev, 1978) such an EIL program. The confrontational and persistent probing approach that Indigo and I employed, the frown on Ashish's face while he talked about his students' presentations, and the label 'complaints' Fatima used, might have unintentionally and implicitly conveyed to students that their attempts to question or challenge the perspectives were unacceptable or forms of "attitudinal sins" (Kachru, 1986), but which could have instead been inner tensions that they naturally experienced when exposed to a new and different discourse. That the students were questioning and challenging the educators, and that they said "but in reality this is …", might seem to be an indication of students listening carefully and dialogically processing the principles we advocated. They could also be part of the students' own ongoing cognitive battles as a result of the clashing discourses they had heard from us and those that they had developed/heard outside and which they brought with them into the class. Therefore, it was no wonder that our approach that persistently asked them to critically reconsider their views as well as the views we and the EIL authoritative voices advocated was met with three Ss (Silences, Sighs, and Shuns) from some students.

My fellow colleagues, Ashish and Indigo, initially proposed to simply inform students that "there are different ways of looking at things" and that "the world is changing". This approach was critiqued by Jenks et al. (2001) as a 'feel-good' approach that focuses on 'let's-get-to-know-each-other-better'. According to Jenks et al. (2001) this approach is problematic because it may well be that it evades or is "ignorant of the root causes of racism and inequality" (p. 93). On the basis of all of the research conducted in this study, it appears that EIL educators should go beyond this feel-good approach. Although since the period of data gathering efforts have been ongoing to address this challenge in the EIL program at Urban University, at the time of writing this book I can only observe that the program curricula have not yet *adequately* engaged students in discussing sociopolitical concerns or questions. However, this does not necessarily mean that I would answer 'no' to Wee's (2013) question of how realistic it was to teach EIL.

6.6. Chapter summary

The main question that this book aims to address is, as Wee (2013) supports, how realistic it would be for educators to implement the principles of teaching EIL. Based on my engagement with the collected data on actual classroom practices and experiences, illustrated in Chapter 4 and Chapter 5, I have illustrated the feasibility of teaching EIL in this chapter. Most importantly, I have also critically revisited and renewed the 'frameworks' or principles for EIL teaching syllabus materials and pedagogy discussed in Chapter 2, and therefore proposed a new set of principles in the light of the voices and experiences of EIL educators at Urban University.

Reviewing change: teachers' perspectives 173

In order to advocate the values and beliefs of the EIL paradigm (McKay, 2002; Sharifian, 2009) and to inspire students to learn to develop a dynamic perspective (Vavrus, 1991) on the pluricentricity of the forms, cultures, and users of English, EIL educators at Urban University:

(1) introduced students to diverse forms of English and engaged them in the understanding that English language variation is sociolinguistically natural, normal, and necessary;
(2) exposed students to diverse users of English and ensured that a variety of speakers of world Englishes and of interactions among them were 'non-ethnocentrically' represented in the materials;
(3) offered opportunities for students to learn about diverse cultures of English and engaged them in learning how these cultures are reflected in the way people use English[1];
(4) provided students with the opportunities to develop skills to work with differences by using role-play or simulation activities in which students were required to work with real-life scenarios or cases consisting of issues that arose from cultural and linguistic differences with which they might or might not have been familiar. Through these scenarios, students began to develop the ability to explain and negotiate differences based on their knowledge of how one language can be used to diverse conceptualisations; and
(5) engaged students in discussing both 'big' and 'little' sociopolitical concerns or issues on the politics of difference. This was done through the incorporation of controversial issues found in everyday life, such as examples of discriminatory practices or issues that unjustly empower certain individuals and marginalise others.

Based on all the EIL educator-participants' experiences of teaching EIL at Urban University, I also showed and discussed that the process of advocating the EIL paradigm is filled with tensions and struggle. It was evident in the educators' voices that these tensions, 'inner battles', and struggles were due to a cognitive battle between competing discourses from EIL and those that they had encountered in the past and brought with them into the classes. Although EIL educators showed awareness of this battle, it was not reflected in the curricula. Sometimes, particular pedagogical approaches or responses tended to silence students as opposed to encouraging further dialogue. These responses can suggest a view of tensions and struggles in learning a new discourse that regards such things as regrettable rather than as a natural and, one might say, healthy response to learning in the face of principled teaching and advocacy for a particular understanding of language, culture and the world. In fact, some of my colleagues indicated that it was not appropriate to discuss the tensions or inner battles they experienced with their students, as it would be interpreted as one's diffidence and disbelief in the advocated values and beliefs.

In order to see the extent to which the objectives of the EIL program at Urban University were met, the next chapter will present and discuss the students'

174 *Reviewing change: teachers' perspectives*

experiences of studying in this program. In other words, the following chapter will allow EIL educators and scholars to read how particular cohorts of students responded to EIL syllabus materials and pedagogical practices. The voices of the students are important here because the feasibility of implementing the principles of teaching EIL does not only lie in the hands of teachers, but also in the students whom I view as 'active participants' in the curricula.

Note

1 Exposure to (1), (2), and (3) was provided through a wide range of sources namely: writings on different varieties of English and by scholars from diverse Kachruvian circles, contemporary popular culture, online web resources, social networking sites, international newspapers, airline magazines, guest lecturers, and *most importantly* the students themselves, who have been recurringly required to reflect on, analyse, and enlighten others about their own cultural and linguistic capital and/or to share their observations of others peoples' experiences of using English in their own surroundings.

7   EIL students' responses to change

Far too often we publish for the attention of our colleagues and to advance knowledge

Bamgbose (2001, p. 361)

but

we overlook the treasure in our very own backyards: our students …

Soo Hoo (1993, p. 390)

in other words

[e]ducators lose a powerful opportunity to learn from students when they do not encourage their involvement

Nieto (1999, p. 192)

7.0. Introduction

In Chapter 4, through my critical autobiographical narrative of my journey of developing an English as an International Language (EIL) program, and an account of how my colleagues taught EIL, I presented the principles/views/ beliefs explicitly advocated by the program, and those that were implicitly embedded within the teaching of EIL in this program. In addition to the research gap Brown (2012) highlights (as discussed in the previous chapter), he also raises other questions that have been rarely pursued by research studies in the area of EIL. These include: (1) has the EIL curriculum been 'successful'? and (2) what are the effects of an EIL curriculum on students who have been living in or who study in English-speaking countries? Previous studies reveal that short-term 'injections' of EIL, e.g. a single two-hour session (Briguglio, 2006), a seven-day course (Kubota, 2001b), and a one-semester subject (Rose & Galloway, forthcoming; Suzuki, 2011) on EIL/World Englishes have not been 'successful' in a sense that at the end of these periods of teaching and learning students still displayed native-speakerist, ethnocentric, or xenophobic attitudes. The authors of the studies I refer to here claim that longer educational "interventions" will produce more 'successful' outcomes. In probing this claim, I will explore how students who studied in the program and learned through it for a longer period

176 *EIL students' responses to change*

of time (ranging from one year to three years), responded to the set of usual principles/views/beliefs advocated by an EIL curriculum. In particular, the chapter aims to address how students respond to learning about the changing sociolinguistic landscape of English. I organise my discussion around the following specific questions.

- Do students perceive any relevance, values, or benefits of learning about EIL? If so, in what ways?
- What do students experience as the factors that have contributed to such perceptions?
- Do students experience any challenges/dilemmas while learning about EIL or even after having learnt about EIL?
- Why do students resist, struggle, or experience tension or conflict in learning to advocate the perspectives underlying the EIL curriculum?

It is also through the responses to the above questions that this study attempts to address Wee's (2013) question of how realistic it might be to teach EIL.

7.1. First-year EIL students

For this phase of my inquiry, I chose to interview, and to closely analyse the accounts of studying in the EIL program, three of the six first-year students-participants who had initially agreed to participate in the study. This is because these three students had completed the full first-year study sequence (i.e. two subjects consecutively in one year) of the undergraduate EIL program whereas the other three participants had not done so. My decision here was mainly driven by concerns about the trustworthiness of the suggestion that students become less prejudiced, less native-speakerist, and more appreciative after studying EIL for longer than a mere semester or if the study involves consecutive sequences in the course of a degree.

I now present the cases of the three first-year EIL students – Manida (who was born in Laos), Cheolsoo (from South Korea), and Ogilvy (from Australia) – drawing on data that I gathered from in-depth interviews with these students.

7.1.1. Who is Manida?

Manida was born in Vientiane, Laos, and was of Vietnamese descent. She spoke Lao, Vietnamese, Thai, and English. She started learning English in high school and undertook extra English courses in a private English language institution. Prior to her tertiary education in Australia, she had completed a one-year university bridging program run by a university in Melbourne. During the data collection, Manida was a final-year student in the Faculty of Business and Economics with specialisation in Banking and Finance. As students in this field were required to undertake electives from a different faculty, she had chosen to undertake two first-year subjects from the EIL program in the Faculty of Arts. I will summarise first, in bullet points, the core ideas from Manida's interviews (Box 7.1).

Box 7.1. Summary of Manida's views and experiences of learning English as an International Language (EIL)

(1) Manida perceived learning EIL to be relevant because of:

- exposure to speakers of English from diverse backgrounds; and
- communicating in English with the 'unknown'.

(2) Lecturers' use of real-life scenarios, challenging questions, and lessons on accent and language variation prompted her to:

- think about the way she perceived her own use of English and about ways to deal with the practices that question the way she perceived her English; and
- perceive both 'native-speakers' and herself as learners of English.

(3) Manida was unsure if the principles underpinning EIL could be applied beyond the course because of racial and linguistic differences not being respected and appreciated in society, and therefore she believed that the course needed to discuss these issues more.

7.1.1.1. EIL: "it was not what I thought"

When Manida first heard the term 'English as an International Language', she thought that it was a program that taught a singular variety of Australian English to non-English-speaking background (NESB) international students. Before attending the classes, she thought this program would be useful for her because she believed that she only needed to know how to speak a singular form of Australian English in order to study and live in Australia. After attending the first few lectures, she realised that "it was not what I thought it would be".

When I asked Manida whether or not she had regretted undertaking the range of subjects associated with EIL, she disagreed and asserted that "learning about the different varieties of English [was] even more important" because of the diversity of English speakers she had observed in Melbourne:

> today's society like Melbourne is a multicultural and multilingual city ... you meet and see people from different cultural backgrounds in the city who are not necessarily, you know, so-called 'Australians' ... I have many friends and housemates from different backgrounds and they speak English differently from the one I used to learn at language school ... so I need to be aware of different, for example, politeness, why they are doing the way they do, how can I respond to that?

As a final year student, she further emphasised that the uncertainty of the interlocutors with whom she will communicate in English in the future had encouraged her to view learning EIL as valuable:

178 *EIL students' responses to change*

like I'm studying business banking and finance, of course I will work in this industry, but knowing different varieties of English and why people speak differently prepares me for communicating with customers from God knows which backgrounds because you never know who you're talking to. We are exposed to international communication.

7.1.1.2. *Experiencing change and pedagogical factors behind change*

The "stories shared by [her] lecturers about their journey of developing their own English and feeling confident about it" had also allowed Manida to believe that she has "an identity to keep", that she claimed she very much admired. In addition, the difficulty for her and her other classmates to participate in an activity where they had to "mimic a mock accent created by the teachers made [her] and maybe other classmates think seriously about the way we sound and the way we see ourselves". Manida told me that when she first came to Australia, she attempted to "change [her] accent like by mimicking the way Australians sound" but she said she "failed" in these attempts. Initially, she thought that this failure meant failure to

> speak English properly, but the lessons on accent and language variation and when I observe the way my lecturers from, you know, different culture speak make me think … like not really. Why is there a need to change? I cannot do that … I still have some sort of different backgrounds and because we are different … how can we be the same, right?

One of the outcomes of completing two EIL subjects was that Manida now wanted "*to* be [her]self rather than be someone else … be [her]self without trying to, for example, change [her] accents". She believed that this "kind of attitude and perception were not in [her] mind before [she] learnt about Englishes". And she claimed that she would employ a different approach if there was someone who attempted to 'correct' the way she spoke English in the future.

> If someone comments on or wants to change my accent, I would be, like, okay in the past, but now, I think I'll be offended. English is an 'international' language, so what rights does he have to comment on my accent? The first question I would ask to the person who corrected my English is what is the right English? American? British? Singaporean? So, what do you think is the correct English? So, what's wrong with my English? It's mine, and it's this way. It's like my idiolect … and everyone has the right to keep their identity right? …. So please respect it.

And yet, despite her understanding of English language variation and her strong attitude to preserve her identity as well as to demand respectful treatment from "someone who wants to change [her] accent", it emerged that this feisty attitude would not be likely shown if that "someone" was an English teacher.

> If it's a comment from my English teacher, it's totally different. I'll accept
> that because it's their job, they know what they are doing, and their task is to
> make me erm … speak English erm … "properly".

Interestingly, the hesitation Manida showed – in the elongated "erm" in this
quote – and her visually placing inverted commas around the word "properly"
as she spoke it may be indicative of the tension that she felt and her uncertainty
about the appropriateness of challenging her English teacher's expertise even
though she was aware of the problematic notion of 'proper English'.

During Fatima's lesson on Language and Identity, I observed that Manida was
very 'tuned in'. When Fatima asked her students to reflect on the question "Do
you see yourself as a learner of English or speaker of English?", Manida quickly
and confidently responded that she perceived herself as a learner of English rather
than a speaker of English, but she did not have enough time to elaborate on the
answer further because the lesson had come to an end. I noted what she said and
put the question to her again during an interview. She repeated exactly the same
as what she initially said during the lesson with Fatima. When I prompted her to
further explain her view, she said that she used to think that because "English
is [her] second language, therefore, [she is] a learner of English". She reported
that she was aware of the fact the way she described herself as a learner of English
"has a rather not nice meaning behind it". However, she claimed that this lesson,
"those on how and why language varies", and "[her] tutors' challenging questions that for example ask me to be or imagine [myself] in the shoes of some-
body" had challenged her initial way of understanding "a learner of English".

> I don't think you can say that you are either a speaker or a learner or ask a ques-
> tion that are you still learning English or speaking English. Because I think
> learning … even the so-called natives still have to learn English, right? When
> they are exposed to new readings, there are some sorts of words that they
> have not seen before. They'll still go to dictionary and they'll start studying.
> So I think that … at the moment I am a learner of English and I'm not satis-
> fied with my English and I don't think that in the future or in the near future,
> I won't be satisfied as well because it's an ongoing process. Because you expose
> at different age, different time, you are exposed to different experience and
> you like studying and learning things all the time because of these experiences.
> I know how to speak the language, know about the language, but I also at the
> same time am learning about and with other speakers of English. New words
> of English are emerging … so it's an ongoing process … so, it never ends.

This, she reported, had further inspired her to learn more about EIL.

7.1.1.3. One "puzzling question"

Despite her clear enthusiasm for learning EIL, Manida said that she encountered
one "puzzling question" which she had not been able to answer. She reported

180 *EIL students' responses to change*

that she was not confident about the extent to which she could apply what she had learnt outside the EIL classrooms: "My one and only challenge in studying EIL is whether we can use what we have studied into real life ... whether it's applicable and how we can make that applicable". She further explained:

> I think the difference itself is a good thing and I have no doubt that we should encourage diversity, but whether people are aware of the differences and trying to understand and appreciate the differences in the use of English is really uncertain because many people in my society or in the societies still think that no one speaks better than the owner of the language.

Her use of the words "*owner* of the language" in the above quote further indicates that, although she demonstrated awareness of the internationalisation of the English language, she still found it challenging to agree with the idea of 'native-speakers' from Inner-Circle countries (Kachru, 1986) not being the 'sole' owners of the language. When I encouraged Manida to explain why she perceived EIL ideas as difficult to apply outside classrooms, she shared her experience of interacting with her other lecturers (not EIL lecturers) at the university, who instructed her to conform to native-speakerist conventions.

> I want my difference in the way I speak and write to be acknowledged, but I was asked to follow the conventions, things like the way native-speakers are speaking. Otherwise they are going to look at you and say, 'You're weird!'

With a frustrated facial expression and tone, she said that it would still be pointless even if she did follow the 'conventions'.

> Even if I want to have and do speak English with an Australian accent ... but given the very basic thing is the physical characteristics ... of course that's the first thing people judge on when they first look at you. So, if you don't look 'Anglo' and because of that, automatically your English is not good and you got a question like, with an ironic tone 'Can you speak English?' ... how can you stand that?

In fact, this was also experienced by some of her "ABC [Australian Born Chinese] friends whose English is so proficient and speak English as their mother tongue". Therefore she suggested that while "the difference itself is a good thing, but it provides a chance for people to discriminate others and *most importantly* [her emphasis], this is why EIL needs to address these issues more". In response to this, I invited Manida for a follow-up interview to discuss further what she meant by the latter. At that second interview, she reported that there were not many opportunities throughout her studies in the two courses of the EIL program to raise the questions and concerns that she (as well as her classmates) had while learning EIL.

EIL students' responses to change   181

[S]ometimes in class I want to talk about those issues, but I don't really know where to begin and how to begin because the tutors are already talking about differences in the way people speak English. Yes, my classmates and I know now about differences, but we are confused whether we can bring it outside .... It sounds like lecturers tell us one thing and people outside the class tell us another thing, so that is why I said we are confused .... I think the lecturers need to allow us to talk about this.

As a final comment, she claimed that she had once suspected that "maybe the lecturers are avoiding this because it is not what they believe and it is not what we should believe too ... (laughing)".

7.1.2. Who is Cheolsoo?

Cheolsoo was born in Daegu, South Korea, and he speaks Korean and English. At the time of our interview, he said that he had been learning English since he was five years old. Because English writing and speaking were not emphasised in secondary schools in Korea, his mother, who had a degree in English and English literature, had motivated him to learn Standard English pronunciation, speaking, and writing. He had been in Australia for three years and he completed a seven-month intensive university bridging program in this country before he commenced his tertiary studies. At the time of the study, Cheolsoo was a first-year student in the Faculty of Business and Economics with specialisation in Marketing. Like Manida, he had chosen to undertake two first-year subjects from the EIL program in the Faculty of Arts as his elective subjects. Summarised first, in bullet points, are the core ideas from Cheolsoo's interviews (Box 7.2).

7.1.2.1. Encountering and experiencing "something I had never thought about before"

When Cheolsoo enrolled for the first semester of EIL, he only intended to study it for one semester as his elective. He expected the program to teach "how to talk like Australians or maybe Americans and improve my English because I have a Korean accent". After the first two weeks, he decided to continue in the program over the whole year (two semesters) despite the fact that the subject was different from his initial perception, for the following reason:

I find it fascinating and important to learn more about EIL especially the diversity of English cos ... the diversity of cultures and ethnicity in Australia. And especially in today's globalisation .... It's so true that I have lecturers who do not necessarily speak Australian English, but they are from China, India, Sri Lanka, and Italy who speak their variety of English ... but I know it's not an Australian English.

182   *EIL students' responses to change*

Box 7.2. Summary of Cheolsoo's views and experiences of learning EIL

(1) Cheolsoo perceived learning EIL was important because of linguistic and cultural diversity in Australia (e.g. his lecturers were from diverse backgrounds)

(2) The emphasis placed on students' prior and current experiences of learning and using English; the classes on English language variation and accent; the stories of the lecturers; and the reading materials by 'Mrs Shim and Baek' (on Korean English):

- allowed him to perceive that the way he uses English is a reflection of his worldview and identity;
- encouraged him to perceive himself as both a learner and a speaker of English; and
- inspired him to learn more about EIL and have the ambition to spread what he has learned through writing essays about EIL and publishing them.

(3) He was uncertain if the notion of EIL is practical or helpful because:

- being and sounding different from the 'mainstream' do not seem to be appreciated by some groups of people in Korea and Australia;
- negative attitudes of English teachers in Korea and some Koreans towards Korean English as an emerging variety of English have given him second thoughts; and
- he was not sure how to deal with diversity.

In further conversation about his decision to continue studying in the EIL program, he explained that he had been encouraged to "think about something that [he] had never thought about before". He reported that a number of his previous perceptions had been challenged by the lecturers and the prescribed readings, which had largely prompted him to view English and himself differently.

Cheolsoo reported that the emphasis placed on his experiences of using and learning English both in written and spoken assessment tasks had prompted him to rethink and revise how he viewed his English. He reported that he now had a clearer understanding of the way in which he, as a Korean, used English.

> Before I learnt EIL, I was not one of the pros for the EIL concept the first time, I thought my English is not something that reflects my worldview … but the more I study, the more I realise that, growing up in Korea and Australia, I have confronted a lot of cultural issues and that would be reflected in my English …. So, for example in greetings stuff, I would

EIL students' responses to change 183

> actually prefer to use 'Have you had a dinner?' rather than 'How are you going?' That's important because in Korea we have been through Korean war, and Korean ancestors were poor and they rarely had nice meal, so Koreans usually do greetings [in this way]. So, it's about caring about someone, one already had dinner or what they did ... you know, different from Australians' use of 'How are you going?' or 'G'day mate', which I don't feel the 'connection'.

Not only had Cheolsoo become aware of the influence of his Korean culture on English, but he seemed to have developed the ability to confidently explain why he spoke the way he did and to justify his choice of phrases. He also reported that he had been prompted by his previous English teachers to believe that the best way to communicate in English is to "sound Australian or maybe American". The knowledge that he had acquired from the lessons titled "English language variation and Accent debates class" had challenged his previous beliefs. The lessons seemed to have led him to view the effort and willingness to negotiate meanings as important factors for successful communication in English as opposed to which 'native-speaker' accent should be adopted.

> Some Americans or Australians would want us to be like Australians or to become Australian or American speakers of English, but after those lectures ... knowing different accent and different varieties ... I'm so impressed ... I don't think we should be like that ... I have started to think that the most important thing is how you can express their thoughts and *try* to understand others' thoughts in today's international communicative settings [Cheolsoo's emphasis].

Like Manida, he also believed that learning about EIL had encouraged him to view the differences in the way he used English was in fact a "natural thing". Therefore, he had developed this willingness to have this difference – which signified his cultural backgrounds, values, and therefore identity – maintained rather than replaced.

> If we speak like Australians, it's like being colonised by Australian culture and English rather than keeping our identity, cos we have other cultural and racial and other backgrounds ... and it's inevitable, it's natural thing.

When I was observing Fatima's lesson on Language and Identity, especially the part where students were asked to answer whether they identify themselves as a learner or a speaker of English, Cheolsoo did not say anything. When we were having a conversation about this later, he reported that at that time, he regarded it as "a silly or duuuh question ... of course, I'm still a learner because I'm a non-native English speaker". He reported that the "stories of [his] lecturers' experiences of using English in different parts of the world" seemed to have inspired him to learn to identify himself both as a speaker and a learner:

184   *EIL students' responses to change*

> I am still a language learner because there are people who speak different dialects of English and different accents and also nowadays a lot of people use abbreviations like gtg, lol .... So, still we are learners because we don't know all of those and are not exposed to those ... and although I'm still not satisfied with my English, but I think I'm not a bad speaker of English because I can express my thoughts, my academic thoughts ...

In addition to the changes outlined above, in further interviews Cheolsoo revealed a number of challenges he had encountered during his study.

7.1.2.2. *"Still not sure if EIL is the mainstream or trend"*

Although Cheolsoo reported that he enjoyed learning about English language variation and regarded it as important and useful, his reflection on his experiences of having lived in Australia and South Korea seemed to have prompted him to feel confused. He was uncertain if he could apply what he had learned from the program in those societies. He thought that the paradigm of EIL was widely known and accepted.

> I thought all people know that English became an international language, but they still think that they should implement one single standard English to learn, not the fact that there are varieties of English or Englishes in the global world. So, I'm still not sure if EIL is going to be the mainstream or trend.

Yet, when I invited him to further explain his reason for the uncertainty he had about EIL being the 'mainstream' or 'trend', he shared his experiences of witnessing and observing how 'difference' or 'English language variation' was negatively viewed by some groups of people both in Australia and Korea. He gave a specific example of how the news about violence towards Indians in some parts of Australia had made him question whether being and sounding different from the 'mainstream' would be viewed as positive.

> The discrimination against Indians ... like some Australians do, they bash them. They just underestimate Indians due to their appearance, due to their biased point of view towards Indians behaviours. They see Indians as rude and speaking bad or crashed English or something like that ... so, it's out there, and diversity in English and race is seen as bad ... so, not sure if it's good to be different from the 'mainstream'.

At the tertiary institution where he had previously studied, Cheolsoo reported that he had been asked to "change [his] pronunciation" and he had been "evaluated negatively because [his] English [was] seen as weird and not 'proficient' ". Therefore, despite his desire to identify and to be identified as a speaker of English, "those who are racist and who would not want to try to understand [his] thoughts would call [him] a 'learner learner' because English was not [his] first language and would not regard [him] as a speaker of English". He shared that he appreciated the effort and enthusiasm of EIL scholars and lecturers in promoting differences and encouraging him to take pride in his difference, but he still found it difficult to see the practicality of it. In fact, he himself was not really ready for or certain about living with diversity and the "confrontation" that it may bring:

> I like the fact that there are lots of varieties of ideas and stuff, but if I start the differences between me and others, I get a bit embarrassed and don't know what to do. So I like the varieties of ideas but don't like the confrontation with different cultures which I couldn't understand even if I try to understand. That's what I don't know. So I like the diversity but I don't know how to deal with that diversity.

Furthermore, this tension had been further caused by his observations of the attitudes of some of his fellow countrymen who supported the supremacy of Kachruvian Inner-Circle Englishes, in particular American English. He claimed that he was very frustrated to see how his other fellow Koreans "worship US English and when you speak US English, you're a really a good man but if you speak other English, then it's not proper". Therefore, even though he learned to view Korean English as another legitimate emerging variety of English after studying in the program for two semesters, he reported that he still experienced a struggle to assert and defend its presence in his society(ies). He explained that this was partly because that variety had not been yet codified, but mainly because:

> Koreans themselves usually consider some localised ... maybe something like that ... an inferior level, and worse than American English. Koreans do not accept Korean English as variety of world Englishes.

He reported that, from his experiences of learning English in Korea, many English teachers in Korea:

> make a joke about Korean English, like Konglish, an inferior level English. Koreans say air-con and hand-phone ... teachers always teach that air-con and hand-phone are wrong. They recognise them as bad transformed English words, not independent nativised or localised words.

He strongly questioned: "When this Korean English become one single variety of English? Will it become until I die?" Thus, he recommended that EIL educators and subjects need to address this issue more because he did not know and was not confident of how to deal with these issues. He even went further by suggesting that:

> EIL needs to do something like Globish which has published a lot, in variety of languages then they can read the book and change their ideas and spread

186   *EIL students' responses to change*

to whole world and sometimes the idea will be settled and established and world Englishes can change them.

These challenges and Cheolsoo's half-flippant reference to "Globish", however, had not completely destroyed his motivation to study more about EIL and his ambition to "do something to spread the EIL". The articles written about Korean English and/or English in Korea had been inspirational and motivating, he said:

> I was also so impressed to see Korean English done by Mrs Shim and Mr Baek. I was like, 'Wow! I think I want to further studies in the EIL'. I want to contribute something by writing an essay and discussion paper on my country and comparison to native-speakers countries like Australia and US. I want to write about my current country's perspective .... That's why I'm learning EIL, so that I can write something like discussion essays so that I can publish my works in scholar's world or Google Scholar through database in this university or other universities. Currently, many foreigners came in and many Koreans still admire native-speakers from US and even hire sometimes person with bad history or something like that, but foreigners who taught English has not changed, Korean still learns English eagerously [Cheolsoo's own term] and if there's some main movement or so, Korean English may change a bit. I also want to recommend people to go to different countries like Korea and listen to the way people speak English to broaden their perspectives of English spoken in the world.

7.1.3. Who is Ogilvy?

Ogilvy was a seventh-generation Australian, born in Melbourne. He completed his secondary education at Melbourne High School, one of the most prestigious and multicultural secondary schools in Melbourne. When I asked him what his mother tongue was, he specifically said "Australian English". As students at Melbourne High School were required to study one European and Asian language, he studied German (for two years) and Bahasa Indonesia (an Indonesian language, for six years). As part of the school's extra-curricular program, he went to Yogyakarta in Indonesia for several weeks to study Bahasa Indonesia and Indonesian culture. He still intended to study the language further at tertiary level for two reasons: the geographical proximity of Indonesia and Australia and his aim to work for the department of foreign affairs and trade, which would require competence to speak in a second language. At the time of the interview, Ogilvy was in his first year of his Bachelor of Arts degree. He intended to specialise in Politics and only undertook EIL as his first-year sequence elective. Summarised first, in bullet points, are the core ideas from Ogilvy's interviews (Box 7.3).

Box 7.3. Summary of Ogilvy's views and experiences of learning EIL

(1) Ogilvy believed learning EIL was important because:

- being a resident of a multicultural city (Melbourne) and working as a diplomat in the future provide him with exposure to people from diverse linguistic and cultural backgrounds; and
- learning EIL, hopefully, would provide him with knowledge about how international students learn English, the difficulties they have, their foibles, and how he can communicate with them better (a misconception of what the program teaches and a deficit perception of speakers of varieties of Outer- and Expanding-Circle Englishes).

(2) After engaging with the lecturers' "playing-devil's-advocate" questions and critically considering the "alternate theories" presented in the subject, he had been prompted to view the importance/value of learning EIL differently. Specifically, it had prompted him to:

- broaden his horizons (his understanding of the 'organic process' of English language variation);
- critically revisit his initial native-speakerist perception of attributing the unfamiliarity of speakers of Outer- and Expanding-Circle Englishes with Australian English to their 'weaker grasp of English';
- become aware of the need for 'native-speakers' to learn different varieties of English; and
- become aware of the negative consequences (or as he said, "offences") of the creation and the teaching of a 'Global Standard English' and a 'clearer region-free accented English'.

(3) Ogilvy still experienced a struggle to adopt the principles underlying the EIL program and claimed that he still had (ingrained) 'elitist' perception of Inner-Circle varieties of English and believed strongly in the implementability of the creation and the teaching of a Global Standard English and a region-free accent.

- Though he was aware that his perception was problematic, snobbish, and elitist, he still believed that speakers of English from Outer- and Expanding-Circle countries should not be encouraged to speak their own varieties (which he perceived as "foibles") and should learn to speak native Standard English, because native-speakers "invented" English.
- He suggested that his resistance to the principles underlying the EIL program is also because his initial perception is this is 'how the outside world works', such as his:

188   *EIL students' responses to change*

- mass exposure to media and popular culture that glorified British and American English and that portrayed British English speakers as intelligent;
- emulation of the way a British English speaker speaks gets him a job; and
- observation of the negative remarks Australians were making about the broad Australian accent of the then prime minister.
- In the light of the above, Ogilvy questioned: how can we allow people to speak in their own varieties of English in a society that does not value variation?

7.1.3.1. *Initial encounter with EIL*

Ogilvy's ideal future profession, which was to work as a diplomat or an ambassador for the department of foreign affairs and trade, and "live in a culturally diverse city like Melbourne" had motivated him to undertake first-year EIL subjects. He claimed that working for this department and living in Melbourne involved "meeting people from different countries" and "being able to communicate across cultures".

After having attended the classes for two weeks, he believed that undertaking this subject would be useful and important for him because "knowing about the fact there's different varieties would help [him] see and understand how international people study English, difficulties they have in approaching English, and their sort of foibles". He reported that the first two weeks of the lesson on English language variation had raised his awareness of the fact that his variety of Australian English was not universally intelligible. To illustrate this awareness, he provided his "very interesting and fun" experience of communicating with his secondary school classmates from Singapore and Malaysia, who could not understand his Australian English and were ridiculed. He attributed their unfamiliarity to their "weaker grasp of English":

> [K]nowing that there's different varieties of English, that would be useful, because there's a lot of people from Singapore and Malaysia who come over to Australia and who definitely, who had much weaker grasp of English than myself …. It was very interesting cos like … one of them for example [his] friend Bryan, he could speak English good. So we [Ogilvy and his Australian friends] used to ridicule Bryan a bit, set him [Bryan] up to say something silly, using native Australian English and slang … didn't know what it means, which is a bit cruel, but it's a lot of fun. But I definitely notice while Bryan might have formally studied English, he [Bryan] wasn't able to grasp a lot of phrases and expressions that we Australians use.

Thus, Ogilvy believed studying about EIL would provide him with a better understanding of "the different varieties of English":

> like those from Singapore whose English is very staccato, a cut off manner, [he] can hear them thinking when they speak ... as opposed to legato, like smooth and flowing which is the way [he's] talking now, so different varieties is umm ... like ... I suppose ... [long pause] in a sense like a mixture of different sources as well because these people were studying English.

Although Ogilvy appeared to have a motivation to learn how to communicate interculturally, he also appeared to have come to the program with a different understanding/view of what the program taught. He understood the EIL program would teach him about how "NESB international students learn" English, the "difficulties" they go through in learning English, and, therefore, the "unique foibles" they have.

Since he used the term 'different varieties of English' at the beginning of the semester, I was curious to know how he understood this term. Both interviews and classroom observations allowed me to see his understanding and view of different varieties of English. During classroom observations, I noticed that he smirked and shook his head while my colleagues were presenting examples of different varieties of world Englishes during the seminars and lectures. When we talked about what I had observed, he explained that he was surprised and "gobsmacked to see that these subcultures [of] English get taught". By 'subcultures [of] English', he explained that he meant "different types of English that you guys presented in the lectures and seminars, which I think are neither correct nor spoken and used by native-speakers". Hence, during the discussions on Standard English, he asserted that a widely supported "Global Standard English" and a "region-free accent" needed to be encouraged in order "to combat these subcultures [of] English" and to make the speakers "understandable to native-speakers and sound correct". He further added:

> I don't espouse the theory that what is 'incorrect' English is not actually 'incorrect' English, these features would be seen as uneducated and these subcultures English-speaking people need to learn Global Standard English because it [subculture English] is incorrect and inaccurate form of English. Definitely not understandable to native-speakers. I'm sure using formal speech or so-called Global Standard English would be the way to combat this.

7.1.3.2. 'EIL got me thinking about the things I used to take for granted'

After having completed the subject, Ogilvy and I spoke again in an interview for this project. I asked him if he wanted to read the comments he made in the previous interviews. He agreed, and after having done so, I asked him if he had any

190 *EIL students' responses to change*

second thoughts on those comments. He explained that he "mainly agreed with all of them", but he claimed the subject had prompted him to reassess some of his views.

He asserted that he "didn't regret choosing to learn EIL". He believed it was valuable to learn EIL because it "has really got [him] thinking about the things [he] used to take for granted." Ogilvy asserted that initially the way his seminar tutor "showed different types of English" and asked him "to reflect on English language variation in [his] own social and cultural contexts" was in fact rather "shallow and a bit 'primary-schooly'" and this experience had not actually encouraged him to learn to "appreciate the diversity of English". It was during the lessons on Language and Identity as well as Language and Worldview, he claimed, that he had learnt to gain a better understanding and appreciation of the diversity of English. He argued that the way the lecturers posed the "playing-devil's-advocate questions ... like 'put-yourself-in-their-shoes or imagine-you-were-asked-to-drop-your-accent, what-would-you-do and how-would-you-feel?' ... kind of questions" and the way they highlighted "some of the alternate theories had forced [him] to think seriously about [his] perceptions" had "broadened [his] horizons and understanding of English variation". Specifically, he reported that both writing in a reflective journal and the 'playing-devil's-advocate' questions had to some extent encouraged him to become aware of the nature of English language variation and of "English being an incredibly varied language as opposed to a monolithic language".

> Thanks to the devil's questions [laughter] and partly the reflective observations I did, I think ... now I have come to understand about the different varieties of English and that these varieties don't pop up for no reasons, and there are significant cultural factors that influence the language, it's an organic process!

When we were conversing further about his current perception about the comments he made in previous interviews, he admitted that his previous view on Australian English being incomprehensible to speakers of English from Outer- and Expanding-Circle countries due to their 'weaker' grasp of English now seemed "quite superficial". He reported that he started to "give it second thoughts" when the lecturers asked him during a seminar on Accent Debates to listen to and provide a summary of a conversation between two Irishmen who were conversing in a variety of Irish English. The "massive struggle that [he] and [his] other Australian classmates had" in understanding the conversation and completing the task had prompted him to understand the superficiality of attributing a person's inability to understand Australian English solely to his/her 'grasp of English'. Something as simple as "G'day or how you're going, the weather is bloody awful outside", he argued, would not translate across to "anyone from any country regardless of their proficiency in English if that person has not studied [his] dialect of English and is not familiar with such a culturally loaded expression". This comment seems to indicate his awareness of the fact that understanding different varieties of English requires the person regardless of his/her country of origin and proficiency in English to receive an education about it (like how he was taught about Irish English in the EIL subject).

This awareness, he added, encouraged him to the view that being a so-called 'native-speaker' of English did not mean that he spoke "correct and intelligible English" or that he knew "everything about English, and [could] converse with anyone in English". Rather, one still had to learn English, especially in today's globalisation era, which, he anticipated, will influence the development of his idiolect.

> Even if I, a native-speaker of Australian English, don't understand other varieties of English like Singaporean English, it doesn't mean that they are "incorrect". As there are so many different varieties of English out there especially as globalisation continues, I'll be forced to be a learner just because we are all exposed to so many different varieties of English, my vocab will continually be expanding as I'm exposed to Indonesian English or Singaporean English or Indian English. I will keep learning as I go and will keep enriching my idiolect.

Moreover, he reported that the 'linguistic-identity-switching activity' that I had conducted in the lesson on accents and identities had "really challenged [him] to rethink" his enthusiasm for the creation and the teaching of his notion of "Global Standard English and a clearer region-free accented English for all". His struggle to participate in the 'linguistic-identity-switching activity' (see Section 5.2.3 for details of this activity) and the discussions of the struggle to participate in the activity had allowed him to have a first-hand-experience of feeling the implementation of his idea of 'a Global Standard English and a clearer region-free accented English for all' and, as he termed, "the offences" it may cause.

> I have become less enthusiastic about that idea now. It's virtually impossible to expect people to speak in one accent, I guess my initial view on creating a global region-free accent and a Global Standard English is very unfair and very unduly difficult task to put upon them. Every country has their own important cultural traits and unique linguistic elements that they bring into their version of English. So, it's difficult to distil those things. One of the ways to express your culture is via language. And thinking about the offences that teaching only variety of Standard English cause in eradicating those cultures … like how you did to us in that activity [laughter] … that activity and the discussion made me think seriously about those issues.

He also felt that this activity had provided him with opportunities to reflect on the importance and value of preserving one's own variety of English and the consequence of imperialistically replacing one's variety of English with another variety. He used the case of telling indigenous Australians' dreamtime story in Standard Australian English as an example.

> Every community or circle has its own view on what is considered to be a standard way of using language and this standard is used to

192 *EIL students' responses to change*

communicate their cultural values. Like the indigenous Aborigines, I now really understand how they feel about the teaching and learning of Standard Australian English ... I'm sure if you told the dreamtime story in Standard Australian English, it wouldn't sound anywhere near as good as it's told in like the actual tongue or their version Standard English it's designed to be told in, I think this goes for everybody, really!

From this activity, he claimed that he had "definitely learnt a useful lesson already".

However, his zealous support for the creation and the teaching of 'a Global Standard English for all' still persisted despite his awareness of the fact that it was difficult and risky to put it into practice. In addition, the fact that he "mainly agreed with all" of the comments he made in previous interviews had also further prompted me to have further conversations with him. I wanted to inquire further into his resistance towards the views advocated by the lecturers of the subjects, which he shared very openly with me.

7.1.3.3. *"I did struggle with some of the topics that you raised"*

Even though Ogilvy appeared to have become aware of English being a heterogeneous language, of the heterogeneity as an "organic process", of the "offences" that teaching one-Global-Standard-English may cause, and of the need to learn different varieties of English, further interviews reveal that he was still struggling to consistently and coherently advocate these 'alternative' views. In particular, he reported that although the lecturers had continuously emphasised in the lectures that he was encouraged to "view different varieties of English from a language perspective" rather than from a layman's perspective, he claimed that he was still hesitant and reluctant to view those differences from a language standpoint. He reported that he was very aware of this and called himself "an English snob". He still further asserted that he could not refrain from glorifying varieties of Inner-Circle English (such as BBC English) and stigmatising or marginalising other varieties of English, which he termed "subcultures English".

I did struggle with some of the topics that you raised, especially with the issue of prestige accent and English. I still believe in it, I know I am an English snob ... I know from a language standpoint, I shouldn't have looked down upon those subcultures English, those different varieties of English spoken by like Singaporeans or Indians etc., but it's too hard not to. Although I can see why this is not the way to go, I still don't think myself or the vast majority of people are ever really going to change their perceptions of that language anytime because that glorious refined BBC approach to English is great to listen to. It's like when I watch BBC World News, I just assumed that it's got better coverage because it's got the BBC approach to English. This perception has been just too deeply ingrained in me, so I don't think I can change the perception anytime soon!

EIL students' responses to change 193

Even though earlier Ogilvy claimed that he had learnt to understand that every variety of English has its own "cultural traits", and that had developed in him an interest to learn about these different varieties of English, he still strongly believed that speakers from "non-English-speaking backgrounds should not be taught and be encouraged to speak their subcultures English, and instead should learn how to speak like native English speakers or standard native English" in order to make themselves more understandable to "native-speakers". His justification for this viewpoint seemed to indicate his dismissal of unique features of World Englishes as 'foibles' and 'speed-bumps', and his strong support for an 'elitist' belief in native-speakerism and 'standard English ideology'.

> Although I had said that languages have cultural significance, I definitely don't think they should be encouraged, I don't think that people should be taught those subcultures of English, I personally don't think those subcultures should be eradicated and I don't think they should be taught, people should learn the correct standard of English so that those subcultures, foibles, and speed-bumps can gradually correct themselves. So speaking the standard native English is the correct course of action. I know it's going to sound elitist, I would probably expect them to come close my version of English than my version of English to theirs. My perception is still we are the Inner-Circle English countries, we created and invent English, so it's up to them to emulate our English, not the other way round, they should not be using their foibles or speed-bumps I said before!

Even as a so-called 'native-speaker', he claimed that he was not also satisfied with the "traits" that he had in the way he spoke English. He desired to change it into a "region accent-free English", which, according to him, would be either "American movie style English" or "British English".

> I don't sound prestige and cleverer, I still pause, and I use 'like', and umms a lot. I know that's the nature of speaking, but it should not be. In future, I want to be an ambassador so I have to sound educated, accent-free, clever. I think I would be aiming for that movie style of accent, like the American films, that's accent-free, or British English, which sounds intelligent.

As we conversed further, the interviews revealed that "what was out there [outside classrooms]" seemed to have prompted Ogilvy to experience tensions and resistance towards the views advocated by the EIL lecturers and the set of principles underpinning the program. He claimed that now he was "very well aware of the new perspectives about the English language" that the subject had "got him thinking" and that he "should not see things in a superficial way after learning EIL". Nevertheless, he was insistent that "the outside world does not welcome this perspective you [pointing at me] bring to the table". Firstly, his "mass exposure to the mass media and popular culture that propagate the view of speaking British and American English symbolises that one is intelligent", and his success

194   *EIL students' responses to change*

in getting employed as a result of speaking English with a British accent, had prompted him to develop deeper resistance towards what he had learnt in the EIL program. He claimed that learning about "subculture English is not necessary" because

> the reality is and the matter is I am going to look down on you if you don't speak native English and a lot of people out there are going to look down on you if you speak what is perceived to be inaccurate. And that's going to harm you in future.

Secondly, his observations with regard to the negative remarks/comments that many Australians had been making about the accent of the then prime minister of Australia (Julia Gillard) – he referred to this as a "boganish accent" (i.e. a broad Australian accent) – had also prompted him to develop a view that he and those "subcultures English speakers have to drop their own English and learn to speak better English". He again emphasised that he needed to view this issue from an EIL perspective, but his future career working in the diplomatic corps and the negative perceptions that certain groups of Australians (including himself) had of the then prime minister's accent had prompted him to question the extent to which the EIL perspective would be implementable outside classrooms.

> I mean EIL has taught me that English is not monolithic and we need to appreciate the diversity, but look at Julia Gillard, and look at the negative things that people give her because of boganish accent, I think I would fail her as a diplomat, or if I speak like that, I would fail to become a diplomat, so I would need to speak English with a neutral accent and a positively-perceived accent. I looked down on her so I don't want to be looked down on by others when I speak. Linguistically this is not the way to go, but this is what the vast majority of people out there think.

In response to the perspectives that the subject had offered to him, he questioned "how can people be allowed to speak in their own varieties of English in a society that does not have a positive value attached to language variation?" Further, he argued that, "if [he] had to learn EIL again, [he] would actually like to know more about this [the question he posed earlier] rather than just simply about these people from these countries speak differently, those people from those countries speak differently."

7.2. Third-year students

In this section, I present the cases of two of my third-year EIL students – Phil and Tomoko – who specialised in EIL for their undergraduate arts degree. The reason I chose these two students is because at the time of data collection, they were the only students who had graduated with a major in EIL. The rest of my students in third-year class mostly chose the subjects as their 'one-off' electives.

I also deliberately included final-year students in my study to see if the attitudes and understandings of these students, who had three years of sustained exposure to EIL teaching and learning, would be different from those of the first-year students. Would these final-year students be less weighed down by prejudices, less influenced by ethnocentricity, or less prone to native-speakerist assumptions? The following presents an account of the data I gathered from two in-depth interviews with Phil and Tomoko.

7.2.1. Who is Phil?

Phil was born in Brunei, but moved to Australia when he was about five years old. Because he had spent most of his life in Australia, he considered himself an Australian. Though he understood and could speak Mandarin, he predominantly used English to communicate with his parents and siblings. He also spoke Japanese and had visited Japan several times as a student and a tourist. At the time of our interview, Phil had already completed his undergraduate arts degree with specialisation in Japanese Studies and EIL. As he did not have a teaching qualification but wanted to teach English in Japan after his study, Phil completed an intensive University of Cambridge English language teacher-education course called CELTA (Certificate for English Language Teaching to Adults) in Melbourne. He had also taught English to international students who studied in Australia. Summarised first, in bullet points, are the core ideas from Phil's interviews (Box 7.4).

7.2.1.1. "I'm the king of the world mentality"

When I asked Phil about why he had chosen to study EIL, he reported that initially he "was just only looking for an outlet"; his friend had told him that EIL was the subject he could "score great marks in because English is [his] first language". After having attended the first lecture and tutorial of the first-year EIL subject, he remembered thinking that studying this subject would be valuable because it would "bump up my grades". After seeing his classmates were "a bunch of non-English-speaking international kids", he described himself as "becoming very cocky" and recalled thinking: if he "can't get an HD [High Distinction] in the subject, I am an idiot".

> [T]he room is full of fobs [fresh-off-the-boats] and these guys can't even speak English. And when my other friends found out, they're like, 'English as an International Language? What is that? Phil, what the hell are you doing in the unit which is for the fobs?' ... A lot of my friends think that it is actually a joke. And I'm like, 'yeah, I'm kicking arse'. So, in the class, since I am very confident in my English ability, I took over the classroom and discussions.

He reported that he had "started to see something different" after having attended several tutorials, but his "I'm the king of the world mentality" was

196   *EIL students' responses to change*

Box 7.4. Summary of Phil's views and experiences of learning EIL

(1) Phil believed that learning EIL was important to him because of his intended future profession as an English teacher in Japan and the limitation of CELTA in preparing him to be an English teacher.

(2) The reflection activities, the opportunities given to students to share their experiences without any fear of being ridiculed, the controversial readings had prompted him to:

- understand the diversity of English;
- challenge his "I'm the king of the world" mentality;
- learn about his classmates from other countries and challenge how he used to think about them: rich fobs who don't speak English;
- raise his awareness of "what is really going out there in the real world" and the practice of linguicism; and
- raise his awareness of the effort of scholars to make changes happen and therefore encourage him to try to make changes happen.

(3) EIL is a 'risky' business because:

- the EIL ideology is not shared by his peers and other fellow teachers;
- his students perceive subscribing to the dominant communicative conventions is a way to perform well and survive in the university; and
- discrimination persists and therefore not everybody is open and ready enough for changes.

---

still dominant. Since he grew up in Australia, he believed that he still "had more advantages compared to [his] classmates who did not speak English as their native tongue". He realised that his "mentality and arrogance" had caused him to perform unsatisfactorily in the assignments. He was surprised to read his lecturer's comments on his assignment:

> I could not believe what one of you said about my work. It was like, you take things for granted. Your approaches and arguments are way too superficial and have not demonstrated critical and in-depth understanding of language variation.

Interestingly, this comment had not de-motivated him to further his study in EIL. As I described in Phil's profile, he had chosen to specialise in EIL for his undergraduate arts degree. When I asked him why he had chosen to specialise in EIL, he reported that there were several reasons.

7.2.1.2. Experiencing and initiating change from 'someone cocky like me'

One reason for Phil to continue studying and specialising in EIL was his choice of future profession. He intended to be an English teacher in Japan.

> This program relates to what I want to do later as an English teacher or what I am currently working as an English teacher. I have always wanted to look at and challenge the way English is taught in Japan.

He claimed that teaching English was more than just knowing how to teach the language. Phil claimed that the CELTA program he had already completed had not provided him with sufficient knowledge, attitudes, and skills to enter the English language teaching profession because "there are a lot of issues out there, that is still existing which CELTA sort of did not discuss". When I asked him to clarify what he meant by the "issues out there", he talked about his own "limitations as an English teacher", which he never thought about before and which he wanted to improve. These 'issues' were mostly related to his awareness of the sociolinguistic reality of English, perceptions of his students and people in general from different lingua-cultural backgrounds.

> A lot of stuff that we were doing in EIL really uncover the weaknesses that I had as an English teacher, which CELTA did not really talk about. You know, you can't take things for granted, like the way I understood English, the way I viewed people and the way I viewed my classmates from different cultures, you know, the fobs who don't speak English or speak English with weird accent. Every time we're in EIL class, through discussions in your classes especially in the first year, things started to spark. For example, I started to think about ways of how in my past, in my experience of how I discriminated against my students and other people. So, EIL started to show these weaknesses that I used to employ as an English teacher.

Further conversations revealed that the changes in the way Phil understood and viewed English, himself, as well as speakers of English from Outer- and Expanding-Circle countries whom he had encountered as a result of studying EIL, had prompted him to view learning EIL as "invaluable and important". Over the course of three (two hours each) interviews with me, he showed that not only had the curricula prompted him to change his perceptions within the course but had also inspired him to act on these perceptions outside the classroom. In his words, the EIL program

> is very useful for me because it's more than just teaching us language awareness, and being open, but also teaching us to change our perceptions. And a lot of things are not just about perceptions of English and yourself, but also perceptions on life, and the way you work and how you handle work, university work, and working outside.

198   *EIL students' responses to change*

Firstly, Phil reported that the reflection activities or reflective assessment tasks that he had completed throughout his three years of studying in the program had given him "the opportunity to look back at or reassess [himself] and [his] life, reflect on what [he] had done, and then learn from there". He felt that "doing the whole course from start to finish with those reflection tasks helped [him] learn and understand all these different ways of, not just the way we speak, but also the way we see, the way we listen, or the way we write, and the importance of maintaining this diversity". Specifically, Phil reported that the lecturers' endless attempts to encourage him to critically reflect on how he used English and on his observations of how other people from similar and/ or different cultural backgrounds used English "had taken [him] away from that ego, from the English language". He used to believe that that there was only one variety of English – i.e. 'Standard English' – and this English was spoken by all 'native-speakers' including himself. As he progressed through the course, he claimed that he had been prompted to challenge his previous view and to develop awareness of the pluralistic nature of English, including his own English.

> I used to believe in one single Standard English and that whole assimilation into the society, that whole do the way Romans do thing, that fobs who don't speak English and speak English with weird accent need to lose your accent, become part of us and speak Standard native English. But now, I realise that there are lots and lots of different versions of English and different Standard Englishes. And I realise that I've encountered different varieties of English in everyday life, spoken by people from different countries. we have 'English', but we are all different, even you know, the so-called native-speakers, like, e.g. when I was at a bar, e.g. I even speak different style of English, different from the one I'm using to talk to you now. So, my English is influenced by where I've been, where I've gone, whom I've met, what I've done, so it's like, through all that, I make it myself.

Further conversations also revealed that his observation of the pluralistic nature of English, especially "after learning that unit on World Englishes", had encouraged him to challenge the way he used to perceive himself or as he termed, "I'm the king of the world mentality". As Phil stated before, because he grew up in Australia and therefore believed that he had a high level of proficiency of English, he regarded himself as a speaker/user of Standard English. However, the reflections and observations about the changing nature of English he had been asked to undertake throughout his study in the program had prompted him to view himself as a learner and inspired him to become more open and willing to learn further.

> I no longer look at language in terms of mastery or weakness because it's English, a language that will change, and you always learn it, even when you're speaking. So I still consider myself learning in every aspect because there's [*sic*]

a million of other people I haven't met from different nations. I still want to travel, want to see different world and want to meet new different people. And I probably won't dare to say that my English is complete. So, I'm still learning.

Secondly, another aspect of the teaching that Phil believed made learning EIL crucial, especially to "someone cocky like me" was "the way lecturers give students opportunities to say what they thought without any fear of being ridiculed or like you're wrong". It is because of this kind of approach, he argued, that he felt encouraged to challenge his initial ethnocentric perceptions of speakers of English from Outer- and Expanding-Circle countries. He used to view his classmates who grew up in Outer- and Expanding-Circle countries as the "rich international fobs who don't speak English" whom he even 'graded' as "the back-rows".

> Many times when I looked back at them, I used to think that grade them, I used to think of them like back-rows. You know … there are back-row people, middle-row people, and front-row people. The front-row people are the ones who are interested, middle-row, they do most of their job. The back-row, they're not really interested in learning.

However, he claimed that the approaches used by the various lecturers had allowed his classmates from other countries to share, without any fear, their thoughts and experiences. Previously, he had been unaware of these experiences, and he had learnt a great deal from hearing about them.

> Most importantly, you guys [lecturers] do that a lot, which allows me to hear good ideas from my classmates, as in, like, the way they feel. A lot of what I find in EIL class is the students want to talk and they did open up their hearts. When you have that difficulty, EIL opens up that difficulty international students and even local students have if they take part in it. They open up their wounds. Because there is this gap in the society where you feel like 'I'm all alone', there's no one that understands me, so they come to this EIL class where there are a lot of people who understand them, they're opening up, they're telling their thoughts, they're telling their ideas, and it's like hearing these thoughts from these wounds and when I'm in the class, I hear all these great ideas and they're revealing themselves, they're revealing these holes.

One of the 'stories and experiences' that he clearly remembered and from which he had gained knowledge was of his classmates from Hong Kong. He reported that the sharing of English language teaching experiences in Hong Kong and their observations of the English language teaching situations in Hong Kong had largely impressed him and challenged his initially condescending views about his classmates who had grown up in other countries.

> When the 'back-row' people talked, they brought up issues that I have never thought about it that way, like there was one case where they're talking

about Hong Kong and how teaching is evolving in Hong Kong and they talked about the English teaching industry, how it's growing, and how people work in it ... and I found out that one of the girls taught English to other Hong Kong students and helped her students go through learning process. So, she was great. And instead of like me thinking about them like they're a bunch of fobs, I started to think that holy crap ... these people have education. This person is probably way smarter than me and I start to think that I am no longer on top of the world, I'm probably below everybody else.

He claimed that not only had these stories, experiences, and thoughts shared by his classmates from other countries driven him to "question [his] mentality of putting people into certain 'frameworks', but he had also "become more open and willing to learn from different cultures" because "there's a lot of information out there in the world which you'll lose out if you stay close-minded".

However, as open and humble as Phil might have become, there still seemed to be a subtle sign of his deficit constructions of cultural and linguistic differences. Although he demonstrated enthusiasm in listening to and learning from the stories and experiences of his classmates from different backgrounds, his use of "wounds", "holes", and "difficulties" to describe those stories and experiences and his view of them as "great ideas" may imply that he felt sorry to hear these 'marginalised groups' struggling to have their differences recognised. These 'difficulties', 'wounds', 'holes' would less likely be experienced by the so-called 'local students', which can be seen in "EIL opens up difficulty ... local students have *if* they take part in". Figuratively, it is as if EIL students, especially the so-called 'international students', were the injured patients who attended a 'clinic' (EIL program) to seek treatment for their wounds/holes and to obtain sympathy from the 'local students' for the difficulties those wounds/holes had caused them. To avoid misinterpretation or, worse, accusation, I emailed Phil a copy of my writing about him. (At that time, he was indeed teaching English in Japan.) I asked him to check and ensure that I had not misrepresented or misinterpreted what he said. His email response to my interpretation verified my interpretation (Figure 7.1).

Phil felt that the 'controversial' prescribed readings he had read throughout his three years of study in EIL had not only raised his awareness of the pluralistic nature of English and the 'reality', but also brought to his attention the amount

> *Yeah Roby, I agree with how you interpret my views. I don't think I was as advanced as I am now in looking at things. Now, I think what I said before is a bit "over" (if you know what I mean), but at that time, the [Phil] that you were talking to still had a very small piece of his "I'm-the-king-of-the-world" mentality. So, it is still quite negative, like you wrote somewhere a 'deficit' way of thinking. But I meant it in a nice way though, I listened to their negative experiences and sad stories, and they were important for me to understand, they needed people like myself to understand them, otherwise, I wouldn't have cleaned up my act. :)*

Figure 7.1 Phil's email response

EIL students' responses to change 201

of effort EIL educators had put in raising his awareness of issues he had never thought about before or he took for granted. He reported that the journal article by Geneva Smitherman (1974) on the issue of inequality in English language education in the United States in African American English, had "really touched [him], opened up [his] eyes a lot". It had "made [him] fully aware of what's going out there in the world like the politics at work or things that I didn't realise before". I asked him to describe what kind of "things" the article had made him realise. He reported that the article had brought to his attention the native-speakerism ideology embedded within his previous views on "all international Asian guys can't speak English well" and in his response ("as long as you practise with native-speakers, you'll be okay") to his friend who was "ashamed of his 'accented' English", which he used to think as "normal". He believed that those issues raised in the readings had further encouraged him to try to make changes happen.

> There are people and professors out there, like Geneva, working hard to make change, trying to make change happen and if I keep on thinking this negative view and keep thinking that nothing is going to happen if we keep waiting for something to happen. It's not going to unless we do something about it. That's why I want to take the steps trying to make these changes happen.

Interestingly, Phil did attempt to bring EIL into his daily life. The following story that he shared seems to indicate his attempt in using his knowledge of EIL to instil in his Japanese friends (whom he met during his visit to Japan) confidence to pursue their ambition of becoming English teachers.

> My friends were like: I wanted to be an English teacher. And then I said, 'What's stopping you?' They said, 'Because I don't speak English that well'. And I thought that this comes to the issue of how they understand which English is the 'right' English? So, I ask them that question, 'Which English'? They were like, 'What do you mean' and then I said, 'Which English do you want to teach? Cos there are billions of Englishes out there, what English do you want to teach? And what English do your students want to learn?' Since they still look confused, I asked them what English do you speak? They are like 'Well, I think I speak Japanese English' and I said 'Yeah, good'. And I told them that 'I speak my own English because I have different experiences that have scalped my way. I watch American TV, so I have a lot of Americanisms in the way I speak even though I was brought up in Australia. When I speak to Japanese people, I sometimes put some Japanese mannerism in the way I speak English. All this influence my English, so it's 'unique'. And I tell them that 'your English is yours', this is your English, be proud of it, don't be afraid, don't think that you need to meet some shadow figure. When they started to realise that, I can see their confidence growing and enthusiasm in becoming an English teacher.

202 EIL students' responses to change

Phil's attempt to promote pluricentricity was further seen in his response to the comment made by his classmate, whose first mission as an English teacher was to change her students' 'weird' English accent.

> [W]hen you're in a classroom, you no longer should think that those students are weak because of they have accent. Or making comments like I can't understand him or those Indians students are idiot. You can't have that. You can't have none of that. You have to be as neutral, and as understanding, and as equal and have the ability to listen to everybody. So, you need to listen, digest, clarify, and help them develop their own flavour.

Phil described that he was a bit "disturbed" by that comment and this experience had urged him to "spread EIL to the public".

7.2.1.3. EIL is 'a risky business'

Similar to other participants in this study, although Phil reported that he had altered his views on the diversity of English and challenged his initial ethnocentric perceptions towards speakers of English from other countries, he felt that there were still some aspects of the principles advocated by the program with which he was struggling. Interestingly, the subject in which he encountered most challenges was the subject that I taught and coordinated – Writing Across Cultures – which focused on the diversification of academic and professional writing conventions in English. He reported that he still found it difficult to implement what he had learnt in this subject into his current and future classes:

> it's always a difficult issue, I'm still trying to work out a way to teach students how to be proud of themselves, and how to be themselves in their writing. In speaking, I guess it would be easy, but when it comes to writing, it's always a difficult issue.

He claimed that it was important for his students to assert their own identity in their writing and for his students to feel that the writing conventions they bring to the classrooms were respected by teachers. However, he was aware that this view or belief was not necessarily shared by some students and teachers that he knew. He argued that some students, including his own classmates, had no choice but to unquestioningly subscribe to the dominant Anglo-Australian conventions of written communication in order to perform well or even just to 'survive' in academic life.

> At the end of the day, students are here to get marks. If they don't do the way the Romans do, other teachers who are not sympathetic or don't understand this EIL view of writing would be like 'No, you're wrong', then the students would be in trouble. Or like IELTS, you don't write in the required style, you're doomed. So, I'm not sure how I can encourage my students

EIL students' responses to change   203

to try to get good marks but using this new mentality of EIL. It's indeed a challenging aspect.

Phil asserted that the knowledge he had acquired from that subject "put [him] in a very difficult spot", because as an English teacher, he would be blamed if the writings of those students who graduated from his English class did not adhere to the dominant writing conventions. He claimed that asking students to write according to their own culturally appropriate conventions and demanding teachers to embrace diverse written conventions was "a risky business". Thus, what he said he would do as an English teacher is to raise students' awareness of "this power thing". In saying that, he also implied that this was what EIL lecturers could have done *more*.

> Although I'm doing English as an International Language and I would be teaching my students to be proud of themselves, but no matter what we do, nothing's gonna change, people will just keep on killing each other, keep on being racist to each other, and people keep doing that cos that's the way human beings operate. So, we still have to teach the students to learn to be aware of the power issues, because if they're aware of it, they know the pitfalls. And because you know about these pitfalls, you can learn to prevent and resolve these issues, like the article by Geneva, rather than simply talking about the way she writes is in an African American English, we need to talk about the issues of inequality in language education raised in her article.

Phil further argued that even if "you [referring to me, as his former lecturer] tried to make me and my classmates aware or I later on as a teacher tried to make my students aware of this EIL thing or power thing", it would still be a challenging journey because "not everybody was ready enough for a sudden change or not aware of change because as I said before, people keep on being racist to each other. Like a case of my DipEd [Diploma of Education – initial teacher education degree] ESL [English as a Second Language] classmate labelled his students, who are refugees and migrants, during a classroom presentation as 'bastards who don't speak English'". Therefore, he suggested that "perhaps there should be more conversations about this in your [pointing at me] class cos I felt this is still somewhat lacking in the program" He then shared his proposal of how to make changes happen "subtly":

> I know I can't change everybody, I know I can't help everybody, same like what I mentioned about EIL program. We can't just grab them and start demanding change. We want you to go out there and make people change slowly; just start small with your friends, with your family, people you often meet up with, small things. We don't want people demonstrating on the street. It's better to teach people slowly and subtly you know … reveal different things here and there so that people start to become aware of it.

204   *EIL students' responses to change*

7.2.2. Who is Tomoko?

Tomoko was born in China but moved to Japan when she was "really young". She described herself as "quarter Japanese and the rest Chinese" because her mother was Chinese but her father was half Japanese and Chinese. She spoke Japanese, Chinese, and English. She claimed that her Japanese was more dominant and proficient than her Chinese because she was educated in Japanese and used Chinese only to communicate with her family. However, she reported that sometimes she could express herself better in Chinese than in Japanese because some words or expressions in Chinese were not available in Japanese. She had been learning English since primary school. She was sent by her parents to the United States to study Grade 6 (upper primary) for half a year. During her stay in America, she had to study English from scratch, as English was not taught as a school subject in primary school in Japan. She had been in Australia for seven years and had completed her secondary schooling in Sydney. At the time of the interview, she had already completed her arts degree, specialising in Chinese Studies and EIL. She had also been offered a place to study a pre-service teacher-education degree at one of the large universities in Melbourne. She began this course as soon as she had graduated, but in the second week of the first semester, she withdrew from it (for a particular reason that will be discussed in the subsequent analysis). Summarised first, in bullet points, are the core ideas from Tomoko's interviews (Box 7.5).

7.2.2.1. Encountering EIL and experiencing change

Since Tomoko's ultimate goal was to become an ESL teacher in Australia, she was initially advised by her course advisor to study either EIL or Linguistics. Since she was a 'NESB international student', she was later recommended to study EIL instead of Linguistics because "it's a program only for international students and if it has 'international' attached to it, they'll correct our English and help us improve it". After attending a few lectures of her first EIL subject, she was "very surprised" to find out that the program was not teaching what she expected and what she had been told. This, however, had not stopped Tomoko from studying EIL further. In fact, she now had a different purpose for studying EIL and had different reasons for choosing to specialise in it.

Firstly, Tomoko had been dissatisfied with the quality of English language teaching in her secondary schools in Japan and Australia (as an international student). She began to feel that learning about EIL may be important. She reported that in the secondary school she attended in Australia, she had had a very "hard time" because the school did not have any "proper ESL class". When I asked what she meant by 'proper', she explained that her teacher had had a superficial understanding of the students' cultural and linguistic backgrounds. In her secondary school English class in Japan, the way her 'Anglo teacher' taught English was "really torturing time" and had caused her to feel less confident in using English.

> When I was in junior school, because it was really torturing time seriously, especially the speaking course, cos in my high school, we would have Japanese teacher and an Anglo teacher standing next to her. And every time we pronounce something, he will come and see our pronunciation and listen to our pronunciation. And if it's 'wrong', he would say: 'No, no, you come out'. So, he'll select few students who can't really pronounce the words and he'll give us special lesson about the accent ... you have to go out and practise for a long time. I was really worried to speak English. When I speak something in a different accent, the teachers will actually come and say, 'No!! it's not the way you should pronounce it'. So, I was frustrated. I hope I can change this.

This particular teaching approach had prompted her to develop a perception that in order to "speak English perfectly, you need to sound like a native and your accent is simply wrong". Therefore, she believed that studying in the EIL program would hopefully be able to provide her with some knowledge of how to make changes to the situation she had described in the future.

Another factor that had motivated her to specialise in EIL was her curiosity and willingness to know and learn more about how to effectively communicate in English and teach English in multicultural settings. In her words, she felt this was "very important for me because I am going to become a teacher in Australia, which is a multicultural society unlike in Japan". "As a child who grew up in a monocultural society like Japan", she claimed this was not something that she would need to think about. Therefore, as she progressed in her study in EIL, she had been exposed to a lot of "interesting but difficult" questions by her first-year lecturers. She was curious and keen to learn more.

> Something that interested me and made me want to learn more was the lots of questions that you guys asked which popped up in my mind all the time. This is actually my favourite part because you present questions on how to manage, resolve differences. These questions I still think that we have not resolved and am interested in knowing how you resolve this question. Like we have cultural diversity, how to speak and write, we know we are different, we are aware of the differences, but if other people are not aware of this difference, how are we going to talk with them? So, I'm actually interested to see how you resolve.

Secondly, Tomoko claimed that her main reason for viewing the need to know and learn about EIL and for specialising in the discipline was the changes that learning in this program had brought to her initial perceptions of the diversity of English and its users. The readings, especially "the first year first semester readings have taught me a lot and have changed my view a lot about the English language". She reported that she used to view English as the only language spoken by "the white people population", whom she used to consider as "the only true and legitimate speakers of English". This perception together with her

Box 7.5. Summary of Tomoko's views and experiences of learning EIL

(1) Tomoko perceived EIL to be important because:

- her goal was to become an English as a Second Language (ESL) teacher and to bring changes to the quality of English language teaching;
- she was curious and willing to know and learn more about how to effectively communicate in English and teach in multicultural settings.

(2) The readings, the practice of sharing language using/learning experiences, and the teaching approach in the EIL course exposed her to different angles of understanding communication in English, which had:

- raised her awareness of different varieties of English and challenged her initial view of English as the language of "white people";
- encouraged and inspired her to learn to understand and appreciate her own use of English as a multilingual speaker of English; and to gain self-confidence and positive self-esteem;
- given her opportunities to learn to understand different worldviews and challenge her hierarchical images of division ('native-speakers' as more superior to non-native-speakers); and
- given her a chance to slowly change her views on English.

(3) Learning EIL was a challenge because "in reality, a lot of things aren't really what we wish it to be".

- She was unsure if EIL can be applied due to racial and linguistic differences not being respected and appreciated in the society and by the people with whom she interacted (e.g. shop assistants, university lecturers, and 'native' English-speaking classmates).
- As a result of her previous English language education, she still perceived being a multilingual user of English as a disadvantage and therefore she still claimed that she needed to be given 'special treatment'.
- Even though the EIL program talked about a bit about politics, it did not seem to be useful because it was a reality and there was nothing she (even as a teacher) could do about it. She did, however, suggest that lecturers should provide more opportunities to discuss those issues in class rather than avoid them.

EIL students' responses to change   207

experiences of living in Australia was damaging to her self-esteem and prompted her to perceive herself as inferior.

> Since I came to Australia, I always felt that I am a bit lower grade, my self-esteem was damaged because I was told that I couldn't speak English as well as the other local people and I felt that I had some 'accent' [laughter] and I tried to mimic so hard and I couldn't use their slang and I felt that if I can't speak English like Australians, I'd be behind them.

As our conversation progressed, Tomoko provided an example of how the ethnocentric comments made by her university lecturers and 'native' English-speaking classmates with whom she was studying had further confirmed her previous perception of English and her feeling of inferiority:

> because many times in my university life, many people like my lecturers and local classmates told me that I have problems with the way I use English to put forward my arguments and that we, Japanese people, don't think critically. So, I always thought that it is because I was from Japan and Japanese people don't argue or we don't use straight words to say something.

Before studying EIL, she believed that her previous perception was true even though she disliked this idea. While studying EIL, the readings on English language variation, she felt, had prompted her to develop awareness of different varieties of English and had to some extent challenged her previous perception of English as the language of the "white people".

> I used to think that American, British or the Inner-Circle people, are the only English speakers in the world and a good communicator in English is someone who speaks English with their accent, slang, and everything. But that Kachru's circles and the readings about Englishes changed my view a lot, you know, to actually learn the fact that there are also many English spoken in Outer- and Expanding-Circle countries and they are more than Inner-Circle people. I was very surprised. And this is very important for us to understand. Now, I know English is belong to everyone, now I know … the English is not belonging to their language, but I didn't know before.

To reconfirm that she actually believed in what she just said, I asked her to provide an example of how she understood English as no longer just the language of "*white people*". She reported that she actually struggled to come to terms with this view when she first learnt about it in the first year of her EIL studies. This view was in fact confirmed by her experiences of reading extracts from a novel written by a Chinese author in English to her 'native' English-speaking Australian classmate, who could not understand what had been read to her.

> It's very funny ummm … before I read this English novel written by umm … Chinese people. I think … I read the book before I had class with language

208 *EIL students' responses to change*

and culture, I studied that course and I went back to read again and I felt ooooooohhhhh ... yeaaaaah ... I know why he writes this way! And I read this specific paragraph to my friend, a native-speaker, do you understand what this means? She was like 'No, what does that mean?' I was like 'Ooooohhh ... but that is English, you ... you don't understand', she was like 'No idea' ... now, I know, that's the difference, and he writes in English, publish it in English country. If you call yourself the owner of the language, you'd know it right? So, I think the program really really helps me understand this issue.

She claimed that if she had not studied EIL, she would have actually blamed the author for "writing non-native English which is incorrect".

Tomoko further argued that not only had the readings in the EIL program developed her awareness of the diversity of English, they also seemed to have encouraged and inspired her to learn to understand and appreciate her own use of English, and to gain self-confidence and positive self-esteem along the way.

Actually knowing about this helped me feel a lot better and helped me accept myself better. I have learnt to appreciate the language like the accent I have and the culture I bring in with myself. I had to come to understand why I speak the way I do. Because I have multilingual background with myself, when I speak English I will have a lot of my cultural expressions brought in to English conversation. For example, even though I sometimes use ambiguous expressions in putting forward my arguments in writing essay, it doesn't mean I don't think critically.

Tomoko had initially perceived the practice of bringing one's own cultural norms into English – speaking one's mother tongue in English (Smith, 2003) – was "wrong" because "when you speak English, you've got to mimic you know the 'native-speakers'". However, her positive self-esteem and appreciation of her own English as a reflection of her cultural norms and multilinguality could be further seen in the way she emphasised the importance of showing originality in using English, which, at the same time, signalled her awareness of the nature of language variation.

People should not be afraid of using their own characteristics from their culture or their variety in their communication and really being 'original'. Being very original ... not hiding your own identity and your own cultural essence into your language, and not afraid to put that into your English and your communication. And that's actually a plus and also that's why English is diverse.

In addition, the reason why she claimed she had changed her view had also been influenced by one of her lecturer's teaching approach that provided her with exposure to different angles of understanding communication in English. She believed that even though the readings were "quite influential ... they seemed to send out only one message". This exposure to different range of views, had encouraged her to understand the strengths and limitations of the different perspectives and to take responsibility in choosing the one that made more sense to her.

> If I was told that I should not perceive native-speakers as the original speaker of English or that I should not be ashamed of my accent and try to make that my view, I would have dropped it and stuck to this view forever without knowing what was wrong with that. Even if you [pointing at me] told me that was wrong, without considering other options, again, that would not change my mind. But I clearly remember never in our class you force us to accept the EIL view or to say that … having accent is good or something like that …. But what you are giving us options to choose what kind of people you want to be, and you are giving us more arguments and more views from different scholars, the pluses and minuses, and telling us what's going on in the world as the situations of English as an International Language and telling us that how we originally thought one only one option. What you do is to help us understand the view that we had before and give us other perspectives. I think it helps me understand different views and be more open with different views. So, I slowly understood the EIL view and at the same time understood the non-EIL view. That's why I find it more helpful in helping me understanding differences and to choose the ones that I could see the point and feel comfortable with, which is now the EIL view.

She concluded that if her previous ESL teacher in Japan or Australia raised her awareness of different varieties of English and different perspectives of communication in English using the above teaching approach, she would have been far more confident. This was also exactly why she wanted to specialise in EIL in the hope that she, as an English teacher, would adopt this approach in her teaching.

> In future, I'd never force my students to learn one particular English. For example, sometimes I would help my friends with their English and what I realised is now I would not say to my friend you never say that, you never do this or something like this, I would be more flexible, I think you can say this, but some other people would say something different because of blah … blah … blah, so, it's up to you, you decide whichever you feel comfortable with.

Furthermore, Tomoko claimed that her knowledge of EIL and her understanding of the nature of English language variation had to some extent prompted her to challenge her own perceptions of speakers of English from other 'racial groups': "I know this sounds really bad, but I have to say that EIL has helped me become less judgemental and accepted other races better". She reported that, before learning EIL, she used to have 'ranks' for different racial groups and for English that these groups speak.

210   *EIL students' responses to change*

> When I came to Australia, I see a lot of multicultural people and I feel I had a label, white people are superior and then maybe Asians [laughter] and the rest of them are you know I was really really bad ... [laughter] If people have their accent or if they are not really fluent in speaking native English or in communication, I would just like okay, okay, please don't speak, I was really bad.

However, Tomoko acknowledged that the approaches used by the lecturers to teaching EIL that "allow people to share their experiences" had further provided her opportunities to listen to and understand different cultural worldviews as well as to critically revisit her perceptions of speakers of Englishes from different cultural backgrounds.

> We have a lot of group activities, we can share our opinion with other people, that was really helpful. If I didn't have that, I wouldn't know that there are other arguments, there are other people thinking the other way and I would ... if we didn't have that opportunity, the only opinion and view that matters is mine, I would think that mine is the only better option. Sharing experiences is very good ... I realise that many people in our class are from very, very different cultural and language backgrounds and their experiences are really different from what I had or what you might have thought or, so that sharing experiences open up our views and change my views about these people, about their Englishes as well. So, I should not be judgemental.

She then provided an example of her 'Language and Culture' class in which the sharing of experiences also allowed her to challenge some stereotypical images she had of others:

> [t]he language and culture class, like figurative and metaphor, and that's very specific culture related and it's very interesting to see people use different metaphors when they speak English and you never know sometimes from different culture, they use similar metaphors in English. You'd understand, even you don't know their culture, but they are similar to your culture, and use similar metaphors. And through the presentation, you know every lecture we have a presentation and people talk about their culture and it's very, very interesting and very helpful in challenging my surface-level views on other cultures.

Therefore, Tomoko argued that in addition to displaying originality in using English in intercultural communicative contexts, one also "should not judge others based on their language and race and should perceive all speakers of English as equal". This was "an important lesson of EIL I'd learnt and I want my students to think [about]". In addition, she claimed that she had learnt to perceive all speakers of English from different racial groups as equal and to develop the effort and patience to communicate with speakers of other varieties of English with which she was not familiar.

I could now accept other races, other accents, and became more patient, I could listen to people, I tried to understand because even the expressions is different, they still have some meanings from their own cultural backgrounds or they mean something, and I try to understand more.

7.2.2.2. 'In reality, a lot of things aren't really what we wish it to be'

Although Tomoko had experienced changes in her understanding of English and her views towards the diversity of English and its users after engaging within the EIL curricula for three years, the interviews also revealed she had encountered several challenges in embracing the views advocated by her EIL lecturers and in implementing them outside the classroom. When she first started to learn about different varieties of English, she was under the impression that these varieties of English had already been legitimately recognised by people in the society in which she lived.

> I learnt EIL from first year and I thought … you know, worlds are more accepting the other varieties and I remember in communication class, I thought people are accepting different varieties. So, I became very confident about myself.

However, she was not really sure if she could confidently bring her knowledge outside the EIL classes because "in reality, a lot of things aren't really what we wish it to be, it was really sad". Even though she reported that she had learnt "to present [her] own voice and to be proud to be different", she still believed that she was living in "the native-speakers era". In this 'era', it was difficult for her "non-native English-speaking" voice to be heard. Tomoko shared two examples to illustrate this point. The first example was her encounter with a shop assistant who 'corrected' her English pronunciation, which she defended, but her defence was dismissed by the shop assistant.

> I was ordering something in Oakleigh [a suburb in Melbourne where she lives] and said something, I can't remember the food name, it's an English name but anyway, I know that the way I pronounce it is different from how that guy would pronounce it. And he was trying to lecture me the way they pronounce it and he said the way you said English is wrong … and he was really stubborn and I was like … that's the way you speak it and I have my own way of pronouncing it, and don't force that to me and to other people. But he didn't listen of course.

The second example came from Tomoko's short time in a teacher-education degree from which she withdrew in the second teaching week of the course. In her ESL teaching methodology class, she was "forced by [her] lecturer to adopt her [the lecturer's] view which is so native-speakers-oriented". Because she was very used to the teaching approach in the EIL and was very comfortable with the

212   *EIL students' responses to change*

EIL paradigm, she offered her view on the teaching of English based on the EIL perspectives in a hope that the lecturer would allow her space for negotiation. However, she claimed that the lecturer said "No! Not that" and "did not even bother to explain why". The third example that Tomoko shared was the parochial comments made by her so-called 'native' English-speaking friends and a lecturer from another program in response to her attempt to defend her use of English as a variety of English.

> I told my lecturer that this is how I speak and it's my English and they're like, you have to learn my language, English is our language and you have to write the way we write, and you have to speak that way, we don't know yours and we don't care. So, they're very strong about their opinion. They have their own voice and this is the challenge for me and I don't know how to compromise.

Although she had learned to develop positive views towards the diversity of English and its users, she reported that encountering the shop assistant who corrected her English, having her EIL perspectives rejected by her ESL teaching methodology lecturer, and listening to their parochial comments, had largely made her feel confused as to which perspectives she needed to adopt and the applicability of the EIL perspective that strongly supports acceptance and celebration of diversity. On one hand, she had come to appreciate the diversity of English as "a good thing", but on the other hand, the above experiences had to a large extent 'pushed' her back to "the views of the old days and made [her] feel desired to stick to the norms of native-speakers in order to be accepted and maybe to 'survive'".

In addition, even though she initially claimed that she had started to learn to perceive all speakers of English as equal, further conversations to some extent revealed that her "views of the old days" still persisted and that being a multilingual speaker of English seemed to be considered a deficiency. This could be seen in the reason she provided for her choice to regard herself as either a user or learner of English.

> As a user of English, I have to use English every day, daily life, study, work, it's the language of this country, you communicate in English. You're learner, because this is your second language because you don't have a proficiency to master the language. The more important thing is you learn the new stuff from people from different backgrounds. I understand that language keeps on transforming and it's same as the people in other fields, they come back and study. We need to keep update ourselves to the language, be able to stay in as a proactive communicator. So I think I'm learning everyday still and I'm trying to learn different ways of using English. For example the way I write and speak is me, is the way I would do, so when I read other people's writing, they have different way of writing and speaking. So, keep learning.

Despite her theoretical knowledge of the nature of language variation and her motivation to keep learning, the interview conveyed a clear message that a widespread view of the supremacy of 'native-speakers' still persisted in Australia. Still informed by the problematic view of native-speakers as having the highest proficiency in the language, she perceived the label of a learner can only be given to the so-called 'second-language speakers' who *cannot* master the language and are not proficient in the language.

Her deeper perception of being a speaker of English from a multilingual and multicultural background as a deficit could further be observed in the way she called for the uniqueness in the way she used English (influenced by her cultural values), to be 'sympathised' with and given a "special treatment" as opposed to respected.

> You have to accept that people write and speak differently, people write the way they do because they come from a different background and they will bring in their expressions into their writing So, you have to give special treatment. If they don't give us special treatment, I will fail [laughter]. Well, I think that [pause] ... yes, ... English is not my first language, I'm not a native-speaker, I cannot write or speak English the way I write Japanese. So, I'm disadvantaged in a way ... if you know, there are special treatment people who can understand that English is not my first language, that would be good.

Even after having engaged in the EIL curricula for three years, she still believed that writing and speaking differently from speakers of English from Inner-Circle countries is a characteristic of a non-native-speaker and is a disadvantage. There seemed to be a tendency for her to perceive a variety of English of which its pragmatic norms, grammar, vocabulary, and accent are different from those of Inner-Circle countries as a deficiency that needed to be given a remedy or a special treatment. Tomoko was fully aware of the problematic "views from the old days" and of the origin of this view, from 18 years of learning English under the normative paradigm. It did indicate, however, that she had made an attempt to fundamentally challenge those views from the previous days, which she claimed would require more time and effort from both her and contemporary society.

> I try to see them equal, I know I should see them as equal, but I still have some views from previous old days that they are ... for 18 years of my life, it's already deeply stretched in our mind ... the native-speakers are always superior cos that's the way I was told in my English class, in my high school, and everywhere ... so I still sometimes have that you know ... and I don't know how to deal with it even though I've done EIL, so it will take long time and lots of effort, and the society needs to change as well.

Furthermore, she felt that the EIL curricula she had learnt for three years had not provided her with sufficient and in-depth discussions of the ways to negotiate

214   *EIL students' responses to change*

or grapple with the tensions that she would invariably face outside classrooms. She acknowledged that the EIL curricula "sometimes talk a bit about politics". However, her deep sigh at this point revealed deep frustration, as if she felt the political issues as rather pointless. She believed that it would be difficult to deal with power imbalance and to make changes happen even when she became a teacher.

> It's a power thing, and with politics you can't do anything. That's just reality [deep sigh]. Like we talk about Singlish and Standard English in Singapore. We only review the situation, but can we really do anything about it? We can't. The government tells us what we have to do? What language? What is it you have to use? Although the fight, argument, and debate are happening, the politics is there and it's still happening. I think we can raise the voice, but we can't do anything about it. But even we become a teacher, it's also challenging, I think I can promote what I think, but if the government or principal says no, can I do anything? It's really, really power thing. So, I think I'm not sure if this is useful to study.

When I invited her to share further her uncertainty about the usefulness of studying this issue, she reported that this issue was often "mentioned so briefly" by the lecturers and was left for her "to think about it in [her] own time, which we actually don't because we need guidance". Perhaps, she suggested, she would have been able to "see how useful these issues are" if the lecturers "discuss more rather than avoid it and ask us [Tomoko and her peers] to think".

7.3. Chapter summary

A question that has been under-researched in literature on EIL curriculum (Brown, 2012) is the responses of students who are studying in Kachruvian Inner-Circle countries to the values and beliefs promoted in an EIL curriculum. In this chapter, I have presented the experiences of some undergraduate students who studied EIL for one year or three years at Urban University in Melbourne, Australia. Their experiences provided an opportunity for EIL educators and researchers at Urban University and from other contexts to read and listen to what students claimed and experienced to be the benefits of learning about EIL in the EIL program at Urban University, and at the same time the tensions and conflicts they experienced while studying the curricula. The latter to some extent confirms my discussion in Chapter 4, Chapter 5, and Chapter 6 about an important element of learning in an ideological environment, which my colleagues and I seemed to have previously overlooked and perhaps even unintentionally 'silenced'. Furthermore, this allowed me to uncover some 'hidden text' that my colleagues and I may have implicitly conveyed to our students. Not only have the findings from this chapter confirmed those of previous studies, but have also demonstrated the need to reconsider the perspectives offered by previous studies, and therefore the principles of teaching EIL. All of this will be discussed in the following chapter.

8 Reviewing change
From students' perspectives

8.0. Introduction

In Chapter 7, I presented the voices of five students enrolled in the EIL program at Urban University. Their experiences of engaging in the curricula have shed light on the principles of teaching EIL. In this chapter, I aim to present and discuss the themes and issues that have emerged from the above findings in light of the discussions in Chapter 2. This section also serves to present a more finely tuned and theorised discussion of the main 'problematics' (Smith, 1987, 2005) or gaps in this book project.

One of the important aspects that the current literature on teaching EIL has acknowledged as still being under-developed, or has overlooked altogether, is students' views on or responses to the beliefs and values advocated in EIL curricula (Brown, 2012). Another way of saying this is to point out, as Wee (2013) and Qu (2016) have done, that debates on how feasible or realistic it might be to implement the principles advocated by the EIL paradigm are still very much lacking. The existing literature tends to focus on informing teachers how to teach EIL in a —narrowly technicist sense. Few studies have attempted to explore from the students' perspective the feasibility of teaching EIL (Briguglio, 2006; Chang, 2014; Galloway & Rose, 2014; Kubota, 2001b; Oxford & Jain, 2010; Rose & Galloway, forthcoming; Shin, 2004; Suzuki, 2011). Most of these studies, however, do not sound too pleased or satisfied with their findings when they report that their students still display attitudes and perceptions that are contrary to the principles underpinning their EIL lessons and curricula. For some, the solution is to provide a longer EIL 'intervention' in the form of a full course or degree. Surely that would produce more desirable results. The hope seems to be that this would prevent English language educators from casting doubt on the feasibility of implementing the principles of teaching EIL, and help them to answer the question: will a longer EIL 'intervention' necessarily lead to a 'successful' EIL curriculum? This also made me wonder if it would be so. But the experiences of the student-participants in this study, those who had engaged in learning about EIL for one year or three years in the EIL course that was specially created at Urban University, have been very helpful as I have sought to answer this question.

216 *Reviewing change: students' perspectives*

The project described in this book has shown, in nuanced ways, the changes that diverse students had experienced in their understanding and perceptions towards different varieties of English and speakers of different world Englishes after having engaged in an EIL curriculum for one year (Manida, Cheolsoo, and Ogilvy) and three years (Phil and Tomoko). The interviews with the students also addressed one aspect that has not yet been addressed in previous studies, i.e. the factors that prompted the students to change their views about the English language and about their own identity. The students spoke about how particular learning materials and pedagogical practices they had experienced had played a role in inspiring them to critically challenge and change their previous understandings, perceptions, and attitudes. Some students had been inspired to propose and initiate approaches to promote respect for English language variation and challenge practices that disrespected it. And yet, despite their one year or three years in-depth engagement with the EIL curricula, the students still experienced challenges, tensions, and struggles in learning about EIL and in envisioning a high feasibility of implementing the principles advocated by the EIL program. Often, they explained these challenges and struggles in terms of the competing cognitive 'battles' of discourses between their EIL lecturers and those of 'non-EIL' advocates from their lives beyond the EIL course (both at university and in their personal lives). According to the students, these 'battles' were often not brought to the fore and talked about in the EIL curricula at Urban University (see Section 7.1.1 [Manida], Section 7.1.3 [Ogilvy], and Section 7.1.5 [Tomoko]). Students believed that this needed to be addressed and the fact that it was not inquired into in the EIL classrooms made them wonder if it was important. Therefore, even though the beliefs and values advocated in an EIL program prompted the students to speak about the value of studying in such a program, they made it clear also that there are still some areas that EIL educators need to take into consideration as they seek to improve or develop an EIL curriculum.

8.1. Experiencing changes through EIL curricula

> definitely learnt a useful lesson already
>
> (Ogilvy)

After having studied in an EIL program for one year or three years at Urban University, the student-participants claimed that they had experienced the beneficial effects of having engaged in learning about EIL and discussing issues or perspectives that inform the EIL paradigm. Similar to the experiences of students in previous studies (cf. Briguglio, 2006; Chang, 2014; Galloway & Rose, 2014; Kubota, 2001b; Oxford & Jain, 2010; Rose & Galloway, forthcoming; Shin, 2004; Suzuki, 2011), all participants reported that the benefits they experienced included: changes in their awareness and understanding of the English language; and changes in their understanding and views about English language variation and speakers of Englishes from Outer- and Expanding-Circle countries.

In addition, while their changing awareness and perceptions of the English language had prompted some participants (Manida, Cheolsoo, and Ogilvy) to think about ways of acting on this awareness and these perceptions, it emerged that some other participants (Phil and Tomoko) had already started to initiate and implement change. All of these, discussed in more detail in the following section, according to the students, could be attributed to the curriculum, and the teaching and learning they had experienced in EIL classrooms.

8.1.1. Awareness of the diversity of English and its perceived relevance

We have 'English', but we are all different

(Phil)

The first beneficial effect that all participants claimed they had experienced was that they had become aware of the changing sociolinguistic landscape of English, and at the time of the interviews, they had a better understanding of the nature of English language variation. As expected and highlighted in previous studies (Galloway & Rose, 2014; Kubota, 2001b; Oxford & Jain, 2010; Rose & Galloway, forthcoming; Suzuki, 2011), all student-participants in this study initially entered the EIL program at Urban University with a problematic assumption that English was only spoken by inhabitants of Inner-Circle countries and, therefore, it was exclusively the language of those countries. To Manida, Cheolsoo, and Tomoko, learning English was about learning to communicate with the so-called 'native' English speakers. Ogilvy and Phil, as the so-called 'native-speakers' of English, came to study in the EIL program with somewhat superficial understandings of the diversity of English. Their understanding of this 'diversity' was restricted to 'Standard' English spoken by 'native-speakers' who are born in the so-called 'native' English-speaking countries where English is a dominant language; and 'non-standard' English spoken by 'non-native-speakers' who are not born in 'native' English-speaking countries.

However, this understanding and assumption were challenged and changed after their encounters with some specific learning materials and pedagogical practices. Firstly, they mentioned explicitly the prescribed reading materials that explained the roles/functions of English in each of the Kachruvian circles. These readings, they observed, highlighted how the increasing numbers of speakers of English from Outer and Expanding Circle countries are exceeding those from Inner-Circle countries. The students also spoke about how examples of different varieties of English "changed [their] views a lot" (Tomoko) or in particular, "broadened [their] horizons and understanding of English variation" (Ogilvy). Tomoko's story about her encounter with an English novel written by a Chinese author which was comprehensible to her but not to her 'native' English-speaking friend was telling. It illustrated that did the readings she had read throughout her study not only raised her awareness of the diversity of English but they also allowed her to better understand the notion of renationalisation of the ownership of English (McKay, 2002) or, in her words, "English belong[s] to everyone" (Tomoko).

Secondly, the examples of different varieties of English and the tasks in which students were asked to reflect on their own or others' experiences of using English were other major elements of the EIL curricula that all participants believed had played a role in raising their awareness of "English being an incredibly varied language as opposed to a monolithic language" (Ogilvy). In a sense, these activities helped them to map the complex demographic backgrounds of the users of English. Looking specifically at Phil's experiences, those reflective tasks provided him opportunities to "realise [his] encounter [with] different varieties of English in everyday life, spoken by people from different countries". This was also experienced by both Manida and Cheolsoo, who talked about their experiences during their stay in Melbourne of encountering and interacting with speakers of varieties of English other than Australian English and who were from diverse lingua-cultural backgrounds.

Finally, the data also revealed that the topic on language variation, which explored how English language varies, was frequently mentioned as the one that had prompted students to gain a better theoretical understanding of the fact that the diversity of English is "a natural thing" (Cheolsoo). As Ogilvy put it succinctly, "I have come to understand that these varieties don't pop up for no reasons ... and there are significant cultural factors that influence the language ... it's an organic process". Manida shared a similar view and her experience in learning about this topic plus the reflective activities had allowed her to contemplate and realise why she and other speakers of English used English differently from each other. Therefore, it can be seen that engaging in EIL curricula for a longer period of time not only raised the students' awareness of the diversity of English, it also prompted them to understand better why English language naturally varies.

McKay and Brown (2016) argue that materials that teach different varieties of English need to be relevant to local contexts. It is evident that all student-participants in my study acknowledged the importance and relevance of having awareness and knowledge of the diversity of English with respect to the local context in which they were living. This awareness was perceived to be important and useful for their encounters and interactions with users of English at home (housemates), at work (customers), and at the university (lecturers and classmates/friends) from diverse lingua-cultural backgrounds who did not necessarily speak varieties of Australian English. This echoes the rich sociocultural and sociolinguistic landscape of Australia observed by Burridge (2010), Clyne (2005), Marlina (2010), and Sharifian (2014). Tomoko's decision to choose EIL as a specialisation for her undergraduate arts degree further allowed a clearer view of the relevance of learning about EIL in Melbourne. She explained that in-depth knowledge of EIL would be crucial for her future profession as a secondary school English language teacher in Melbourne, who would be more likely to interact with and teach students from different cultural and linguistic backgrounds. Going beyond Australia, Manida and Ogilvy, in particular, believed that knowledge of EIL across the world was needed in today's era of globalisation.

Echoing the view expressed by Xu (2002) and Matsuda (2012a), both justified that the knowledge and awareness of the diversity of English would prepare them for communicating with future interlocutors whose lingua-cultural backgrounds would often be unknown and diverse.

The students' views of the relevance of learning about EIL in Melbourne discussed above confirm what I argued in Chapter 2 about Melbourne as a linguistically and culturally feasible context for offering the new EIL curriculum/program at Urban University. In spite of Australia being a country in which English is used as the national language, the rich linguistic and cultural landscape of this globalised nation provides a strong background for teaching EIL. Some recent publications on teaching EIL, such as Alsagoff et al. (2012), still emphasise the importance of teaching and learning EIL in contexts outside of Kachruvian Inner Circle English-speaking countries, where English is not a national language and where it is developed in multilingual and multicultural settings. As I have argued elsewhere (Marlina, 2013c), a perspective such as this may imply two things: (1) that Inner-Circle countries are not multilingual and multicultural, and, therefore, (2) the teaching of EIL is not relevant in those countries. This can be misleading because many Inner-Circle English-speaking countries, for example the United States and Australia, are becoming increasingly multilingual, multicultural, and 'pluri-varietal'. The forces of globalisation such as mass migration and advancement of technology have allowed citizens of Inner-Circle countries, as experienced by myself, my teacher-participants and my student-participants, to be in frequent contact with diverse speakers of world Englishes. Therefore, I argue that the teaching and learning of EIL should also be perceived as relevant to any globalised, multilingual, and multicultural context such as Australia regardless of the status and role of the English language in the country.

8.1.2. Changing views on world Englishes and their speakers

> It's more than just teaching us language awareness, but also teaching us to change our perceptions
>
> (Phil)

Phil's comment suggests another beneficial outcome that all student-participants claimed to have experienced after engaging in learning in the EIL program at Urban University. Not only did this raise their awareness of English language variation, but it also prompted a level of change in the way students viewed different varieties of English, themselves as users of English, and other speakers of Englishes from Outer-and Expanding-Circle countries. With support from some specific learning materials and pedagogical practices students not only developed their awareness and theoretical understanding of (the nature of) English language variation, they also learned to develop a critical view of the underlying assumptions behind their previous taken-for-granted perceptions. As similarly reported in some previous studies (Galloway & Rose, 2014; Kubota, 2001b; Oxford & Jain,

220 *Reviewing change: students' perspectives*

2010; Rose & Galloway, forthcoming; Suzuki, 2011), the student-participants in my study initially enrolled in the EIL program with beliefs and views that reflected (1) the ideology of native-speakerism (Holliday, 2005) – a belief in the supremacy of speakers of English from Inner-Circle countries – and (2) a deviational and deficit perspective (Vavrus, 1991) of speakers of Englishes from Outer- and Expanding-Circle countries. Although all participants seemed to be aware of some form or aspect of 'differences' in the way English was spoken or written prior to their in-depth engagement with an EIL curriculum or curricula, these differences were regarded as deficiencies that needed to be remedied.

Manida, Cheolsoo, and Tomoko had all entered the program with (1) a self-deprecating and deficit view of the way they used English; and (2) an assumption that "Americans, Australians, and British are the only true and legitimate speakers of English", whose forms of English are exclusively effective for international communication. Being aware of how differently they used English or sounded in English, Manida labelled it as "just another weird language" whereas both Cheolsoo and Tomoko perceived their Korean/Japanese-accented English as "simply wrong". Informed by this deficit view, Tomoko confessed to have unfairly 'ranked' speakers of English on the basis of their racial group and their use of English ("white people are superior, and then maybe Asians, and the rest of them are really really bad"); she would avoid communicating with those who were not "really fluent in native English". Driven by this deficit perspective on themselves and their minimal understanding and awareness of English language variation, they enrolled in the EIL program expecting their teachers to "correct [their] English" (Manida) and "help [them] speak perfectly like Australians or maybe Americans" (Cheolsoo) so that they would not feel "a bit lower grade [and] behind" (Tomoko).

Similarly the ideologies associated with native-speakerism (Holliday, 2005) and deviational/deficit perspectives of world Englishes (Vavrus, 1991) are also reflected in how the Australian-born/raised student-participants, Ogilvy and Phil, initially viewed different varieties of English and speakers of English from Outer- and Expanding-Circle countries. Although Ogilvy's initial intentions to study EIL seemed to be consistent with what the EIL program at Urban University aimed to teach ("being able to communicate across cultures" and "knowing different varieties of English"), further analyses of our conversations and my observations of his responses to world Englishes in class confirmed a deficit and native-speakerist view of the diversity of English and its speakers.

As an EIL student, Ogilvy conveyed his interest in learning about the "difficulties that international people" have in "learning English", "the speed-bumps" or "the unique foibles". All of these italicised words tend to reflect a binary opposition that Ogilvy had constructed of who are and who are not legitimate 'users' of English, and what is and what is not a legitimate variety of English. People from Outer- and Expanding-Circle countries ("my Singaporean and Malaysian classmates" [Ogilvy]) were not perceived as legitimate speakers of English but as 'learners' from non-English-speaking background countries because they had "a weaker grasp of English" (than Ogilvy himself); that they were unfamiliar with

Australian English (although they "had formally studied English" [Ogilvy]); that they "used phraseology incorrectly or expression incorrectly" (Ogilvy); and that they spoke English with "a staccato tone" (Ogilvy). Learning how to communicate across cultures tended to be viewed as learning to understand and perhaps sympathise with the "difficulties", "foibles", and "speed-bumps" (Ogilvy) that speakers of English from Outer- and Expanding-Circle countries have. In addition, Ogilvy's use of words such as "unique foibles" and "speed-bumps", hesitation (umm … like … I suppose …), and the long pause when explaining what he referred to as 'different varieties of English' seem to indicate his reluctance to view them as legitimate 'different' varieties of English. This attitude or perception could be observed and hence confirmed when he smirked and shook his head in response to the different varieties of English presented in class, and that he was "gobsmacked" at the fact that these, what he further labelled as, "subcultures English" were studied and taught. Based on these findings, a 'different' variety of English was perceived and defined as a deficient form of English that deviates 'incorrectly' from a 'native' variety of English as opposed to a legitimate distinctive use of English that is used by people from different countries.

Phil's initial views towards speakers of English from Outer- and Expanding-Circle countries and their use of English conveyed a much stronger deficit and native-speakerist view. His initial intention to study EIL, to a large extent, is indicative of an ideology of native-English speaker supremacy or as he coined, "*I'm-the-king-of-the-world mentality*". Unlike Ogilvy, Phil's intention was nowhere near what the EIL program aimed to teach as he only aimed to achieve a high score/grade. He confidently believed that his ability to speak English confidently and proficiently as a 'native' English speaker would allow him to receive a better score/grade than his other non-English-speaking background classmates as, in his view, they were less likely to be more proficient and confident in using English than him. Furthermore, unlike Ogilvy who still viewed them as learners of English who spoke "*subcultures* English" (Ogilvy) or English with "speed-bumps" (Ogilvy), Phil viewed and labelled them pejoratively as "backrows, rich fobs [fresh-off-the-boats], or non-English speaking international kids who can't even speak English, and who have weird accent which you can't understand". With this view, Phil claimed that he would avoid communicating with "Asians" both in class as well as in workplace, again because "Asians don't speak English". Driven by their deficit perspectives on speakers of English from Outer- and Expanding-Circle countries as well as their problematic view of success in communication in English lying in one's 'nativeness' to English, both Ogilvy and Phil believed and advocated that speakers of English from Outer- and Expanding-Circle countries who resided in Australia needed to "do the way Romans do things" (Phil) by "los[ing] their accent" (Phil) and speaking "a region-free accent or Global Standard English" (Ogilvy) in order to "combat these inaccurate forms of English" (Ogilvy) and make them "understandable to native-speakers" (Ogilvy).

However, it is evident that some student-participants' encounters with "alternate theories" (Ogilvy) promoted through some specific learning materials and pedagogical practices prompted them to contest the native-speakerist ideology and deficit/deviational perspectives underlying their previous views, and to develop different perspectives. Firstly, the pedagogical practices that recurringly placed emphasis on critically reflecting on and sharing experiences of using and learning English, were unanimously affirmed by Manida, Cheolsoo, Phil, and Tomoko. For Manida it played a contributory role in prompting students to "really really think more about your own self, your English, your approach to using English" and Tomoko believed that they "open[ed] up our views and change my views about Englishes [used by speakers of English from Outer- and Expanding-Circle backgrounds]". Specifically, the "real scenarios in their [lecturers'] and our [students'] life" (Manida) shared in a classroom environment where students were invited to share their views and experiences of using/learning English "without fear of being ridiculed" (Phil) raised their awareness of English language variation. In addition, they prompted students, in accord with Briguglio (2005) and Matsuda (2002), to better understand and appreciate how speakers of world Englishes (including the students themselves) use English to communicate their linguistic identities, cultural values, and worldviews.

Unlike the student-participants in Briguglio (2006) and Shin (2004), who only felt confident about themselves as speakers of English, some of student-participants in my research had been prompted to feel confident in being speakers of different varieties of world Englishes as well as to have confidence in explaining and justifying why they used English the way they did. This is evidenced in (1) Tomoko's better comprehension of a book written in English by a Chinese author, and her self-confidence and pride in being a speaker of English who comes from a multilingual and culturally complex background; (2) Manida's decision to view and classify her English as "one of many dialects of English" that reflected her Laotian "worldview and pragmatic strategies like any other Englishes in the world"; (3) Ogilvy's awareness and understanding of English language variation as "an organic process" and the significant cultural factors behind this variation; (4) Cheolsoo's attempt to classify his own use of English as a legitimate variety of English through his unapologetic explanation and justification for his preferred choice of a form of greeting in English that reflects his Korean sociocultural values; and (5) Phil's awareness of his English as a reflection of "where [he's] been or gone, whom [he's] met, what [he's] done". Additionally, the two EIL graduates' three years of engagement in these experience-sharing practices and those that encourage students to critically assess/reflect on the strengths and limitations of different views of conceptualising English and communication in English, prompted them to contest how problematic their previous practices had been, of unjustly dividing and naming people according to their racial and linguistic backgrounds, and of avoiding people who speak with "a weird accent" (Tomoko). Supporting Higgins (2003) and some findings from studies by Kubota (2001b) and Briguglio (2006), Tomoko and Phil claimed that these pedagogical practices had inspired them to learn to be "less judgemental" (Tomoko), to be patient in encountering unknown and unfamiliar varieties of English, to be critical of a discriminatory mentality or mindset that "puts people into certain frameworks" (Phil), and to be open-minded as not doing so would disadvantage them in the areas of accessing knowledge, beliefs, perceptions, and experiences of people from different parts of the world. They would end up "thinking that mine is the only better option" (Tomoko).

Secondly, student-participants' responses to the principles advocated in the EIL program further revealed another aspect of change that has not yet been highlighted in previous studies and in the current literature of teaching and learning EIL. As an EIL educator and researcher, it was rewarding for me (as it was for my teaching colleagues, too) to observe that the prescribed readings and classroom discussions that centred on English language variation as well as a specific course on World Englishes had inspired all student-participants to perceive themselves as learners of English and to develop a willingness to keep learning. The understanding or category of a learner for these students was no longer based on whether a person was a 'native-' or 'non-native-speaker' or whether English is his/her predominant or additional language. Rather it tended to be informed by their observations and perceptions of English as an "ongoing" (Manida) dynamic language that keeps naturally "expanding" (Phil), "transforming" (Tomoko), and pluralising. And yet, although Manida, Cheolsoo, and Tomoko had learned to perceive themselves as users of different varieties of English mentioned before, they also wanted to be identified as learners whose task is to "keep learning and updating themselves" (Tomoko) because a "different age, different time" (Manida) exposes people to "different experience" (Tomoko), and therefore to "different dialects of English" (Cheolsoo) that "never ends" (Manida). Ogilvy and Phil, on the other hand, also wanted to be identified as learners as they had come to realise and experience that being a so-called 'native-speaker' of English does not mean that one's "English is ever complete" (Phil) or that one "speaks correct and intelligible English ... and ... knows everything about English" (Ogilvy). Rather, one still has to keep learning because "there are still so many different varieties of English out there especially as globalisation continues"(Ogilvy) and "so many people out there I have not met ... and ... information out there in the world, which you'll lose out if you stay close-minded" (Phil).

Finally, in addition to the sharing of experiences and observations of linguistic and cultural differences, this study has shown the effects in an EIL curriculum of discussing controversial issues or 'tough topics' and "playing-devil's-advocate questions" (Ogilvy) on students' existing views. In teaching those controversial issues, one particular activity that the participants believed had a long-lasting impact on them was the 'linguistic-identity-switching activity' that I conducted in my lesson. This required students to speak in only one particular unfamiliar variety of English which I had selected and they were penalised for any slight deviation. It was claimed that this activity and subsequent discussions about students' struggle to participate in it had prompted the participants to perceive the importance of "being original" in one's use of English (Manida, Tomoko, and Cheolsoo) or of not "play[ing] pretending games" (Das, 1965). They felt it was important to call for acknowledgement and respect for their originality in the way they use English (Manida and Tomoko); to perceive the need to develop effective intercultural communicative strategies (Cheolsoo) and to learn from each other (Phil)

224 *Reviewing change: students' perspectives*

as opposed to seeking to emulate particular English language users or speakers; and to become aware of the imperialistic nature and undesirable consequences or "offences" (Ogilvy) of enforcing a particular group's standard language upon all. Therefore, it can be seen that not only did the student-participants in this study to some extent respond positively to the perspectives underpinning the EIL program, and not only did they view the relevance/importance of learning about EIL, but they also "definitely learnt a useful lesson" (Ogilvy).

8.1.3. Proposing and initiating change

> ... nothing is going to happen unless we do something about it. That's why I want to take the steps to make these changes happen
>
> (Phil)

Another outcome of the analysis of the interview material regarding studying in an EIL program has also not yet been observed and addressed in previous studies. Previous studies have found that on completion of a series of EIL lessons, of a single workshop, or a semester-long course, students have demonstrated awareness and understanding of the diversity of English (Galloway & Rose, 2014; Rose & Galloway, forthcoming; Suzuki, 2011) and a critical perception towards the deviational and deficit perspectives of diversity in English language usage (Chang, 2014; Oxford & Jain, 2010; Shin, 2004). However, my study found that, based on their awareness and perceptions, some students-participants proposed some ways to promote respect for the diversity of English and to challenge practices that disrespect diversity whereas others were already making some attempts to bring about change or 'take actions'. Interestingly, the study showed that student-participants who were only at the level of a proposal were those who had completed the first-year sequence (Manida and Cheolsoo). Those who claimed to have made initiatives to bring about change were the third-year students (Phil and Tomoko) who, at the time this study was conducted, had already completed three years of study in the EIL program at Urban University and had chosen EIL as their undergraduate major.

With her changing awareness and perceptions towards the diversity of English and towards herself as a speaker of English, Manida proposed that she would no longer passively accept people's criticisms or corrections of the way she sounded in English. She proposed that she would defend it by probing the corrector's right to correcting the way she sounded in English and by questioning their knowledge of 'right' or 'correct' English in the light of the diversification of the English language. Impressed by the diversity of English and inspired by South Korean scholars' publications on the uniqueness of Korean English, Cheolsoo also proposed that he would like to further his study in EIL so that he could "write an essay and discussion paper on [his] country, publish [his] works in scholar's world or Google Scholar through database in this university or other universities [and] recommend people to go to Korea and listen to the way people

[Koreans] speak English to broaden their perspectives of English spoken in the world".

As Phil stated, "nothing is going to happen if we keep waiting for something to happen … unless we do something about it. That's why I want to take the steps trying to make these changes happen … but subtly". These 'steps for making changes happen' could be observed in both Tomoko's and Phil's interviews. Unlike Manida, who only proposed an assertive way of responding to people's attempts to correct her way of speaking English, Tomoko executed this proposal in an actual context. When she encountered a person who corrected her pronunciation of a food name and lectured her on how to pronounce it correctly, she assertively defended that "[she has her] own way of pronouncing it" and demanded that the person not "force that to [her] and to other people". As a private English tutor for her friend and a future English teacher, she also claimed to resist "saying to [her friends or future students] you never say that or you never do something like this". Instead, she preferred to adopt a "more flexible" approach in which she provided her friends (or would provide her future students) with a number of different ways of using English and then remind them of their rights and power to decide which ways of using English made sense to them or that they could connect with. Inspired by the effort of many EIL scholars "working hard trying to make change happen" (Phil) and particularly by Geneva Smitherman's (1974) work, Phil also made attempts like Tomoko when he encountered similar scenarios. This can be observed in his critique of his friend whose first aim of becoming an English teacher was to change students' 'weird' accents. It can also be seen in his story about him imparting his knowledge of EIL to his Japanese friends and urging confidence in them to pursue their ambition of becoming English teachers, to "be proud of it [their own use of English]" (Phil), and to avoid "thinking about meeting some shadow figure" (Phil). The consensus seemed to be that it is not enough for an EIL curriculum or program to raise students' awareness of the pluricentricity of English and to prompt them to perceive that all varieties of English are equal and legitimate members of the English language family. An EIL curriculum or program needs to inspire students to know, to care, and most importantly to "act upon their awareness" (Kubota, 2012, p. 64).

Moreover, the data indicate that, as Clyne and Sharifian (2008) argue, teaching students about EIL to understand and implement the principles and views advocated by the EIL paradigm is a time-consuming process. Expecting students to achieve the desired outcomes after having studied EIL in two (Shin, 2004) or eight EIL lessons (Kubota, 2001b), in a two and half hour EIL-focused workshop (Briguglio, 2006), or twelve weeks course (Suzuki, 2011) is perhaps way too idealistic. Briguglio (2006) could also be right to suggest that EIL educators are likely to observe more achievements from their students who have had a longer exposure to and more in-depth engagement in an EIL curriculum or program. In many ways, my study supports such a suggestion. However, further conversations with my student-participants revealed that gaining awareness about EIL, learning to become confident advocates of the EIL paradigm, and learning to act upon their awareness did not necessarily constitute a smooth journey.

226 *Reviewing change: students' perspectives*

8.2. Experiencing struggles and tensions in learning about EIL

> In reality, a lot of things aren't really what we wish it to be
>
> (Tomoko)

> EIL lecturers tell us one thing and people outside the class tell us another thing
>
> (Manida)

Having engaged in EIL curricula for one year (Manida, Tomoko, and Ogilvy) or three years (Phil and Tomoko) clearly enabled the students who participated in this study to experience changes to their initial perceptions. However, just as clearly, all student-participants experienced difficulties in envisioning the feasibility beyond their enrolment in the EIL course of operating in their own contexts consistent with the advocated EIL principles. Indeed, they still shared some views or discourses that might be regarded as 'attitudinal sins' by Kachru (1986) or 'undesirable behaviours' by some other EIL scholars. Rather than using Kachru's (1986) term to conceptualise students' perceptions that run counter to the EIL paradigm, I prefer to view them as products of ongoing struggles, conflicts, and tensions in learning to advocate for the anti-normative EIL paradigm. This is because, informed by the Bakhtinian perspective that underpins this book project, I believe that encountering challenges, struggles, and tensions in learning in an "ideological environment" (Bakhtin & Medvedev, 1978) such as an EIL class, is natural, inevitable and probably desirable.

Unlike previous studies which showed only the 'undesirable attitudinal sins' after learning EIL, I have taken an interest in exploring further what might have prompted students to experience this cognitive disequilibrium (struggle, tensions, and conflicts). Additionally, unlike previous studies that used an 'either-this-or-that' approach in talking about whether their participants did or did not display the expected and advocated outcomes of studying EIL, I took a different approach. All student-participants at Urban University explicitly indicated their appreciation for the principles advocated by the curricula or program and, to some extent, their attempts to take a critical perspective on their native-speakerism-oriented previous views. At the same time, they experienced tensions prompted by their encounters with a clash of multiple competing voices or discourses (Assaf & Dooley, 2006; Canagarajah, 1993; Doecke & Kostogriz, 2008). These voices comprise: the 'anti-normative' ones from the EIL program; those they had been exposed to, experienced, and developed prior to studying in the EIL program; and those they anticipated they were likely to experience or be exposed to beyond university after studying in the program. Thus, the findings of this study directly challenge Kubota's (2001b) explanation of students' struggle to advocate the EIL principles or elitist discourses as being the result of their lack of exposure to world Englishes in daily life or their lack of interest in learning a foreign language.

In many of the observations they made, all student-participants in this study lent support to Nieto's (1999, 2004, 2010) claims about the role that the discourses, voices, or practices from their previous and current sociopolitical contexts play in prompting them to experience struggle in envisioning the feasibility of advocating the EIL paradigm in a realistic context and in operating in their social and educational contexts with the views/beliefs imparted by the program. In fact, the results of my study did reveal students' awareness of these social discourses or "views from the previous old days" (Tomoko) or more specifically, "elitist views" (Ogilvy) that were "deeply stretched" (for 18 years of [Tomoko's] life) or "too deeply ingrained" (Ogilvy) in them to the extent that it would have been "processed dialogically to become half one's own words" (Bakhtin, 1981, p. xvii). These 'elitist' and 'native-speakerist' discourses or voices to which they had been exposed for years continued to echo loudly and powerfully in their internally persuasive discourses, such that students were prompted to lean more towards these discourses to show "allegiances" (Bakhtin, 1981, p. 342). This explains why they experienced conflicts or tensions when encountering the anti-elitist discourses that had just recently joined – and become part of – their internally persuasive discourses.

As previously mentioned, all student-participants appreciated the opportunity to perceive themselves confidently as users of different varieties of English and to recognise the nature of different varieties of English as reflections of the users' significant identities and cultural values. At the same time, the social discourses from their previous and current educational contexts such as the native-speakerist and assimilationist views and attitudes conveyed by their other lecturers, English teachers, and peer groups/classmates that constructed those who sound different from 'the mainstream' as the "weird" (Manida), "inferior" (Cheolsoo), or culturally problematic Others (Holliday, 2005), had prompted them to share their uncertainty as to whether they could and/or would allow themselves or other people to 'be original' and 'stop playing pretending games' in their educational contexts. Some student-participants attempted to communicate their willingness to deconstruct themselves as culturally problematic Others. They demanded having their "idiolects" and "voices" respectfully acknowledged, and called for the legitimate recognition and respectful acknowledgement of these different 'voices'. However, some students expressed uncertainty how this would be welcomed in their educational contexts as a result of their lingering voices and discourses from their previous learning experiences. Others already experienced and observed discourses in their educational context that rejected their effort to assert one's own 'voice' (Manida and Tomoko), and to share perspectives that advocated for a legitimate recognition for differences (Tomoko) and that ethnocentrically and xenophobically constructed difference as deficiency (Ogilvy, Cheolsoo, and Phil) such as "refugees and migrants ... as bastards who don't speak English". Therefore, when they encountered the differently powerful discourses voiced by EIL educators who advocated for the importance of appreciating different varieties of English and of 'owning' one's use of English, tensions arose. These tensions prompted some participants to perceive EIL as a "risky business" (Phil); they felt that pledging 'temporary allegiances' to elitist discourses could be a less risky option. An example of this can be observed in Phil's comment about students who tried (but did not necessarily succeed) to 'do as the Romans do'

228 *Reviewing change: students' perspectives*

and thus avoided being "doomed". This was also evident in Ogilvy's hesitation (not absolute rejection) to support and advocate the idea of allowing speakers of Englishes from Outer- and Expanding-Circle countries to speak their "sub-cultures English" instead of 'native' English because "a lot of people out there are going to look down on you if you speak what is perceived to be inaccurate".

In addition to what might be termed native-speakerism-oriented social dis-courses from students' various educational contexts, there were even more powerful discourses or voices reflected in the practices in the social contexts they encountered and experienced. These had prompted them to experience more tensions as they were exposed to another powerful authoritative discourse from the EIL program. Specifically, a range of social and political conditions at the time of the study had prompted participants to further question whether being and sounding different are positively viewed and appreciated by the context in which they lived. These included: the negative portrayal of and critique against the 'boganish' accent of the (then) Australian prime minister; the recent racial violence towards the Indian student community in Melbourne reported in the news; the success of securing a job as a result of 'playing a pretending game'; and the treatment as the cultural problematic Other that a person may receive who speaks 'a different variety of English' even though in some respects they have been successful in assimilating him/herself to the 'mainstream'. As Ogilvy put it succinctly, "how can people be allowed to speak in their own varieties of English in a society that does not have a positive value attached to diversity"? Tupas (2006) has a similar view. Though English language variation may be sociolin-guistically legitimate, it largely remains politically unacceptable to many groups of people in society. Having been informed of this and having experienced it in their lives, all participants demonstrated some dilemmas at the prospect of returning to the 'old days' discourses and whether they were still attracted to the option of avoiding "being looked down on by others" (Ogilvy).

Through presenting and reflecting on the EIL syllabus and materials at Urban University, the students' perspectives and experiences showed full awareness of the conflicts and tensions that their lecturers also experienced; and of the missing piece or subtexts in the curricula. Specifically, the EIL syllabus materials in my program that included different varieties of English, that incorporated the voices of people from diverse cultures (Matsuda, 2002, 2005; McKay, 2010), and that taught them to appreciate and legitimately recognise different varieties of English (Li, 2007; Shim, 2002), did not seem to have included much inquiry into the sociopolitical contexts in which students studied and lived. In other words, the syllabus materials, as illustrated in Chapter 5, mainly focused on teaching stu-dents about differences and encouraged them to respect and appreciate differ-ences or to " 'let's-get-to-know-each-other-better' " (Jenks et al., 2001, p. 93). What appeared to remain unaddressed were questions around how these dif-ferences and tensions were experienced and responded to by groups of people within the students' sociopolitical contexts. As shared by most of the student-participants, there did not seem to be a space for them to discuss or inquire into these tensions, which had prompted some participants to question if the lecturers were "trying to avoid it". In fact, Chapter 5 shows that some lecturers did (perhaps unintentionally) avoid it and seek to shut down some of the more uncomfortable discussions about these issues in the tutorials. There also appeared to be somewhat of a silencing of this dimension in the EIL literature. Even though controversial readings or politicisation of difference were included in some of the curricula, students were aware of and confirmed that these issues were mostly mentioned only in passing. Students' interviews repeatedly confirmed the findings and discussions in Chapter 5 and Chapter 6, which showed that the curricula of the EIL program at Urban University still predominantly remained at the level where students were regularly taught to see the importance of maintaining diversity and respecting diversity. Fewer opportunities were provided to share without fear their "heteroglot world of competing discourses" (Doecke & Kostogriz, 2008, p. 77) with respect to diversity. Students did not feel that they were free to question/problematise how they had come to be, to perceive, or to think in that way; nor did they feel free to propose "the alternative possibilities for organising social life" (Simon, 1992, p. 58) beyond the advocated EIL principles. Based on the findings in Chapter 4 and Chapter 5, this was indeed still missing in my teaching and most importantly in an ideological environment like the EIL program at Urban University.

Nevertheless, in responding to concerns about the feasibility of having a 'successful' EIL curriculum or lesson expressed by the scholars (Kubota, 2001b; Brown, 2012; Wee, 2013) raised in Chapter 2 and in the data of this study, I still refuse to be pessimistic about the prospect of teaching EIL and the possible beneficial outcomes it may bring, for two reasons. Firstly, the results indicate that the anti-normative discourses that advocated for a respectful and legitimate recognition of the diversity of English and its users seemed to have become embedded in the students' internally persuasive discourses and might have been dialogically processed to become perhaps a significant part of their own words and worlds. Secondly, despite the tensions and struggles the student-participants experienced, the anti-normative discourses that had just become embedded in their internally persuasive discourses seemed to have prompted all of them to express a keen interest in wanting to learn more about these discourses. While the first-year students showed keen interest in wanting to learn more about EIL to make a difference, the third-year students, as discussed previously, had already started to initiate changes "slowly and subtly" by "start[ing] small with your friends, with your family, people you often meet up with". Although Ogilvy, in particular, might sound as if he was comfortable with and favourably chose to uphold his native-speakerist views, the fact that he labelled these views as "elitist" and calling himself "an English snob" might echo the influence of the discourses to which he had been exposed in the EIL program and, therefore, imply his recognition how problematic those views were. Like other first-year participants, he also showed keen interest in wanting to learn more about these alternative discourses and to engage in more dialogues about how to acknowledge and promote respect for diversity in a context that still views diversity as deficiency. This was an important stepping stone for him as well as for the other participants as they continued to develop their own beliefs beyond their EIL experience at university (Assaf & Dooley, 2006).

Thus, I have come to the view that an EIL curriculum or program that provides students with knowledge and awareness of the pluricentricity of English and the skills to communicate across cultures with an aim to "abolish ethnocentrism" (Brown, 1995, p. 236) or to produce a fully converted advocate of the program is simply infeasible, idealistic, or perhaps utopian. What is perhaps more realistic and less utopian is an EIL curriculum or program, as an ideological environment, that aims to provide students with (1) knowledge and awareness of the pluricentricity of English and its users; (2) a space to experience, reflect on, and dialogue about the confusion, tension, or conflict they are likely to experience as a result of their entrance into a heteroglot world of multiple competing normative and anti-normative discourses that are intersecting and clashing; and (3) inspiration to keep learning and critically inquiring into these discourses in order to develop their own ideological standpoint and approach in the face of the diversity of English.

In response to Brown's (2012) sceptical question: "has there [ever] been a successful EIL curriculum?", I would say 'No' because a 'successful curriculum' there seems to imply that there is nothing else to learn, and that a person's belief is expected to have been fully developed and informed by EIL principles on completion of the curriculum. Metaphorically, in an EIL class, students are being taught to swim against the current, and to swim against the current in one, two, or even five years is a challenging task as there will be floating objects that swim towards them and push them back to where the current is heading. Therefore, with an anti-normative and ideologically challenging curriculum such as EIL, the question that may need to be asked is whether there has been an EIL curriculum that prompts students to critically reflect on and dialogue about their exposed and experienced multiple competing discourses, and to keep learning, contemplating, and dialogically processing these alternative discourses about English language variation from an EIL perspective. I am still not confident to claim that the EIL curricula at Urban University can respond with a resounding 'Yes' to this question. However, I am confident that my colleagues and I are likely to continue working towards a 'Yes' answer to this question by taking into consideration the alternative principles and pedagogical approaches to the teaching of EIL I will discuss Chapter 9.

8.3. Chapter summary

In this chapter, I discussed the voices or experiences of students who studied EIL for one year or three years at Urban University. Regardless of the length of their study in the program, the students initially enrolled in the program with views that were informed by the ideology of native-speakerism and deficit/deviation perspectives. All participants agreed and experienced that their engagement in an EIL program at Urban University had prompted them to develop awareness and better theoretical understanding of the diversity of English and its users. This awareness and understanding had prompted them to critically challenge those initial views, and to develop a different or perhaps a more positive and respectful perception of perceiving the diversity of English and its users (including themselves). The students from Expanding-Circle countries claimed to have developed confidence in perceiving themselves as legitimate speakers of English and in advocating for their use of English to be respected, whereas those from Inner-Circle countries claimed to have developed a critical view of their native-speakerist supremacy notion of themselves and believed that there was much information about the English language that they still needed to learn and better understand (this is true also for the former group). Informed by this, while some participants proposed ways to advocate an EIL perception in an actual context, others who had had longer engagement with the EIL program already started to initiate changes in an actual context based on the beliefs and views advocated by the program. All of these could be attributed to the support of a number of authoritative voices from the prescribed reading materials on (the nature of) English language variation and on 'controversial' topics, the pedagogical activities that required them to critically reflect on their and others' experiences of using, learning, and teaching English, and those activities or questions that allowed them to experience the feeling of being in the shoes of linguistically marginalised and oppressed individuals.

At the same time, all student-participants, regardless of the duration of their engagement in the EIL curricula at Urban University, experienced tensions and conflicts in learning about the diversity of English and its users, and learning to advocate for the values and beliefs underpinning the curricula. These tensions, conflicts, or even confusions were prompted by a clash of powerful anti-normative discourses promoted in the EIL curricula and other discourses brought with them which they had developed from their exposure to and experiences in studying and living in contexts that promoted the supremacy of 'native-speakers' of English and the 'elitist' view of differences as deficiency. Such elitist social discourses seemed to be almost overpowering to the extent that they had prompted them to (1) question the feasibility of operating with the anti-normative discourses in a context that constructed diversity as deficiency; and (2) consider whether holding onto the elitist discourses would be a less risky option. The students' experiences revealed that not many opportunities were given to address and inquire into these tensions and conflicts within the EIL course at Urban University, confirming what I had observed and presented in Chapter 5.

In the light of all of this, does this mean that it would be infeasible to implement the principles of teaching EIL? In the next chapter, I will return to this question and discuss the implications of the results of this project for the teaching of English as a pluricentric language.

9 Re-envisioning a program of ongoing inquiry

9.0. Introduction

I conclude this book with a discussion of what I have learned from my research journey – the knowledge generated through this project – and recommendations for a program of ongoing inquiry for English as an International Language (EIL) educators at Urban University (or in other similar contexts). I highlight the main findings of this project and how they contribute knowledge to the existing literature about the principles and practices of teaching EIL, and I present a set of recommendations in the light of the findings. In highlighting the major findings of this book project, this chapter returns to and addresses the key question of this project, voiced by Wee (2013) and supported by Qu (2016), 'How realistic it might be to implement the suggestions or principles of teaching EIL', in the light of the teaching and learning experiences of EIL educators and students in the EIL program at Urban University. Informed by the findings and discussions presented in Chapter 4, Chapter 5, Chapter 6, Chapter 7, and Chapter 8, this chapter recommends what I have presented as an alternative approach to curriculum development and teaching and learning that EIL educators at Urban University, and by implication other educators in similar contexts, might consider in developing and teaching an EIL curriculum, lesson, or program. Lastly, I outline the limitations of this study as well as some guidelines for future research.

9.1. Summary of main findings and their contributions

In response to the widely recognised pluralising forms, users, and cultures of English across the world, scholars have called for educators and curriculum developers in higher education settings to appreciate more fully the sociolinguistic complexity, indeed the reality, of the English language, and have often proposed an EIL paradigm or framework for doing so. As important and helpful as this guiding framework may be, there remain a number of 'missing pieces' in the existing research and practice conversations about teaching EIL.

Firstly, this paradigm or suggested framework is often seen as remaining at a conceptual level (Matsuda 2012a; forthcoming), and practitioners have found it difficult to operationalise this framework in practical terms (Brown, 2012).

Secondly, the voices, experiences, and perspectives of those who advocate new paradigms or frameworks and/or who participate in newly implemented curriculum initiatives (both teachers and students) are rarely if ever audible in the research literature (Brown, 2012; Li, 2009). These missing pieces prompted Wee (2013) and Qu (2016), in their recent review of the literature on teaching EIL, to advise that it would be more effective for future study or conversations on this issue to address and trigger more debates on how realistic it would be teach EIL or to implement the suggested framework. Their advice became a significant prompt for the major research question of the project, and I begin this concluding chapter by summarising how this project has responded to this question.

9.1.1. How realistic?

The experiences of lecturers and students in the EIL program at Urban University showed that the teaching of EIL seems to be more realistic than idealistic. The students' voices presented in Chapter 7, in particular, have shown how the syllabus materials and pedagogical approaches that all EIL lecturers employed in advocating the EIL paradigm (illustrated in Chapter 4 and Chapter 5) have been relevant, valuable, and/or beneficial.

9.1.1.1. Teachers' approaches

In order to operationalise the paradigm and to inspire students to learn to appreciate different varieties of English, key theorists (such as Baumgardner, 2006; Brown, 2012; Hino, 2010, 2012; Matsuda, 2003, 2012b; McKay, 2012a, 2012b; McKay & Brown, 2016) advise that EIL teaching syllabus materials and pedagogical practices should expose students to the pluralising forms, users, and cultures of English. However, what seems to be sorely missing from this advice is any sense of direction as to how to practically operationalise the EIL paradigm in a realistic classroom setting, as well as how to strategically engage students in learning about and understanding world Englishes. Thus, to contribute to these missing pieces and demonstrate the feasibility of teaching EIL, this book project has attempted to show as concretely and specifically as possible how EIL educators at Urban University exposed their students to and engaged them in learning about the pluralising forms, users, and cultures of English.

Firstly, rather than overloading students at the outset with scholarly literature about and examples of different varieties of English, all EIL educators at Urban University began by engaging their students in exploring and discussing the *nature* of language variation in order to gain a dynamic view (Vavrus, 1991) of language diversity. They opened up a conversation about how differences in English can be conceptualised as sociolinguistically normal and necessary as opposed to one that is framed by pointing out errors and deficiencies. Specifically, prior to an in-depth study of world Englishes in a higher level of study (EIL3102: World Englishes), students in first (EIL1010: English, Society, and Communication, EIL1020: International Communication), second (EIL2120: Language and

234   Re-envisioning a program of ongoing inquiry

Globalisation), and even third-year level (EIL3110: Language and Culture) were invited to explore how 'language is a dialect with an army and a navy'; how language and the way people use language *naturally* varies, and most importantly the factors behind the variations in the way people use language. To teach the latter, in almost all subjects in the program the EIL educators involved their students in exploring how language(s) or the way people use language(s) reflect the user's identity, cultural values, and/or conceptualisation of the world.

Authentic samples of English language variation, collected from a wide range of sources in various Kachruvian circles, were used either as examples to illustrate concepts or as a basis for an activity. The nature of these samples varied: from prescribed reading materials to online materials (including films), and from 'live' authoritative voices (guest lecturers) to teachers' personal collections of authentic texts from their everyday life (e.g. newspapers, email exchanges, airline magazines). Another source for these samples, one that to my knowledge has not been discussed in the EIL literature, were examples of language variation drawn from the students' own lives. Since covering all different varieties and cultures in the world in a single lesson, course, program (Matsuda, 2012b) is virtually impossible and since the program at Urban University was blessed with cohorts of students from diverse lingua-cultural backgrounds, EIL educators at Urban University used their own students' linguistic and cultural knowledge as invaluable resources for inquiring into linguistic and cultural diversity. Thus, pedagogical activities and assessment tasks from the first to the third years were designed in a way that invited students to reflect on, analyse, and most importantly enlighten their classmates and teachers of their experiences of using English and other languages, their cultural practices, values, and conceptualisation of the world. Not only did this allow students and teachers to participate in a community of practice in EIL (Hino, 2010), but it also provided students with opportunities to learn how to communicate their linguistic and cultural knowledge in English to those from other cultural contexts (McKay, 2002).

A second way in which the EIL program of teaching and learning at Urban University was different from previous studies was in its recognition that having awareness and theoretical understanding of different varieties of English and their reflections of diverse identities and cultural values is not sufficient. Key theorists such as Brown (2012), Canagarajah (2006), Firth (1996) and Higgins (2003) argue that the EIL curricula should also equip students with the ability to work across Englishes and cultures, or to be metaculturally competent (Sharifian, 2014). Once again, this advice in the literature has often remained at a conceptual level, and practitioners have found it difficult to embed within their practice. In response, this study has provided theorised illustrations of practice showing, for example, the different ways in which EIL educators used simulation, intercultural role-play, and scenario/case-based approaches in developing students' metacultural competence. These scenarios or simulations often involved intercultural (mis)communication cases or issues that arose from cultural and linguistic differences with which students might or might not have been familiar, and to which they were required to respond strategically and respectfully. Students were 'put on the spot' to draw on their conceptual variation awareness and knowledge, and then to employ strategies to work with unfamiliar different varieties of English and cultural practice.

Lastly, one final element of EIL curricula that emerged from this study and has not yet been widely discussed in the literature on teaching EIL is the incorporation of big-P and little-p issues (Janks, 2010) or sociopolitical concerns in an EIL curriculum. All EIL educators at Urban University, supported by Rizvi and Walsh (1998), emphasised that it is impossible to talk about cultural and linguistic differences or to raise questions about how these differences are unjustly constructed, treated, or perceived *without* being controversial. Therefore, in addition to discussing a big-P issue such as linguistic imperialism or linguicism, EIL educators at Urban University also engaged students in a classroom debate on little-p issues such as linguistic and racial discrimination in the hiring practices of English language teachers. For instance, a linguistic-identity-switching activity was conducted to allow students to experience the feeling of being in the shoes of those who were required to assimilate linguistically by those in power. This was conducted with the intention that students would problematise their own existing beliefs and/or the existing ideologies and practices that unjustly empowered some and marginalised others. Ultimately, it was hoped that students would be transformed through this learning and exit the course desiring to advocate for the beliefs and values promoted by an EIL paradigm.

9.1.1.2. Students' responses

Students' experiences of having studied and engaged in the above EIL curricula at Urban University confirmed the feasibility of the teaching of EIL and the importance of appreciating knowledge about English language variation in today's multilingual and multicultural globalising Australian society. In spite of Australia being a country in which English is used as the national language, the rich linguistic and cultural landscape of this globalised nation (Burridge, 2010; Clyne, 2005; Marlina, 2010; Sharifian, 2014) makes a compelling argument for teaching English as an international language. And yet some recent publications on teaching EIL such as Alsagoff et al. (2012) still appear to focus on teaching and learning EIL in contexts outside of Kachruvian Inner-Circle English-speaking countries where English is only one of a number of languages spoken and taught. As I have argued elsewhere (Marlina, 2013c), a perspective like this may imply two things: (1) that Inner-Circle countries are not multilingual and multicultural, and, therefore, (2) the teaching of EIL is not as important in those countries. This can be misleading because many Inner-Circle English-speaking countries, for example the United States and Australia, are becoming increasingly multilingual, multicultural, and 'pluri-varietal'. The forces of globalisation such as mass migration and advancement of technology have allowed citizens of Inner-Circle countries – as experienced by myself, my colleagues, and students at Urban University – to be in frequent contact with diverse speakers of world Englishes. Throughout this study, I have argued that the teaching and learning

236 *Re-envisioning a program of ongoing inquiry*

of EIL should also be perceived as relevant and important to any globalised, multilingual, and multicultural context such as Australia, regardless of the status and role of the English language in the country.

Confirming findings from some previous studies (Ali, 2015; Briguglio, 2006; Chang, 2014; Oxford & Jain, 2010; Shin, 2004; Suzuki, 2011), student-participants in this project repeatedly observed that the EIL curricula at Urban University had raised their awareness of the pluralising forms, users, and culture of English, and had equipped them with understanding of the fact that this pluralisation of English was an 'organic' process. With this awareness and understanding, all students also reported to have critically challenged the 'elitist', native-speakerist, and ethnocentric views that they brought with them to their studies. Further, they described how they had developed a different or perhaps a more positive and respectful perception of the diversity of English and its users (including themselves).

Furthermore, in-depth conversations with the student-participants also revealed some aspects of personal transformation that previous studies have not yet spoken about. This was an aspect of the study that was particularly gratifying to the EIL educators at Urban University. Firstly, some students, especially those from Expanding-Circle countries, believed that the EIL curricula had instilled in them personal confidence in perceiving themselves as legitimate speakers of English and, most importantly, in justifying why they used English the way they did. Secondly, all students seemed to have developed a willingness to continue learning and deepening their knowledge of the English language, which had been prompted by their awareness of the changing nature of the English language and the diversity of its users whom they had not yet encountered. Lastly, some students had been inspired by the curricula to become an advocate of EIL principles in their everyday life context. Third-year students, in particular, already started to initiate changes in an actual context based on the beliefs advocated in the curricula of the program. However, the study also revealed that the teaching and learning of EIL did not come without a level of challenge to students' personal beliefs and identities.

9.1.2. *Challenges in teaching and learning EIL*

Contrary to assumptions underpinning some studies (Briguglio, 2006; Kubota, 2001b; Oxford & Jain, 2010; Suzuki, 2011), the students in my research who had studied in the EIL program for a period of one to three years still expressed views that could be interpreted as native-speaker-supremacist, elitist, or anti-normative. Some remained unconvinced or uncertain about the feasibility of implementing the values or mindsets promoted by the EIL curricula outside the classroom. Unlike other scholars who regarded this as a negative outcome of the course, or as an 'attitudinal sin' (Kachru, 1986) and then concluded that further 'intervention' was needed as the previous one had failed profoundly to 'abolish' such an attitude or view, this study takes a different view. Rather than blaming the course or the student, this book project took the opportunity to inquire further into what might have laid underneath this view/attitude. My research lends support to a wide range of scholarly inquiry into the interconnections between language, culture, and identity (and beliefs) (see e.g. Assaf & Dooley, 2006; Bakhtin, 1981; Canagarajah, 1993; Doecke & Kostogriz, 2008; Nieto, 2010; Tupas, 2006). It has revealed how (1) the deeply stretched 'views from the old days', and (2) other powerful discourses the participants had been exposed to and experienced in their sociopolitical contexts, had echoed loudly to the extent that it prompted them to experience tensions and struggle to advocate with confidence the values and beliefs offered and promoted by the EIL curricula. These discourses were those of students' other lecturers, previous English teachers, peer groups/classmates, and some groups of people in their societies, who ethnocentrically and xenophobically constructed and treated those who were different from 'the mainstream' as the 'weird' and 'inferior' culturally problematic Others (Holliday, 2005). For some students such as Ogilvy and Phil the enduring connections to such discourses were unavoidable. Other students acknowledged that a range of authoritative discourses in the EIL program at Urban University had raised their awareness of how problematic the aforementioned discourses were and had provided them an alternative, more liberating discourse or perspective. However, at the same time their encounters with these voices had prompted them to experience cognitive 'inner battles' between all of these discourses. This battle of discourses is evident in several statements recorded in Chapter 7, such as: EIL lecturers tell us one thing and people outside the class tell us another thing; or how can people be allowed to speak in their own varieties of English in a society that does not have a positive value attached to diversity?

There had not been much space within the EIL curricula at Urban University for students to bring forward their dilemmas and to inquire into this 'battle'. Evidently, the EIL educators at Urban University were aware of this tension and even experienced a similar tension in their own beliefs and views. However, actions tend to speak louder than words. Some educators' pedagogical approaches, including mine, seemed to unintentionally and implicitly convey a message to students that this battle was not welcomed and was not supposed to be dialogued about. This was observed in the scenarios where students who offered their opinions that questioned or challenged the values or mindsets that the curricula advocated were frowned upon, labelled as 'complaints', avoided, and confrontationally approached by the educators. Rather than dialoguing and inquiring further into their opinions (which is profoundly missing in the EIL curricula at Urban University), EIL educators at Urban University still encouraged students to 'let's-get-to-know-each-other-better-*more*' by insisting on considering the value and view of respecting differences or by informing students that the decision to change was entirely their choice.

Returning to Wee's (2013) question, does this mean that teaching EIL is idealistic and infeasible? My answer is still 'No'. Developing and implementing a meaningful EIL curriculum is still realistic if EIL educators at Urban University (and perhaps other EIL scholars elsewhere) are keen and committed to taking into consideration the suggested alternative principles and pedagogical approaches to

238   Re-envisioning a program of ongoing inquiry

the teaching of EIL (Section 9.2). These principles, slightly amended from the principles commonly presented in more recent EIL literature (Matsuda, 2012a, 2012b; McKay, 2012a, 2012b; McKay & Brown, 2016), are my attempts to emphasise the theoretical and practical significance of this study.

9.2. Recommendations

> As a profession we appear to have a strong propensity for bandwagons, an inclination to seek simple, final solutions for complex problems. As individuals we need to resist the assumption that there is one Truth.
>
> Clark (1982, pp. 444–445)

Based on the works of key critical theorists (Bakhtin, 1981; Canagarajah, 1993; Doecke & Kostogriz, 2008; Pennycook, 1999; Simon, 1992) as well as my own engagement with the voices/experiences of EIL educators and students at Urban University presented in this study, I critically revisit assumptions and pedagogical approaches offered by key EIL scholars and researchers in the area of EIL syllabus materials and pedagogical practices (Brown, 2012; Brown, 1995, 2006; Hino, 2010; Kubota, 2001a, 2012; Matsuda, 2003, 2012a, 2012b; McKay, 2002, 2003, 2012a, 2012b; McKay & Brown, 2016) and propose a different set of principles or 'frameworks' for EIL teaching syllabus materials and pedagogical practices:

- EIL curricula inspire students to understand the nature of English language variation and to keep learning;
- EIL curricula engage students in developing metacultural competence;
- EIL curricula address sociopolitical issues or questions; and
- EIL curricula recognise struggles and tensions as normal, natural, and necessary.

I will now explain these alternative principles and pedagogical approaches, not as a set of definitive prescriptions for practice but as a critically grounded and practical set of propositions that educators or scholars might want to consider when developing, selecting, and/or reviewing syllabus materials and pedagogical activities for teaching EIL.

9.2.1. EIL curricula inspire students to understand the nature of English language variation and to keep learning

In response to the changing sociolinguistic reality of English, this study recommends that EIL curricula strategically expose students to, and engage them in, learning about diverse forms, users, and cultures of English. It should also inspire students to understand and appreciate how diversity is sociolinguistically normal and valuable in creating a more democratic society. Not only is this awareness and knowledge of this reality of English important and relevant in today's globalised world, but it is also likely to allow students to experience, as revealed in this study, the benefits of being aware and knowledgeable about world Englishes.

What is often unclear in the previously proposed frameworks for teaching EIL is how to realistically implement them. To raise their students' awareness of world Englishes and instil in them a legitimate and respectful recognition of these Englishes, do teachers simply prescribe writings on Singaporean English, Chinese English, and Scottish English and include plenty of examples of these Englishes in their lessons? Do teachers simply tell students that there are different varieties of English which need to be legitimately recognised as equal, and of which the speakers need to be proud? This study has demonstrated the value, prior to any in-depth engagement in learning about different national and regional varieties of English, of students developing some basic knowledge and understanding of the nature of English language variation. Yet merely informing them that there are different varieties of English in the world, and presenting them with examples are less likely to inspire students to develop a dynamic perspective of world Englishes. Rather, students need to be engaged in an in-depth exploration of questions that may inspire them to learn to see that language variation is a natural or 'organic' process: What is language variation? Why does language naturally vary? How does language vary? Who contributes to this variation? Where do you hear and find this variation? On the one hand, this book project has shown the importance of situating such questioning of the key knowledge that is being taught in the EIL classroom firmly within the students' lived experience. In this way students learn, from early in their study, that one of the most invaluable resources for engaging in learning about English language variation and how this variation reflects diverse sociocultural values and realities is the students themselves, particularly their cultural and linguistic capital. Another pragmatic dimension to this is that there little in the way of EIL learning resources that present students with the changing sociolinguistic landscape of English, and anyway it would be hard for any pre-packaged resource to connect with the particular ethnic, linguistic, and cultural backgrounds in all of the different EIL classrooms across the world. Therefore, reflecting on, analysing, and sharing their own (and others') experiences and/or observations of using language is crucial here. As Kramsch says (2013), language teaching in the era of globalisation should establish both sharing cultures as well as the culture of sharing. This is important because not only can this be used as a way to expose students to or engage them in learning about linguistic and cultural diversity, but also as a way to inspire them to conceptualise learning about linguistic and cultural diversity as a never-ending journey. An outcome of an EIL-oriented course should surely be that students desire to keep learning as "there's a lot of information out there in the world which [one] will lose out if [he/she] stays close-minded" (Phil).

9.2.2. *EIL curricula engage students in developing metacultural competence*

With enhanced knowledge and awareness of the sociolinguistic reality of English, students need to be given opportunities to translate this knowledge and awareness

240 *Re-envisioning a program of ongoing inquiry*

into practice. In other words, EIL curricula should establish spaces for students to learn to develop the ability to work effectively in today's "multifaceted and potentially confusing linguistic world" (Crystal, 1999, p. 97) and to develop metacultural competence (Sharifian, 2014). This is important because, with the increasing frequency of transplanetary contacts thanks to the forces of globalisation, the interlocutors with whom students are going to be interacting are often unknown, but are certainly diverse in linguistic and cultural behaviour. Awareness of variations in the way people use English and how it reflects diverse cultural values and sociocultural realities is important, but is still insufficient. Students should be equipped with the ability to acknowledge and articulate their awareness or interpretations, as well as to apply effectively these different values and realities through various forms of negotiation in their everyday lives. Pedagogically, learning activities can be designed to engage students in developing strategies to work effectively and respectfully with differences. Specifically, educators can use intercultural role-plays (Hino, 2010) or scenarios and simulations of communicative encounters with different varieties of English or different cultural practices where they need to demonstrate their awareness, explain/interpret this awareness, and negotiate these differences.

9.2.3. *EIL curricula address sociopolitical issues or questions*

Although Sharifian's (2009) EIL paradigm acknowledges the relevance of world Englishes in language teaching and emphasises the importance of incorporating it into English language syllabus materials and pedagogical practices, it seems to overlook or fails to acknowledge explicitly the relevance of and importance of discussing sociopolitical aspects of the global spread of English, as well as the politicisation of linguistic and cultural diversity in everyday contexts. Without this dimension, the teaching of EIL can decline into superficial "romantic and anti-intellectual celebration of individual difference" (Pennycook, 1990, p. 308). Specifically, merely describing or teaching different varieties of English "overlooks the power and ideologies behind the spread of English, and legitimates yet another language of power, thus undermining the rich linguistic multiplicity existing within a country (Kubota, 2012, pp. 60–64). Drawing on suggestions by Matsuda (2003), Dogancay-Aktuna (2006), and Kubota (2012), this book argues that EIL syllabus materials and pedagogical practices need to consider including and engaging their students in learning about sociopolitical issues, such as the politics of the hegemonic spread of English, linguistic imperialism, linguicism, and linguistic genocide. In addition to these big-P issues (Janks, 2010), I urge the importance of addressing and engaging EIL students in discussing any existing unjust practices and ideologies in their everyday lives or little-p issues (Janks, 2010) within an EIL curriculum. Although, as suggested by McKay and Brown (2016), it is important to expose students to different varieties of English, to take pride in the varieties of English they speak, and to recognise all varieties as equal, this approach often "pays little attention to the role of the dominant culture in preventing equality" (Jenks et al., 2001, p. 92) and how diversity is constructed or treated in the sociopolitical context (Nieto, 1999, 2010) in which students live and study. These micropolitics of everyday life are important not just because they are hard to avoid. They are a part of the everyday of which people may or may not be conscious. Thus EIL-inspired educators could consider developing learning activities that raise their students' critical awareness and discussions of potential political linguistic issues in their surroundings, such as racial/linguistic inequalities, racial violence, assimilationist policy, and linguistic/racial discrimination in language teaching employment. As Janks (2010) says, "working with the politics of local enables us to effect small changes that make a difference in our everyday lives and those of the people around us" (p. 41). This can be seen in the attempts of some students in my study who, having completed a three-year undergraduate study in EIL, proceeded to challenge native-speakerist and self-deprecating views communicated by their friends as well as to inspire them to develop a respectful view of themselves and of others.

9.2.4. EIL curricula recognise struggles and tensions as normal, natural, and necessary

This study shares the view of some scholars that paradigms of World Englishes and EIL are anti-normative paradigms (Kubota, 2012). From the word 'anti-normative', it can be seen that these paradigms are advocating a perspective(s) that consciously challenges a 'normal current'. As argued by Tupas (2006), though different varieties of English are sociolinguistically acceptable, they are still sociopolitically unacceptable in real life. If EIL educators are to teach ideas, views, and beliefs that are challenging or different from a 'normal current', and if they are to do this and still maintain a standpoint of encouraging critical reflection in their students, then this teaching becomes a delicate activity that needs to be practised with some care and pedagogical expertise. As Bennett (1993) argues, "the concept of difference and the implications this concept brings along with it is one of the most threatening ideas for students" (p. 181) and thus may prompt students (as well as teachers) to experience cognitive disequilibrium, resistance, struggle, or tensions.

However, my review of the current 'landscape' of teaching EIL across the world and my analysis of the hidden curriculum of the EIL program at Urban University suggest that Bennett's argument is often forgotten. In my study, when students offered perspectives that showed hesitation about or active resistance towards the views or beliefs advocated by the EIL paradigm, researchers and scholars tended to construct these negatively: they were 'problems' in the teaching and learning, or 'attitudinal sins' on the part of the students. And there was little evidence of scholars or practitioners attempting to explore the phenomenon in any depth. For some, the solution is to execute more 'interventions' (Briguglio, 2006; Galloway & Rose, 2014; Kubota, 2001b; Seargeant, 2012; Suzuki, 2011), since a 'single-shot intervention' was clearly not enough to 'abolish' this problem. This was similarly observed in the pedagogical approaches of EIL educators at Urban University where views and beliefs that were different

242   Re-envisioning a program of ongoing inquiry

from the ones advocated by the educators were avoided, frowned upon, and even confrontationally approached. As I illustrated in my reflections on a range of teaching contexts in Chapter 2, all of this would appear to be constructing the teaching of EIL as similar to administering medical injections to cure an 'illness'. In such a paradigm, students are expected to 'fully recover' from their 'deficiency', 'sins' or 'illness' after an 'intervention'. If these 'symptoms' still persist, more 'EIL-shots' should be administered to 'abolish' them. In this case, these beliefs or the practices that are based on this belief are not much different from those of the EIL-ex program at Urban University or a 'remedial class' (Haigh, 2002) in which a binary opposition of 'us' and 'them' is created. 'Us' are students who have 'fully converted' into EIL advocates and whose perspectives given in class are not frowned upon but praised, whereas 'them' are those who are still 'EIL-deficient' and need to be remedied to ensure that their frowned-upon 'EIL-resistant' perspectives are 'abolished'.

Inspired by the work of Bakhtin (1981), Canagarajah (1993), Doecke and Kostogriz (2008), Gleeson and Davison (2016), Simon (1992) and the experience of conducting this project, I now have learned not to regard or view struggles, tensions, and conflicts in learning EIL as negative or signs of rebellion against the paradigm, but as *natural* or "inherent" (Bakhtin, 1981, p. 348) reactions or responses to a new and different discourse or perspective, especially one that encourages 'swimming against the current' that has been flowing in one direction for a very long time. Thus, ultimately the approach that this project recommends is to recognise the phenomenon of students struggling with dilemmas or tensions as crucial to their learning. When people engage in learning or understanding a particular subject matter such as EIL, they are, at the same time, cognitively entering a 'discourse/ideology battle arena' in which they are dialoguing, debating, and/or competing with a range of conflicting voices or discourses (authoritative and internally persuasive discourses) on that particular subject matter to which they have previously been exposed, and into which they have been socialised. In relation to teaching EIL, the powerful discourses voiced in EIL classrooms on the importance of appreciating different varieties of English and of 'owning' one's use of English are likely to create tensions in students whose internally persuasive discourses might have already been shaped by other discourses that promote the supremacy of native-English speakers. As tantalising and liberating as this 'new' discourse or ideological standpoint may sound to the learners, it may not yet have the power in first encounters (or many subsequent encounters) to replace those 'old' discourses that have been deeply ingrained for a long period of time. As evidenced in this project, even after completing a three-year course in EIL, the discourses from 'the old days' still echoed rather loudly in Phil and Tomoko's minds to the extent that it prompted them to experience a struggle to become an EIL advocate. For Phil and Tomoko and for many others too, "challenging deeply held assumptions and views that constitute their internally persuasive discourses and provide multiple viewpoints and voices is a process that takes time and commitment" (Doecke & Kostogriz, 2008, p. 5).

In light of this, a different pedagogical approach is needed especially based on a view that struggles and tensions (1) are crucial to the learning process as individuals build new understandings (Bakhtin, 1981; Doecke & Kostogriz, 2008), and (2) need to be engaged with in "a perhaps unresolvable, but nevertheless educationally productive process" (Simon, 1992, p. 25). In other words, if different varieties of English should be argued as sociolinguistically normal and necessary, then inner tensions, struggles, or conflicts should also be perceived as normal and necessary in an educational program that is based on an anti-normative paradigm. In fact, new learning will not take place unless students are "discomforted by inconsistencies or dissonance between their beliefs and new theories" (Gleeson & Davison, 2016, p. 46).

Pedagogically, "challenging ideology can never be a matter of simply persuading people to think otherwise" (Doecke & Kostogriz, 2008, p. 82). In the case of teaching EIL, it is not sufficient simply to inform people they should take pride in the English they speak, and to insist that they consider the offered perspective. To deal with tensions, conflicts, struggles, "we may need to study them" (Williams, 1996, p. 200) as opposed to avoiding them, approaching them confrontationally, or searching for more ways to 'abolish' them. In other words, EIL educators might need to inquire into, bring forward, or discuss openly the range of discourses that have prompted students to experience this cognitive disequilibrium, especially those discourses from the micropolitics of everyday life. This is because these tend to be the encounters that continuously shape people's ways of understanding the world (Janks, 2010). These are the encounters that, as revealed in this study, prompt students and teachers to experience tension and struggle. As these discourses or acts of critiquing everyday life can be rather sensitive and delicate, students can be encouraged to reflect on, discuss openly, and critically evaluate these discourses in a non-threatening environment. Alternatively, when students express their disagreement with the views offered, educators can encourage them to feel that learning about diversity "does not always mean agreement and does not ever mean the same" (Simon, 1992, p. 25). Both teachers and students could proceed to inquire into what might or could have been the underlying reasons behind their disagreement with the offered perspectives.

In order to observe this at a practical level, EIL educators could consider engaging students in exploring critically and addressing what Simon calls "the 'naturalness' of dominant ways of seeing, saying, and doing" (Simon, 1992, p. 58). This can be done by asking (Simon, 1992):

(1) Why are things the way they are?
(2) How did they become that way?
(3) Why might change be desirable?
(4) What would it take for things to be otherwise?

Inspired by Simon's (1992) work, I also would suggest that rather than simply 'discussing' these discourses as they can end up simply being tired social issues (Pennycook, 1999), both students and teachers can work together in:

244   Re-envisioning a program of ongoing inquiry

- re-telling well-known stories: both educators and students can inquire into the already known existing micropolitics of everyday life, and explore how these old stories can be unpacked and used to produce new meanings;
- telling new stories: both educators and students can draw a picture of reality, characters, events, or actions that were previously invisible, untold, unthinkable, and unimaginable; and
- critiquing their own "embeddedness in histories, memories, and social relations that are the ground for their understanding of the social world and their actions within it" (Simon, 1992, p. 57).

These recommended principles and pedagogical approaches, emphasising the quote from Clarke (1982) at the beginning of Section 9.2, are not intended to serve as prescriptions for practice, nor as definitive solutions to particular EIL practice challenges, but rather to trigger more robust debate about EIL curricula or to open up further conversations on how realistic it might be to teach EIL. In this respect, I am representing the dialogues and learning about the curriculum and pedagogy of EIL as dynamic, ongoing, and 'unfinalised' (Bakhtin, 1981). This leads me to highlight the limitations of this book project and to offer some suggestions for future research that could carry on these unfinalised and ongoing dialogues and debates about the development of EIL curricula and about the learning and teaching of EIL.

9.3. Limitations of this study and suggestions for future research

Although I have proposed a modified set of principles and pedagogical practices for the particular teaching of EIL in Urban University, and have suggested that these principles and practices *could* be considered for other contexts, my intention is to be suggestive and not prescriptive. As mentioned briefly in Chapter 3, the outcomes of my study and their implications are based on a case of a single, recently revised program in one particular faculty and one particular institution in Australia. This case has involved a close focus on the teaching and learning experiences of a limited number of participants (students and teachers). Furthermore, due to the nature of the Faculty of Arts undergraduate degree at Urban University, this study could not provide a complete record of the learning development and learning experiences (from the time they enrolled in the first year until they graduated) of those students who had expressed their interest in participating in the study but I was not able to include in the project. Unlike programs in other faculties at Urban University where the progression is fixed, students in the Faculty of Arts at Urban University are free to choose the subjects they wish to undertake as a major, a minor, or as electives. There is no guarantee that students who are enrolled in first-year EIL courses are going to continue studying with the program and choose EIL as their major. Usually their decision to specialise in a particular discipline is not made until they are at the second-year level. Because the EIL program at Urban University does not have any prerequisites, students from any level of study and any discipline backgrounds can opt into the program at a time in their learning pathway that suits them. As a result, there are some second- or third-year students who are undertaking first-, second-, and third-year EIL subjects in one semester either because they have just realised that their initial choice of specialisation was perhaps not the best choice for them or because they have performed poorly in their initially chosen major/minor and have decided to explore a different one. Therefore, this study may have generated a wider range of student responses had I had the luxury to observe and study the learning development of more students as they progressed from first to third year.

There are a few EIL undergraduate students who choose to undertake a postgraduate degree in EIL and even doctoral research in EIL at Urban University. One claim that I have argued throughout the study is that learning to be an EIL advocate is a complex and time-consuming process and is often filled with tensions, struggles, and conflicts as one encounters multiple competing authoritative and internally persuasive discourses. It is through ongoing inquiries and dialogues into these tensions and struggles that learners formulate their own ideological standpoint. Hence, it would be interesting to explore this perspective from the learning experiences and perspectives of these postgraduate and/or graduate students well after they have completed their study of EIL.

One last limitation of this study is that the EIL program in which I carried out my study is not a program for teaching English language *proficiency* to students, i.e. it does not teach students to be more proficient speakers of English. It is better understood as a content program (refer to the explanation of this term in Chapter 3). Therefore, students who are studying in this program are generally already highly proficient as speakers of the English language. Their knowledge of the English language is sufficient to allow them to take part in a range of collaborative tasks that require them to reflect on and analyse their own use of English, and to critically consider how their knowledge and use of English might be different from varieties of Inner-Circle Englishes they had grown up learning. Investigating a curriculum or program that uses the EIL paradigm to teach general English language proficiency can be another direction that researchers or educators might like to pursue.

I am certain that there is much more that can be done to advance knowledge on EIL curriculum and pedagogy, which is currently in its infancy stage. In further studies, I would like to re-emphasise, as Bamgbose (2001) commented, that we should not only write about or advocate the teaching of EIL for attracting our colleagues' attention. It is time that we, as EIL educators and researchers, dive into our classrooms and listen to the voices of students and language teachers. Language teachers, in particular, are frustrated not necessarily because there have been no practical examples of how to implement the teaching of EIL. Though there are few published materials (e.g. Matsuda & Duran, 2012; Siemund, Davydova, & Maier, 2012), teachers may be still frustrated because they are uncertain about how those materials and the philosophical assumptions underlying those materials are welcomed in their educational institutions and in their societies. Although a wealth of studies has strongly emphasised the relevance and urgency of teaching an EIL curriculum, especially in today's increasingly

246 *Re-envisioning a program of ongoing inquiry*

multicultural world, "there is actually little awareness of what it means to live between cultures" (Besemeres & Wierzbicka, 2007, p. xiv). It is hoped that more EIL-inspired researchers and educators will help continue this journey of developing and researching curricula or programs that aim to prepare today's global citizens for learning to live respectfully between or within cultures, languages, and Englishes.

Appendices

Appendix 1: Objectives of EIL-ex subjects

The EIL-ex program aims to provide 'second English language speaker of English' with:

- knowledge about forms and language features of communication in English and at the same time opportunities to increase their own language skills as they study the adaptability and flexibility of choice and variety which the English language produces at all levels of use (EIU1010 – Communication);
- knowledge of the unique grammatical, syntactical, and semantic features of the English language (EIU1020 – Form and Structure);
- the ability to identify the English form and structure of a variety of language functions through recognising some of the major contextual influences on language choice and the differences between speech and writing which affect the second language speaker (EIU2110 – Form and Function: English in Context);
- knowledge of the way spoken English adapts to accommodate a vast variety of contexts and the ability to investigate the ways in which a second language speaker may apply these theories to their interactions with the world (EIU2120 – One mode, Many methods);
- the ability to identify how communication is organised in a wide variety of professional contexts within the professional genres of English as well as identify the difference between correct language use and appropriate language choice within a variety of professional situation (EIU3102 – The language of professional communication).
- a deeper understanding of the complex relationships between language and culture and how this affects the second language speaker (EIU3110 – Language and Culture);
- the ability to analyse a variety of English language models, and an understanding of the relationship between the organisation of structure and content in a way that represents the message in the most appropriate form (EIU3210 – English discourse: exploration and demonstration); and
- the ability as a second language speaker to analyse texts that often offer a subtler message that communicates attitudes, feelings, beliefs, values and emotions. (EIU3130 – Making sense of the environment: English as the language of action and reflection).

248 *Appendices*

Appendix 2: Questions for EIL-ex essays

EIL1010 – Communication

- The genre of essays is one of the most recognisable genres in this academic discourse community. However, it is a genre that causes many *multilingual students* a great deal of *difficulties*. What do you believe are the main *reasons for these difficulties?*
- *First language speakers share what is understood as conventional or community meaning.* What effect does connotative meaning have on the way in which a message is understood? What makes this aspect of textual comprehension *difficult for the second language speaker*, both in the general use of language and in this discourse community in particular?

EIL1020 – form and structure

- What do *multilingual students need to know* about critical thinking *to be successful writers* in the Humanities or in the academic discourse community?
- What are the influences that affect the lexicogrammatical choices expected in tertiary writing in the Humanities and how might a genre-based grammar *assist a multilingual student* understand them?

EIL2110 – Form and function: English in context

- Are there *advantages* of introducing functional concepts such as field, tenor, and mode into a language program *for multilingual speakers* who are about to engage in academic study in this discourse community?
- What are the most important influences that affect the construction of meaning within a spoken and written text? Demonstrate how these influences can *pose problems for second language speakers* when they must communicate in English.

EIL2120 – The language of spoken English

- *Conversation* is not so much the 'natural use of language' but the site of negotiation and interaction and so is often *the hardest language function for the multilingual speakers* to participate in. Discuss.
- What *spoken genres* are valued in this academic discourse community and why can they be *difficult for the multilingual speakers to acquire?*

EIL3102 – Professional communication

This subject requires students to create and host a conference. Thus, they are required to design their own topics/questions. Here are the topics of the conference that the students designed and were approved by Lorna:

Appendices 249

- Discuss the *common problems multilingual speakers* have with persuasive speech and what *techniques* can be used *to help* them construct a more persuasive speech.
- Understanding the role of audience in persuasive speaking and psychological aspects of persuasion are *problems that multilingual speakers* have in giving a persuasive speech. Discuss this statement.
- *Multilingual speakers* are often *not confident* speaking in English and so their speech may not come across to the audience as particularly persuasive as it *lacks the power* that most first language speakers' speeches possess. Justify this statement and use your own examples to support your arguments.
- Essay writing is vital in the academic discourse community. What are *advice* and *practical strategies* that can be developed to *assist multilingual speakers communicate effectively* within this discourse community?
- Coming from a different cultural background makes it harder for *multilingual speakers to communicate through their writing*, compared with monolingual speakers of English as their expression might often *look unnatural* to their tutors. Discuss this statement and use your own examples to support your arguments.

EIL3110 – Language and culture

- What specific features of language and culture should be given priority when *preparing multilingual speakers* for academic study?
- How is the *concept of 'an Australian' used in advertising in this culture*? Select some advertisements that you feel have this cultural image successfully. Explain the success in both language and visual terms and what *difficulties multilingual speakers* have in understanding this advertisement.

EIL3130 – Making sense of the environment: English as the language of action and reflection

- Consider the social and cultural influences that exist in written text and why they are *areas of difficulty for multilingual speakers*.
- Examine the ways in which our social perceptions are manipulated by the *language of the mass media* and consider the *difficulties* this presents for *multilingual speakers of English*.

EIL3210 – The language of written English

- We all bring a range of meanings to the texts we create and there are many influences that affect how that meaning is formed. What are some of *the most difficult characteristics* of meaning that *a multilingual writer must overcome*?
- *If a multilingual writer* has a well-developed understanding of English then using figurative language should not cause them *difficulty*. Discuss.

Appendix 3: Topics and readings for EIL1010 trial subject

Week	Topic	Prescribed Readings
1	Introduction	No reading
2	What is language variation?	• Hudson, R.A. (1996). *Sociolinguistics.* Cambridge: Cambridge University Press. • Yule, G. (1996). *The Study of Language.* Cambridge: Cambridge University Press.
3	English in Singapore (Singaporean English)	• Pakir, A. (1993). Spoken and written English in Singapore: The differences. In A. Pakir (Ed.), *The English Language in Singapore* (pp. 23–25). Singapore: UniPress. • Platt, J.T. (1977). The subvarieties of Singapore English: their sociolectal and functional status. In W. Crewe (Ed.), *The English Language in Singapore* (pp. 83–95). Singapore: Eastern Universities Press.
4	Classroom test on language variation	
5	The concept of English as an International Language and World Englishes	• McKay, S. (2002). *Teaching English as an International Language.* Oxford: Oxford University Press.
6	'Do I sound cool and clear' to you?	• Bamgbose, A. (1998). Torn between the norms: innovations in world Englishes. *World Englishes, 17* (1), 1–14.
7	Native-speakers/ non-native-speakers	• Smith, D.L. (2003). Essay: Confessions of a native speaker. *Asian Englishes,* 6 (*1*), 92–96.
8	Mid-term test	
9	One English fits all?	• Kirkpatrick, A. (2006). Which model of English: Native-speaker, nativised or lingua franca? In R. Rubdy & M. Saraceni (Eds.), *English in the World: Global Rules, Global Roles* (pp. 71–83). London: Continuum.
10	Register and style	• Smith, F. (1994). *Writing and the Writer.* Mahwah, NJ: Lawrence Erlbaum.
11	Writing across cultures	• Kachru, Y. (2001). World Englishes and rhetoric across cultures. *Asian Englishes, 4* (2), 54–71. • Kachru, Y. (2006). Speaking and writing in world Englishes. In B.B. Kachru, Y. Kachru, & C.L. Nelson (Eds.), *The Handbook of World Englishes* (pp. 374–385). Malden: Blackwell.
12	Revision	
13	Final test	

Appendices 251

Appendix 4: Test questions for EIL trial

Final test

EIL1010
English as an International Language
Communication

Information

- Duration: 2 hours
- This sheet contains ONLY the test questions. You must write the answers in the provided answer booklet.
- Both question sheet and answer booklet must be handed to the tutor at the completion of the test.
- This is an open book test.

Choose **FIVE questions** from the following and write 200 words for **each** question

(1) According to McKay (2002), there does not seem to be a need for users of EIL to internalise the cultural norms of Inner-Circle countries in order to use English effectively as a medium of wider communication. Do you agree/disagree? Why? Do you think it is possible to learn a language without internalising the cultural norms of these countries?

(2) When you speak a language, you are speaking 'the navy and army of the language'. Reflect on how you speak English and your additional language (if applicable) and discuss to what extent do you agree with this? Explain what does this mean in the light of various topics on language variation.

(3) New Englishes are now developing in parts of the world where the most important use of English is for communication in multi-lingual communities. Each has its own standard that could and should be the English taught in schools (Kachru, 1992). To what extent do you agree or disagree with Kachru's views on World Englishes and why?

(4) In order to be intelligible, which one of the following questions matters the most: do I sound cool? Or do I sound clear? Justify your choice.

(5) What does it mean to be a competent EIL communicator? What advice would you give future students of EIL?

(6) James is a Chinese Indonesian who speaks Creole Mandarin as his mother tongue. He uses this language to communicate with his parents and other family members; uses Bahasa Indonesia (Indonesian language) with his Malay

252 *Appendices*

Indonesian friends; and uses English and Mandarin at schools. At the age of 12, he moved to Singapore and studied for 2 years in an international school where English and Mandarin were the medium of instructions. At the age of 14, he moved to Australia and completed his secondary and tertiary education. Now he is working as a certified translator/interpreter (Indonesian/ Mandarin/English) in South Africa. Therefore, would you consider James a 'native' speaker of English? Explain why or why not? Justify!

Appendix 5: Objectives of newly revised EIL subjects

Upon completion of the subjects from the EIL program, students will have demonstrated:

- a high level of understanding of the differences in how people communicate in English and critical awareness of and reflections on any misconceptions or pre-conceived assumptions about communication in English (EIL1010);
- legitimate recognition and appreciation for the diversity of cultural conventions speakers of different cultural and linguistic backgrounds bring to communication within international contexts (EIL1020);
- a high level of familiarity with and the ability to conduct research on current issues and research in English as an International Language and World Englishes (EIL2110);
- appreciation for the diverse forms and meaning that English language can have as a result of globalisation, and an in-depth understanding of the role of English in online communication and popular culture in multilingual and multicultural contexts (EIL2120);
- a high level of understanding and a legitimate recognition for world Englishes, and the ability to communicate respectfully across different Englishes (EIL3102);
- appreciation and understanding of the diversity of cultural values and world-views reflected in different Englishes, and a critical understanding of the undesirable impact of the spread of English on other languages and cultural identity constructions/maintenance (EIL3110);
- critical views on the ideology behind the learning and teaching of English; and a high level of awareness and understanding of the impact of ethnocentric teaching and learning materials or activities on learners and teachers of English (EIL3130); and
- awareness of features of writing in world Englishes and in different societies in the world; and the ability to critically challenge the assumptions behind one hegemonic model of writing in English in international communication (EIL3210).

Appendix 6: Subjects, topics, and prescribed reading materials of the newly developed EIL program

Subject	Topics covered	Prescribed Reading Materials
EIL1010: English, Society, and Communication (1st year, semester 1)	• How language varies? • Language and Dialect • Variation 1: Sociolect, Register, and Style • Variation 2: Pidgin and Creoles • Variation 3: Ethnicity and Multilingualism • Why variation? • Language and Identity • Language and Worldview • Issues/debates in language variation • Accent Debates • 'The' Standard English Debates • 'Native' and 'Non-Native' Debates	• Hudson, R.A. (1996). *Sociolinguistics*. Cambridge: Cambridge University Press • Wardhaugh, R. (1993). *Investigating Language: Central Problems in Linguistics*. Oxford: Blackwell • Yule, G. (1996). *The Study of Language*. Cambridge: Cambridge University Press • Stockwell, P. (2007). *Sociolinguistics: A Resource Book for Students*. London: Routledge • Bauer, L., Holmes, J., & Warren, P. (Eds.). (2006). *Language Matters*. Basingstoke: Palgrave • Thornborrow, J. (1999). Language and identity. In L. Thomas & S. Wareing (Eds.), *Language, Society, and Power* (pp. 135–149). London: Routledge • Esling, J.H. (1998). Everyone has an accent except me. In L. Bauer & P. Trudgill (Eds.), *Language Myths* (pp. 169–175). London: Penguin Books • Mugglestone, L. (2007). Accent as social symbol. In D. Graddol, D. Leith, J. Swann, M. Rhys, & J. Gillen (Eds.), *Changing English* (pp. 153–171). Abingdon: Routledge • Thomas, L. (1999). The standard English debate. In L. Thomas & S. Wareing (Eds.), *Language, Society, and Power* (pp. 151–171). London: Routledge • Brutt-Griffler, J. & Samimy, K.K. (2001) Transcending nativeness paradigm, *World Englishes, 20* (*1*), 99–106 • Smith, D.L. (2003). Essay: Confessions of a native speaker. *Asian Englishes, 6* (1), 92–96

Appendix 6 (*cont.*)

Subject	Topics covered	Prescribed Reading Materials
EIL1020: International Communication (1st year, semester 2)	• What is English as an International Language? • Interaction as Cooperation • Contexts in International Communication • Politeness across Cultures • Intelligibility in International Communication • Writing across Cultures • Models for Communication: Globish, Native-Speaker, Nativised, and Lingua-Franca	• McKay, S. (2002). *Teaching English as an International Language.* Oxford: Oxford University Press • Kachru, Y. & Smith, L.E. (2008). *Cultures, Contexts, and World Englishes.* London: Routledge • Nerriere, J.P. & Hon, D. (2009). *Globish The World Over.* US: International Globish Institute • Kirkpatrick, A. (2006). Which model of English: native-speaker, nativised or lingua franca? In R. Rubdy & M. Saraceni (Eds.), *English in the World: Global Rules, Global Roles* (pp. 71–83). London: Continuum.
EIL2110: Researching EIL (2nd year, semester 1)	• English as an International Language: State-of-the-Art • Research and Methodology • Qualitative and Quantitative Research • Research Literature Review • Data Collection and Analysis • Research Writing • Research Presentation	• Sharifian, F. (2009). *English as an International Language: Perspectives and pedagogical issues.* Bristol: Multilingual Matters • Creswell, J. (2009). *Research Design: Qualitative, Quantitative and Mixed-Methods Approaches.* London: Sage • Dornyei, Z. (2007). *Research Methods in Applied Linguistics.* Oxford: Oxford University Press • McKay, S.L. (2006). *Researching Second Language Classroom.* Mahwah, NJ: Lawrence Erlbaum

| EIL2120: Language and Globalisation (2nd year, semester 2) | • English, Globalisation, and Technology
• Internet English: Netspeak
• Texting English
• Online Intercultural Communication
• Englishes in the Media
• Englishes in Hip Hop
• Englishes in the Advertisements | • Crystal, D. (2006). *Language and the Internet*. Cambridge: Cambridge University Press
• Gao, L.W. (2001). Digital age, digital English. *English Today 67, 17* (3), 17–23
• Crystal, D. (2008). *Txtng: The Gr8 Db8*. Oxford: Oxford University Press
• Chiluwa, I. (2008). Assessing the Nigerianness of SMS text-messages in English. *English Today 93, 24* (1), 51–56
• Ma, R. (1996). Computer-mediated conversations as a new dimension of intercultural communication between East Asian and North American college students. In S.C. Herring (Ed.), *Computer-Mediated Communication: Linguistic, Social and Cross-Cultural Perspectives* (pp. 174–185). Philadelphia, PA: John Benjamins
• Bhatia, T.K. (2006). World Englishes in global advertising. In B.B. Kachru, Y. Kachru, & C.L. Nelson (Eds.), *The Handbook of World Englishes* (pp. 601–619). Malden: Blackwell
• Lee, J.S. (2006). Linguistic constructions of modernity: English mixing in Korean television commercials. *Language in Society*, 35, 59–91
• Martin, E.A. (2006). World Englishes in the media. In B.B. Kachru, Y. Kachru, & C.L. Nelson (Eds.), *The Handbook of World Englishes* (pp. 583–600). Malden: Blackwell
• Lee, J.S. (2007). I'm the illest fucka. *English Today 90, 23* (2), 54–60
• Lee, J.S. (2004). Linguistic hybridisation in K-Pop: discourse of self-assertion and resistance. *World Englishes, 23* (3), 429–450. |

Appendix 6 (*cont.*)

Subject	Topics covered	Prescribed Reading Materials
EIL3110: Language and Culture (3rd year, semester 1)	• Relationship between Language and Culture • Culture and Figurative Language • World Englishes across Cultures • Humour across Cultures • Cultural Identity in the Globalised world • Globalisation of English: Threats?	• Scollon, R. & Scollon, S.W. (2001). *Intercultural Communication*. Malden: Blackwell • Kramsch, C. (1998). *Language and Culture*. Oxford: Oxford University Press • Dobrovol'skij, D. & Piirainen, E. (2005). *Figurative Language: Cross-Cultural and Cross Linguistic Perspectives*. Oxford: Elsevier • Wong, J. (2006). Contextualising aunty in Singaporean English. *World Englishes, 25* (3), 451–466 • Smith, L.E. (1987). *Discourse Across Cultures: Strategies in World Englishes*. Hertfordshire: Prentice Hall • Kotthoff, H. & Spencer-Oatey, H. (2007). *Handbook of Intercultural Communication*. Berlin: Mouton de Gryuter • Kumaravadivelu, B. (2008). *Cultural Globalisation and Language Education*. New Haven, CT: Yale University Press • Ho, D.G.E. (2006). I'm not west. I'm not east. So how leh? *English Today, 22* (3), 17–24 • Rubdy, R. (2001). Creative destruction: Singapore's Speak Good English movement. *English Today, 20* (3), 341–355 • Phillipson, R. (1992). *Linguistic Imperialism*. Oxford: Oxford University Press.

EIL3102: World Englishes (3rd year, semester 1)	• Inner-Circle Countries: British English, American English, and Australian English • Outer-Circle Countries: Indian English, Hong Kong English, Singaporean English and Malaysian English • Expanding-Circle Countries: East Asia and Europe	• Kirkpatrick, A. (2007). *World Englishes: Implications for International Communication and English Language Teaching*. Cambridge: Cambridge University Press • Kretzschmar, W.A. (2010). The development of Standard American English. In A. Kirkpatrick (Ed.), *The Routledge Handbook of World Englishes* (p. 112). London: Routledge • Burridge, K. (2010). English in Australia. In A. Kirkpatrick (Ed.), *The Routledge Handbook of World Englishes* (pp. 132–151). London: Routledge • Mukherjee, J. (2010). The development of English language in India. In A. Kirkpatrick (Ed.), *The Routledge Handbook of World Englishes* (pp. 167–180). London: Routledge • Hashim, A. (2002). Culture and identity in the English discourses of Malaysians. In A. Kirkpatrick (Ed.), *Englishes in Asia: Communication, Identity, Power, and Education* (pp. 75–93). Melbourne: Language Australia • Low, E.L. (2010). English in Singapore and Malaysia: differences and similarities. In A. Kirkpatrick (Ed.), *The Routledge Handbook of World Englishes* (pp. 229–246). London: Routledge • Pang, T.T.T. (2003). Hong Kong English: A stillborn variety? *English Today, 19* (2), 12–18 • Mamoru, M. (2009). Japanese English for EIAL: What it should be like and how much it has been introduced. In K. Murata & J. Jenkins (Eds.), *Global Englishes in Asian Contexts: Current and Future Debates* (pp. 73–93). London: Palgrave • Park, K. (2009). Characteristics of Korea English as a glocalized variety. In K. Murata & J. Jenkins (Eds.), *Global Englishes in Asian Contexts: Current and Future Debates* (pp. 94–107). London: Palgrave • Shim, R.J.Y. (1999). Codified Koran English: Process, characteristics and consequence. *World Englishes, 18* (2), 247–258 • Xu, Z. (2010). Chinese English: A future power? In A. Kirkpatrick (Ed.), *The Routledge Handbook of World Englishes* (pp. 282–298). London: Routledge • Gorlach, M. (2002). *English in Europe*. Oxford: Oxford University Press.

Appendix 6 (*cont.*)

Subject	Topics covered	Prescribed Reading Materials
EIL3130: Language and Education (3rd year, semester 2)	• Linguistic and Cultural Diversity Education • Curriculum for Teaching EIL • Pedagogy for Teaching EIL • Assessing and Testing EIL • EIL perspective on Teaching Macroskills and Microskills	• Tudor, I. (2003). Learning to live with complexity: Towards an ecological perspective on language teaching. *System, 31*, 1–12 • Crystal, D. (1999). From out in the left field? That's not cricket: Finding a focus for the language curriculum. In R.S. Wheeler (Ed.), *The Workings of Language: From Prescriptions to Perspectives* (pp. 91–105). Westport: Praeger • Brown, K. (2006). Models, methods, and curriculum for ELT preparation. In. B.B. Kachru, Y. Kachru, & C.L. Nelson (Eds.), *The Handbook of World Englishes* (pp. 630–693). Malden: Blackwell • Baumgardner, R.J. (2006). Teaching world Englishes. In B.B. Kachru, Y. Kachru, & C.L. Nelson (Eds.), *The Handbook of World Englishes* (pp. 661–679). Malden: Blackwell • Jenkins, J. (2006). The spread of English as an international language: A testing time for testers. *ELT Journal, 60*, 51–60 • Kachru, B.B. (1992). Models for non-native Englishes. In B.B. Kachru (Ed.) *The Other Tongue: Englishes Across Cultures* (2nd ed.) (pp. 48–75). Urbana, IL: University of Illinois Press • Matsuda, A. (2003). Incorporating world Englishes in teaching English as an International Language. *TESOL Quarterly, 37*, 719–729 • McKay, S.L. (2003). EIL curriculum development. *RELC Journal, 34* (1), 31–47 • Kramsch, C. & Sullivan, P. (1996). Appropriate pedagogy, *ELT Journal, 50* (3), 199–212 • Kirkpatrick, A. (2007). Teaching English across cultures: What do English language teachers need to know how to teach English. *EA Journal, 23* (2), 20–36 • Hino, N. (2010). *EIL in Teaching Practice – A Pedagogical Analysis of EIL Classrooms in Action*. Osaka: Graduate School of Language and Culture, Osaka University.

| EIL3210: Writing Across Cultures (3rd year, semester 2) | • What Do I Know About English?
• What Do I Know About Writing?
• "not everyone writes": Oracy and Literacy
• Writing and Social Identity
• Contrastive Rhetoric: Writing and Culture
• World Englishes and Writing
• Critical Contrastive Rhetoric | • Scott, J.C. (2005). *Communication for a Global Society*. Reston: National Business Education Association
• Malcolm, I.G. (1999). Writing an intercultural process. In C.N. Candlin & K. Hyland (Eds.), *Writing: Texts, Processes and Practices* (pp. 121–141). London: Longman
• Fraida, D. & Kuhlman, N.A. (1992). *Cross Cultural Literacy, Global Perspectives on Reading and Writing*. New Jersey: Regents Prentice Hall
• Rubin, D. (1997). *Composing Social Identity in Written Language*. Mahwah, NJ: Lawrence Erlbaum
• Grabe, W. & Kaplan, R.B. (1996). *Theory & Practice of Writing*. Essex: Pearson Education
• Kachru, Y. & Nelson, C.L. (2006). Culture and conventions of writing. In Y. Kachru & C.L. Nelson (Eds.), *World Englishes: in Asian Contexts* (pp. 283–291). Hong Kong: Hong Kong University Press
• Smitherman, G. (1974). Soul 'n Style. *The English Journal, 63* (3), 14–15 (an example of writing in World Englishes)
• Severino, C. Guerra, J.C. & Butler, J.E. (1997). *Writing in Multicultural Settings*. New York, NY: The Modern Language Association of America
• Kubota, R. & Lehner, A. (2004). Toward critical contrastive rhetoric. *Journal of Second Language Writing, 13*, 10–15
• Canagarajah, S. (2002). Multilingual writers and the academic community: towards a critical relationship. *Journal of English for Academic Purposes*, 1, 29–44. |

References

Akbari, R. (2008). Transforming lives: Introducing critical pedagogy into ELT classrooms. *ELT Journal, 62* (3), 276–283

Ali, Z. (2015). The prospect and potential challenges of teaching Englishes in Pakistan. *Asian Englishes, 17,* 152–169.

Alsagoff, L., McKay, S.L., Hu, G., & Renandya, W.A. (Eds.). (2012). *Principles and Practices for Teaching English as an International Language,* New York, NY: Routledge.

Appadurai, A. (1990). Disjuncture and difference in the global cultural economy. *Theory, Culture and Society, 7,* 295–310.

Applebee, A. (1996). *Curriculum as Conversation: Transforming Traditions of Teaching and Learning.* Chicago, IL: University of Chicago, IL Press.

Araluce, H.A. (2008). Multicultural competence in teacher education. In I.R. Gay, A.J.M. Guijarro, & J.I.A. Hernandez (Eds.), *New Trends in English Teacher Education* (pp. 141–150). Spain: Universidad de Castilla-La Mancha.

Assaf, L.C. & Dooley, C.M. (2006). 'Everything they were giving us created tension': Creating and managing tension in a graduate-level multicultural education course. *Multicultural Education, 14* (2), 42–49.

Baik, J.H. & Shim, J.Y. (2002). Teaching world Englishes via the Internet. *World Englishes, 21* (3), 427–430.

Banks, J.A. & Banks, C.A.M. (2006). *Multicultural Education: Issues and Perspectives* (6th ed.). Indianapolis, IN: Jossey-Bass.

Baumgardner, R.J. (2006). Teaching world Englishes. In B.B. Kachru, Y. Kachru, & C.L. Nelson (Eds.), *The Handbook of World Englishes* (pp. 661–679). Malden: Blackwell Publishing.

Bakhtin, M.M. (1981). *The Dialogical Imagination* (C. Emerson & M. Holoquist, Trans. & Ed.). Austin, TX: University of Texas Press.

Bakhtin, M.M. & Medvedev, P.N. (1978). *The Formal Method in Literary Scholarship: A Critical Introduction to Sociological Poetics* (A.J. Wehrle, Trans.). Cambridge, MA: Harvard University Press.

Bamgbose, A. (2001). World Englishes and globalization. *World Englishes, 20* (3), 357–363.

Barnes, D. (1992). *From Communication to Curriculum* (2nd ed.). Portsmouth, NH: Boynton/Cook.

Bassey, M. (2003). Case study research. In J. Swann & J. Pratt (Eds.), *Educational Research in Practice: Making Sense of Methodology* (pp. 111–123). London: Continuum.

Bayyurt, Y. & Altinmakas, D. (2012). A WE-based English communication skills course at a Turkish University. In A. Matsuda (Ed.), *Principles and Practices of Teaching English as an International Language* (pp. 169–182). Bristol: Multilingual Matters.

Bell, J.C. (2002). Narrative inquiry: More than just telling stories. *TESOL Quarterly, 36* (2), 207–213.

Bell, J.S. (1997). Teacher research in second and foreign language education. *Canadian Modern Language Review, 54* (1), 3–10.

Bennett, M.J. (Ed.). (1993). *Principles of Training and Development.* Portland, OR: Portland State University.

Besemeres, M. & Wierzbicka, A. (Ed.). (2007). *Translating Lives: Living with Two Languages and Cultures.* Queensland: University of Queensland Press.

Bhatia, T.K. (2006). World Englishes in global advertising. In B.B. Kachru, Y. Kachru, & C.L. Nelson (Eds.), *The Handbook of World Englishes* (pp. 601–619). Malden: Blackwell Publishing.

Bisong, J. (1995). Language choice and cultural imperialism: A Nigerian perspective. *ELT Journal, 49* (2), 122–132.

Bogdan, R.C. & Biklen, S.K. (1992). *Qualitative Research For Education: An Introduction to Theory and Methods.* (2nd ed.). Needham Heights, MA: Allyn & Bacon.

Bolton, K. (2005). Where WE stands: Approaches, issues and debate in world Englishes. *World Englishes, 24* (1), 69–83.

Bourdieu, P. (1991). *Language and Symbolic Power.* Cambridege: Polity Press.

Bredella, L. (2003). What does it mean to be intercultural? In G. Alfred, M. Byram, & M. Fleming (Eds.), *Intercultural Experience and Education* (pp. 225–239). Clevedon: Multilingual Matters.

Briguglio, C. (2005). *The use of English as a global language in multinational settings and the implications for business education.* Unpublished PhD thesis, The University of Western Australia, Western Australia, Australia.

Briguglio, C. (2006). Empowering students by developing their intercultural communication competence: A two-way process. In ISANA (Ed.), *Educate, Advocate, Empower* (pp. 1–10). Queensland: ISANA International Education Association Inc.

Briguglio, C. (2007). Educating the business graduate of the 21st century: Communication for a globalised world. *International Journal of Teaching and Learning in Higher Education, 19,* 8–20.

Brown, J.D. (2012). EIL curriculum development. In L. Alsagoff, S.L. McKay, G. Hu, & W.A. Renandya (Eds.), *Principles and Practices for Teaching English as an International Language* (pp. 147–167). New York, NY: Routledge.

Brown, K. (1995). World Englishes: to teach or not to teach? *World Englishes, 14* (2), 233–245.

Brown, K. (2006). Models, methods, and curriculum for ELT preparation. In. B.B. Kachru, Y. Kachru, & C.L. Nelson (Eds.), *The Handbook of World Englishes* (pp. 630–693). Malden: Blackwell Publishing.

Brown, L. & Durrheim, K. (2009). Different kinds of knowing: Generating qualitative data through mobile interviewing. *Qualitative Inquiry, 15,* 911–930.

Brutt-Griffler, J. (2002). *World English: A Study of Its Development.* Clevedon: Multilingual Matters.

Boyatzis, R. (1998). *Transforming Qualitative Information: Thematic Analysis and Code Development.* Thousand Oaks, CA: Sage.

Burgess, R.G. (Ed.). (1982). *Field Research: A Source Book and Field Manual.* London: Allen & Unwin.

Burridge, K. (2010). English in Australia. In A. Kirkpatrick (Ed.), *The Routledge Handbook of World Englishes* (pp. 132–151). Abingdon: Routledge.

Canagarajah, A.S. (1993). Critical ethnography of a Sri Lankan classroom: Ambiguities in student opposition to reproduction through ESOL. *TESOL Quarterly, 27* (4), 601–626.

262 *References*

Canagarajah, A.S. (1999a). *Resisting Linguistic Imperialism in English Teaching*. Oxford: Oxford University Press.

Canagarajah, A.S. (1999b). On EFL teachers, awareness, and agency. *ELT Journal, 53* (3), 207–214.

Canagarajah, A.S. (2006). Changing communicative needs, revised assessment objectives: Testing English as an International Language. *Language Assessment Quarterly, 3* (3), 229–242.

Canagarajah, S. (2002). Multilingual writers and the academic community: Towards a critical relationship. *Journal of English for Academic Purposes, 1*, 29–44.

Carr, D. (1986). *Time, Narrative and History*. Bloomington, IN: Indiana University Press.

Carter, K. (1993). The place of story in the study of teaching and teacher education. *Educational Researcher, 22* (1), 5–12.

Casanave, C.P. (2010). Case studies. In B. Paltridge & A. Phakiti (Eds.), *Continuum Companion to Research Methods in Applied Linguistics* (pp. 66–79). London: Continuum.

Casanave, C.P. & Schecter, S.R. (Eds.). (1997). *On Becoming a Language Educator: Personal Essays on Professional Development*. Mahwah, NJ: Erlbaum.

Celce-Murcia, M. (2001). *Teaching English as a Second or Foreign Language* (3rd ed.). Boston, MA: Heinle & Heinle.

Chandruang, K. (1907). *My Boyhood in Siam*. London: Andre Deutch.

Chang, Y.J. (2014). Learning English today: What can world Englishes teach college students in Taiwan? *English Today, 30* (1), 21–27.

Chase, S.E. (2005). Narrative inquiry: Multiple lenses, approaches, voices. In N.K. Denzin & Y.S. Lincoln (Eds.), *The Sage Handbook of Qualitative Research* (3rd ed.). (pp. 651–679). Thousand Oaks, CA: Sage.

Chew, P.G.L. (1999). Linguistic imperialism, globalism, and the English language. *AILA Review, 13*, 37–47.

Clandinin, D.J., & Connelly, F.M. (2000). *Narrative Inquiry: Experience and Story in Qualitative Research*. San Francisco, CA: Jossey-Bass.

Clark, M.A. (1982). On bandwagons, tyranny, and common sense. *TESOL Quarterly, 16* (4), 437–448.

Clyne, M. (2005). *Australia's Language Potential*. Sydney: University of NSW Press.

Clyne, M. & Sharifian, F. (2008). English as an International Language: Challenges and possibilities. *Australian Review of Applied Linguistics, 31* (3), 1–16.

Cochran-Smith, D. (2000). Blind vision: Unlearning racism in teacher education. *Harvard Educational Review, 70* (2), 157–190.

Collins, P. & Blair, D. (Eds.). (1989). *Australian English: The Language of a New Society*. Queensland: Queensland University Press.

Cortazzi, M. & Jin. L. (1999). Cultural mirrors: Materials and methods in the EFL classroom. In E. Hinkel (Ed.), *Culture in Second Language Teaching* (pp. 196–219). Cambridge: Cambridge University Press.

Cox, F.M. & Palethorpe, S. (2001). The changing face of Australian English vowels. In D. Blair & P. Collins (Eds.), *Varieties of English Around the World: English in Australia* (pp. 17–44). Amsterdam: John Benjamins.

Crang, M. & Cook, I. (2007). *Doing Ethnographies*. Thousand Oaks, CA: Sage.

Creswell, J. (2003). *Research Design: Qualitative, Quantitative and Mixed-Methods Approaches* (2nd ed.). London: SAGE.

Creswell, J.W. (2007). *Qualitative Inquiry and Research Design: Choosing Among Five Traditions* (2nd ed.). Thousand Oaks, CA: Sage.

Crotty, M. (1998). *The Foundations of Social Research: Meaning and Perspective in the Research Process*. St Leonards, NSW: Allen & Unwin.

Crystal, D. (1997). *English as a Global Language*. Cambridge: Cambridge University Press.

Crystal, D. (1999). From out in the left field? That's not cricket: Finding a focus for the language curriculum. In R.S. Wheeler (Ed.), *The Workings of Language: From Prescriptions to Perspectives* (pp. 91–105). Westport: Praeger.

Crystal, D. (2006). *Language and the Internet*. Cambridge: Cambridge University Press.

Crystal, D. (2008). *Txtng: The Gr8 Db8*. Oxford: Oxford University Press.

D'Angelo, J. (2012). WE-Informed EIL curriculum at Chukyo: Towards a functional, educated, multilingual outcome. In A. Matsuda (Ed.), *Principles and Practices of Teaching English as an International Language* (pp. 121–139). Bristol: Multilingual Matters.

Das, K. (1965). *Summer in Calcutta*. Delhi: Everest Press.

Datta, T.K. (1939). *What English Education has Made of Us*. Lahore: Doaba.

Denzin, N.K. & Lincoln, Y.S. (2005). Introduction: The discipline and practice of qualitative research. In N.K. Denzin & Y.S. Lincoln (Eds.), *The Sage Handbook of Qualitative Research* (3rd ed.). (pp. 1–32). Thousand Oaks, CA: Sage.

Denzin, N.K. & Lincoln, Y.S. (2011). *The Sage Handbook of Qualitative Research* (4th ed.). Thousand Oaks, CA: Sage.

Diamond Sutra Recitation Group (2007). *Chung Hyo Ye: Tales of Filial Devotion, Loyalty, Respect and Benevolence from the History and Folklore of Korea*. Pohang, Korea: Yong Hwa Publications.

Diaper, G. (1990). The Hawthorne effect: A fresh examination. *Educational Studies, 16* (3), 261–267.

Dixon, R.M.W., Moore, B., Ramson, M.W., & Thomas, M. (1992). *Australian Aboriginal Words in English: Their Origin and Meaning*. Melbourne: Oxford University Press Australia.

Doan, B.N. (2011). Contrasting representations of English as an International Language (EIL) in two EIL undergraduate programs. *Journal of English as an International Language, 7* (1), 1–21.

Doecke, B. (2004). Educating the educator (an autobiographical essay). *English in Australia, 141*, 9–18.

Doecke, B. & Kostogriz, A. (2008). Becoming a professional (and other dissident acts): Language and literacy teaching in an age of neoliberal reform. *L1-Educational Studies in Language and Literature, 8* (4), 63–84.

Doecke, B. & Parr, G.B. (2009). 'Crude thinking' or reclaiming our 'story-telling rights': Harold Rosen's essays on narrative. *Changing English (An International Journal of English Teaching), 16* (1), 63–76.

Dogancay-Aktuna, S. (2006). Expanding the socio-cultural knowledge base of TESOL teacher-education. *Language, Culture, and Curriculum, 19* (3), 278–295.

Dogancay-Aktuna, S. & Hardman, J. (2012). Teacher education for EIL: Working toward a situated meta-praxis. In A. Matsuda (Ed.), *Principles and Practices of Teaching English as an International Language* (pp. 103–118). Bristol: Multilingual Matters.

Dwyer, S.C. & Buckle, J.L. (2009). The space between: On being an insider-outsider in qualitative research. *International Journal of Qualitative Methods, 8* (1), 54–63.

Eades, D. (1993). The case for Condren: Aboriginal English, pragmatics, and the law. *Journal of Pragmatics, 20*, 141–162.

Eades, D. (2000). I don't think it's an answer to the question: Silencing Aboriginal witness in court. *Language in Society, 29* (2), 161–196.

264   References

Eagleson, R.D., Kaldor, S., & Malcolm, I. (1982). *English and the Aboriginal Child.* Canberra: CDC.

Edwards, R., Crosling, G., Petrovic-Lazarovic, S., & O'Neill, P. (2003). Internationalisation of business education: Meaning and implementation. *Higher Education Research & Development, 22* (2), 183–192.

Ellis, C. (2004). *The Ethnographic I: A Methodological Novel about Autoethnography.* New York, NY: Altamira Press.

Ellis, G. (1996). How culturally appropriate is the communicative approach? *ELT Journal, 50* (3), 213–218.

Eisner, E.W. (1994). *The Educational Imagination: On the Design and Evaluation of School Programs.* New York, NY: Macmillan College Publishing Company.

Erdinast-Vulcan, D. (2008). The I that tells itself: A Bakhtinian perspective on narrative identity. *Narrative, 16* (1), 1–15.

Evans, C. (1978). *Psychology: a Dictionary of Mind, Brain and Behaviour.* London: Arrow.

Fenstermacher, G.D. (1994). The knower and the known: The nature of knowledge in research on teaching. In L. Darling-Hammond (Ed.), *Review of Research in Education* (pp. 3–56). Washington, DC: American Educational Research Association.

Finnegan, R. (2006). Using documents. In R. Sapsford & V. Jupp (Eds.), *Data Collection and Analysis* (pp. 138–151). London: Sage.

Firth, A. (1996). The discursive accomplishment of 'normality': On conversation analysis and 'Lingua Franca'. *Journal of Pragmatics, 26* (2), 237–259.

Fishman, J. (1982). Sociology of english as an additional language. In B.B. Kachru (Ed.), *The Other Tongue: English Across Cultures* (pp. 15–22). Urbana, IL: University of Illinois Press.

Foreman, P.B. (1948). The theory of case studies. *Social Forces, 26* (4), 408–419.

Foster, P. (2006). Observational research. In R. Sapsford & V. Jupp (Eds.), *Data Collection and Analysis* (pp. 57–92). London: Sage.

Frank, R.M., Dirven, R., Ziemke, T., & Bernandez, E. (Eds.). (2008). *Body, Language, and Mind (Vol. 2): Sociocultural Situatedness.* Berlin/New York, NY: Mouton de Gruyter.

Freedman, S.W. & Ball, A.F. (2004). Ideological becoming: Bakhtinian concepts to guide the study of language, literacy, and learning. In A.F. Ball & S.W. Freedman (Eds.), *Bakhtinian Perspectives on Language, Literacy, and Learning* (pp. 3–33). Cambridge: Cambridge University Press.

Freire, P. (1970). *Pedagogy of the Oppressed.* New York, NY: Continuum.

Galloway, N. & Rose, H. (2014). Using listening journals to raise awareness of Global Englishes in ELT. *ELT Journal, 68* (4), 386–396.

Gannaway, D. & Sheppard, K. (2012). *Benchmarking the Australian Bachelor of Arts: A Summary of Trends across the Australian Bachelor of Arts Degree Programs.* Queensland: Teaching & Educational Development Institute (TEDI), University of Queensland.

Gannaway, D. & Trent, F. (2008). *Nature and Roles of Arts Degrees in Contemporary Society: A National Scoping Project of Arts Programs Across Australia* (Dean of Arts, Social Sciences and Humanities – DASSH – BA Scoping Project August 2008). Strawberry Hills, NSW: Australian Learning and Teaching Council Ltd.

Gannon, S. (2008). Messing with memories: Feminist poststructuralism and memory-work. In A. Hyle, E.M. Ewing, S.D. Montgomery, & J.S. Kaufman (Eds.), *Dissecting the Mundane: International Perspectives on Memory-Work* (pp. 63–76). Lanham, MD: University Press of America.

Gannon, S. (2009). Writing narrative. In J. Higgs, D. Horsfall, & S. Grace (Eds.), *Writing Qualitative Research in Practice* (pp. 73–82). Rotterdam: Sense Publishers.

Gleeson, M. & Davison, C. (2016). A conflict between experience and professional learning: Subject teachers' beliefs about teaching English language learners. *RELC Journal, 47* (1), 43–57.

Glesne, C., & Peshkin, A. (1992). *Becoming Qualitative Researchers: An Introduction*. White Plains, NY: Longman.

Graddol, D. (1997). *The Future of English*. London: British Council.

Graddol, D. (1999). The decline of the native speaker. *AILA Review, 13*, 57–68.

Graddol, D. (2001). English in the future. In A. Burns & C. Coffin (Eds.), *Analysing English in a Global Context* (pp. 26–37). New York, NY: Routledge.

Graddol, D. (2006). *English Next*. London: British Council.

Gray, J. (2002). The global coursebook in English language teaching. In D. Block & D. Cameron (Eds.), *Globalization and Language Teaching* (pp. 151–167). London: Routledge.

Guba, E.G. & Lincoln, Y.S. (1981). *Effective Evaluation*. San Francisco, CA: Jossey-Bass.

Haigh, M.J. (2002). Internationalisation of the curriculum: Designing inclusive education for a small world. *Journal of Geography in Higher Education, 26* (1), 49–66.

Haug, F. (2008). Memory work. *Australian Feminist Studies, 23* (58), 537–541.

Halliday, M.A.K. (1985). *Introduction to Functional Grammar*, London: Edward Arnold.

Hammersley, M. (1987). Some notes on the terms 'validity' and 'reliability'. *British Educational Research Journal, 13* (1), 73–81.

Harumi, I. (2002). A new framework of culture teaching for teaching English as a global language. *RELC Journal, 33* (2), 36–57.

Hayward, F. (2000). *Preliminary Status Report 2000: Internationalization of US Higher Education*. Washington, DC: American Council of Education.

Heath, S.B., Street, B.V. &., & Mills, M. (2008). *On Ethnography: Approaches to Language and Literacy Research*. New York, NY: Teachers College Press.

Higgins, C. (2003). 'Ownership' of English in the outer circle: An alternative to the NS-NNS dichotomy. *TESOL Quarterly, 37*, 615–644.

Hino, N. (2010). EIL in teaching practice – a pedagogical analysis of EIL classrooms in action. In N. Hino (Ed.), *Gengobunka-kyoiku no aratanaru riron to jissen [New Theories and Practice in Education in Language and Culture]* (pp. 1–10). Osaka: Graduate School of Language and Culture, Osaka University.

Hino, N. (2012). Participating in the community of EIL users through real time news: Integrated Practice in TEIL (IPTEIL). In A. Matsuda (Ed.), *Teaching English as an International Language: Principles and Practices* (pp. 183–200). Bristol: Multilingual Matters.

Holliday, A. (1994). *Appropriate Methodology and Social Context*. Cambridge: Cambridge University Press.

Holliday, A. (2005). *The Struggle to Teach English as an International Language*. Oxford: Oxford University Press.

Holliday, A. (2007). *Doing and Writing Qualitative Research*. (2nd ed.). London: Sage.

Holliday, A. (2010). Analysing qualitative data. In B. Paltridge & A. Phakiti (Eds.), *Continuum Companion to Research Methods in Applied Linguistics* (pp. 98–110). London: Continuum.

Horvath, B.M. (1985). *Variation in Australian English: The sociolects in Sydney*. Cambridge: Cambridge University Press.

266 *References*

Hosseini, K. (2013). *The Kite Runner*. New York, NY: Riverhead Books.

Hu, G. (2002). Potential cultural resistance to pedagogical imports: The case of Communicative Language Teaching in China. *Language, Culture, and Curriculum, 15* (2), 93–105.

Hu, G.W. (2012). Assessing English as an International Language. In L. Alsagoff, S.L. McKay, G.W. Hu, & W. Renandya (Eds.), *Principles and Practices for Teaching English as an International Language* (pp. 123–143). New York, NY: Routledge.

Hudson, R.A. (1996). *Sociolinguistics*. Cambridge: Cambridge University Press.

Janks, H. (2010). Language, power, and pedagogies. In N. Hornberger & S.L. McKay (Eds.), *Sociolinguistics and Language Education* (pp. 40–61). Bristol: Multilingual Matters.

Jenkins, J. (2003). *World Englishes: A Resource Book for Students*. (2nd ed.). London: Routledge.

Jenkins, J. (2004). ELF at the gate: The position of English as a lingua franca. In *Proceedings of the 38th IATEFL International Conference*. (pp. 33–42). Canterbury: IATEFL.

Jenkins, J. (2006a). Current perspectives on teaching world Englishes and English as a lingua franca. *TESOL Quarterly, 40* (1), 157–181.

Jenkins, J. (2006b). The spread of English as an International Language: A testing time for testers. *ELT Journal, 60*, 51–60.

Jenkins, J. (2009). *World Englishes: A Resource Book for Students*. (2nd ed.). London/ New York, NY: Routledge.

Jenks, C., Lee, J.O., & Kanpol, B. (2001). Approaches to multicultural education in preservice teacher education: Philosophical frameworks and models for teaching. *The Urban Review, 33* (2), 87–105.

Kachru, B.B. (1986). *The Alchemy of English*. Oxford: Pergamon Press.

Kachru, B.B. (1992). Models for non-native Englishes. In B.B. Kachru (Ed.), *The Other Tongue: Englishes Across Cultures* (2nd ed.). (pp. 48–75). Urbana, IL: University of Illinois Press.

Kachru, Y. & Smith, L.E. (2008). *Cultures, Contexts, and World Englishes*. London: Routledge.

Kachru, B.B., Kachru, Y., & Nelson C.L. (Eds.). (2006). *The Handbook of World Englishes*. Malden: Blackwell Publishing.

Karavas-Doukas, K. (1998). Evaluating the implementation of educational innovations: Lessons from the past. In P. Rea-Dickins, & K.P. Germaine (Eds.), *Managing Evaluation and Innovation in Language Teaching* (pp. 25–50). Harlow: Longman.

Kenny, W.R. & Grotelueschen, A.D. (1980). *Making the case for case study*. Occasional Paper, Office for the Study of Continuing Professional Education. Urbana-Champaign, IL: College of Education, University of Illinois.

Kiesling, S.F. (2006). English in Australia and New Zealand. In B.B. Kachru, Y. Kachru, & C.L. Nelson (Eds.), *The Handbook of World Englishes* (pp. 74–89). Malden: Blackwell Publishing.

Kirkpatrick, A. (2006). Which model of English: Native-speaker, nativised or lingua franca? In R. Rubdy & M. Saraceni (Eds.), *English in the World: Global Rules, Global Roles* (pp. 71–83). London: Continuum.

Kirkpatrick, A. (2007). *World Englishes: Implications for International Communication and English Language Teaching*. Cambridge: Cambridge University Press.

Kirkpatrick, A. (2010). *The Routledge Handbook of World Englishes*. London: Routledge.

Kirkpatrick, A. (2011). English as an Asian lingua franca and the multilingual model of ELT. *Language Teaching, 44* (2), 212–224.

Kramsch, C. (1998). *Language and Culture*. Oxford: Oxford University Press.

Kramsch, C. (2013). Teaching foreign languages in an era of globalization. Paper presented at the Language and Society Centre Annual Lecture, 24 June 2013, Monash University, Melbourne, Australia.

Kramsch, C. & Sullivan, P. (1996). Appropriate pedagogy. *ELT Journal, 50* (3), 199–212.

Krober, A. & Kluckhohn, C. (1952). *Culture: A Critical Review of Concepts and Definitions*. New York, NY: Vintage Books.

Kubota, R. (2001a). Learning diversity from world Englishes. *The Social Studies, 92* (2), 69–72.

Kubota, R. (2001b). Teaching world Englishes to native speakers of English in the USA. *World Englishes, 20* (1), 47–64.

Kubota, R. (2012). The politics of EIL: Toward border-crossing communication in and beyond English. In A. Matsuda (Ed.), *Principles and Practices of Teaching English as an International Language* (pp. 55–69). Bristol: Multilingual Matters.

Kubota, R. & Austin, T. (2007). Critical approaches to world language education in the United States: An introduction. *Critical Inquiry in Language Studies, 4* (2–3), 73–83.

Kubota, R. & Lehner, A. (2004). Toward critical contrastive rhetoric. *Journal of Second Language Writing, 13*, 10–15.

Kuhn, T.S. (1962). *The Structure of Scientific Revolutions*. Chicago, IL: University of Chicago, IL Press.

Kumaravadivelu, B. (2003). *Beyond Methods: Macrostrategies for Language Teaching*. New Haven, CT: Yale University Press.

Kumaravadivelu, B. (2006). *Understanding Language Teaching: From Method to Postmethod*. Mahwah, NJ: Lawrence Erlbaum.

Lam, W.S.E. (2000). Second language literacy and the design of the self: A case study of a teenager writing on the Internet. *TESOL Quarterly, 34*, 457–482.

Lantolf, J. (Ed.). (2000). *Sociocultural Theory and Second Language Learning*. Oxford: Oxford University Press.

Leask, B. (2008). Internationalisation, globalisation and curriculum innovation. In M. Hellsten & A. Reid (Eds.), *Researching International Pedagogies: Sustainable Practice of Teaching and Learning in Higher Education* (pp. 9–26). The Netherlands: Springer.

LeCompte, M.D. & Schensul, J.J. (1999). *Designing and Conducting Ethnographic Research*. Walnut Creek, CA: AltaMira.

Lee, H. (2012). World Englishes in a high school English class. In A. Matsuda (Ed.), *Principles and Practices of Teaching English as an International Language* (pp. 154–168). Bristol: Multilingual Matters.

Li, D. (1998). It's always more difficult than you plan and imagine: Teachers' perceived difficulties in introducing the communicative approach in South Korea. *TESOL Quarterly, 32* (4), 677–703.

Li, D.C.S. (2007). Researching and teaching China and Hong Kong English: Issues, problems and prospects. *English Today, 23* (3&4), 11–17.

Li, D.C.S. (2009). Attitudes towards English as an International Language: The pervasiveness of native models among L2 users and teachers. In F. Sharifian (Ed.), *English as an International Language: Perspectives and Pedagogical Issues* (pp. 81–118). Bristol: Multilingual Matters.

Lincoln, Y.S. & Guba, E.G. (2000). Paradigmatic controversies, contradictions, and emerging influences. In N. Denzin & Y. Lincoln (eds.), *Handbook of Qualitative Research* (2nd ed.) (pp. 163–188). Thousand Oaks, CA: Sage.

268 References

Lowenberg, P. (2012). Assessing proficiency in EIL. In A. Matsuda (Ed.), *Principles and Practices of Teaching English as an International Language* (pp. 84–102). Bristol: Multilingual Matters.

Luders, C. (2004). Field observation and ethnography. In U. Flick, E.V. Kardorff, & I. Steinke (Eds.), *A Companion to Qualitative Research* (pp. 222–230). London: Sage.

MacDonald, B. & Walker, R. (1975). Case study and the social philosophy of educational research. *Cambridge Journal of Education, 5* (1), 2–11.

Malcolm, I. (2004a). Australian creoles and Aboriginal English: Phonology. In E.W. Scheider, K. Burridge, B. Kortmann, R. Mesthrie, & C. Upton (Eds.), *A Handbook of Varieties of English (Vol. 1): Phonology* (pp. 656–670). Berlin: Mouton de Gruyter.

Malcolm, I. (2004b). Australian creoles and Aboriginal English: Morphology and syntax. In E.W. Scheider, K. Burridge, B. Kortmann, R. Mesthrie, & C. Upton (Eds.), *A Handbook of Varieties of English (Vol. 2): Morphology and Syntax* (pp. 657–681). Berlin: Mouton de Gruyter.

Manara, C. (2012). *Intercultural Dialogue and English Language Teaching: Indonesian teacher educators' narratives of professional learning.* Unpublished PhD thesis, Monash University, Melbourne, Victoria, Australia.

Marlina, R. (2010). Teachers of Englishes, *English Teaching Professional, 66,* 47–49.

Marlina, R. (2011). *Critical Reflections on Teaching English as an International Language.* Symposium at the 17th Annual International Association for World Englishes Conference, "Englishes in the world: the world in Englishes', 23–25 November 2011, Monash University, Melbourne, Australia.

Marlina, R. (2012). Teaching world Englishes in an English as an International Language program to 'native-speakers' in the globalising Australia. Paper presented at the 4th Annual Roundtable of Language and Society Centre, 'Teaching and Learning Languages for International Communication', 16 February 2012, School of Languages, Cultures, and Linguistics, Faculty of Arts, Monash University, Melbourne, Victoria, Australia.

Marlina, R. (2013a). Learning about English as an International Language in Australia: From three students' perspectives. *Asian EFL Journal, 15* (3), 202–229.

Marlina, R. (2013b). *Globalisation, internationalisation, and language education: An academic program for global citizens.* In S.L. McKay & F. Sharifian. (Eds.), Special issue on 'Globalization, localization, and language use/learning', *Multilingual Education, 3* (5), 1–21.

Marlina, R. (2013c). Book review: Lubna Alsagoff, Sandra Lee McKay, Guangwei Hu, Willy A. Renandya, eds. 2012. Principles and Practices for Teaching English as an International Language. *World Englishes, 32* (3), 443–445.

Marlina, R. (Forthcoming). *Teaching language skills.* In *TESOL Encyclopaedia of English Language Teaching (Teaching English as an International Language Volume).* Chichester: John Wiley & Sons, Ltd.

Marlina, R. & Ahn, H.J. (2011). 'Internationalised' English teaching materials? Please think again: A Korean case study. Paper presented at the Korean Association of Teachers of English (KATE) Conference, 'Empowering English Teachers in the Globalization Era', 1–2 July 2011, Yonsei University, Seoul, South Korea.

Marlina, R. & Giri, R. (2013). 'We provide the best international education and use international-oriented learning materials': Questioning the 'international' from the perspective of English as an International Language. In N.T. Zacharias & C. Manara (Eds.), *Contextualising the Pedagogy of English as an International Language: Issues and Tensions* (pp. 75–98). Newcastle upon Tyne: Cambridge Publishing Scholars.

References 269

Marshall, C. & Rossman, G.B. (2006). *Designing Qualitative Research.* (4th ed.). Thousand Oaks, CA: Sage.

Martin, E.A. (2006). World Englishes in the media. In B.B. Kachru, Y. Kachru, & C.L. Nelson (Eds.), *The Handbook of World Englishes* (pp. 583–600). Malden: Blackwell.

Mason, J. (2002). *Researching Your Own Practice: The Discipline of Noticing.* Oxon: Routledge.

Matsuda, A. (2002). 'International understanding' through teaching world Englishes. *World Englishes, 21* (3), 436–440.

Matsuda, A. (2003). Incorporating world Englishes in Teaching English as an International Language. *TESOL Quarterly, 37*, 719–729.

Matsuda, A. (2005). Preparing future users of English as an International Language. In A. Burns (Ed.), *Teaching English From a Global Perspective: Case Studies in TESOL Series* (pp. 62–72). Alexandria: TESOL.

Matsuda, A. (2009). Desirable but not necessary? The place of world Englishes and English as an International Language in English teacher preparation program in Japan. In F. Sharifian (Ed.), *English as an International Language: Perspectives and Pedagogical Issues* (pp. 169–189). Bristol: Multilingual Matters.

Matsuda, A. (2012a). *Principles and Practices of Teaching English as an International Language.* Bristol: Multilingual Matters.

Matsuda, A. (2012b). Teaching materials in EIL. In L. Alsagoff, S.L. McKay, G. Hu, & W.A. Renandya. (Eds.), *Principles and Practices for Teaching English as an International Language* (pp. 168–185). New York, NY: Routledge.

Matsuda, A. (Forthcoming). *Preparing Teachers to Teach English as an International Language.* Bristol: Multilingual Matters.

Matsuda, A. & Duran, C.S. (2012). EIL activities and tasks for traditional English classroom. In A. Matsuda (Ed.), *Principles and Practices of Teaching English as an International Language* (pp. 201–250). Bristol: Multilingual Matters.

Matsuda, A. & Friedrich, P. (2010). When five words are not enough: A conceptual and terminological discussion of English as a lingua franca, *International Multilingual Research Journal, 4*, 20–30.

Matsuda, A. & Friedrich, P. (2011). English as an International Language: A curriculum blueprint. *World Englishes, 30* (3), 332–344.

Matsuda, A. & Friedrich, P. (2012). Selecting an instructional variety for an EIL curriculum. In A. Matsuda (Ed.), *Principles and Practices of Teaching English as an International Language* (pp. 17–27). Bristol: Multilingual Matters.

McKay, S.L. (2002). *Teaching English as an International Language.* Oxford: Oxford University Press.

McKay, S.L. (2003). EIL curriculum development. *RELC Journal, 34* (1), 31–47.

McKay, S.L. (2010). English as an International Language. In N. Hornberger & S.L. McKay (Eds.), *Sociolinguistics and Language Education* (pp. 89–115). Bristol: Multilingual Matters.

McKay, S.L. (2012a). Principles of teaching English as an International Language. In L. Alsagoff, S.L. McKay, G.W. Hu, & W. Renandya (Eds.), *Principles and Practices for Teaching English as an International Language* (pp 28–46). New York, NY: Routledge.

McKay, S.L. (2012b). Teaching materials for English as an International Language. In A. Matsuda (Ed.), *Teaching English as an International Language: Principles and Practices* (pp. 70–83). Bristol: Multilingual Matters.

McKay, S.L. & Bokhorst-Heng, W.D. (2008). *International English in its Sociolinguistic Contexts: Towards a Socially Sensitive EIL Pedagogy.* London: Routledge.

270   References

McKay, S.L. & Brown, J.D. (2016). *Teaching and Assessing EIL in Local Contexts Around the World.* New York, NY: Routledge.

McNiff, J. & Whitehead, J. (2011). *All You Need to Know About Action Research.* London: Sage.

Merriam, S.B. (1998). *Qualitative Research and Case Study Applications in Education.* San Francisco, CA: Jossey-Bass.

Merriam, S.B. (2009). *Qualitative Research: A Guide to Design and Implementation.* San Francisco, CA: Jossey-Bass.

Milner, H.R. (2010). *Culture, Curriculum, and Identity in Education.* New York, NY: Palgrave Macmillan.

Min, E. (2001). Bakhtinian perspectives for the study of intercultural communication. *Journal of Intercultural Studies, 22* (1), 5–18.

Minichiello, V., Aroni, R., Timewell, E., & Alexander, L. (1995). *In-depth Interviewing: Researching People.* Sydney: Longman Cheshire.

Mitchell, W.J.T. (Ed.). (1981). *On Narrative.* Chicago, IL: University of Chicago, IL Press.

Moustakas, C. (1994). *Phenomenological Research Methods.* Thousand Oaks, CA: Sage.

Newman, W.L. (2000). *Social Research Methods: Qualitative and Quantitative Approaches.* (4th ed.). Boston, MA: Allyn and Bacon.

Nieswiadomy, R.M. (1993). *Foundations of Nursing Research.* Norwalk, CT: Appleton & Lange.

Nieto, S. (1999). Critical multicultural education and students' perspectives. In S. May (Ed.), *Critical Multiculturalism: Rethinking Multicultural and Antiracist Education* (pp. 191–215). London: Falmer Press.

Nieto, S. (2004). *Affirming Diversity: The Sociopolitical Context of Multicultural Education* (4th ed.). Boston, MA: Pearson.

Nieto, S. (2010). *Language, Culture, and Teaching: Critical Perspectives.* New York, NY: Taylor & Francis.

Odora-Hoppers, C.A. (2009). Education, culture, and society in a globalising world: Implications for comparative and international education. *Compare: A Journal of Comparative and International Education, 39* (5), 601–614.

Oller, J.W. & Richard-Amato, P. (Eds.). (1983). *Methods that Work: A Smorgasbord of Ideas for Language Teachers.* Rowley, MA: Newbury House.

Oxford, R.L. & Jain, R. (2010). Students' evolving perspectives on world Englishes, non-native English speakers, and non-native English-speaking teachers based on a graduate course. In A. Mahboob (Ed.), *The NNEST Lens: Non Native English Speakers in TESOL* (pp. 239–262). Newcastle upon Tyne: Cambridge Scholars Publishing.

Park, J.S.Y. & Wee, L. (2009). The three circles redux: A market-theoretic perspective on world Englishes. *Applied Linguistics, 30* (3), 389–406.

Parr, G.B. (2007). Writing and practitioner inquiry: Thinking relationally. *English Teaching: Practice and Critique, 6* (3), 22–47.

Parr, G.B. (2010). *Inquiry-Based Professional Learning: Speaking Back to Standards-Based Reforms.* Teneriffe, Queensland: Post Pressed.

Patton, M.Q. (1985). Quality in qualitative research: Methodological principles and recent developments. Invited address to Division J of the American Educational Research Association, April 1985, Chicago, Illinois, USA.

Patton, M.Q. (2002). *Qualitative Evaluation Methods* (3rd ed.). Thousand Oaks, CA: Sage.

Pennycook, A. (1990). Critical pedagogy and second language acquisition, *System, 18* (3), 303–314.

References 271

Pennycook, A. (1994). *The Cultural Politics of English as an International Language*. Harlow: Longman.

Pennycook, A. (1999). Introduction: Critical approaches to TESOL. *TESOL Quarterly*, *33* (3), 329–348.

Pennycook, A. (2000). The social politics and the cultural politics of language classrooms. In J.K. Hall & W.G. Eggington (Eds.), *The Sociopolitics of English Language Teaching* (pp. 89–103). Clevedon: Multilingual Matters.

Pennycook, A. (2003). Global Englishes, rip slyme, and performativity. *Journal of Sociolinguistics*, *7* (4), 513–533.

Phan, L.H. (2001). How do culturally situated notions of 'polite' forms influence the way Vietnamese postgraduate students write academic English in Australia. *Australian Journal of Education*, *5* (3), 296–308.

Phillips, D.C. & Burbules, N.C. (2000). *Postpositivism and Educational Research*. Lanham/Boulder: Rowman & Littlefield Publishers.

Phillipson, R. (1992). *Linguistic Imperialism*. Oxford: Oxford University Press.

Phillipson, R. (2009). *Linguistic Imperialism Continued*. London: Routledge.

Platt, J.T. (1977). The subvarieties of Singapore English: Their sociolectal and functional status. In W. Crewe (Ed.), *The English Language in Singapore* (pp. 83–95). Singapore: Eastern Universities Press.

Polkinghorne, D.E. (1988). *Narrative Knowing and the Human Sciences*. Albany, NY: SUNY Press.

Quirk, R. (1990). Language varieties and standard language. *English Today*, *21*, 3–10.

Qu, R. (2016). Book Review: Roby Marlina & Ram Giri, eds. 2014. The Pedagogy of English as an International Language: Perspectives from Scholars, Teachers, and Students. *The Journal of Asia TEFL*, *13* (1), 70–71.

Richards, J. & Rodgers, T. (1985). Method: Approach, design, and procedure. In J. Richards (Ed.), *The Context of Language Teaching* (pp. 16–32). Cambridge: Cambridge University Press.

Riessman, C.K. (1993). *Narrative Analysis*. Newbury Park, CA: Sage.

Rizvi, F. & Walsh, L. (1998). Difference, globalisation and the internationalisation of curriculum. *Australian Universities' Review*, *2*, 7–11.

Rose, H. & Galloway, N. (Forthcoming). Debating standard language ideology in the classroom: Using the 'Speak Good English Movement' to raise awareness of global Englishes. *RELC Journal*.

Rosen, H. (1998). *Speaking from Memory: Guide to Autobiographical Acts and Practices*. London: Trentham Books.

Rosenberg, P. (1997). Underground discourses: Exploring whiteness in teacher education. In M. Fine, L. Weis, L. Powell, & L. Wong (Eds.), *Off-white: Readings on Race and Power in Society* (pp. 79–86). New York, NY: Routledge.

Rossman, G.B., & Rallis, S.F. (2012). *Learning in the Field: An Introduction to Qualitative Research*. California: Sage.

Rubin, D. (1997). *Composing Social Identity in Written Language*. Mahwah, NJ: Lawrence Erlbaum.

Ryan, C. & Carroll, J. (2005). Canaries in the coalmine: International students in Western universities. In J. Carroll & J. Ryan (Eds.), *Teaching International Students: Improving Learning for All* (pp. 3–16). London: Routledge.

Sanger, J. (1996). *The Compleat Observer? A Field Research Guide to Observation*. London: Falmer Press.

Saraceni, M. (2009). Relocating English: Towards a new paradigm for English in the world. *Language and Intercultural Communication*, *9* (3), 175–186.

272 References

Schneider, E.W. (1997a). *Englishes around the World 1: General Studies, British Isles, North America Studies in Honour of Manfred Gorlach*. Amsterdam: John Benjamins.

Schneider, E.W. (1997b). *Englishes Around the World 2: Caribbean, Africa, Asia, Australasia Studies in Honour of Manfred Gorlach*. Amsterdam: John Benjamins.

Schutz, A. (1967). *The Phenomenology of the Social World*. (G. Walsh & F. Lenhert, Trans). Chicago, IL: Northwestern University Press.

Schwandt, T.A. (2000). Three epistemological stances for qualitative inquiry: Interpretivism, hermeneutics and social constructionism. In N.K. Denzin & Y.S. Lincoln (Eds.), *The Sage Handbook of Qualitative Research* (pp. 189–214). Thousand Oaks, CA: Sage Publications.

Schwandt, T.A. (2007). *The Sage Dictionary of Qualitative Inquiry* (3rd ed.). Thousand Oaks, CA: Sage.

Seargeant, P. (2012). *Exploring World Englishes: Language in a Global Context*. Abingdon: Routledge.

Seidlhofer, B. (2003). *A Concept of International English and Related Issues: From 'Real English' to 'Realistic English'*. Strasbourg: Directorate of School, Out-of-School and Higher Education Council of Europe.

Seidman, I. (2006). *Interviewing as Qualitative Research: A Guide for Researchers in Education and the Social Sciences* (3rd ed.). New York, NY: Teachers College Press.

Sharifian, F. (2006). A cultural-conceptual approach and world Englishes: The case of Aboriginal English. *World Englishes, 25* (1), 11–22.

Sharifian, F. (2009). *English as an International Language: Perspectives and Pedagogical Issues*. Bristol: Multilingual Matters.

Sharifian, F. (2011). *Cultural Conceptualisations and Language: Theoretical Framework and Applications*. Amsterdam: John Benjamins & Co.

Sharifian, F. (2014). Teaching English as an International Language in multicultural contexts: Focus on Australia. In R. Marlina & R. Giri (Eds.), *The Pedagogy of English as an International Language*. The Netherlands: Springer.

Sharifian, F. & Marlina, R. (2012). English as an International Language: An innovative program. In A. Matsuda (Ed.), *Teaching English as an International Language: Principles and Practices* (pp. 140–153). Bristol: Multilingual Matters.

Sharifian, F. & Palmer, G.B. (Eds.). (2007). *Applied Cultural Linguistics: Implications for Second Language Learning and Intercultural Communication*. Amsterdam: John Benjamins & Co.

Shim, R.J.Y. (2002). Changing attitudes toward TEWOL in Korea. *Journal of Asian Pacific Communication, 12* (1), 143–158.

Shin, J.K. (2004). The use of Freirean pedagogy in teaching English as an International Language: Raising the critical consciousness of EFL teachers in Korea, *LLC Review, 4* (1), 64–84.

Siemund, P., Davydova, J., & Maier, G. (2012). *The Amazing World of Englishes*. Berlin: Walter de Gruyter.

Sifakis, N.C. (2007). The education of teachers of English as a lingua franca: A transformative perspective. *International Journal of Applied Linguistics, 17* (3), 355–375.

Simon, R.I. (1992). *Teaching Against the Grain: Texts for a Pedagogy of Possibility*. New York, NY: Bergin & Garvey.

Simons, H. (2009). *Case Study Research in Practice*. London: Sage.

Singh, M. & Shrestha, M. (2008). Internationalising pedagogical structures: Admittance into the community of scholars via double knowing. In. M. Hellsten & A. Reid (Eds.), *Researching International Pedagogies: Sustainable Practice of Teaching and Learning in Higher Education* (pp. 65–82). The Netherlands: Springer.

Singh, M., Kell, P., & Pandian, A. (2002). *Appropriating English: Innovation in the English Language Teaching Business*. New York, NY: Peter Lang.

Skutnabb-Kangas, T. & Phillipson, R. (Eds.). (1994). *Linguistic Human Rights. Overcoming linguistic discrimination*. Berlin: Mouton de Gruyter.

Smith, D.E. (1987). *The Everyday World as Problematic: A Feminist Sociology*. Boston, MA: Northeastern University Press.

Smith, D.E. (2005). *Institutional Ethnography: A Sociology for People*. Oxford: Altamira Press.

Smith, D.L. (2003). Essay: Confessions of a native speaker. *Asian Englishes, 6* (1), 92–96.

Smith, L.E. (1976). English as an international auxiliary language. *RELC Journal, 7* (2), 38–42.

Smith, L.E. (1978). Some distinctive features of EIIL vs ESOL in ELE. Culture Learning Institute Report, *5* (3), 5–11.

Smith, L.E. (1981). English as an international language. No room for linguistic chauvinism. *Nagoya Gakuin Daigaku, Gaikokugo, Kyoiku Kiyo* (Nagoya Gakuin University Round Table on Languages, Linguistics and Literature), *3*, 27–32.

Smith, L.E. (1983). *Readings in English as an International Language*. Oxford: Pergamon Press.

Smitherman, G. (1974). Soul and style. *The English Journal, 63*(3), 14–15.

Soo Hoo, S. (1993). Students as partners in research and restructuring schools. *Educational Forum, 57*, 386–393.

Stake, R.E. (2005). Qualitative case studies. In N.K. Denzin & Y.S. Lincoln (Eds.), *The Sage Handbook of Qualitative Research* (pp. 443–466). California: Sage.

Stella, A. & Liston, C. (2008). *Internationalisation of Australian Universities: Learning from Cycle 1 Audits*. Melbourne: Australian Universities Quality Agency.

Stern, H.H. (1983). *Fundamental Concepts of Language Teaching*. Oxford: Oxford University Press.

Stier, J. (2004). Taking a critical stance towards internationalization ideologies in higher education: Idealism, instrumentalism and educationalism. *Globalisation, Societies and Education, 2* (1), 83–98.

Stockwell, P. (2007). *Sociolinguistics: A Resource Book for Students*. London: Routledge.

Storti, C. (1994). *Cross-Cultural Dialogues: 74 Brief Encounters with Cultural Difference*. Boston, MA: Intercultural Press.

Strauss, A. & Corbin, J. (1990). *Basics of Qualitative Research: Grounded Theory Procedures and Techniques*. Thousand Oaks, CA: Sage.

Strauss, A. & Corbin, J. (1998). *Basics of Qualitative Research: Grounded Theory Procedures and Techniques* (2nd ed.). Thousand Oaks, CA: Sage.

Suzuki, A. (2011). Introducing diversity of English into ELT: Student teachers' responses. *ELT Journal, 65* (2), 145–153.

Tanaka, S. (2006). English and multiculturalism – from the language user's perspective. *RELC Journal, 37* (1), 47–66.

Thornborrow, J. (1999). Language and identity. In L. Thomas & S. Wareing (Eds.), *Language, Society, and Power* (pp. 135–149). London: Routledge.

Tollefson, J.W. (2007). Ideology, language varieties, and ELT. In J. Cummins & C. Davison (Eds.), *International Handbook of English Language Teaching* (pp. 25–36). New York, NY: Springer.

Tomlinson, B. (2003). A multidimensional approach to teaching English for the world. In R. Rubdy & M. Saraceni (Eds.), *English in the World: Global Rules, Global Roles* (pp. 130–150). London: Continuum.

Trevaskes, S., Eisenchlas, S., & Liddicoat, A.J. (2003). *Australian Perspectives on Internationalising Education*. Melbourne: Language Australia.

274 References

Tudor, I. (2003). Learning to live with complexity: Towards an ecological perspective on language teaching. *System, 31*, 1–12.

Tupas, T.R.F. (2006). Standard Englishes, pedagogical paradigms and their conditions of (im)possibility. In R. Rubdy & M. Saraceni (Eds.), *English in the World: Global Rules, Global Roles* (pp. 169–185). London: Continuum Press.

Ulin, P., Robinson, E., Tolley, E., & McNeill, E.(2002). *Qualitative Methods: A field Guide for Applied Research in Sexual and Reproductive Health.* Research Triangle Park: Family Health International.

Universities Australia. (2009). *The Nature of International Education in Australian Universities and Its Benefits.* Retrieved 19 February 2016 from www.universitie-saustralia.edu.au/page/submissions---reports/commissioned-studies/benefits-of-international-education/

Vavrus, F. (1991). When paradigms clash: The role of institutionalised varieties in language teacher education. *World Englishes, 10* (2), 181–196.

Walker, R. (1980). The conduct of educational case studies: Ethics, theory, and procedures. In W.B. Dockerell & D. Hamilton (Eds.), *Rethinking Educational Research* (pp. 30–63). London: Hodder & Stoughton.

Wardhaugh, R. (1993). *Investigating Language: Central Problems in Linguistics.* Oxford: Blackwell.

Waugh, R.F. & Punch, K.F. (1987). Teacher receptivity to system-wide change in the implementation stage. *Review of Educational Research, 57* (3), 237–254.

Webb, G. (2005). Internationalisation of curriculum: An institutional approach. In J. Carroll & J. Ryan (Eds.), *Teaching International Students: Improving Learning for All* (pp. 109–118). London: Routledge.

Wee, L. (2013). Book Review: Lubna Alsagoff, Sandra Lee McKay, Guangwei Hu, Willy A. Renandya, eds. 2012. Principles and Practices for Teaching English as an International Language, *TESOL Quarterly, 47* (1), 202–204.

White, J., Drew, S., & Hay, T. (2009). Ethnography versus case study: Positioning research and researchers. *Qualitative Research Journal, 9* (1), 18–27.

Widdowson, H.G. (1994). The ownership of English. *TESOL Quarterly, 28*, 377–388.

Widdowson, H.G. (1997). EIL, ESL, EFL: Global issues and local interests. *World Englishes, 16* (1), 135–146.

Wiebe, E., Durepos, G., & Mills, A.J. (Eds.). (2010). *Encylopedia of Case Study Research (Vol. 2).* Thousand Oaks, CA: Sage.

Wierzbicka, A. (2006). *English: Meaning and Culture.* New York, NY: Oxford University Press.

Williams, J.A. (1996). The curriculum, the students, and the world. *American Behavioral Scientist, 40*, 195–202.

Willis, J.W. (2007). *Foundations of Qualitative Research: Interpretive and Critical Approaches.* London: Sage.

Wolcott, H.F. (1994). *Transforming Qualitative Data: Description, Analysis, and Interpretation.* Thousand Oaks, CA: Sage.

Xu, Z. (2002). From TEFL to TEIL: Changes in perceptions and practices: Teaching English as an International Language (EIL) in Chinese Universities in P.R. China. In A. Kirkpatrick (Ed.), *Englishes in Asia: Communication, Identity, Power, and Education* (pp. 225–240). Melbourne: Language Australia.

Yin, R.K. (2009). *Case Study Research: Design and Methods.* Thousand Oaks, CA: Sage.

Yule, G. (1996). *The Study of Language.* Cambridge: Cambridge University Press.

Index

Please note that page references to Boxes, Figures or Tables will be followed by the letters 'b', 'f', or 't' in italics, respectively; references to Notes will contain the letter 'n' followed by the Note number. Names of teachers or students are pseudonyms, whenever they appear.

Aboriginal Australians/Aboriginal English 14, 17, 18, 126
accents 16; Accent Debates 142, 143*f*, 144*f*, 145–6, 147; Malaysian English 110; native-English speakers 46, 150; negativity towards linguistic and cultural diversity 40–1; non-native English speakers 110, 150; region-free 187*b*, 189, 191, 221
action research 58
African language, English as 12
Alsagoff, L. 219
American English 12, 15, 20, 41, 108, 110, 152; African American English 94, 166, 201, 203
anti-normative paradigm 20–2, 70
Applied Linguistics 11, 20, 45, 47
appropriation of English language 2, 15
Aristotle 56
artefact collection and analysis 6, 65, 67–9
Asian Englishes (journal) 163
Asian language, English as 12
assimilation 44, 106, 111, 198, 235; assimilationist approach to delivery of knowledge delivery 7, 8; pressures 17, 18; students' perspectives 227, 228
'attitudinal sins' (Kachru) 42, 226, 236
audio-recordings 40
Austin, T. 26
Australia: Anglo Australians and Aborigines 17; Asian international students 18; Bachelor of Arts (BA) degrees 7; Deans of Arts, Social Sciences and Humanities (DAASH) 7; ELT-related conferences in 31; Englishes in 2, 3, 17–20; and globalisation 19–20; higher education curriculum development 7; Indigenous Australians 14; as Inner-Circle country 13, 14, 17, 111; Melbourne, nationality and suburbs 18–19; as microcosm of the world 3, 19; migration to 2, 17, 18, 26; multiculturalism in 2, 3, 17–20, 187*b*, 219, 236; outsourcing by corporations 19; television network 3; universities, nature of international education in 7; White Non-Standard Australian English 17; *see also* Aboriginal Englishes; EIL (English as an International Language) program, Urban University; Urban University, Australia
Australian English 17, 18, 26, 188, 190, 221; Standard 191–2
authoritative discourses 44
autobiographical narrative 6, 9, 65, 68, 72, 79–103; EIL as only the 'exterior' 81–3; EIL subject for first-year students (as first trial) 92–3; from EIU to EIL 80–102; end of semester 99–100; going from single subject to a program 101–2; language variation (week 2) 93–5; Singaporean English (week 3) 95–8; teaching EIL1020 in semester 2 89–92; writing in international communication contexts (week 9) 98, 99*f*

Bachelor of Arts (BA) degrees 7
'backyard' research 50, 51, 68
Bakhtin, M.M. 43, 44, 242

276 *Index*

Bamgbose, A. 33, 175, 245
Banks, J.A. and C.A.M. 45
Bassey, M. 58
BBC English 192
Bell, J.C. 72
Bend It Like Beckham (film) 165
Bennett, M.J. 241
bias, clarifying 76–7
bi-/multilingual speakers of English 1, 2, 14–15, 16, 25
Bisong, J. 15
Boyatzis, R. 74
Bredella, L. 30
Bride and Prejudice (film) 165
Briguglio, C. 4, 40, 41, 42, 100, 222, 225
British English 12, 15, 41, 96, 165, 220; and implementation of change by EIL teachers 105, 106, 108, 152, 156; and students' responses to change 178, 188*b*, 193; *see also* United Kingdom
Brown, J.D. 5, 32–3, 43, 45, 104, 160, 175, 218, 230, 234, 240
Brown, K. 31
Brown, L. 71
Brutt-Griffler, J. 15
Buckle, J.L. 52, 53, 62, 67, 76
Burbules, N.C. 51
Burridge, K. 18, 218

Canada: as Inner-Circle country 13
Canagarajah, A.S. 22, 30, 43, 44, 45, 98, 234, 242
Casanave, C.P. 57, 58, 64, 65, 72, 75, 76, 79
case studies 57–9, 60, 65, 74; interviews 70–1
Certificate for English Language Teaching to Adults (CELTA) 195, 197
Chang, Y.J. 42
change 25–30; backgrounds of users of English 14; demand for implementation 11–48; experiencing and initiating 197–202; implementation 104–61; need for new paradigm of teaching and learning of EIL 1–10; proposing and initiating 224–5; reviewing 162–231; students' perspectives, reviewing from 215–31; students' responses to 175–214
China: as Expanding-Circle country 13
Chung Hyo Ye (folk tale) 166
circles (concentric), Kachruvian 2, 4, 13, 13*f*, 17, 21, 27, 217, 234; previous studies, effects of teaching EIL 33–4; *see also* Expanding-Circle countries;

Inner-Circle countries; Outer-Circle countries
Clark, M.A. 238
classroom teaching of EIL 112–60; differences, working with 132–7; films and online resources 126–7; 'free-floating' dimensions 137, 149; 'live' authoritative voices, other 127; observations 6; pedagogical activities 118–32; raising awareness of diversity of English, users and culture 113–32; rhetoric 134; role-play 135*f*, 240; silence 132, 133; students' own experiences and observations 127–32; teachers' own collection of texts 118–26; topics and readings 114–18, *250*; websites 127
CLT (Communicative Language Teaching) 31
Clyne, M. 17, 22, 218, 225
Cochran-Smith, D. 23–4
coding, data analysis 74
colonialism 12, 13
communication skills, promoting 29–30, 168–9; intercultural miscommunication scenarios 134*f*, 136*f*; writing in international communication contexts (week 9) 98, 99*f*
Communicative Language Teaching (CLT) 31
competences of students, metacultural 239–40
concentric circles model *see* circles (concentric), Kachruvian
conceptual explication strategies 30, 168
conceptual negotiation strategies 30, 168–9
conceptual variation awareness 30, 168
Cortazzi, M. 29
Creole speakers of English 14; decreolisation 17
Creswell, J. 53, 54, 55, 56, 73–4, 76
Critical Applied Linguistics 8
Critical Literacy Study 8
Critical Multicultural Education 8
Crocodile Dundee in Los Angeles (film) 165
Crotty, M. 54
Crystal, D. 12, 25
culture: classroom teaching of EIL 113–32; cultural arenas, English as dominant language in 12; cultural values, representation of/exposure to 28–9, 167–8; international target 29; metacultural competence 30, 239–40;

notion of 28; source 29; stereotypes, avoiding 29; *see also* EIL3110 - Language and Culture

curricula, EIL 23–5, 229, 236; addressing of sociopolitical issues or questions 31, 169–72, 240–1; encouraging of maintenance of learning 238–9; engaging students in developing metacultural competence 239–40; experiencing changes through 216–25; explicit curriculum 24; forms 23–4; hidden curriculum 24; inspiring students to understand language variation 238–9; pedagogical practices 30–2; political issues 46; politics of difference, addressing 137–49; whether providing exposure to varieties of English 25–7, 162–4; recommendations in relation to 238–44; research concerns 24; student responses to perspectives offered and advocated by 6; 'successful' 42; syllabus materials 25–30; unreviewed frameworks/principles 24–5; *see also* EIL subject components; syllabus materials (EIL), goals

D'Angelo, J. 61

data analysis methods 73–5, 78

data collection 7, 59, 65–73; artefacts 6, 65, 67–9; interviews 69–72; narrative 72–3; observations 66–7; sources 41–2

data-driven approach 74

Davison, C. 242

Deans of Arts, Social Sciences and Humanities (DAASH), Australia 7

deficit EIL perspective 22

deviational EIL perspective 22

differences, working with 132–7; intercultural miscommunication scenarios 134f, 136f; at work 135, 136f; *see also* politics of difference

discourses 16, 44

diversity education, struggles and tensions *see* struggles and tensions, diversity education

documentary sources, and artefacts 69

Doecke, B. 46, 242

Dogancay-Aktuna, S. 240

Durrheim, K. 71

Dwyer, S.C. 52, 53, 62, 67, 76

dynamic EIL perspective 22, 27

economic arenas, English as dominant language in 12

educators of EIL 237; alternative pedagogical assumptions and approaches to consider 6; Ashish (Nepalese lecturer) 62, 102, 105–7, 108, 113, 114, 117, 119, 120, 125, 141, 145, 151, 152, 172; critique 24; Fatima (Indonesian lecturer) 62, 102, 105, 107–11, 113, 114, 117, 120f, 124, 141, 145, 156–8, 179; implementation of values and beliefs advocated by EIL paradigm 6; Indigo (Australian lecturer) 62, 102, 105, 111–14, 117, 118, 123, 126, 132, 141–2, 146, 147f, 148f, 152, 153, 154f, 155, 172; implementing of change by 104–61; profile 105–12; realism in approaches of 233–5; voices of teachers 9; worthwhile goals 8; *see also* teaching of EIL

EIL (English as an International Language) program, Urban University: autobiographical narrative 79; case study approach 57; challenges in teaching and learning 236–8; in classrooms *see* classroom teaching; curricula *see* curricula, EIL; description and analysis of EIL-ex syllabus materials 85, 86f, 87–9; implementation of values and beliefs advocated by EIL paradigm 6; initial encounters with 188–9; newly developed program (subjects, topics and prescribed reading materials) 115, 253–9t; objectives of EIL-ex subjects 84, 247; as only the 'exterior' 81–3; perception as a 'risky business' 202–3; prerequisites for studying in EIL-ex 83–5; previous and revised programs 101f; questions for EIL-ex essays 88, 248–9; significance and contribution to the professional community 7–8; student responses to perspectives offered and advocated by curriculum 6; subject areas for first-year students 92–3; teaching *see* teaching of EIL; thick description 105; unsure if mainstream or a trend 184–6; and WE, as an anti-normative paradigm 20–2; *see also* EIU (English in Use); English as an International Language (EIL)

EIL subject components: EIL1010 - English, Society, and Communication *see* EIL1010 - English, Society, and Communication; EIL1020 - International Communication *see* EIL1020 - International

278 Index

Communication; EIL2110 - Form and function: English in context *see* EIL2110 - Form and function: English in context; EIL2120 - Language of spoken English *see* EIL2120 - Language and Globalisation; EIL3102 - Professional communication *see* EIL3102 - World Englishes; EIL3110 - Language and culture *see* EIL3110 - Language and Culture; EIL3130 - Making sense of the environment: English as the language of action and reflection *see* EIL3130 - Language and Education; EIL3210 - Writing Across Cultures *see* EIL3210 - Writing Across Cultures; *see also* syllabus materials (EIL), goals

EIL1010 - English, Society, and Communication: and awareness of differences 161n2; and classroom teaching of EIL 115, 117, 119, 122, 128, 129*f*, 139, 144*f*; description and analysis of EIL-ex syllabus materials 85, 86*f*, 87*f*, 91; objectives of EIL-ex subjects 247; objectives of newly revised EIL subjects 92*f*, 252; and profile of EIL educators at Urban University, Australia 106, 108, 111; questions for EIL-ex essays 248; realism of findings 233; teachers' perspectives 166; test questions for EIL trial 251; topics and readings for trial subject *250*

EIL1020 - International Communication: and classroom teaching of EIL 115, 118, 119, 127, 128, 132, 133, 139; description and analysis of EIL-ex syllabus materials 85; genre-based grammar exercise sheet 90*f*; objectives of newly revised EIL subjects 252; and profile of EIL educators at Urban University, Australia 106, 108, 111; questions for EIL-ex essays 248; realism of findings 233; teachers' perspectives 168, 169; teaching in semester 2 89–92

EIL2110 - Form and function: English in context: and awareness of differences 161n2; and classroom teaching of EIL 115, 116; objectives of newly revised EIL subjects 252; questions for EIL-ex essays 248

EIL2120 - Language and Globalisation: and classroom teaching of EIL 115, 119, 121, 127, 129, 130*f*, 139, 140*f*,

141*f*; objectives of newly revised EIL subjects 252; questions for EIL-ex essays 248; realism of findings 233–4; teachers' perspectives 169

EIL3102 - World Englishes: and awareness of differences 161n2; and classroom teaching of EIL 116, 122, 127, 129; objectives of newly revised EIL subjects 252; questions for EIL-ex essays 248–9; teachers' perspectives 166, 167

EIL3110 - Language and Culture: and classroom teaching of EIL 116, 117, 119, 129–30, 131*f*, 132, 135, 137, 138; objectives of newly revised EIL subjects 252; questions for EIL-ex essays 249; realism of findings 234; teachers' perspectives 168, 169

EIL3130 - Language and Education: and classroom teaching of EIL 116, 127, 132, 134, 136; objectives of EIL-ex subjects 247; objectives of newly revised EIL subjects 252; questions for EIL-ex essays 249; teachers' perspectives 168

EIL3210 - Writing Across Cultures: and classroom teaching of EIL 116, 117, 119, 132, 134, 136; objectives of newly revised EIL subjects 252; questions for EIL-ex essays 249; teachers' perspectives 168

Eisenchlas, S. 7

Eisner, E.W. 23–4

EIU1020 - Form and structure: objectives of EIL-ex subjects 247

EIU2110 - Form and function: English in context: objectives of EIL-ex subjects 247

EIU2120 - One mode, Many methods: objectives of EIL-ex subjects 247

EIU3102 - The language of professional communication: objectives of EIL-ex subjects 247

EIU3110 - Language and Culture: objectives of EIL-ex subjects 247

EIU3210 - English discourse: exploration and demonstration: objectives of EIL-ex subjects 247

email conversations, as artefacts 68

English as a Foreign Language (EFL) 14, 24–5

English as a Lingua Franca (ELF) 8, 20; *see also* lingua-cultural backgrounds, diverse

Index 279

English as a Second Language (ESL) 79; and implementation of change by EIL teachers 106, 111; students' responses 203, 206*b*; and teaching of EIL 24–5, 49

English as an International Language (EIL) 11, 20, 49; deficit perspective 22; deviational perspective 22; dynamic perspective 22, 27; ethical teaching 5; vs. 'International English' 21; need to teach 1–10; paradigm *see* paradigm, EIL; *see also* EIL (English as an International Language) program, Urban University

English in Use (EIU) 60; objectives of EIL-ex subjects 247; transition to EIL 80–102; *see also* EIL (English as an International Language) program, Urban University

English language: American English *see* American English; appropriation and re-nationalisation of 2, 15; awareness of diversity and perceived relevance 217–19; BBC English 192; bi-/ multilingual speakers 1, 2, 14–15, 16, 25; British English 12, 15, 41; changes to backgrounds of users 14; complexity 11, 12; countries where formally recognised as a national language 13; Creole speakers 14; de-Anglicisation of 28; de-nationalisation of 16; difficult to claim exclusive ownership of 17; 'Englishes' 15–16; exposure to varieties of, by EIL syllabus materials 25–7; global expansion of 1, 2, 12–17, 28, 31, 46; as an international language *see* English as an International Language (EIL); localisation of 15; Malaysian English 110; non-English-mother-tongue countries active in using 12; perceived as 'owned' by the Britons and Americans 12, 15, 41; pidgin English 14, 17; pluralised forms 2, 15, 16, 17; reasonable competence in 14; roles or functions 12; sociolinguistic landscape 1, 2, 8, 11, 18, 21, 31, 104; Standard English *see* Standard English; status of an international language 1, 2, 12, 13–14, 16; subcultures English 192, 221; supremacy of English spoken, perceptions of 28, 40–3, 45, 99, 154, 185, 213, 220, 231, 242; 'treasures' of, going to 'strange shores' 12, 14;

where an additional institutionalised language 13, 14

English Language Intensive Course for Overseas Students (ELICOS) 49

English Language Teaching (ELT) 22

English Today (journal) 2, 163; 1 16

English World Wide (journal) 2

Erdinast-Vulcan, D. 80

ESL *see* English as a Second Language (ESL)

ethnocentrism 26, 40, 43, 47, 230

ethnocultural varieties of English 18

ethnography 57, 58–9

ethnoscapes 3*t*, 4

Expanding-Circle countries 1, 2, 27, 40, 153; and Australian English 190; equal recognition of varieties of English from 21; examples 13, 14; status of English in 14; students' responses 197, 199, 216, 217, 219–22, 231; teachers' perspectives 168; *see also* circles (concentric), Kachruvian; Inner-Circle countries; Outer-Circle countries

explicit curriculum (text) 24

external auditing 76

external trustworthiness 77

Facebook 19

films and online resources 126–7

financescapes 3*t*, 4

first-year students 66; application of knowledge outside the classroom, concerns regarding 179–81; encountering/experiencing something not previously thought about 181–4; expectations and reality 177–8; experiences of Cheolsoo (South Korea) 176, 181–6, 216, 217, 220, 222–4; experiences of Manida (Laos) 176–81, 216–18, 220, 222–4, 226, 227; experiences of Ogilvy (Australia) 64, 176, 186–94, 216–18, 220, 221, 224, 226–9; experiencing change and pedagogical factors behind 178–9; getting to think about previously taken-for-granted matters 189–92; initial encounters with EIL 188–9; struggling with topics raised 192–4; subject areas for 92–3; unsure if EIL mainstream or a trend 184–6

Firth, A. 30, 234

follow-up interviews 71

Foreman, P.B. 76

280 *Index*

Foster, P. 65, 67
Freire, P. 46
Friedrich, P. 24

Galloway, N. 39, 41, 42
Gannon, S. 72, 76
General English language learning 24–5, 62
Gillard, J. 194
Gleeson, M. 242
Glesne, C. 50
globalisation: and Australia 19–20; and communication 31; forces of 3*t*, 18; '-scapes' created by 2, 3*t*, 4
gold-rushes 17
Graddol, D. 2, 14
grammars, multiple 16
grounded theory 57
Gung Ho (film) 165

Haug, F. 79
Hawthorne effect 42
hidden curriculum 24
hidden text 150
Higgins, C. 30, 222, 234
Hino, N. 32, 133, 163
Holliday, A. 73, 75
Hong Kong: multinational companies in 4
Huberman, A.M. 73–4

ideoscapes 3*t*, 4
immigration 14, 203, 227; Australia, migrants in 2, 17, 26; mass migration 17, 18; non-Anglo-Celtic migrants 18; second-generation migrants 18
India: as Outer-Circle country 13; outsourcing to 19
Indonesia: bi-/multilingual speakers of English 16; ELT-related conferences in 31; as Expanding-Circle country 13
Industrial Revolution, role of Britain in 12
information and communication technology (ICT) 2, 15, 22
Inner-Circle countries 1–2, 3, 5, 27, 32, 101, 245; BBC English 192; examples 13, 14, 17; and natural changes in languages 164; students' responses 214, 219, 235; supremacy of Englishes spoken by, perception of 45, 99, 185, 187*b*, 220; and teachers 153, 168; *see also* circles (concentric), Kachruvian; Expanding-Circle countries; Outer-Circle countries

inquiry strategies, qualitative research 56–9
Intensive General English program 24–5
interlanguages 22
internally persuasive discourses 44
'International English' 21
International English Language Testing System (IELTS) 159
international target culture 29
intertexts 24
interviews 69–72; in-depth semi-structured 6, 65, 70, 71; follow-up 71; mobile interviewing 71–2; open-ended 70; relationships 71; timing of 70
Ireland: as Inner-Circle country 13

Jain, R. 39, 40, 42
The Jakarta Post 123*f*
Janks, H. 45, 46, 241
Japan: as Expanding-Circle country 13
Jenkins, J. 14
Jenks, C. 8, 45, 172
Jin, L. 29
journals 2, 22, 163; as artefacts 68–9

Kachru, B.B. 1, 2, 12, 13, 14, 22, 27, 42, 105, 107, 145, 159–60, 226; *see also* circles (concentric), Kachruvian
Kanpol, B. 8
Karavas-Doukas, K. 61
Kell, P. 26
Kiesling, S. F. 18
The Kite Runner (Hosseini) 118, 165
Kluckhohn, C. 28
knowledge: assimilationist approach to delivery of 7; claims 54–6; 'correct' sources of 26; paradigm shift or advance in 20; pedagogical, sharing of 4–5
Kostogriz, A. 46, 242
Kramsch, C. 31, 118, 239
Krober, A. 28
Kubota, R. 20, 26, 40, 41, 46, 88, 99–100, 169, 222, 226, 240
Kuhn, T. 20
Kumaravadivelu, B. 31

language testing 23
LeCompte, M.D. 55
Lee, J.O. 8
Lehner, A. 88
lexical features of English language 16
Li, D. 15
Li, D.C.S. 33

Liddicoat, A. J. 7

lingua-cultural backgrounds, diverse 21; autobiographical narrative 84, 92, 98, 102; and global expansion of English 14, 19; and implementation of change by EIL teachers 105, 116, 119; and need to teach EIL 2, 3; ongoing inquiry, re-envisioning program of 234; reviewing of change 163, 165, 166, 167, 168, 218, 219; students' responses to change 197; and teaching of EIL 27, 29, 50, 62; *see also* English as a Lingua Franca (ELF)

linguicism 40, 137, 138

linguistic imperialism 15, 40, 137

linguistic nationism 137, 138

linguistic-identity-switching activity 147–8, 191, 223

McKay, S. 3, 26, 43, 45, 218, 240; *Teaching English as an International Language* 1

McNiff, J. 58

Malaysia: multinational companies in 4

Malaysian English 110

Marlina, R. 30, 218

Marshall, C. 57

Mason, J. 80

mass migration 17, 18

Matsuda, A. 4, 24, 25, 26, 29, 45–6, 104, 167, 169, 219, 222, 240

mediascapes 3*t*, 4

Melbourne, nationality and suburbs 18–19

member-checking 76

Merriam, S.B. 55, 57, 58, 59, 68, 77

metacultural competence 30, 239–40

Miles, M.B. 73–4

Milner, H.R. 24, 29–30

miners, Chinese 17

MMORPG (massively multi-player online role playing games) 19

mobile interviewing 71–2

mobility, global 2

monocultural chauvinism, avoiding 29, 83

monolingual native-speakers of English 15

mono-modal approach 23, 26

morphological features of English language 17

multiculturalism 8, 14, 15, 28, 29, 39, 107, 113, 133; in Australia 3, 17–20, 187*b*, 219, 236; contexts/settings 3, 15,

205, 206*b*, 219, 236, 252; education 45, 133, 186; identity 110; society 113, 205

multilingualism 46, 101

multinationals 4, 40

My Boyhood in Siam (Chandruang) 118

The Namesake (film) 165

narrative/narrative-based inquiry 57, 72–3; autobiographical *see* autobiographical narrative; modes 72; reflexive narrative 73

Native and Non-Native Debates 144*f*, 145, 146, 147, 152

native-English speakers 1, 22, 99; accents 46, 150; classmates 206*b*, 207; difficult to claim exclusive ownership of English language 17; from England or United States 16; fluency 220; and global expansion of English 16, 17; ideology 221; and implementation of change by EIL teachers 138, 147*f*, 152; interactions with non-native speakers 27; monolingual, as minority 15; and student responses to change 212, 217; vs. sub-cultures, English of 228; supremacy of Englishes spoken by, perception of 28, 40, 41, 42–3, 45, 154, 213, 231, 242; and teaching of EIL 23, 26, 39, 40; *see also* Native and Non-Native Debates

native-English speaking countries 13, 15, 217; syllabus materials (EIL) 26, 27, 28, 29

native-speakerism 43, 220, 228, 241

NESB *see* non-English-speaking background (NESB)

New Zealand: as Inner-Circle country 13

Nieto, S. 175, 226

Nigeria: as Outer-Circle country 13

non-English-speaking background (NESB) 60, 83, 177, 189

non-native English speakers 92, 217, 223; accents 150; and global expansion of English 16; and implementation of change by EIL teachers 106, 117, 118, 142, 145*f*, 147; interactions with native-speakers 27; previous studies, effects of teaching EIL 39–40; and review of change 166; and student responses to change 211, 213; students 39–40, 109; and teaching of EIL 27, 33, 39, 61; writing 208; *see also* Native

282 Index

and Non-Native Debates; native-English speakers
non-native English-speaking countries 25, 26, 28, 29

observational understanding 69
observations, research 6, 66–7; limitations of solely using 62–3
ongoing inquiry, re-envisioning program of 9, 232–46; challenges in teaching and learning EIL 236–8; realism, degree of 233–6; recommendations 238–44; study limitations/suggestions for future research 244–6; summary of main findings and contributions 232–8
online forums 19
Outer-Circle countries 1, 2, 17, 27, 40, 153; and Australian English 190; equal recognition of varieties of English from 21; examples 13; and Expanding-Circle countries 14; 'new Englishes' 21–2; students' responses 197, 199, 216, 217, 219–22; teachers' perspectives 168; see also circles (concentric), Kachruvian; Expanding-Circle countries; Inner-Circle countries
Outsourced (film) 165
outsourcing 19
Oxford, R.L. 39, 40, 42

Pandian, A. 26
paradigm, EIL 3–4, 7, 9; implementation of values and beliefs advocated by 6; need for new paradigm of teaching and learning of EIL 1, 3; in relation to World Englishes 11; and teaching of EIL 23; at Urban University 66; WE and EIL as a normative paradigm 20–2
Park, J.S.Y. 14, 22
Parr, G.B. 68, 72
Patton, M.Q. 60
pedagogy: alternative assumptions 6; change, pedagogical factors behind 178–9; classroom activities 118–32; curriculum practices 4, 30–2; principles 8; revision of pedagogical strategies for English language education 21; transformative 46
peer briefing 76
Pennycook, A. 22, 45, 46
Peshkin, A. 50
Phan Le Ha 136, 137
phenomenology 57

Philippines: as Outer-Circle country 13; outsourcing to 19
Phillips, D.C. 51
Phillipson, R. 15
phonological features of English language 16, 17
Phua Chu Kang Pte Ltd (film) 165
pidgin English 14, 17
Plato 56
pluralised forms of English 2, 15, 16, 17
pluralism, linguistic and cultural 45
pluricentricity 22, 168
politics: big-*P* (Politics) 45, 46, 137, 139*f*, 140*f*, 141*f*; of difference *see* politics of difference; little-*p* (politics) 45, 46, 137
politics of difference: addressing in the curricula 137–49; challenges in engaging with 137–60; current debate 144, 145–6; problems encountered 149–60; *see also* differences, working with
positivism 51, 52; post-positivism paradigm 56
pragmatic features of English language 16, 17
pre-packed materials 26
previous studies, effects of teaching EIL 32–43, 34–8*t*; critical reflections 41–3; desired instructional effects 11, 33, 39–40; undesired instructional effects 11, 40–1
prior-research-driven approach 74
prior-research-driven approach, data analysis 74
prolonged time in the field, spending 76
Punch, K.F. 85
purposeful sampling 60

Qu, R. 5, 6, 47, 215, 232, 233
qualitative research 6, 50–9, 77; as 'backyard' research 50, 51, 61–4, 68; case studies *see* case studies; description 51; ethnography 57, 58–9; 'hyphen of insider-outsider' 53; inquiry strategies 56–9; knowledge claims 54–6; and learning 51; meaning making 56; methodology 57, 58–9, 60; narrative inquiry 57; perspectives 54–5; quality research, characteristics 53; social constructivism 55–6; university classrooms, worlds of 55
Queen's English 20
Quirk, R. 145

Rallis, S.F. 51, 53, 55, 56
realism in experiences of lecturers and students in EIL program, degree of 5; implementation of suggestions/principles of teaching EIL 6; students' responses 235–6; teachers' approaches 233–5
reflexive narrative 73
re-nationalisation of English language 2
research, EIL teaching: anonymity, preserving 64; choice of students 63–4; context 59–64; data analysis methods 73–5, 78; data collection methods 59, 65–73; design framework 50–9; impact of presence of researchers on participants' behaviours and practices 67; inquiry strategies 56–9; instructional effects, scarcity of studies 33; key questions 6–7; multisite designs 77; observations 6, 62–3, 66–7; participants 61–4; problematics of 60; qualitative approach 6, 50–9; research gaps, filling in 41, 47–8, 175; selecting 'treasures in the backyard' 61–4; setting 59, 60–1; social constructivism 55–6, 77–8; study limitations/suggestions for future research 244–6; trustworthiness 75–7; undergraduate EIL units, students enrolled on 63
respondent validation 76
Rizvi, F. 235
Rose, H. 39, 41, 42
Rosenberg, P. 24
Rossman, G.B. 51, 53, 55, 56, 57
Rubin, D. 118, 136, 137

sampling 60
Saraceni, M. 22
'-scapes,' created by globalisation 2, 3t, 4
Schensul, J.J. 55
Schutz, A. 69
Seargeant, P. 26
second-generation migrants 18
semantic features of English language 16
semi-structured interviews 6
Sharifan, F. 3, 18–19, 20, 21, 22, 218, 225, 240
Shin, J.K. 39, 40, 42, 222
silence 133
Simon, R.I. 46, 242, 243–4
Simons, H. 66–7
Singapore: as Outer-Circle country 13; Singaporean English 95–8; sit-com drama 96; teaching materials 87

Singh, M. 26
Smith, D. 60, 69
Smith, L. 1, 22
Smith, L.E. 159–60
Smitherman, G. 166, 201, 225
social constructivism 55–6, 77–8
social discourses, categorisation of (Bakhtin) 44
social networking sites 19
sociolinguistic landscape, English 1, 2, 8, 11, 18, 21, 31, 104
sociopolitical issues/questions, addressing in EIL curricula 31, 169–72, 240–1
Soo Hoo, S. 175
source culture 29
South Korea: bi-/multilingual speakers of English 16; ELT-related conferences in 31; as Expanding-Circle country 13
speakers of WE: changing views on 219–24; variety of multilingual speakers and interactions between 27–8, 165–7; *see also* WE (World Englishes)
Special Broadcasting Service (SBS), Australia 3
speech acts 132
Stake, R.E. 57, 66
Standard English 18, 96, 97, 217; Australian 191–2; Debates 142, 143f, 144f, 156; two views on 145f
status of an international language, English having 1, 2, 12, 13–14, 16
The Straits Times 122, 124f
struggles and tensions, diversity education 43–7; experiencing in learning about EIL 226–30; recognition as normal, natural and necessary 241–4
students of EIL 9; first-year 66, 92–3, 176–94; third-year 194–214; backgrounds 63; EIL curricula, experiencing changes through 216–25; experiences of Cheolsoo (South Korea) 176, 181–6, 216, 217, 220, 222–4; experiences of Manida (Laos) 176–81, 216–18, 220, 222–4, 226, 227; experiences of Ogilvy (Australia) 64, 176, 186–94, 216–18, 220, 221, 224, 226–9; experiences of Phil 194, 195–203, 216, 217, 221–3, 225, 242; experiences of Tomoko 194, 204–14, 216, 217, 220, 222, 223, 226, 227, 242; responses of *see* students' responses; voices 9

284 *Index*

students' responses to change 175–231; EIL curriculum, perspectives offered and advocated by 6; previous studies 5–6; realism in 235–6; reviewing change from perspectives of students 215–31; written, artefact collection 68; *see also* students of EIL

subcultures English 192, 221

subject areas, EIL *see* EIL subject components

subject outlines, as artefacts 68

subjective understanding 69

subtexts 24

Sullivan, P. 31

supremacy of English spoken, perceptions of: Inner-Circle countries 45, 99, 185, 220; native-English speakers 28, 40, 41, 42–3, 154, 213, 231, 242

Suzuki, A. 39, 41, 42, 100

Sweet Home Alabama (film) 165

syllabus materials (EIL): communication skills, promoting 29–30, 168–9; description and analysis of EIL-ex syllabus materials 85, 86f, 87–9; different cultural values, representation and exposure 28–9, 167–8; goals 23, 25–30; monocultural chauvinism, avoiding 28, 83; parochialism, avoiding 28; principles 25; speakers of WE, variety of and interactions between 27–8, 165–7; typical example 27–8; varieties of English, exposure to 25–7, 162–4; *see also* curricula, EIL

syntactical features of English language 16

taken-for-granted assumptions, getting students to think about 33, 189–92

teachers: approaches, degree of realism 233–5; texts, own collection of 118–26; voices of 9; *see also* educators of EIL; teaching of EIL

Teaching English to Speakers of Other Languages (TESOL) disciplines 21, 45, 47, 62; teacher-education programs 23, 31

teaching of EIL 9, 22–32; abstract nature 4; in classrooms 112–60; and diverse lingua-cultural backgrounds 14, 19, 21, 27, 50, 62; English language teaching enterprises 15; implementing of change 104–61; instructional variety 23; liberal approach 46; materials, as artefacts 68; methodology 23; mono-modal approach

23, 26; previous studies on effects of 32–43; principles, need for 5; profile of EIL educators at Urban University, Australia 105–12; studying 49–78; technological approach to 95; *see also* educators of EIL

technoscapes 3t, 4

TESOL *see* Teaching English to Speakers of Other Languages (TESOL) disciplines

Test of English as a Foreign Language (TOEFL) 159

thematic analysis 74

theory-driven approach, data analysis 74

third year students: encountering EIL and experiencing change 204–11; events not matching up to desires 211–14; experiences of Phil 194, 195–203, 216, 217, 221–3, 225, 242; experiences of Tomoko 194, 204–14, 216, 217, 220, 222, 223, 226, 227, 242; experiencing and initiating change 197–202; "king of the world mentality" 195–6, 221; perception of EIL as a 'risky business' 202–3

Thornborrow, J. 118

tolerance 30

Tollefson, J.W. 46

transformative pedagogy 46

Travaskes, S. 7, 83

triangulation of data 75–6

trustworthiness, of study 75–7

Tudor, I. 95

Tupas, T.R.F. 228

Twitter 19

United Kingdom: British English 12, 15, 41, 96, 105, 106, 108, 152, 156, 165, 178, 188b, 193, 220; as colonial nation 12; as Inner-Circle country 13; perception of English language as 'owned' by 12, 15

United States: American English *see* American English; 'general American' 20; as Inner-Circle country 13; perception of English language as 'owned' by 12, 15

Urban University, Australia 6; Department of Language and Linguistics 78n2; EIL paradigm, use of 66; EIL program at *see* EIL (English as an International Language) program, Urban University; Ethics Committee

64; Faculty of Arts 61; goals, accomplishing 7; limitations of EIL paradigm 7; profile of EIL educators at 105–12; *see also* Australia

Vavrus, F. 22
Vietnam 31
Vietnam Airlines inflight magazine 122, 123*f*
vocabulary 16

Walsh, L. 235
Wardhaugh, R. 130
Waugh, R.F. 85
WE (World Englishes) *see* World Englishes (WE)
websites 127
Wee, L. 5, 6, 10, 14, 22, 47, 104, 160, 172, 215, 232, 233, 237–8
'Western bias' 31

'Western' English-speaking countries 16
Whitehead, J. 58
Williams, J.A. 46
Willis, J.W. 59
World Englishes *see* WE (World Englishes)
World Englishes (journal) 2, 16, 163
World Englishes (WE) 8, 11, 17, 20, 21; in Australia 17–20; changing views on 219–24; 'circle' framework (Kachru) 2; whether curricula providing exposure to 25–7, 162–4; and EIL, as an anti-normative paradigm 20–2; Kachruvian 22; paradigm 22; speakers of *see* speakers of WE; variety of multilingual speakers of and interactions between 27–8

xenophobic attitudes 40
Xu, Z. 3, 219

Yin, R.K. 57, 58, 70

Taylor & Francis eBooks

Helping you to choose the right eBooks for your Library

Add Routledge titles to your library's digital collection today. Taylor and Francis ebooks contains over 50,000 titles in the Humanities, Social Sciences, Behavioural Sciences, Built Environment and Law.

Choose from a range of subject packages or create your own!

Benefits for you
- Free MARC records
- COUNTER-compliant usage statistics
- Flexible purchase and pricing options
- All titles DRM-free.

Benefits for your user
- Off-site, anytime access via Athens or referring URL
- Print or copy pages or chapters
- Full content search
- Bookmark, highlight and annotate text
- Access to thousands of pages of quality research at the click of a button.

REQUEST YOUR FREE INSTITUTIONAL TRIAL TODAY

Free Trials Available
We offer free trials to qualifying academic, corporate and government customers.

eCollections – Choose from over 30 subject eCollections, including:

Archaeology	Language Learning
Architecture	Law
Asian Studies	Literature
Business & Management	Media & Communication
Classical Studies	Middle East Studies
Construction	Music
Creative & Media Arts	Philosophy
Criminology & Criminal Justice	Planning
Economics	Politics
Education	Psychology & Mental Health
Energy	Religion
Engineering	Security
English Language & Linguistics	Social Work
Environment & Sustainability	Sociology
Geography	Sport
Health Studies	Theatre & Performance
History	Tourism, Hospitality & Events

For more information, pricing enquiries or to order a free trial, please contact your local sales team:
www.tandfebooks.com/page/sales

Routledge
Taylor & Francis Group

The home of
Routledge books

www.tandfebooks.com